SECOND EDITION

Inclusive Physical Activity

Promoting Health for a Lifetime

Library of Congress Cataloging-in-Publication Data

Kasser, Susan L.
Inclusive physical activity : promoting health for a lifetime / Susan L. Kasser, Rebecca K. Lytle. -- 2nd ed.
p. cm.
Includes bibliographical references and index.
1. Physical education for children. 2. Physical fitness for children. 3. Physical education for children with disabilities. 4. Inclusive education. I. Lytle, Rebecca K., 1961- II. Title.
GV443.K36 2013
371.9'04486--dc23

2012025269

ISBN-10: 1-4504-0186-4 (print)
ISBN-13: 978-1-4504-0186-9 (print)

The web addresses cited in this text were current as of September 14, 2012, unless otherwise noted.

Acquisitions Editor: Scott Wikgren; **Developmental Editor:** Melissa Feld; **Assistant Editor:** Rachel Brito; **Copyeditor:** John Wentworth; **Indexer:** Dan Connolly; **Permissions Manager:** Dalene Reeder; **Graphic Designer:** Fred Starbird; **Graphic Artist:** Denise Lowry; **Cover Designer:** Keith Blomberg; **Photograph (cover):** © Human Kinetics; **Photographs (interior):** © Human Kinetics, unless otherwise noted; **Photo Asset Manager:** Laura Fitch; **Visual Production Assistant:** Joyce Brumfield; **Photo Production Manager:** Jason Allen; **Art Manager:** Kelly Hendren; **Associate Art Manager:** Alan L. Wilborn; **Illustrations:** © Human Kinetics, unless otherwise noted; **Printer:** Sheridan Books

Printed in the United States of America 10 9 8 7 6 5 4 3 2 1

The paper in this book is certified under a sustainable forestry program.

Human Kinetics
Website: www.HumanKinetics.com

United States: Human Kinetics, P.O. Box 5076, Champaign, IL 61825-5076
800-747-4457
e-mail: humank@hkusa.com

Canada: Human Kinetics, 475 Devonshire Road Unit 100, Windsor, ON N8Y 2L5
800-465-7301 (in Canada only)
e-mail: info@hkcanada.com

Europe: Human Kinetics, 107 Bradford Road, Stanningley, Leeds LS28 6AT, United Kingdom
+44 (0) 113 255 5665
e-mail: hk@hkeurope.com

Australia: Human Kinetics, 57A Price Avenue, Lower Mitcham, South Australia 5062
08 8372 0999
e-mail: info@hkaustralia.com

New Zealand: Human Kinetics, P.O. Box 80, Torrens Park, South Australia 5062
0800 222 062
e-mail: info@hknewzealand.com

E5298

SECOND EDITION

INCLUSIVE PHYSICAL ACTIVITY

Promoting Health for a Lifetime

Susan L. Kasser, PhD
UNIVERSITY OF VERMONT

Rebecca K. Lytle, PhD
CALIFORNIA STATE UNIVERSITY, CHICO

Human Kinetics

Contents

Preface

Much attention is focused on the value of physical activity and exercise. This makes sense given the increased number of individuals with chronic health conditions associated with inactivity and the skyrocketing cost of health care in Western societies. What is more astonishing, though, is the dramatic rise in obesity for both children and adults, even with our growing knowledge of the risks associated with unhealthy eating habits and leading a sedentary lifestyle. Unfortunately, there are members of our schools and communities who have not received as much attention as others in terms of health promotion and disease prevention: those with "disabilities." The health disparities between people with and without disabilities are growing. People with disabilities experience significantly higher rates of conditions such as diabetes, depression, hypertension, and obesity, just to name a few. They also experience lower rates of recommended health behaviors, including exercise. This constraint on physical activity and exercise is to be blamed, in part, on the limited opportunities available for people with significant disabilities to engage in physical activity programs.

As physical activity and exercise practitioners, we are all uniquely positioned to close this health gap and increase the opportunities for meaningful participation in lifelong physical activity for those with disabilities. We are dedicated to providing all individuals within our programs well-designed and appropriate physical activity that enhances and maintains their physical, social, and emotional health and well-being. Yet creating access for individuals with disabilities to physical activity programs and effectively programming for diverse participants may seem difficult at first. However, by becoming more aware of participant needs, identifying important resources and supports, and increasing professional competence in accommodating all individuals, the breadth of physical activity opportunities can be widened for people with disabilities. Regardless of the setting, physical activity professionals can become more committed and prepared to teach and program for all individuals, whether these participants have differences in balance, coordination, or fitness or significantly different levels of concept understanding, varying attention spans, or limited skills in communication or social behavior.

Health promotion for people with disabilities starts with you—the physical educator in the school, the coach on the field, or the exercise practitioner in your community. Promoting inclusive physical activity rests on the knowledge that including individuals with different ability levels, experiences, and knowledge in physical activity benefits all involved. In this book we attempt to open the doors to lifelong physical activity for all individuals by changing perspectives and practices regarding physical activity. The book forwards a philosophy that supports optimal programming for everyone, regardless of capability. To include individuals with disabilities in physical activity while ensuring optimal programming for all requires practitioners to become critical thinkers and proficient problem solvers. They must be able to observe, assess, and implement many strategies to meet the unique needs of individuals within many contexts.

This text is designed primarily for students preparing to work with diverse populations in a physical activity setting. Our goal is to develop students' knowledge and the skills they need to provide meaningful and inclusive physical activity. This text is also a resource for practitioners committed to offering optimal physical activity programming for participants. Throughout the text, the term physical activity practitioner is used rather than physical educator, personal trainer, or coach. We believe the broad term practitioner is more encompassing of all professionals who work in physical activity settings (such as schools, exercise or rehabilitation facilities, community recreation sites, and sport programs) and will encourage each of them to develop more inclusive practices. The text also takes a life-span approach to physical activity participation. Considerations and programming strategies are applied to infants and toddlers, school-age children in physical education and recreation programs, and adults within sports or community-based exercise and activity programs. The book's most outstanding feature is its unique approach to modifications in instruction and activities. The FAMME (Functional Approach to Modifying Movement Experiences) model provides readers with a conceptual framework and a four-step process for accommodating all individuals within physical activity. The model is designed to encourage practitioners to consider individuals within programs by connecting modifications directly to capability differences in order to provide optimal challenges and successful experiences for every participant. Each functional component (e.g., eye–hand coordination, strength, attention span) is presented in chart form with information on influencing factors and effective adaptations to accommodate varied skill levels. Throughout the text, content progresses from understanding professional responsibilities and resources to practical strategies for programming. Strategies and techniques are offered to increase awareness of ability differences, foster positive attitudes, and increase advocacy efforts aimed at expanding physical activity opportunities. We present practical suggestions that can be readily used by practitioners to more effectively individualize programming and enhance physical activity participation for all involved.

WHAT'S NEW IN THIS EDITION?

Although this second edition of *Inclusive Physical Activity* still encompasses a life-span approach to physical activity, it differs from the first edition in substantive ways. First, the International Class of Functioning, Disability and Health (ICF) sets the stage for a more integrated framework for conceptualizing disability and the concept of inclusive physical activity embedded in a health promotion framework. The foundation for the text, and one that will resonate through each chapter, rests on existing health disparities among individuals with and without disabilities and the role physical activity practitioners must play in promoting health in individuals with disabilities. Second, new information on diversity is infused throughout the text. Practitioners should be aware and culturally competent in terms of socioeconomic status, race, and ethnicity as well as ability when including individuals into their physical activity programs. The inclusion of diversity issues and considerations is, thus, intentional and occurs throughout the text rather than presented in a single chapter or section. Third, this edition includes an additional chapter on aquatics in which previously presented concepts and strategies are applied to inclusive programming.

FEATURES

Several important features of the book promote reflection and critical thinking. Among these are opening scenarios (called Including All Individuals) in each chapter that place readers in a particular context. The scenarios are followed by several Think Back questions that appear throughout the chapter to encourage readers to connect content to each scenario in a thoughtful and insightful way. Each chapter ends with What Do You Think? questions and What Would You Do? case examples that further encourage reflective thinking and problem solving.

ORGANIZATION

The book is organized into three major parts. Part I, Foundations for Inclusive Physical Activity, deals with historical and sociological aspects of physical activity for individuals with disabilities and changing perspectives as they relate to health promotion for those with disabilities. Person-, context-, and task-related factors influencing physical activity participation for individuals with capability differences as well as strategies to overcome barriers associated with access and accommodation are also discussed. Part II, Inclusive

Physical Activity Program Planning and Implementation, deals with the how, when, and why practitioners make modifications in instructional settings. This section offers insight into effective collaborative partnerships, determination of programming focus and related assessment, and individualized program planning. Much of part II focuses on modification strategies and provides a continuum of modifications for various skill-related abilities. Part III, Application of Inclusive Practices, illustrates examples of inclusive practices as they relate to commonly offered physical activities. Chapters are devoted to adapting instruction and providing activity alternatives in five major content areas: movement skills, games and sports, health-related fitness, aquatics, and outdoor recreation and adventure.

Although some practitioners support a categorical or "disability"-based approach and others a noncategorical or ability-based approach, a balance of these two might be best, as long as program emphasis remains on performance and skill components rather than on labels and general "disability" guidelines. Although the book is noncategorical in nature, points are made about particular person-related health conditions that practitioners must know before effective programming can take place. With this in mind, we have included appendix A, Person-Related Factors Influencing Capability. This appendix includes summaries of related terminology and selected facts about common person-related health conditions organized by the ICF framework. More important, general considerations and contraindications, especially as they relate to physical activity participation, are presented. The text ends with other appendixes related to different aspects of physical activity programming for individuals with disabilities. Appendix B offers eligibility criteria for infants and toddlers. Related resource materials and information sources are offered in appendix C. Appendix D contains a variety of tests and assessment tools appropriate for inclusive physical activity programs, and appendix E is a sample medical history and referral form.

ANCILLARIES

Also available with *Inclusive Physical Activity* is a presentation package that offers instructors ready-to-use slides of main concepts and points from each chapter. An instructor guide is available to assist instructors with assessment of student understanding and application. Finally, a test package is available with multiple choice, short answer, and essay questions for each chapter in the book.

This text is founded on a philosophy and belief that all individuals, with all their distinctive abilities and interests, can and should benefit from participation in physical activity. This involvement should be lifelong, empowering, and inclusive of the range of possible programs, settings, and activities available to everyone. This is our goal. As practitioners, we are in the best position to make this goal a reality as we promote the health and well-being of all individuals. This text is the first step toward the awareness and knowledge necessary for all physical activity programs to become truly inclusive.

Acknowledgments

Throughout our journey of writing this book, many people have inspired us, encouraged us, and challenged us. We would like to thank all our mentors who brought us to this point in time both professionally and philosophically. This includes our best teachers—all the children, adults, and families we have worked with over the years and the OSU crew with whom we have shared ideas.

We would also like to thank our many colleagues who have helped shape this book by sharing their expertise and ideas. We thank the following individuals who contributed to this edition: Dr. Susan Nye for cowriting chapter 7, Dr. Don Lytle for cowriting chapter 8, and Dr. Luis Columna and Dr. Esther M. Ortiz-Stuhr for their work on the new aquatics chapter.

I would also like to thank my husband, Don, for his eternal patience and sharp intellect. Finally, to my colleague Susan Kasser, thank you for your commitment to this project for a second round—you are truly a joy to work with!

Rebecca Lytle

My thanks go to Kathy for her unconditional support and encouragement. And, without a doubt, thank you, Rebecca. I would not have wanted to take on this project with anyone else! I value our friendship and conversations.

Sue Kasser

PART I

Foundations for Inclusive Physical Activity

Understanding the philosophical basis for and sociocultural context of inclusive physical activity is an important prerequisite to offering physical activity programs that include all individuals regardless of age, ability, or experience. Part I includes three chapters that establish the foundation for including all individuals in physical activity programs. Chapter 1 sets the stage for inclusive physical activity programs by providing an overview of the different paradigms used to define ability and disability. The chapter then offers an important basis for inclusive physical activity by discussing the health disparities that exist and the health promotion needs of people with disabilities. The chapter finishes by defining inclusive physical activity and detailing the benefits for participants, peers, and practitioners.

Chapter 2 presents an inclusive model of ability in physical activity as an alternative to traditional views of disability and programming. This model integrates person-, context-, and task-related factors with important concepts related to changing capability, movement potential, and professional practice.

With the philosophical and pragmatic basis for inclusive programming set, chapter 3 provides insight into the challenges and barriers precluding the participation of all individuals in physical activity. The chapter offers contextual and individual obstacles as well as important strategies for overcoming such hurdles to ensure that all individuals have access to and consideration in physical activity opportunities.

CHAPTER 1

Health, Physical Activity, and Individuals With Ability Differences

Photo courtesy of S. Kasser, photographer T. Bolduc.

LEARNING OUTCOMES

After completing this chapter, you should be able to

- compare models of disability;
- discuss why health promotion differs for people with and without disabilities;
- define inclusive physical activity; and
- provide a rationale for involving all individuals in physical activity.

INCLUDING ALL INDIVIDUALS

The staff meeting at Fitness First, the local health and fitness club, just ended. Jessica, the new director of fitness programming at the club, shared this year's program initiatives and membership goals with all in attendance. One of the major priorities Jessica discussed involved expanding fitness classes and personal training services to new members with differing health conditions and capabilities who have been previously underserved. Jessica informed the staff that this year, through a coordinated and collaborative effort, all community members would be afforded health-promoting opportunities and be included in the club's programs and fitness activities as much as possible.

Some of the experienced fitness practitioners objected. They believed that the club could not be all things to all people and suggested that individuals with ability differences receive their therapy in rehabilitation centers and physical therapy clinics; in their view, fitness instructors should not be expected to program for members with low skills or "impairments" in the same classes as the high-skilled and able members. Other fitness trainers expressed approval of the initiative, saying that including members with significantly different abilities together in the same facility and programs could be beneficial for increasing acceptance and enhancing the health of all members. Todd, a personal trainer at the club, left the meeting with many questions. He knew that Jessica expected all fitness trainers to contribute to attaining this new membership goal. He had been told about club membership inquiries from community members who had coordination and balance difficulties; he had also heard about agencies serving individuals with intellectual differences. How would their presence affect the other members' experiences and his plans for his clients? Would problems arise that he could not yet envision? Could this be why some of the experienced practitioners were reluctant to include all community members in the facility and their classes? Todd had thought he was all set to go, but now he felt a new concern: Would he still be able to give all clients the best fitness experience possible?

The practitioners at Fitness First clearly had contrasting perspectives on including members with differing movement and fitness capabilities in the same programs and classes. If you were Todd, how would you feel? Would you want to include these members with other participants in your fitness classes? Why or why not?

As practitioners responsible for participants' experiences within our physical activity programs, we each need to examine our perceptions of ability and disability and our definitions of health and illness. Our views and beliefs not only influence our attitudes toward and interactions with others but also direct our professional practice when implementing physical activity and exercise programs.

The extent to which individuals with ability differences are included in physical activities and movement programs is influenced by society's perceptions and attitudes toward these individuals. The concept of disability has been and continues to be defined by the culture or times in which individuals with significant differences in ability live. Health promotion efforts have also been based on how societies define and perceive wellness. Definitions of wellness have changed over the years, but an important step toward further progress in including all individuals in physical activity and health promotion programs is to focus on *ability*, not disability. Doing so should help us examine how assumptions and attitudes about ability differences influence professional practice.

In this chapter we present a philosophy of inclusive physical activity and a contemporary approach to including all individuals, regardless of ability, in physical activity programs. Although a single chapter cannot fully explain what it means for an individual to be meaningfully included in physical activity, examining the existing views on "disability" and health and how aspects of these views come together to either hinder or allow for inclusive programming may promote greater appreciation for the concept of inclusive physical activity.

CHANGING DEFINITIONS OF DISABILITY

Compared to the past, individuals with ability differences are now receiving increasingly more attention and consideration in terms of health and wellness. Still, the health of people with ability differences is influenced by varying social, political, and historical perspectives that together influence the life experiences of those perceived as different (Pfeiffer, 2003). One of these influences has been, and continues to be, the way that disability is defined. The way in which disability is conceptualized significantly affects how health policies and practices are developed (Boyles, Bailey, & Mossey, 2008). Even today, definitions of disability vary widely, as do the attitudes and assumptions associated with them (Shakespeare, 2006). How then is disability defined? Who creates the definitions? What consequences result from them? In all societies, disability is defined in relation to beliefs about ability and usually by those without "disabilities." The term disability attains meaning through various frameworks or models used to convey attitudes and perceptions. These models differ in their underlying assumptions and expectations of those with disabilities. These beliefs provide the basis not only for understanding "disability" but also for influencing interactions, providing services, and directing programs. In an attempt to internalize and understand ability differences, four prevailing frameworks exist: the medical model of disability, the social minority model of disability, the social construction model of disability, and the international class of functioning, disability, and health model.

Medical Model of Disability

Although the medical model is the oldest of the dominant views of disability, this model still influences programming and professional practice today. The medical model assumes an individual's deficiency is caused by disease, trauma, or impairment (Altman, 2001) and, as such, places the cause of "disability" on the individual. In this model, individuals are typically grouped by their shared "disabling" condition or by category with a primary focus on symptoms and characteristics. Because disability is considered a personal problem (Galvin, 2005), environments that might adversely affect a person's functioning are disregarded. This model implies that the "problem" resides within the individual and that it is the individual who needs to change or be fixed, not the conditions of the environment. Thus programs and services are provided to diagnose, prescribe, and rehabilitate the individual rather than to alter the environment.

Social Minority Model of Disability

Increased insight into the stigma of disability gave rise to the social minority model. In contrast to the medical model, the focus here is not on a physiological cause underlying disability but on the social consequences of having minority status. In other words, disability emerges out of beliefs and actions that isolate, alienate, and discriminate against those with differences (Altman, 2001; Scullion, 2010). This social model has been characterized as a "barriers model" in which access to health care and health promotion is restricted because of negative attitudes and subsequent practices that further exclude people with disabilities (Scullion, 2010). Although this broader perspective acknowledges society's role in shaping disability, it also assumes that all people with a disability share a common experience of being disabled. In fact, however, individuals with disabilities encounter a wide range of conditions and an array of experiences. The social minority model discounts individual identity and negates individual challenges, joys, successes, and other life experiences shared by all individuals with and without disabilities. This view emphasizes disability rather than ability and perpetuates segregation rather than inclusion.

Social Construction Model of Disability

To view disability as a medical condition or group experience offers only a superficial understanding of disability. A more recent framework focuses on the social construction of disability in which disability is perceived as the creation of differences between able and not able (NCDDR, 1999; Oliver, 1996). These differences do not exist naturally but instead are regularly created and reinforced through the interactions and daily practices of an "able-bodied" society (figure 1.1). Rather than a problem arising from a person's particular personal health condition or difference, the difficulty arises from a too narrowly created environment for the diversity of people and their unique circumstances (Kaplan, 2011). For instance, routinely building staircases instead of ramps and cutting 24-inch door openings instead of 32-inch openings create barriers that highlight differences in ability. Norms associated with ability are thus constructed by those without disabilities. Once differences have been created by the "able-bodied" population, they are then used to reinforce the status quo or "reality" of disability. It is these socially formed and established views of disability that underlie the beliefs and expectations of those perceived as incapable. According to this perspective, the concept

DID YOU KNOW?

". . . the 'problem' is not the person with disabilities; the problem is the way that normalcy is constructed to create the 'problem' of the disabled person. . . . The word 'normal' as 'constituting, conforming to, not deviating or different from, the common type or standard, regular, usual' only entered into the English language around 1840." (Davis, 1997, pp. 9-10).

Figure 1.1 Disability and the accompanying values and beliefs are often created by the norm or by those perceived as able-bodied.

of disability cannot be truly understood outside of the social context that gives it definition (Smart & Smart, 1997). Attention is focused on deconstructing past beliefs and stereotypes in order to empower and foster personal development and achievement of all individuals. Such rethinking broadens services and programs and leads to greater inclusive practices.

The International Class of Functioning, Disability and Health Model

It has become clear that none of the previous models described have been able to independently and fully describe the concept of disability. Disability cannot solely be considered either a limitation of the individual or a socially created problem, but instead must be conceptualized as an interaction of the individual and the environment in which he or she lives. The International Class of Functioning, Disability and Health (ICF) offers a more integrated framework for conceptualizing disability (World Health Organization, 2001). The ICF stems from a changing perspective of disability globally and is based on a neutral stand with regard to causes, consequences, and determinants of functional ability. In this model, emphasis shifts from people's disabilities to their level of health and functioning. People with differing abilities are not dichotomized from those without because the model recognizes that every person—regardless of age, ethnic background, socioeconomic status, and other variables—can experience a decrement in health and, in doing so, experience some level of disability at one time or another. In addition, functioning is viewed as an outcome of the interaction between health condition and contextual factors. The extent and level of participation in activities are not solely attributed to changes in body structures and functions but also to personal and environmental factors (figure 1.2). One of the critical goals of the ICF is to create a barrier-free world. This new model asks the questions: How does this person function in the current environment? How might he or she function in a barrier-free environment? Answers to these questions help effect change in individual function and health by providing insight into more diverse strategies and practices.

THINK BACK

Think back to your thoughts about Todd at the beginning of the chapter.

1. How might Todd define disability?
2. Which lens do you believe Todd might look through relating to disability?
3. How might Todd's definition and assumptions influence his work at his fitness center?
4. How does Todd's view of disability compare to your own?

THE HEALTH OF PEOPLE WITH DISABILITIES

Health can be defined in many ways. Often health refers to a sense of physical, emotional, social, and spiritual well-being. Health can also be defined as a lifelong process of achieving optimal wellness and maximizing potential. Regardless of the definition chosen, the importance of health is undeniable. Good health is often regarded as fundamental to quality of life and the capability of being an active and involved participant in a community. However, the health status of people across the United States is not the same; nor is there always equality in health-promoting efforts and services afforded to those with differing abilities and health.

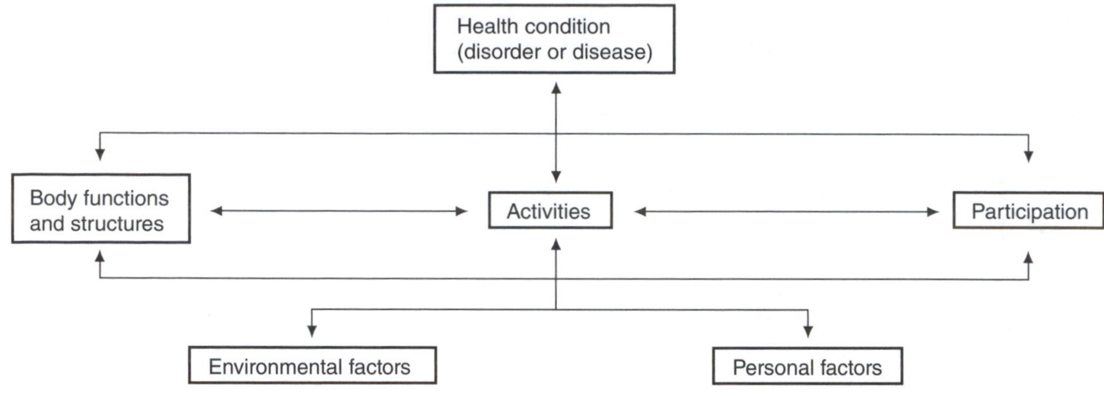

Figure 1.2 The World Health Organization (WHO) International Classification of Functioning, Disability and Health (ICF) offers a framework for interrelations between functioning and disability. It describes health and health-related domains from body, individual, and societal perspectives.

Reprinted, by permission, from World Health Organization, 2001, *The international classification of functioning, disability and health-ICF* (Geneva, Switzerland), 18.

Health Disparities

Compared to the general population, individuals with disabilities experience poorer health and have earlier onset and higher rates of chronic conditions, including diabetes, obesity, and depression (U.S. Department of Health and Human Services, 2000). Moreover, individuals with disabilities have lower rates of social participation in organized health events and health education and, in general, have lower rates of recommended health behaviors. The majority of individuals with disabilities are sedentary. In fact, only about 25 percent of adults with disability meet recommended moderate activity guidelines for physical activity (Boslaugh & Andresen, 2006). In turn, people who have activity limitations report having had more days of pain, depression, anxiety, and sleeplessness and fewer days of vitality than people not reporting activity limitations (Drum, 2003).

DID YOU KNOW?

- An estimated 48 million people in the United States, or nearly 20 percent of the population, currently live with disabilities (Brault, 2008).
- The proportion of people living with disabilities is increasing among all age groups.
- People with disabilities have 3.5 to 5 times higher health care expenditures than people without disabilities (Yelin, Cisternas, & Trupin, 2006), and total national health care expenditures associated with disabilities top nearly $400 billion (Anderson, Weiner, Finkelstein, & Armour, 2011).

The health gap for individuals with disabilities is magnified even more for those racial, ethnic, and other underserved groups who typically have a higher incidence of disability and lower levels of participation in the health care system (Lewis, 2009). Research has documented acknowledged risk behaviors such as physical inactivity and obesity among various racial and ethnic minorities with disabilities (Rimmer, Rubin, Braddock, & Hedman, 1999; Weil et al., 2002), and these health disparities are greater in persons with "disability" and minority status together than in individuals with disability or minority status alone (Jones & Sinclair, 2008).

Health Promotion and People With Disabilities

It is apparent that the health gaps between people with and without disabilities are wide and the disparities broad. The cause of these health disparities can be largely attributable to beliefs and biases within a health care system that devalues wellness for individuals who are perceived as different (Lewis,

2009). And although a clear need exists for improving the health and functional independence of people with disabilities, health promotion efforts for these individuals has been neglected for a number of reasons.

For one, the traditional health promotion model has often been considered a means of preventing disabilities in people without chronic illness or injury (Lollar, 2001). Efforts are primarily aimed at identifying the causes of conditions associated with disabilities and then working to reduce or prevent these conditions from occurring. In other words, health is defined as the absence of disease, and health promotion is thus equated with disability prevention (Rimmer, 1999).

Coupled with this prevention approach was the belief that disability is inevitably equated with poor health and should be addressed primarily within medical and rehabilitation services rather than from a backdrop of community-based health and wellness programs (USDHHS, 2000). The belief that disability was also a negative consequence of not practicing health-promoting behaviors, in part, also explains the void in health promotion for people with disabilities (Harrison, 2006). As a result, health promotion efforts are usually not aimed at preventing secondary conditions among persons already perceived as disabled (Rimmer, 1999).

If it is true that individuals with disabilities would benefit significantly from health promotion programs, then what will it take to promote health for people with disabilities? Among other things, improving the health of people with disabilities will necessitate a consensus that health is holistic, involving a balance of physical, emotional, mental, social, and spiritual aspects and not merely the absence of disease (Kim & Fox, 2006). The health of people with disabilities must also extend beyond merely functional limitation and perceived inability. There needs to be an appreciation that people with disabilities have the capacity to be healthy within the context of their health condition and that many people with disabilities can live healthy active lives (Stuifbergen & Roberts, 1997; figure 1.3).

DID YOU KNOW ?

In *Healthy People 2000*, individuals with disabilities were not assigned objectives for their health. It was not until *Healthy People 2010* that objectives for health were included for individuals with disabilities.

Realistic

Figure 1.3 "Given the proper guidance and direction from rehabilitation professionals, fitness centers are poised to become the future centers of health promotion for people with disabilities" (Rimmer, 1999).

MISCONCEPTIONS OF THE TRADITIONAL PUBLIC HEALTH MODEL (USDHHS, 2000)

- All people with disabilities automatically have poor health.
- Public health should focus only on preventing "disabling" conditions.
- A standard definition of "disability" is not needed for public health purposes.
- The environment plays no role in the disabling process.

Think back to the Fitness First health and fitness club you read about at the start of the chapter.

1. From a health promotion standpoint, what reasons may have existed for the absence of people with ability differences exercising in the club prior to Jessica's new initiatives?
2. Why do you think Jessica believes it is important to begin including new members with different health conditions and capabilities?
3. How do you think Jessica can convince her staff that promoting the health of new members with differences in ability and function is necessary and important?

INCLUSIVE PHYSICAL ACTIVITY

If we are committed to promoting the health of individuals with disabilities, we must consider ways to increase physical activity (PA) among those with individual differences as an important foundation for their healthy lifestyle. To move successfully in this direction, we need to establish a common understanding of the definition, philosophy, and rationale of inclusive physical activity. We then need to examine our own belief systems and rethink how our professional practice can encompass and value inclusive practices.

Definition of Inclusive Physical Activity

Inclusive physical activity is the philosophy and practice of ensuring that all individuals, regardless of ability or age, have equal opportunity in physical activity. This opportunity should include options and decision making and create meaningful participation and success that empower all participants. In other words, inclusive physical activity is defined as *accessible physical activity programs provided to all individuals across the life span in diverse settings.* Truly inclusive physical activity includes all of the following:

- Infant and toddler movement experiences
- School-based physical education programs
- Community-based recreation and leisure activities
- Exercise and fitness programs
- Multilevel sport opportunities
- Culturally specific activities or events

Whether we are speaking of children learning a wide range of movement skills through games or adults improving their physical fitness and health through exercise programs, individuals of all ages can and should be able to derive the joy and benefits of inclusive physical activity (figure 1.4).

The term "inclusive physical activity" is used instead of other physical activity program-related terms to denote a shift from participation based on a disability label toward creating success for all interested participants. For example, "adapted physical activity" is commonly regarded as activity in which adaptations are made primarily for individuals with identifiable disabilities and provided most often within traditional school-based and postsecondary settings (DePauw & Doll-Tepper, 2000; Sherrill, 1998). Inclusive physical activity, on the other

Photo on right: Bill Crump/Brand X

Figure 1.4 People of all ages and abilities should have opportunities for meaningful physical activity participation.

hand, attempts to ensure that all individuals have the chance to benefit from inclusive and accommodating programming regardless of age or ability level. The concept includes not only individuals identified with disabilities but also those without disability labels who might differ in capability because of age, experience, skill, or fitness level. From this philosophical and pragmatic standpoint, accommodations are made within programs to ensure that both highly skilled and lesser-skilled participants receive the benefits of tailored instruction and optimal programming.

Inclusive physical activity is based on the concepts of opportunity and choice. All individuals should have the opportunity to participate in age-appropriate and ability-appropriate activity. As such, a range of meaningful and tailored programs must exist so that individuals with differences in ability or health conditions are not automatically relegated to certain programs for the sake of administrative or programmatic ease. Instead, all participants have options from which they may choose. Inclusive physical activity is not based on a particular setting but rather on participation in meaningful activity selected from a range of options. For this to happen, all practitioners must be able to plan and modify activities to meet diverse needs and abilities so that all participants are offered choice and opportunity that's equitable for everyone. Physical educators should have the attitude and skills they need to allow all children to succeed, both in their general physical education classes and within smaller groups of students with and without differences in abilities. Fitness practitioners in health clubs must also become accepting and versatile enough to want to invite adults with various health conditions into their facilities and design meaningful and individualized fitness programs for them. Only when practitioners across all settings and types of physical activity programs can effectively accommodate the range of differing abilities among participants will inclusive physical activity programs become a reality.

Philosophy of Inclusive Physical Activity

Those who work in physical activity settings are uniquely positioned to influence the health and well-being of all individuals. The concept of inclusive physical activity involves much more than simply integrating individuals with diverse abilities into physical activity. Placing or integrating children with cognitive or behavioral differences into general physical education classes or adults with movement and balance difficulties into community exercise programs does not mean they will be accepted by others, improve on their performance, or find satisfaction through participation. Inclusive physical activity goes beyond providing access to programs and making accommodations to support participation. Inclusive physical activity is a philosophy that embraces the belief in "experiential equity" in which there exists a balance of opportunity, consideration, and effort given to all participants. This philosophy recognizes the value of participant choice and decision making as well as the importance of practitioner responsibility in helping learners achieve a meaningful experience. Inclusive physical activity involves a transformation in the way we view individuals and in the way we educate and teach. Practitioners committed to the concept of inclusive physical activity are keenly aware of the significant systematic changes required in the typical instructional method to ensure that programs are fair and equitable. They appreciate and value the uniqueness of the individuals with whom they work and strive to create an environment that is accepting, empowering, and accommodating for all people to succeed (figure 1.5).

Rationale for Inclusive Physical Activity

Different people have different views about exactly what inclusion involves and how beneficial it is. Support of inclusive physical activity often varies across contexts and participant groups. Some practitioners oppose inclusive physical activity programs in educational settings but support them in recreational and leisure venues. Others support inclusive physical activity in recreational or educational settings but promote nonintegrated sport opportunities, such as the Paralympics. Also, some parents of children with less significant ability differences might support inclusive physical education for their child but oppose it for other children. For many people, opinions on inclusive practices vary according to the abilities of the individuals participating and the particular contexts and circumstances existing.

Inclusive environments have been generally supported in physical education (Block, 2007), community fitness facilities (Rimmer, 1999; Riley, Rimmer, Wang, & Schiller, 2008), and other physical activity and sport programs (DePauw & Doll-Tepper, 2000). A rationale for adopting an inclusive physical activity philosophy includes the following essential points:

- **Resource redundancy.** There are two primary concerns regarding the resource redundancy issue. First, offering separate physical activity programs means requiring additional resources, including personnel, financial support, and facilities. This overlap or duplication increases resource requirements. Second, when resources are allocated to traditional programs that are not inclusive, some participants may not be provided the opportunities they otherwise could be. Inclusive physical activity programming reduces resource redundancy and extends the breadth of physical activity experiences to everyone desiring such opportunities.
- **Instructional individualization.** The concept of instructional individualization is based on the practice that only individuals with disabilities are given individualized instruction and instructional support, whereas those without disability labels are typically grouped together and considered homogeneous in ability. In fact, no two participants function at exactly the same level. For example, within a class of third-graders, one child might excel in math and another in reading. The same is true in physical activity. One person might have great flexibility and another excellent eye–hand coordination. An inclusive physical activity philosophy supports all individuals receiving the necessary support and accommodations to achieve personal participation goals, regardless of label or setting.
- **Breadth of benefits.** The benefits of inclusive physical activity are far-reaching, both for children in school-based physical education programs and for children and adults in

Beliefs Underlying an Inclusive Physical Activity Philosophy

Beliefs About Participants

- Each person is unique with differing physical, cognitive, emotional, and social capabilities and needs.
- Everyone has a right to and can benefit from inclusive physical activity opportunities.
- Each person can be healthy and have a high quality of life within the context of their health condition.
- The capabilities of an individual are dynamic and result from relations among the individual, the context, and the task or activity.
- Participants have a right to personal choice and decision making.
- Each individual in an inclusive physical activity setting benefits from the experiences of others.

Beliefs About Practitioners

- Practitioners are committed to promoting health for all individuals.
- Practitioners promote equal access to environments and equipment and offer shared activities with individual outcomes.
- Practitioners value the diversity and range of participants within their programs.
- Practitioners consider individual interests and needs and demonstrate equitable practice in attending to these considerations.
- Practitioners offer physical activity experiences that are enjoyable, empowering, and personally meaningful.

Figure 1.5 Beliefs necessary for inclusive physical activity to succeed.

programs conducted outside school settings, such as community-based exercise or activity programs, leisure and recreational experiences, or sport arenas. For all involved, benefits include a greater respect for individual differences and for the unique experiences each participant brings to the program (figure 1.6).

Consider how you might reframe or redefine your answers to the questions asked at the beginning of the chapter.

1. Do you think Todd should include individuals of very different abilities in his fitness classes? Why or why not?
2. How do you think doing so would benefit him and his other clients?

Benefits of Inclusive Physical Activity

Participant Benefits

- Increased respect for individual abilities and differences
- Enhanced awareness and insight into one's own strengths and nonstrengths
- Increased breadth of opportunity and experience
- Experience of a more motivating environment
- Expanded support system with less isolation for participants and significant others
- Increased sense of community and acceptance
- Increased sense of contribution to activity, program, and community goals and outcomes
- Enhanced sense of value and self-esteem

Practitioner Benefits

- Increased awareness and insight of participant differences
- Changed perspective on professional practice
- Increased breadth of strategies useful for many others
- Increased knowledge of variations of tasks and skills
- Enhanced value of diverse abilities

Figure 1.6 Inclusive physical activity benefits both participants and practitioners.

SUMMARY

If we can think in terms of ability rather than disability and appreciate that health is for *everyone*, all people can have meaningful and rewarding involvement in physical activity. Inclusive physical activity is a philosophy that goes beyond mere access to programs. It embraces the idea of accommodating and valuing all participants and includes practitioners revamping the way they structure and implement programs. An inclusive physical activity philosophy challenges practitioners to examine their own assumptions regarding ability and health, reflect on their instructional practice as it relates to the success of their participants, and think outside the traditional box that narrows choices and stifles creativity in physical activity settings.

What Do You Think?

1. Do you believe that individuals with disabilities are more socially accepted now than in the past? How so? Do you have examples to support your belief?
2. How does an inclusive physical activity philosophy differ from previous beliefs about physical activity and ability?
3. What is your current philosophy regarding inclusive physical activity practices? Where did this philosophy come from?

What Would You Do?

Scenario 1.1

Joan recently graduated from college with a degree in exercise physiology and was just hired as a program specialist for a brand new sports and rehabilitation facility in a large metropolitan area. She is excited about putting her training to work. In addition to her bachelor's degree, Joan has special certifications in aerobics and aquatics. She worked extensively at a local club during college and feels confident in her skills to work with people. During the first week of her new job, she learns more about her responsibilities, which include scheduling all classes and facilities, training staff, and serving as a personal trainer. The owner of the facility has explained to Joan that she needs to meet the needs of every individual in the community. She also learns more about the clientele at this facility.

The club by her university was filled with healthy young college students, whereas the population of this facility is much more diverse. Individuals range in age from infants to seniors. Her new facility expects to offer parent–infant classes, programs for seniors, a cardiac program, and many other classes for all ages and abilities. In fact, one of the local community-based programs for individuals with developmental disabilities is planning on coming in the afternoons to swim and do weight training. As Joan becomes more familiar with the diversity of individuals she will be working with, she begins to feel less sure of her skills. In fact, she has never worked with young children or individuals with disabilities. Her only experience with disability was in an athletic training class she took working with athletes to rehab injuries to knees and ankles. As she begins to consider the classes she needs to offer, she is not sure how to organize them—by activity, age, ability, or a combination of these. In addition, she is wondering how she will hire and train her staff to work with this diverse population.

1. What model of disability do you think Joan has been exposed to? Why do you think so?
2. How might you organize classes if you were Joan? How would you justify your decisions?
3. What critical issues might Joan want to address in her staff training?

Scenario 1.2

Allison is an elementary physical education teacher at Central Square Elementary School. She has also been the adapted physical education specialist in her district for the last 12 years. Across the district, she has 25 students distributed among three schools. Her district is a blooming district in the process of inaugurating a new elementary school that will increase Allison's case load. Recently she found out that she will have 10 new students who are part of the English Language Learners (ELL) program. Of these 10 students, 6 are from Mexico, 2 from Guatemala, 1 from China, and 1 from Vietnam. When Allison learned of her new students, she was both excited and nervous. Although she has been teaching APE for the past 12 years, most of her students have been Caucasian. One of her students from Guatemala, a little girl named Rebecca, does not speak any English. Rebecca is 9 years old and has spina bifida. Her mother also speaks no English. Allison has heard that some teachers in the district do not think the mother is very collaborative in terms of the educational goals for her daughter. According to the classroom teacher, they have sent several notices to Rebecca's mother requesting a meeting and permission to conduct an assessment for physical education. Teachers know that without parental permission they cannot conduct such an assessment. The classroom teacher has also tried to call home, but the phone was disconnected.

1. If you were Allison, what might you think are some of the reasons Rebecca's mother is not participating in her daughter's school planning?
2. What are steps Allison can take to ensure she is meeting both Rebecca's cultural needs and physical activity needs?
3. What benefits might be gleaned by students and teachers who participate in Allison's class?

CHAPTER 2

An Inclusive Physical Activity Approach

LEARNING OUTCOMES

After completing this chapter, you should be able to

- discuss the underlying concepts of an inclusive approach to physical activity;
- examine how capability relates to person, task, and contextual factors;
- discuss the essential components of inclusive physical activity programs; and
- describe three strategies useful in facilitating an inclusive model of physical activity.

INCLUDING ALL INDIVIDUALS

The first faculty in-service at the city middle school has just ended. The meeting started with the usual welcome by the principal, and this was followed by beginning-of-the-year details about strategic plans and curricular changes. Next on the agenda was the superintendent, who discussed the current educational programming provided for students with special needs and shared her new initiative on inclusion for the district. The superintendent informed the faculty that this year, through a coordinated and collaborative effort, all students with special needs would be included in general education classes as much as possible. As the in-service came to a close, the superintendent's remarks stayed with Theresa, the middle school's program coordinator for physical education. She wondered how instructors in her department would view this new initiative.

Theresa knew that some instructors believed they should not be expected to teach students with low skills or behavior differences in the same classes as the high-skilled students and preferred separate classes for these students. There were others in the department who would embrace the idea of including students with significantly different abilities together in the same classes, believing all students would benefit from such a change. Theresa knew that Nick Powell was starting at the school in the upcoming year. She had been told that Nick had some coordination and balance difficulties as well as some cognitive processing delays. How would his presence affect the other students' learning in the class? Would the physical education teacher be able to modify activities effectively for Nick? Theresa considered the concerns that some of the teachers might have and their abilities to give each of their students, including Nick, the best possible physical education experience.

Clearly, teachers may have contrasting perspectives on including children with diverse movement capabilities in the same physical education classes. If you were one of Nick's teachers, would you want to include him with the other students in your physical activity class? Why or why not? What do you think he is capable of doing and not doing? What could you do to increase Nick's capabilities to assure that his physical education program would be successful?

Promotion of physical activity for individuals with disabilities is needed. As we learned in chapter 1, inclusive physical activity requires a shifting of traditional disability frameworks to a more contemporary approach to functioning and health. Achieving an inclusive physical activity program requires changes in how individuals with disabilities are viewed, the ways in which programs are developed, and the instructional practices employed by practitioners. Inclusive physical activity necessitates an eclectic approach that considers not only how disability and health are redefined but also how movement skills and capability are achieved.

MOVING TOWARD INCLUSIVE PHYSICAL ACTIVITY

The ICF model presented in chapter 1 describes how an individual's functional ability results from the interaction of both personal and environmental factors. This model offers an effective framework for understanding the range of variables that influence the physical activity behavior of individuals with disabilities. In fact, a number of psychosocial determinants influence the activity participation of those with disabilities. Environmental factors, such as social facilitators or barriers, as well as personal factors, such as health condition, self-efficacy, and attitude, have been considered and offered as potential targets for interventions aimed at physical activity promotion for those with disabilities (van der Ploeg, van der Beek, van der Woude, & van Mechelen, 2004). In order to improve physical activity participation of individuals with varying functional levels, however, we must understand not only *what* influences exist to encourage access but also *how* appropriate and effective programming can be implemented to maximize capability and meaningful participation (figure 2.1).

Figure 2.1 Moving toward inclusive physical activity means understanding how to encourage access, maximize capability, and bring about meaningful participation.

An Inclusive Model of Ability in Physical Activity

Inclusive physical activity emphasizes ability and constructing contexts for maximizing success within a range of physical activity programs. The inclusive model of ability in physical activity (IMAPA) integrates concepts from the ICF model but goes one step further by more clearly operationalizing how individuals with disabilities are included and how specific functional changes occur for individuals within these physical activity settings. The approach is ability based and multifocused, thus providing key concepts and strategies for increasing capability, performance, and participation (figure 2.2).

Inclusive physical activity is both person centered and contextually situated. Information regarding health conditions or body functions is significant in terms of activities that might or might not be recommended or contraindicated for the individual. Labels are removed, and individuals are valued, respected, and given equality. How individuals are valued and the psychosocial consequences of these views are considered because they relate to acceptance by others and self-determining behaviors of participants. The approach focuses on personal development and achievement; it considers and plans an environment and social context that can positively influence the successful and meaningful involvement of all individuals

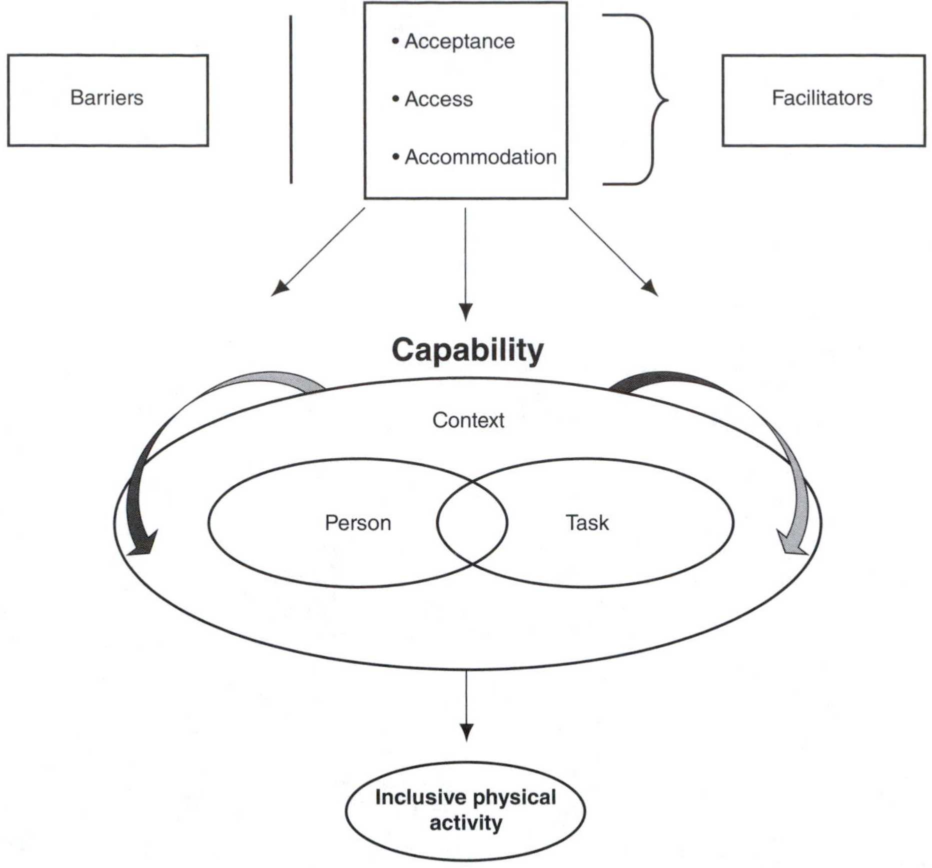

Figure 2.2 The inclusive model of ability in physical activity includes the three A's—acceptance, access, and accommodation—when providing physical activity opportunities to all individuals.

in physical activity. As with the ICF, IMAPA does not focus on individuals with identifiable labels but includes all individuals within any given program. The focus is on meeting the needs of all individuals by striving to create universally designed programs and enhancing functioning, independence, and health.

IMAPA differs from previous models in that it embeds these important philosophical values into a practical approach for considering successful physical activity participation for all individuals. First, the IMAPA model offers considerations and strategies aimed at increasing *acceptance* of all individuals with disabilities as healthy and active people. Second, by identifying and overcoming a range of personal and contextual barriers, the model creates equal *access* to the broad range of physical activity opportunities possible. Third, the model embraces *accommodation* of individual differences through a range of modification strategies to achieve effective and successful activity involvement.

DID YOU KNOW?

"Broad recommendations for people with disabilities to engage in exercise or become more physically active are likely to fail without a systematic framework for identifying key problem areas" (Rimmer, 2006). Understanding how individuals with varying health conditions and capability differences function within the context of person-environment factors is the first step toward fostering greater access to and participation in effective and beneficial activity programs.

Underlying Concepts

As we have mentioned, IMAPA integrates aspects from the current views of functioning and participation to achieve the three A's identified earlier. IMAPA also professes two important practical concepts related to physical activity involvement. The first relates to the dynamic interplay of the person, task, and environment as they relate to capability differences. The second focuses on the dynamic nature of capability, also known as "capability shifting."

Individual Capability

A person's capability cannot be evaluated based only on his or her abilities; the task being executed as well as the context must also be considered. In contrast to the assumptions of the medical model discussed in chapter 1, "disability" does not follow an individual across tasks and contexts. Performance is based on a dynamic interaction among an individual's abilities, the nature of the task or movement skill, and the circumstances under which the tasks are being completed. For example, an adult with limited leg strength might have difficulty walking across a room. However, this individual may walk quite proficiently in a swimming pool given the increased buoyancy of the water. Thus it would be inaccurate to say this individual is "disabled" across all contexts. Rather, ability depends on the individual, the task, and the context.

Capability Shifting

The second important component of an inclusive physical activity approach relates to the concept of capability shifting, in that an individual's capability to perform a given task is altered by changing any one of the three factors involved in performance: the individual's skill level, the context in which the task is performed, or the task itself (figure 2.2). An appreciation of the concept of capability shifting provides a greater opportunity for inclusion and success by allowing for strategies that focus on the task and environment rather than solely on the individual. The focus shifts from disability to ability. For instance, a child with balance problems might have difficulty catching a ball with two hands while standing. An observer might conclude that the child has poor eye–hand coordination and is not capable of catching the ball. But if we place this same child in a chair, he or she might catch the ball effectively from the same distance (figure 2.3). Without the element of balance required for standing, the child's capability and thus success is increased.

Figure 2.3 Changing task requirements can alter performance success.

THINK BACK

Think back to Nick from the beginning of the chapter.

1. What environmental and personal factors may exist to aid or hinder Nick's participation in the physical education program?
2. What would you do to increase Nick's access to the physical education activities offered?

FACTORS INFLUENCING INDIVIDUAL CAPABILITY

The multidimensional nature of the inclusive physical activity approach allows for a range of factors that may or may not affect a person's capability when involved in a movement activity. As stated earlier, these variables are not necessarily static or fixed and may be changed to increase capability and subsequent performance success.

Person-Related Factors Influencing Capability

As described in the ICF, an individual's health condition plays a significant role in performance as well as in perceptions of his or her "ability" or "disability." Within the model, person-related health conditions such as diseases (acute or chronic), disorders, injuries, or trauma can influence capability (WHO, 2001). These various health conditions relate to the physiological or psychological functions of different body systems. Table 2.1 identifies the ICF classifications by body structure and function.

Table 2.2 shows examples of how individuals with various health conditions are considered within the ICF framework. Although the various health conditions can be organized according to the ICF classifications, understand that a condition may affect the functioning of multiple systems, not only the system under which it is organized. For instance, cerebral palsy may be identified as a neuromuscular condition, but some individuals with cerebral palsy may also have differences in mental functions, speech, or vision. Space limitations allow only a few examples. See appendix A for an expanded list of health conditions and related facts for each condition.

Although classifications such as these can be helpful in providing general information, they do not provide deep insight into any one person's capability to perform. Remember that task and context can significantly affect performance outcomes. Individuals differ in terms of their functional capabilities regardless of any specific factor, so assumptions about individuals based on categorical labels must be avoided.

DID YOU KNOW?

A capability approach goes beyond the ICF view of participation and considers "achieved functioning" as influenced not only by the individual's capability but also by opportunity and choice. Understanding participation without appreciating capability misses the chance to include the individual's right and autonomy to choose from a range of life experiences. (Morris, 2009).

Context-Related Factors Influencing Capability

Many contextual factors can directly influence performance capability and activity involvement. These factors include the physical, social, and attitudinal environments in which individuals move and are active. The ICF contains a classification of environmental factors that can be either facilitators (aids) or barriers to participation. These include products and technology; the natural and built environment; support and relationships; attitudes; and services, systems, and policies. These factors, as they relate to barriers to overall activity participation, are discussed in chapter 3.

The designing of novel equipment and innovation of technological advances have significantly impacted capability. For instance, many products are now available to improve function and capability, such as specially designed treadmills with wide belts and slower speeds for individuals with mobility differences, or the Sip 'n' Puff device that allows those with limited upper-body function to control setting the sails and steering a boat solely by use of the sailor's breath (figure 2.4).

Modifications to the activity setting may also increase an individual's capability. For example, specialized matting or turf laid across the sand provides beach access for those using wheelchairs and improves stability and balance for those using a cane or a walker. Physical support or assistance can also improve a person's movement capability. For instance, service dogs can assist those with mobility limitations to more easily complete activities such as crossing the street or shopping for groceries.

Table 2.1 ICF Classification of Body Structures and Functions

ICF category	Specific functions
Mental functions	• Consciousness • Orientation (time, place, person) • Intellectual (including retardation, dementia) • Energy and drive functions • Sleep • Attention • Memory • Emotional functions • Perceptual functions • Higher level cognitive functions • Language
Sensory functions and pain	• Seeing • Hearing • Vestibular (including balance functions) • Pain
Voice and speech functions	• Voice
Functions of the cardiovascular, hematological, immunological, and respiratory systems	• Heart • Blood pressure • Hematological (blood) • Immunological (allergies, hypersensitivity) • Respiration (breathing)
Functions of the digestive, metabolic, and endocrine systems	• Digestive • Defecation • Weight maintenance • Endocrine glands (hormonal changes)
Genitourinary and reproductive functions	• Urination functions • Sexual functions
Neuromusculoskeletal and movement-related functions	• Mobility of joint • Muscle power • Muscle tone • Involuntary movements
Functions of the skin and related structures	• Protection • Repair • Cooling • Sensation

Table 2.2 Examples of Body Functions, Related Health Conditions, and Impairments

Category	Examples
Mental functions	Down syndrome and intellectual functions Multiple sclerosis and speed of cognitive processing Autism and temperament
Sensory functions	Loss of vision Differences in hearing or hearing loss Spinal cord injury and impaired thermo-regulation
Voice and speech functions	Cerebral palsy and difficulty speaking
Functions of the cardiovascular, hematological, immunological, and respiratory systems	Tetraplegia and variations in blood pressure and heart rate Asthma and breathing
Functions of the digestive, metabolic, and endocrine systems	Diabetes and exercise tolerance
Genitourinary and reproductive functions	Spinal cord injury and urinary incontinence
Neuromusculoskeletal and movement-related functions	Cerebral palsy and spasticity Parkinson's disease and balance
Skin and related structures	Paraplegia and pressure sores

Adapted from Rimmer 2006.

Task-Related Factors Influencing Capability

The nature of the task being executed also affects an individual's capability and performance success. The complexity of the movement pattern required to execute the task; the manner in which the task is executed, such as speed of movement or whether the task is self-initiated or in response to an external cue; and whether the skill is continuous or finite can all affect performance outcome. For instance, a child repeatedly bouncing and catching a playground ball with two hands may demonstrate greater capability than if dribbling with just one hand—particularly when first practicing this eye–hand coordination task.

Again think back to Nick Powell at the beginning of the chapter. Now that you have considered ways to increase Nick's access to physical education, consider his participation in the class.

1. Do you think both context- and task-related factors are at play in Nick's case?
2. What would you suggest as possible strategies to shift Nick's capability and increase his actual involvement in activities and ensure his success?

Photo by Donna Towne and used with permission, Vermont Adaptive Ski & Sports.

Figure 2.4 The Sip 'n' Puff allows this sailor full control of the sailboat.

PUTTING IT INTO PRACTICE

The IMAPA offers valuable insight into how ability is viewed and influenced, but practitioner strategies and skills are also essential to achieve the goal of inclusive physical activity programming. Three key strategies promote the implementation of the model and the translating of theory into practice: role extension, reflective practitioners, and restructuring.

Role Extension

The first strategy toward making physical activity inclusive relates to role extension, which involves breaking through boundaries of job expectations and professional territory and extending the commitment and responsibility of physical activity to all and for all. The idea is to prepare all practitioners to be comfortable and adept at working with all participants, regardless of ability. Collaboration and consultation among professionals and participants is needed to achieve this end. Professionals who work with participants with varying abilities work as a team, sharing roles and responsibilities to create successful learning environments. We will discuss this collaborative approach more in chapter 4.

Reflective Practitioners

For programming to include all ability levels and succeed in improving capability, practitioners must become critical thinkers and problem solvers. Their practice must reflect their willingness to accept all participants into their programs and to continually self-assess and adapt their instruction and style as necessary. The three Rs of inclusive reflective practice—ready, rethink, retry—are key to being an effective practitioner (figure 2.5). The first R emphasizes the need for practitioners to prepare themselves and their programs for all participants. This requires them to work collaboratively and gather information that helps them understand the differing capabilities and needs of their participants; they must then

DID YOU KNOW?

Reflection and reflective practice are frequently described as essential attributes of competent health professionals (Mann, Gordon, & MacLeod, 2009).

develop the most meaningful and effective physical activity program for each individual. The second R relates to reflection about the program and its participants, the goal being to continually improve on their practice and the program's effectiveness. They must rethink instructional or activity plans based on what they observe and be open to new ideas and to changing already developed programs. The third R encourages practitioners to retry revised plans that incorporate different strategies or modifications for increased participant involvement and success. It's important to understand that the three-R process is not linear but cyclical in nature. Only with ongoing preparation, reflection, and revision can physical activity programs become truly inclusive. This process is discussed more fully in chapter 6.

Figure 2.5 Reflective practitioners continually practice the cycle of "ready, rethink, and retry" to create physical activity programs that are truly inclusive.

Restructuring

Reflective practice is accompanied by the concept of restructuring. For individuals with differing capabilities, needs, interests, and experiences to be included in physical activity programs, a restructuring of traditional curriculums and program implementation must occur. Strategies that encompass multiuse of space, multiactivity, and multilevel programs must replace strategies in which all participants are involved in similar activities at the same time and in the same way. In chapter 7 we go into more depth about various strategies effective in broadening physical activity programs and present a functional approach to modifying movement experiences (FAMME) model. The FAMME model is a sequence of four steps that connects modifications directly to capability differences to provide meaningful and successful participation for all participants, regardless of skill level. The model guides practitioners to consider all factors that contribute to a movement skill or task outcome—what the individual can do, how the setting should be constructed, and the nature of the goal or task being attempted. This approach, coupled with role extension and reflection, allows physical educators to program effectively for the diverse participants within their programs and assist them by offering truly inclusive physical activity experiences.

Think back to Nick Powell and his participation in the school's physical education program.

1. Will the physical educator need to make modifications for Nick in all activities, regardless of which activity is being taught? Why or why not?
2. If you were the physical educator, would you modify activities just for Nick?
3. Have your initial thoughts about what Nick is and is not capable of changed since the beginning of this chapter? How so?

SUMMARY

More contemporary thinking about function and health has led to models that regard both the environment and personal factors as important contributors to activity and participation. This same appreciation of the multidimensional nature of functioning also includes physical activity performance. The inclusive model of ability in physical activity encompasses both health conditions and context- and task-related factors that combine to influence capability. Practitioners play a critical role in shaping environments and selecting tasks that accommodate individuals with capability differences in such a way that capability is shifted, performance enhanced, and participation is beneficial and satisfying.

What Do You Think?

1. Do you believe that the IMAPA extends previously existing models of disability? Is there anything you would change about the model?
2. When considering the person, task, or context in terms of capability shifting, is one component more or less influential, or are they all equally important in determining capability?
3. Do you believe role extension, reflection, and restructuring are sufficient to allow inclusive physical activity to be fully realized? Why or why not? What other aspects may be needed?

What Would You Do?

Scenario 2.1

Mr. Jackson is in his third year of teaching in an urban city school in northern Texas. In his three years he has learned a lot from his students and their families. For the most part, these families experience both financial and time constraints that significantly limit their participation in recreational physical activities. In addition, because most of these families are recent immigrants, Mr. Jackson realizes they do not have the support of extended family members. Mothers are primarily in charge of recreational activities because their husbands work full time. One woman, Sophia, is the mother of a 14-year-old boy with autism. She mentions to Mr. Jackson that she does not have the skills to make modifications for her son when it comes to physical activity games and recreational opportunities. She also confides that she needs someone to help her with her son and teach her how to support him in the activities that are beneficial for him.

If you were Mr. Jackson:

1. Do you believe Sophia and her son will experience greater challenges in terms of attitudes, access, or accommodation within the recreational programming of their community? Why? How so?
2. What would you recommend as ideas related to physical activity and capability shifting for Sophia's family?
3. What person-related factors may come into play for Sophia's son? What contextual factors may exist?

Scenario 2.2

Darren is an elementary physical education teacher at Ponderosa Elementary School. He has just learned that his district is taking over all the special education programs. Students previously in separate classrooms run by the county will now be in the district classes with their peers. What this means for Darren is that he will have two students in his second-grade physical education class next year who have been identified as having a disability. Darren is a little nervous about this, but he thinks he will be able to meet these students' needs. In fact, the current students in his class come from a variety of socioeconomic and ethnic backgrounds. He has 20 students in his class, and next year he will have an additional aide from special education coming to provide support. One of the new students has cerebral palsy and uses a power wheelchair and a computer to communicate. The other student has a short attention span and difficulty in problem solving and learning. Darren knows that each student in his class has different skills, and he tries to use this to his advantage. In fact, a lot of cross-teaching occurs in his class, with students helping each other. He often puts students into heterogeneous groups and gives them roles or jobs that meet their level of skill for a given activity. In this way, each student contributes to the game or activity. Darren is excited to have these two new students in his class and feels they will contribute to the classroom dynamic. He is eager to learn more about their experiences and the services they might have been receiving through special education so that he and his students can benefit from their expertise.

1. How could IMAPA assist Darren in providing an inclusive second-grade physical education class for all his students?
2. How has Darren used capability shifting to promote learning in his classroom?
3. How could the concept of role extension further assist Darren as he works to meet all his students' needs?

CHAPTER 3

Overcoming Barriers to Inclusive Physical Activity

LEARNING OUTCOMES

After completing this chapter, you should be able to

- recognize barriers in the access to and accommodation of participants in physical activity programs;
- distinguish among person- and context-related barriers that can hinder involvement of participants in physical activity; and
- discuss strategies to overcome barriers and promote inclusive physical activity programs.

INCLUDING ALL INDIVIDUALS

For a few years Brian White has worked as the fitness program coordinator at his community's fitness club. Through a survey of members, he has recently been reminded that his club does not offer programs for people with special interests in certain activities; nor does the club involve members who have identified themselves as needing individualized program plans. Most of his club's members are 25 to 45 years old and exercise during regularly scheduled times and programs.

Brian believed it was time for his club to accommodate a more diverse membership, including older adults with age-related functional disabilities, adults with physical or mobility disabilities, and participants of all ages with learning disabilities. He began to offer several new alternative programs. For the past four months, the club has offered aquatic programs as well as tai chi and yoga. Unfortunately, no new members signed up for the programs. Given the accessible program schedule and exciting new offerings, Brian wondered why there was no increase in membership. In your view, what factors might be preventing new participants from enrolling in Brian's programs? If you were Brian, what changes would you make to attract a diverse group of new members?

A move toward inclusive physical activity requires understanding the philosophical and conceptual foundations underlying inclusive programming, as discussed in previous chapters. Such a move also requires an awareness of the barriers that might exist to hinder the involvement of individuals in physical activity programs. For most of us, which programs we want to join and when we want to be active are the basis for our physical activity decisions. Of course, several factors influence our decisions, such as how much time we can allot to being active, where programs are taking place, and when sessions we are interested in are being offered. Nonetheless, our interests, needs, and preferences should be, and usually are, the primary reasons behind our physical activity choices.

Although barriers to physical activity participation exist for all individuals across the life span, many more factors exist that deny individuals with disabilities the freedom to choose or participate in activities that are available (U.S. Department of Health and Human Services, 2000). Barriers are present at many levels in the realization of all-inclusive programs—from

THINK BACK

Think back to the choices you've made regarding your own participation in physical activity.

1. What activities have you participated in?
2. What factors allowed you to make these choices?
3. Did any factors prevent you from making certain physical activity decisions? If so, what were they? How could these factors have been changed?

initially accepting individuals with different movement capabilities and providing access to physical activity programs to finally accommodating individuals once they join. As much as possible, a person's involvement in physical activity should be based on individual choice rather than on such factors as what's available or accessible. If physical activity professionals are going to work toward providing access and accommodation in physical activity programs, they must broaden their understanding of the breadth and depth of barriers that preclude inclusive physical activity and work toward overcoming them.

Barriers to inclusive physical activity involve one of two categories: (1) context-related barriers, which are external and arise from people and places of physical activity programs; and (2) person-related barriers, which are internal and specific to the individual participant. Each of these barriers can influence the acceptance of, access to, and accommodation of all individuals in physical activity programs (figure 3.1).

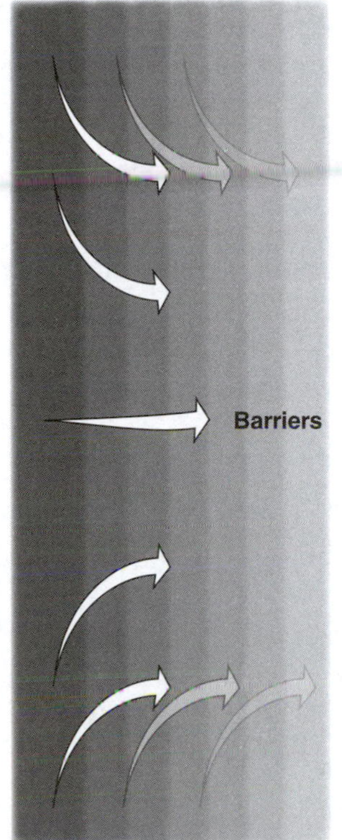

Figure 3.1 Many barriers exist singularly or in combination that might prevent full access to and accommodation of all individuals in physical activity. These barriers relate to the individual or the context of the activity or both.

CONTEXT-RELATED BARRIERS AND STRATEGIES

Many of the barriers to inclusive physical activity exist within the very walls of the communities, schools, and physical activity facilities in which individuals live and are involved. These contextual or environmental barriers are imposed on the individual by others in those settings or by the way in which these settings are constructed. For instance, context-related barriers might include negative attitudes, the use of labels and inappropriate language, lack of professional confidence and competence, inadequate accessibility, or lack of administrative commitment and support.

Attitudes

The attitudes and perceptions of others are among the most significant factors preventing individuals with disabilities from participating in many activity programs (Heward, 2006). Attitudes are generally based on learned beliefs and commonly reflect the thought processes and behavioral evaluations people have toward someone or something (Brostrand, 2006). Although attitudes are typically considered individual and internal processes, they form the lens through which people view, interpret, and interact with the social world around them. Personal experience, familiarity with others, knowledge, and prevalent views of significant others combine to shape a person's belief system. These beliefs in turn might also influence behavior toward and relationships with those who are perceived as different. Individuals with disabilities might be perceived negatively, treated as incapable of making decisions, or even devalued and ignored completely. As discussed in chapter 1, perceptions regarding whether individuals with "disabilities" can be healthy or should be provided health-promoting opportunities such as physical activity may also contribute to reduced opportunity.

Effects of Negative Attitudes

In physical activity programs, the way practitioners, administrators, and program directors view and react to individuals whom they perceive as different or less able significantly affects the success of inclusive efforts. For example, research supports that teachers'

Photo courtesy of David Punia.

Figure 3.2 Negative attitudes of practitioners toward participants can decrease the level of physical activity involvement and inclusiveness of programs.

attitudes toward students with disabilities influence interactions and successful inclusion for school-age children in physical education (Block & Obrusnikova, 2007). Also, a relationship exists between a teacher's attitudes toward inclusive programming and the type or severity of a child's disability. Research suggests that the more significant the difference in ability, the less favorable the practitioner attitude (Conaster, Block, & Lepore, 2000; Conaster, Block, & Gansneder, 2002; see review by Kozub & Lienert, 2003). In addition, students with learning disabilities were viewed more positively than those with behavioral or cognitive disabilities (see review by Kozub & Lienert, 2003; Obrusnikova, 2008). Practitioner attitudes also play a role in inclusive practices for individuals of all ages, including adults involved in recreation and leisure activities (Smith et al., 2005; figure 3.2).

A lack of acceptance by program participants toward individuals with "disabilities" also inhibits inclusive physical activity programming. Research has shown that attitudes of school children toward their peers with significant disabilities play a part in their intention to participate with them in physical education (Hutzler & Levi, 2008; Verderber, Rizzo, & Sherrill, 2003). As is true of professionals, participants develop attitudes based on what they experience around them and what they see in those to whom they look up to for leadership or guidance. In other words, the level of acceptance displayed by professionals subsequently affects the attitude, acceptance, and behavior of peers and participants in the program. Practitioners who do not exhibit positive behaviors and attitudes toward participants with disabilities might negatively influence peer acceptance and attitudes toward those same individuals. Research exploring the perspectives of children with disabilities has confirmed that being allowed to play and feeling like a legitimate participant by their peers were most important to the children with disabilities feeling included (Spencer-Cavaliere & Watkinson, 2010).

The effects of attitudinal barriers on individuals with different abilities are considerable and difficult to overcome. They are especially influential in physical activity programs, in which communication, cooperation, and teamwork are important prerequisites to group participation and individual achievement.

Strategies for Promoting Inclusive Attitudes

Because attitudes are most critical in determining who will and who will not have the opportunity to participate in particular programs, efforts aimed at promoting positive perceptions and attitudes take priority over considerations of access and accommodation. If attitudinal barriers are likely to be the most significant, how can people come to accept and support individuals perceived as different and with whom they have had very little exposure? The answer involves changing perceptions through increased knowledge, awareness, and experience (figure 3.3).

Attitudes toward people with significant disabilities are highly affected by social, physical, and experiential factors. Such attitudes can be influenced by significant others, including parents, teachers, friends, and family members. They might develop from past experience or arise from current ideas or beliefs. For instance, if children grew up in a community in which there were no other children with great differences in ability, the children in this community might come to believe that people with disabilities are unlike themselves and do not belong in the community. Or they might be afraid of the "different" children because of their lack of exposure to them. Had the school or neighborhood been more inclusive, the beliefs and attitudes of the children would likely have been quite different. What then are the strategies that foster positive, more accepting attitudes?

Figure 3.3 Changing perceptions and promoting positive attitudes can significantly influence the level of physical activity involvement of individuals with disabilities.

Preparing peers and participants for inclusive programming is an important step in the process. The peers of participants with disabilities need to understand the nature of ability differences and, more important, increase their awareness of similarities. In general, attitude change is elicited in two ways: through exposure to information and through experience. Strategies that expose people to information include educational presentations, guest speakers, and instructional units infused into a program's curriculum. Professional development activities offered to program personnel can also help support cooperative social interactions among individuals with and without "disabilities" (Lieberman, James, & Ludwa, 2004; Milsom, 2006). Educational programs must be positive; they must emphasize people as individuals rather than collective groups with medical characteristics or conditions; and they must continue to acknowledge the person-environment relationship from an abilities-based perspective (Dunn & Elliott, 2005).

Simulation activities can also increase awareness and information about disability. These simulations are designed to enable students to experience an ability difference through the use of special equipment and instruction. Research supports awareness activities being effective in changing attitudes of children toward peers with disabilities in physical activity settings (Hutzler et al., 2007). Although simulation activities might seem an ideal way to share information about what it is like to have a significant ability difference, some people ethically question the use of simulations (Burgstahler & Doe, 2004). They argue that simulations represent a negative experience and might expose participants to feelings and challenges that individuals with disabilities have only some of the time or under some circumstances. In fact, some maintain that disability-related simulations do not simulate the disability experience at all, and that participants in simulation activities cannot truly understand what it is like to have a disability label or difference in ability.

Research has also failed to offer equivocal support for the effectiveness of simulation activities in promoting positive attitudes (Block & Obrusnikova, 2007; Ellery & Rauschenbach, 2000). A decline in positive attitude as a result of these activities might be associated with increased awareness of perceived limitations or with peer acceptance based on athletic ability. For these reasons, simulation activities should not be used as introductory activities; rather they should be used only after participants have been taught the abilities and coping skills of people with disabilities (Wood, 2002). Burgstahler & Doe (2004) recommend a constructivist view of simulations that promote a deeper understanding of "disability" by including activities that portray individuals with disabilities as active agents for change, focusing on the skills they require and possess rather than on any deficit they might have (figure 3.4). Through simulations, "disability" can be exposed as a function of

Photo courtesy of S. Kasser, photographer T. Bolduc.

Figure 3.4 Peers involved in a simulated game of goalball can deepen their understanding of the skills and capabilities individuals with visual differences possess during a competitive physical activity or sport.

environmental barriers, and simulation activities can highlight contextual modifications that maximize access and foster improved performance and increased success for everyone.

Direct contact can also promote positive attitudes. However, if negative stereotypes and fears are reinforced, direct contact can also cause negative feelings to develop. Because the type of setting and contact can have different effects on attitudes, interactions must be planned and intentional. The experience must demonstrate that the individual with a disability is participating within his or her capabilities rather than highlighting his or her inadequacies. In addition, direct contact promotes favorable attitudes when the experience is perceived as voluntary and enjoyable. Contact alone does not positively change perceptions and acceptance. A social climate in which value and respect for individual similarities and differences exist is essential.

Labeling and Language

Associated with the concepts of attitudes and acceptance is the notion of labeling. We all have many labels attached to us. Some labels are used to denote relationships (e.g., mother, sister, nephew, mentor, friend, colleague), whereas others give insight into roles and responsibilities (e.g., teacher, student, advisor, director). We use these labels with an underlying assumption that the labels only *partially* define the person. We all understand that a person wears many hats and that these hats can and do change from one time to another and from one place to another. No one is only a mother or only a teacher; we know these people are much more as well.

Problems With Labels and Language

Unfortunately, labels are associated with perceived ideas and assumptions about a person that can supersede all other characteristics and realities about the individual and are too often generalized to represent the whole person regardless of place and time. For instance, research has shown that the use of a label rather than understanding a student's actual movement capability had a biasing effect and negatively influenced teachers' intentions to teach the student in physical education classes (Tripp & Rizzo, 2006). Labels can also have hurtful, demeaning consequences for those being labeled (Higgins, Raskind, Goldberg, & Herman, 2002). People with perceived disabilities have endured a countless number of derogatory labels over the years for the sole purpose of excluding them from everyday activities, services, and privileges (Heward, 2006). Often people's intolerance toward those from whom they differ is displayed through their language and words. Previous research examining the everyday language used in conversations about individuals with disability labels showed that "disability" was typically equated with abnormality and that individuals with such labels were frequently devalued (Danforth & Navarro, 1998). As with societal and attitudinal changes, so too has the language of disability gradually changed. People with ability differences have long advocated for changes in the labels and words used to describe them and their "disabilities" (Foreman, 2005).

Two opposing perspectives relate to labeling individuals with "disabilities." Some professionals believe that labeling serves a purpose to the benefit of those being labeled. Labels are often a prerequisite to receiving services, funding, and legal clout and are required for access and accommodation in certain programs (Heward, 2006; Kauffman, 1998). In addition, labels have enabled disability-specific advocacy groups to garner increased attention and lead to the development of specialized instructional methods and interventions (Henley, Ramsey, & Algozzine, 2009). Other professionals argue that labels used to classify or categorize individuals perpetuate stereotypes and exclusionary practices (Henley, Ramsey, & Algozzine, 2009; Stainback & Stainback, 1991). Despite some valid arguments that support labeling, labels tend to focus attention on differences rather than similarities and on individual deficits rather than societal and contextual factors that create ability differences. The most cited disadvantages of labeling include the following:

- Labels reduce individuality and ignore the uniqueness of each participant, classifying individuals solely by group membership. The label becomes the primary identifier of the individual rather than the many other possible identifiers, such as teacher, mother, sister, employee, or friend. Labels do not attempt to convey the total essence and nature of an individual.
- Labels lead to stereotyping and overgeneralizations about ability or inability that in turn encourage limited expectations.
- Labels are usually disability based rather than ability based. They focus attention on what individuals cannot do rather than on what they can do.
- Labels are often viewed as permanent, emphasizing stagnancy rather than change.
- Labels are sometimes used inappropriately to relieve responsibility of practitioners for changing contexts or situations that could allow successful participation of the individual. It may be easier for some practitioners to attribute a participant's failure to his or her "disability" rather than the lack of time and effort given to reflecting on and revising activity plans to accommodate his or her ability differences.

Regardless of the physical activity setting or the age of the participant, labels that deemphasize the abilities of an individual and devalue his or her skills cannot possibly encourage acceptance. Such labels do little to promote high expectations, successful inclusion, or individual accommodation.

Strategies for Promoting Acceptance Through Language

The words we use to label or define people influence how they are viewed and subsequently treated. The first step toward fostering acceptance and respect is changing the language we choose. Terms such as "handicapped" and "crippled" previously evoked images of inability, pity, or fear and tended to group all people together regardless of their needs, strengths, and individuality. Recent perspectives favor the term "disability" and, for the most part, the use of person-first language (Foreman, 2005). For example, we should say "a child with a disability" rather than "a disabled child." This seemingly small difference emphasizes the individual rather than the "disability" and is person centered, not group focused. Here are other guidelines for using terminology and language choices that help shift our language toward being more positive and accepting:

- Avoid using a "disability" label to refer to someone. For example, say "the man who lives down the street in the green house" instead of "the blind man who lives down the street."

- Emphasize the uniqueness of each individual. When we use person-first language and focus on roles and other social labels, we avoid defining people by their "disabilities" (e.g., Susie, a second-grader with a learning difference).
- When it is important to distinguish between individuals with and without "disabilities," use the phrase people without disabilities. Avoid using the terms "normal" or "healthy" to indicate those individuals without disabilities.
- Jargon such as "challenged" or "differently abled" are not always helpful in promoting acceptance and empowering others. The "disability" is not a challenge in itself but rather because of people's views and how contexts are constructed.
- Avoid using words such as "crippled," "defect," "afflicted," and other terms that are negative or devaluing. Restrict your use of the noun "patient" to hospital settings. Table 3.1 lists other preferred terms and phrases and those that should be avoided.

Table 3.1 The Preferred Language of Inclusive Practices

Preferred term	Avoid
Head injury	Brain damage
Deaf or hearing impaired	Deaf and dumb
Nonverbal or without speech	Mute or dumb
Blind or visually impaired	Sightless
Developmentally delayed	Slow
Uses a wheelchair	Confined or bound to a wheelchair
Person who has . . .	Afflicted with, suffers from, or victim of
Mental illness or emotional disability	Crazy or insane
Congenital disability	Birth defect or defective

Although it is important to communicate with and about people with "disabilities" in positive and respectful ways, simply changing the language we use will not automatically lead to greater acceptance and inclusion. Using positive language must be accompanied by changed societal attitudes and values critical for creating inclusive physical activity environments. As mentioned previously, negative attitudes can be significant barriers to the success of inclusion because the public significantly influences how much importance is given to an issue. This situation is made more difficult when individuals with disabilities are underrepresented when decisions about policy and service provision are made (Massie, 2006).

DID YOU KNOW?

Some groups prefer to claim their identity through their difference and are empowered by rejecting the person-first concept. For example, many deaf individuals prefer to be called "deaf" or "hard of hearing" rather than "a person with a hearing impairment."

Perceived Professional Competency

Although some practitioners feel quite comfortable and capable working with individuals with very different abilities, many do not. Often, programs and activities are planned for individuals who are similar in ability or for those who fall within the middle range of skill level. It is both common and valid for professionals to feel inadequate to meet the needs of all individuals, including those participants with significantly different abilities. Many times, practitioners charged with the responsibility for teaching, coaching, or instructing have had little exposure and experience involving people with significantly different learning, movement, and behavioral capabilities. Their fears are often based on their lack of knowledge about various person-related conditions, and their own perceived competence to instruct individuals with disabilities.

Barriers Created by Lack of Perceived Professional Competency

In educational settings, barriers to inclusive programming include lack of teacher collaboration and inadequate training of practitioners (Liu & Pearson, 1999). Particularly in physical education settings, research has shown that practitioners' attitudes toward teaching students with disabilities in general physical education is most influenced by the practitioner's perceived competence to do so (see Kozub & Lienert, 2003 for review). As a result of this lack of professional preparation, teachers often have limited expectations of students with disabilities in the general physical education setting (Lieberman & Houston-Wilson, 2009). Perceived professional competence might also play a role in whether practitioners in community-based exercise or activity programs choose to include adults with disabilities.

Professional knowledge and perceived competency are critical for programs to be inclusive of all individuals interested in lifelong physical activity participation. Without them, many individuals will continue to be excluded from physical activity opportunities.

Strategies for Enhancing Perceived Professional Competence

Staff development and training are necessary for creating successful inclusive physical activity programs (figure 3.5). Professional development and training focused on inclusion and teaching students with disabilities is important for both the teachers' acceptance of those students and the teachers' self-efficacy to instruct these students (Hersman & Hodge, 2010). College courses and academic preparation can also help promote positive attitudes (Folsom-Meek, Nearing, & Kalakian, 2000; Goyakla Apache & Rizzo, 2005), and direct or practicum experience can be effective in increasing perceived competency among preservice practitioners (Hodge, Davis, Woodard, & Sherrill, 2002). Collaborative strategies must be developed and skills and resources shared across all facets of activity programs in order to benefit all participants. In chapter 4 we look in depth at collaboration as a means of obtaining information and developing professional competency.

Effective instruction that meets the needs of all participants includes a hierarchy of pedagogical practices in which organization, instruction, and management form the basis of the physical activity environment. Participant success is the ultimate goal.

Photo courtesy of S. Kasser, photographer T. Bolduc.

Figure 3.5 Conferences and in-service workshops related to inclusive physical activity can increase perceived competency of practitioners working with individuals with disabilities.

The success of an inclusive physical activity experience involves the realization of participant and practitioner goals and the amount and quality of the participant's involvement. The degree of success achieved depends on the participant's ability level and on the practitioner's beliefs about his or her own ability and effectiveness to run the inclusive program and meet everyone's needs.

ELEMENTS OF EFFECTIVE PRACTICE

- Increase active learning and practice time of participants.
- Promote high rates of success for participants through task and context variation.
- Set high but realistic expectations for participants.
- Assist participants to learn from observation and self-reflection.
- Allow individual and group input into the process (e.g., suggested modifications).
- Engage in ongoing reflective and critical thinking—be a problem solver.
- Promote participant self-responsibility and decision making.
- Provide a supportive and accepting climate for all participants.
- Garner support and use all available resources to support professional practice and participant involvement.

Source: Rink, J.E. (1998). *Teaching physical education for learning* (3rd ed.). Boston: McGraw-Hill.

Accessibility

When we think of accessibility, we typically imagine someone in a wheelchair unable to enter a building with stairs or attend an activity session held on the second floor of a building without an elevator. It is true that these kinds of architectural barriers can hinder an individual's involvement in physical activity programs, but there are many other accessibility factors that limit participation. Accessibility barriers constitute anything that prevents an individual's equal access and opportunity to facilities and programs, including communication obstacles, transportation constraints, economic limitations, and equipment availability.

Barriers Related to Accessibility

Architectural barriers, the most glaring of the accessibility hurdles, involve structures that present obstacles or make a building unusable by individuals with disabilities. Even when a ramp leads directly to an entrance, a person using a wheelchair might not be able to use the facility if there is no accessible parking or if the front door is too heavy to open. Other common barriers include the lack of handrails, doorknobs difficult to operate, or doorways too narrow for a wheelchair. How rooms or spaces are arranged might also affect accessibility. Extraneous equipment can impede the movement of people with mobility or balance difficulties; exercise equipment might be too close together, preventing individuals who use wheelchairs to move between or beside them (figure 3.6). A recent survey of health clubs found that most had a low to moderate level of accessibility and that significant deficiencies were related to the built environment (Rimmer, Riley, Wang, & Rauworth, 2005).

Beyond the facility design, barriers related to communication might hinder access to services and programs related to health care and health promotion. For instance, communication barriers can hinder practitioner-client interactions for those with hearing or speech differences, or individuals who are blind may not be able to obtain health information in accessible formats or identify specific rooms in facilities because of a lack of Braille (Kaye, 2001).

Even if a facility is accessible in the broadest of definitions, individuals might still be denied access if they cannot get to and from the facility or program. Whether it is a parent trying to take her infant to a class or an older adult wanting to get to a community exercise program, transportation barriers hamper attempts by individuals with disabilities to participate in many physical activity programs. Individuals living in rural areas might not have access to public transportation. For others, public transportation might exist, but the transit system does not accommodate individuals with disabilities. For instance, the law requires public transit agencies to include wheelchair lifts on buses or railway cars, but this law applies only to new equipment. Some communities have implemented specially arranged accessible transportation services for individuals unable to drive or find transportation, but the schedule restrictions and cost associated with these services might prevent individuals from using the service and further hamper individuals from joining physical activity sessions. For example, in some locations individuals are allowed to use the special services bus only for appointments to the doctor, not for any kind of recreational or leisure activity, and must call at least two days in advance to request the service. These types of restrictions can certainly prevent some people from attending a physical activity class or going out with a friend to participate in a special activity event.

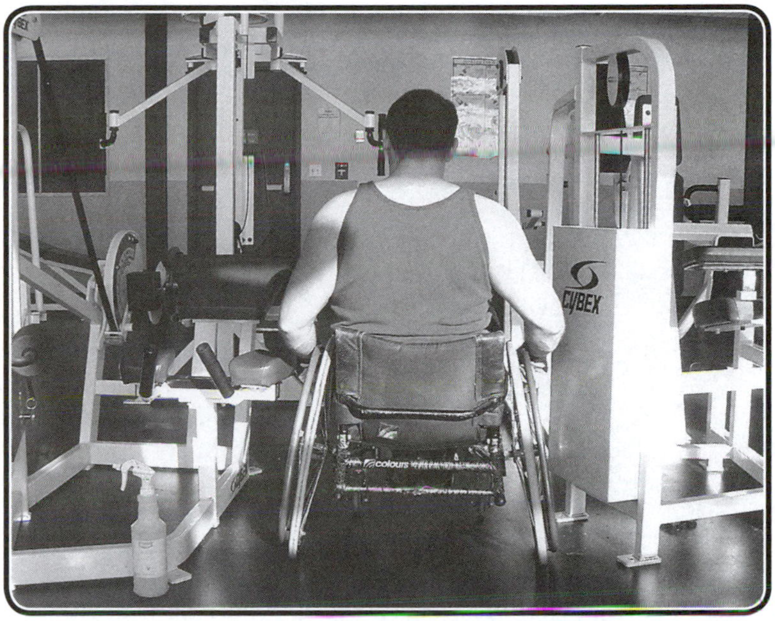

Photo courtesy of S. Kasser, photographer T. Bolduc.

Figure 3.6 In addition to architectural barriers, the spacing of equipment in fitness facilities can further limit accessibility and the opportunity for all individuals to exercise.

Freedom to participate in physical activity means all individuals can physically enter a program *and* financially access the program. Economic barriers exist for many people, but they are common for individuals with disabilities. Although there are indications that employment levels for people with "disabilities" are increasing, data point to a widening gap in income levels for those with disability labels compared to those without (Kaye, 2001). Those who are employed often find themselves in low-paying positions. This situation, compounded by higher than average expenses such as medical needs and equipment, assistive technology, and special transportation, often puts the cost of health and fitness clubs or community programs out of reach. In fact, the cost of exercise programs has been cited as a major obstacle to physical activity participation for minority families who have children with disabilities (Columna, Pyfer, & Senne, 2011) as well as for adults with disabilities (Rimmer, Rubin, & Braddock, 2000). Financial barriers exist not only for adults interested in exercise programs but also for those interested in sport participation. Sophisticated new equipment for individuals with disabilities allows greater freedom and better performance, but costs may be prohibitive for many aspiring athletes (DePauw & Gavron, 2005). In addition, travel expenses for competitions can be expensive, and businesses are less likely to sponsor athletes with disabilities because of the lack of media coverage to sell their products.

We do not generally think of equipment as a barrier to physical activity involvement. Rather, we view equipment as a necessary component to participation in some activities. For example, if you want to go downhill skiing, you will need skis, boots, and poles. However, for an individual who is nonambulatory, this equipment alone does not afford the opportunity to participate. In another example, a child in the first or second grade might not find a standard height basketball hoop accessible for learning how to shoot baskets. In this case the child lacks the strength needed to succeed with this equipment. These examples show how either the lack of availability or lack of appropriateness of equipment results in a barrier to physical activity participation.

DID YOU KNOW

In 1997, 40 to 45 percent of buses used by public transit systems nationally had no wheelchair lifts (Kaye & Longmore, 1997). Since that time, transportation systems have become more useable by individuals with disabilities, with lifts on many more buses, elevators to mass transit stops, and detectable warnings for people with vision disabilities (Kaye, 2001).

DID YOU KNOW ?

Individuals with disabilities have a much higher poverty rate. In the year 2009, an estimated 26.4 percent of noninstitutionalized persons aged 21 to 64 years with a disability in the United States were living below the poverty line (Erickson, Lee, & von Schrader, 2010). This income level leaves very little cash for out-of-pocket expenditures such as those associated with health and physical activity.

Despite greater awareness and improvement in reducing architectural barriers for individuals with disabilities, equal access to buildings and programs in the broadest sense of accessibility has not yet been realized.

Strategies for Overcoming Accessibility Barriers

Over the past two decades, equal access to programs and services for all individuals, including those with disabilities, has improved. This trend toward increased inclusion has come about mainly through a heightened awareness and legislation calling for an end to discriminatory practices in all aspects of daily life, including physical activity opportunities. One of the most important steps in ensuring this equality came with the passage of the Americans with Disabilities Act (ADA) in 1990. The law provided a clear mandate to eliminate discrimination and afford equal access so that all individuals could participate more fully in society's activities and benefit from various programs and services. As a result, health clubs, exercise and recreational programs, and other community-based physical activity programs became more accessible to individuals with disabilities.

School-based accessibility issues were addressed by another significant piece of legislation, the Education of All Handicapped Children's Act of 1975, now called the Individuals with Disabilities Education Act (IDEA). As part of the IDEA, students with "disabilities" are to be provided a free public education alongside their peers to the maximum extent appropriate. Consequently, more and more children have had access to, and the necessary supports in, general physical education programs within their schools. See appendix C for a list of websites with information related to the IDEA act and other critical legislation supporting inclusion over the past three decades.

Accessibility to physical activity programs and activities, however, does not occur simply through the passage of laws. Although legislation and policy has helped, improving the accessibility of fitness and recreational facilities requires collaboration among staff within these facilities, individuals with "disabilities," and accessibility consultants regarding disability awareness, barrier removal, and information and economic resources (Barth, Rimmer, Wang, & Schiller, 2008). Practitioners need to advocate for both access and accommodation for those with whom they work. They must become familiar with the legislation and how components of the laws affect their programs and services. Practitioners who are aware of the barriers that limit access can implement strategies to allow more participants to be involved in their programs. They might be able to provide or assist with transportation, offer sliding scale memberships, secure sponsorships from local businesses to offset participant costs, or choose more accessible locations for their activities. Additionally, the physical activity practitioner in any setting must consider the variability of participants' needs when planning and preparing equipment for activity sessions. In our skiing example, the adult could participate in downhill skiing quite proficiently with the appropriate equipment, such as a monoski (figure 3.7). For the child who wants to learn to shoot a basketball, a shorter hoop or lighter ball can be used. The use of varied equipment or adapted products can make all the difference in creating access for participation.

Although legislation has been helpful in promoting awareness and increasing access to programs, true equality has not been realized. Continued efforts must be made in educating others and informing them of the laws. Unfortunately, though, we cannot legislate change in attitudes and acceptance. Such change must come from increased commitment on the part of practitioners and those overseeing their programs to ensure the intent of the laws is realized.

Administrative Support

Many practitioners have favorable attitudes toward including individuals with significant disabilities in their programs, but they lack the support and commitment of others involved in the decision making. A teacher might feel positive about having a student with a cognitive difference enter her physical education class but not be provided the needed supports by the administration in order for her to do this effectively. A fitness practitioner might welcome individuals with mobility disabilities into his exercise class but lack the support of the program director when it comes to accommodations and support. Administrators and directors must value the philosophy of inclusive practices and be committed to providing a supportive and effective place for inclusive physical activity to occur. Without such a commitment, not much can be done.

Rossmiller Photography

Figure 3.7 Specialized equipment has increased access to many activities for individuals with disabilities.

Lack of Administrative Support

Some of the barriers to inclusive physical activity programming extend beyond the practitioner directly responsible for the program and initially might even seem beyond the practitioner's control. Administrative issues related to facility availability and scheduling, finances needed for equipment or increased support services, or time for increased training and professional development might all hinder the opportunity for inclusive programs to exist. For instance, in public schools, many educators contend that a lack of time significantly impedes their ability to include students with disabilities into their classes (Liu & Pearson, 1999). In addition, teachers might not be provided with enough collaborative planning time to include students in the general physical education program (Lytle & Collier, 2002). Scheduling conflicts prevent needed collaborative meetings from taking place in which strategies and modifications are to be planned. Support personnel are not always available to assist within the program, and when they are they might not be adequately trained in how to assist most effectively. Similarly, practitioners might feel the need to gain knowledge and skills necessary to assist with the inclusion of children or adults with disabilities in physical activity and exercise programs. However, for this to occur there must be a commitment and time available to attend conferences or workshops. This often takes practitioners away from their daily responsibilities, which likely costs supervisors money for training fees and personnel to substitute for the absent practitioners. But regardless of the setting or program activity, administrative support is critical in any physical activity environment for inclusive practices to be realized.

Strategies for Gaining Administrative Support

One of the most critical factors in the continued success of any inclusive model is the availability of adequate support to assist practitioners in developing and implementing inclusive programs. Initially, program personnel must commit to the time and energy required for collaboration, program planning, and reflection on including individuals with diverse needs in established physical activity programs. Practitioners must then advocate for what they need in terms of support to ensure that inclusion of all individuals can occur. This includes educating administrators or supervisors about the philosophical and legal basis for their inclusive efforts, barriers that might exist, and potential strategies to overcome them. The importance of administrative or supervisor support cannot be overlooked in efforts to provide inclusive physical activity programs. Not only can they affect necessary administrative procedures to accommodate individuals with diverse needs in inclusive settings (financial resources, scheduling, matching of participants and practitioners, and providing needed time for planning and collaboration), they can also provide access to necessary training opportunities for practitioners and staff members who are implementing programs and modifications. As discussed earlier, perceived professional competency of those implementing physical activity programs is key to attitudinal change and future professional practice. After training, practitioners should also be provided with ongoing support to facilitate the inclusive program. Ongoing support might be needed in the form of follow-up conferences or training sessions, reduced class or group size, release time for planning, additional support personnel, or other such assistance. In addition, practitioners can promote inclusive programming through parent support, special events, and high visibility of their programs. Every individual who works in the environment must commit to the philosophy of inclusion, including practitioners, participants, and administrative staff. Each must believe that every individual in the program deserves respect, access, and meaningful participation. In chapter 4 we present a collaborative approach toward gaining administrative commitment and support.

THINK BACK

Think back to your own experiences in physical activity programs.

1. Can you think of a time when context-related barriers prevented you from successful participation? If so, what were the barriers?
2. What strategies could have been used to create a more accessible situation for you?
3. Now think back to Brian White at the start of the chapter.
    - What contextual barriers might have played a role in the lack of new members joining his programs? Why might these barriers exist?
    - If you were Brian's consultant for creating inclusive environments, what ideas would you give him?

PERSON-RELATED BARRIERS AND STRATEGIES

Along with external barriers related to physical activity opportunities, there are also obstacles to physical activity participation that are internal to the participants and related to their own knowledge and behavior. These person-related or intrinsic barriers can further limit choices and behavior regarding physical activity (figure 3.8).

Knowledge

A person cannot make a choice to participate in a physical activity program if he or she does not know the program exists. Many people do not participate in programs because their knowledge about the programs is limited. Individuals with disabilities might be unaware of program availability, their legal rights to access programs, and the benefits of participating in physical activity.

Barriers Related to Knowledge

A lack of knowledge about program availability might be the reason some people do not participate in physical activity. For example, the parent of a child who's beginning to show delays in reaching motor milestones might not be aware that early intervention programs exist or how to access them. An adult with joint pain and limited range of motion might not know that the local YMCA has a heated pool and offers low-impact water exercise programs. Not knowing where to exercise can be a primary barrier to exercise participation for African-American women with physical disabilities (Rimmer, Rubin, & Braddock, 2000) and others with mobility disabilities (Scelza, Kalpakjian, Zemper, & Tate, 2005).

Even when people with disabilities know that a program exists, they might not know of their legal rights to access these programs. Parents of a child with an identified disability might be uninformed about educational laws and their child's legal right to participate in an inclusive physical education program with necessary supports provided. An adult wanting to join a community-based activity program might be unaware of laws that guarantee accessible transportation and program access.

Figure 3.8 What participants know and believe about themselves and their involvement in physical activity influences their participation in physical activity programs.

In some cases it's not a lack of knowledge about programs or legal rights that prevents people from gaining access to exercise programs. Rather, the primary barrier for some people is their lack of education regarding the benefits of physical activity. Beliefs and attitudes toward physical activity and the awareness of its importance for health and quality of life significantly influence activity participation and exercise choices. Parents might believe that their child with a mobility difference cannot possibly benefit from physical education, especially in classes with more highly skilled peers. For older adults, the lack of knowledge and understanding of the relationship between moderate activity and health is a significant barrier to exercising (Schutzer & Graves, 2004).

Strategies for Increasing Knowledge

Individuals with disabilities can increase their knowledge of program availability in several ways. They themselves can seek out information regarding program options, or practitioners can gather information to help educate potential participants about activity opportunities. For example, the Internet is a great source of information on activities available for those interested in disability sports programs (see appendix C). Many sites describe competitions, rules, and trainings. Community recreation programs should also be able to inform people of the many diverse programs available within their community. A phone call to a community exercise facility might reveal that the facility has special features to encourage individuals with disabilities to become members, such as heated therapy pools, water aerobics classes, spacious facilities that allow for greater mobility, and knowledgeable staff to assist with all skill and ability levels. Community recreational facilities might have alternative equipment available, such as a monoski or guides at the ski slope. Contacting facilities directly and inquiring about physical activity opportunities is a simple first step toward opening the door to inclusive participation.

Lack of knowledge concerning legal rights prevents some individuals from making informed choices and might restrict participation in many aspects of society, including physical activity opportunities. Individuals with disabilities must advocate for themselves and learn advocacy-related skills that facilitate their involvement (Pfeiffer, 2001). They need either to become self-informed or be educated by others about their legal rights. Such capacity-building efforts have also been shown to empower those with disabilities from ethnic minority groups to increase their degree of control over services and policy decisions and to promote greater compliance with the American with Disabilities Act in their community (Balcazar, Keys, & Suarez-Balcazar, 2008). Friends, family members, teachers, and practitioners also carry the responsibility to serve as advocates and assist individuals with disabilities to become empowered by the legislation in place to serve them and create equitable environments.

For individuals to adopt and adhere to physical activity and exercise, they must first believe that doing so is beneficial. Providing potential participants with literature and materials describing the benefits of physical activity might be enough to spark their interest in joining. Another strategy is to involve health professionals as sources of information and support. For school-based programs, teachers might prepare parents and their students by discussing the benefits, both physical and social, that result from inclusive physical education classes. Health care professionals and fitness practitioners may do the same for the individuals they serve.

Self-Determination, Self-Efficacy, and Motivation

Motivation to be physically active is another significant determinant of physical activity behavior. Individuals are motivated to participate in physical activity for many reasons. Some are encouraged by others or externally pressured to be involved, whereas others choose to engage in an activity out of self-interest, personal commitment, or intrinsic value. Motivation might be based on an internal factor, such as participating because the activity is enjoyable and brings pleasure, or it might be that the activity allows social interaction with friends. Ultimately, intrinsic motivation will influence an individual's decisions in terms of involvement in a task or activity. The higher an individual's motivation, the more apt he or she is to try an activity, put forth effort while participating, and stay with it, even when adherence becomes challenging. According to Bandura (1977), intrinsic motivation has its roots in a person's self-efficacy or belief about his or her capabilities to perform a specific activity or attain a desired outcome. The greater an individual's self-efficacy or self-perceptions about ability in a specific task, the greater the motivation to participate and adhere to the task. But perceived competence is not the only factor that plays a role in one's motivation to engage in activity. Many factors contribute to whether a person is self-motivated. Self-determination of behavior involves internalization or regulation of extrinsic motives as well as perceived locus of causality (Ryan & Deci, 2000). Based on this premise, practitioners must realize that social contexts and conditions can either enhance or diminish positive motivation; they must understand their role in establishing settings that foster autonomy, competence, and connectedness.

Barriers to Motivation

Some people lack the confidence to participate in a physical activity or exercise program and are consequently unmotivated to join. If individuals with disabilities believe they will not be able to do the activity or achieve success as others in the program do, they are less likely to begin the activity or to stay with it after starting it. These kinds of efficacy expectations have been shown to influence the exercise behavior of older adults (Resnick, 2001) and adults with physical "disabilities" (Cardinal, Kosma, & McCubbin, 2004). Individuals with high self-efficacy begin exercising and stay with their programs longer than those with lower self-perceptions of ability. Research also shows that, for adults with long-term mobility disabilities, those with increased motivation and higher exercise self-efficacy have a higher probability of staying with the program (McAuley et al., 2007). A lack of confidence regarding activity participation may also exist in families and caregivers that support individuals with disabilities. Parents of children with vision disabilities report lower expectations and confidence related to their children's successful involvement in physical activity programs

(Stuart, Lieberman, & Hand, 2006). Regardless of age and program type, motivation and confidence are necessary prerequisites to program participation. In terms of self-determination to engage in physical activity, alienation, a lack of connectedness, and less than optimal challenges can create further barriers to activity for participants of varying abilities.

Strategies for Increasing Confidence and Motivation

The key to increased participation and meaningful involvement in physical activity programs is to ensure that participants are internally motivated to join and be physically active. Programs must be perceived as enjoyable and nonthreatening. Participants need to believe they have the skills to be successful. Thus activities must be designed to include a wide range of skill levels with optimal challenges and success planned. Making this happen involves finding out what needs to be manipulated or modified (e.g., equipment, instruction, physical setting) so that everyone involved can participate in the activity. Practitioners must provide positive reinforcement and feedback so that participants feel more confident in their abilities to perform a task or engage in the activity. By modeling a program that is inclusive of all individuals, other participants might too believe they will be accepted and successful. In chapter 7 we offer strategies for individualizing physical activity programs and increasing participant success and confidence.

Perceived Value of the Activity

The tasks included in physical activity programs, be they skills in physical education class or exercises in physical fitness programs, must be chosen with consideration for the meaningfulness, age-appropriateness, and functional value they have for participants. For example, an elementary class might be practicing the skills of catching and throwing in order to use these skills in games, whereas seniors in a water aerobics class might be working to improve strength and balance for increased independence in activities of daily living. Barriers might exist within these and other types of activities when consideration for perceptions of value and future utility are not taken into account.

Barriers Related to Perceived Value of Activities

One potential barrier to participation of individuals with disabilities in physical activity programs is the meaningfulness of the activities available. An increasing number of adults and students with diverse abilities and capabilities are included in prestructured physical activity programs. In school settings, curriculums are set, units developed, and traditional activities implemented. In communities, exercise programs are offered within typically organized facilities, often with set routines and group exercises implemented. Besides the limited activities to choose from, there is a risk that participants or parents will find little meaning in the activities offered and thus devalue the physical activity experience. This results in avoidance of or little enthusiasm shown for the activity. For instance, if a high school physical education program offers team sports only one semester, those students who find individual or leisure activities more meaningful and satisfying might avoid taking additional physical education credit once they have met graduation requirements. Likewise, adults who find aquatics classes more meaningful might avoid exercising if only step aerobics is offered at noon during their lunch hour when they want to exercise.

Another factor concerning the inclusion of individuals with disabilities into physical activity programs is the appropriateness of the activity. Some individuals' physical or developmental capabilities are not the same or even similar to others of the same age. An adult, for instance, whose intellectual capabilities are not commensurate with other adults might not understand the complex rules and strategies of some team-oriented recreational activities or might have trouble understanding the concept of pacing while jogging. For this reason, practitioners often avoid age-appropriate activities and implement activities geared to much younger individuals or children. For example, it would not be appropriate for a high school teacher to have his or her high school students with developmental delays participate in a game of London Bridge to practice walking or skipping to music. Walking for exercise could be practiced in the community, or activity levels could be increased with age-appropriate music and dancing. The absence of age-appropriate physical activity can be connected to a lack of training and competency by professionals and, as such, tends to perpetuate stereotypes and lowered expectations of those individuals with disabilities.

Another possible barrier to physical activity participation is beliefs about whether the activity serves a functional purpose for the individual. Concerns over whether students with disabilities should participate in general physical education classes have centered on whether the tasks or activities in that program are of functional value. Will the physical activity program help the individual with vocational skills, daily life skills of dressing and grooming, and so on? While this question is not asked about most children entering a physical activity program, it is commonly asked of those with significant disabilities. The importance an activity has for enhancing functional capabilities in adults with disabilities is also a concern for some. Although lifting weights might improve fitness, an individual with balance problems might feel that weightlifting is unimportant because it does not directly improve balance and the functional skill of walking.

Strategies for Increasing Perceived Value of Activities

Effective physical activity programs usually spring from a well-planned and organized design. Of course, curriculums and program guides also offer guidance in this regard. However, these should be viewed as general guides, not program mandates. Regardless of setting or participant age, program activities should be derived from meaningful goals and objectives for the participant. For school-age children, the physical education curriculum or activities within curricular units must be adapted to meet the unique learning outcomes important for the student. Adapting the curriculum in physical education is a key strategy to inclusion (Block, 2007). For some children with disabilities, we should not assume that the general physical education program is nonfunctional. In fact, the general physical education program can be functional for most students in promoting lifetime physical activity.

Community-based activity programs must also include opportunities for adults to self-select meaningful activities (figure 3.9). Participants could be offered such recreational activities as canoeing or bowling, which they may be more likely to participate in than team-oriented recreational activities such as volleyball or basketball. Adults in exercise programs should have individualized exercise plans that consider outcomes of functional independence rather than simply strength gains in isolated muscle groups.

Activities and activity-related goals within them are chosen based on participant interests, needs, age, and availability of resources. Consideration is given to skills needed for present settings of physical activity and future settings of intended activity. Activities should be planned with thought for the potential of continued involvement in the activity. For instance, adults in exercise programs might be taught how to do resistance exercises with rubber tubing and free weights because exercise machines might not be available when they exercise outside of program sessions. Children in schools might not have aquatics as part of their program if there are no swimming pools in the community and instead learn to ride bicycles or cross-country ski.

For practitioners to promote physical activity involvement for all individuals, activities should be considered personally meaningful by the participants. They also need to be age-appropriate and functionally important if lifelong physical activity and associated health benefits are to be realized.

Perceived Risks

Whenever someone contemplates participating in a physical activity, he or she weighs the benefits of being physically active, such as improved physical and psychological well-being, against the risks of participating, such as possible fatigue, soreness, injury, and embarrassment. If the perceived benefits of being physically active outweigh the perceived risks, the individual is more likely to engage in physical activity. However, when the perceived risks are greater than the perceived benefits (whether the risks are real or not), one is not likely to choose to participate.

Barriers of Fear and Perceived Health Risks

For many individuals with varied abilities, this cost-benefit analysis can be further complicated by increased symptoms related to a medical condition, increased energy demands to participate in the activity, or feelings of inadequacy compared to others in the group. It has been suggested that sedentary living occurs when people believe that the risks of physical activity exceed the benefits. Such benefit-cost comparing has been shown to influence many adults' decisions to be physically active (O'Brien-Cousins, 2000). Specifically, fear of injury and concerns for safety and suitability of exercise are cited as barriers to exercise in populations with varied health conditions (Huebschmann et al., 2011; Scelza, Kalpakjian, Zemper, & Tate, 2005). The potentially unpleasant sensations, such as fatigue or pain, associated with exercise further limit the adoption of physical activity for many older adults (Cohen-Mansfield, Marx, & Guralnik, 2003).

Regarding children with disabilities, parents might make decisions about their children's involvement in inclusive physical activity programs with similar concerns in mind. They might prevent their children from participating in group physical education classes because they are concerned about safety or fearful of social isolation or ridicule by peers. Young people with disabilities might also choose not to participate in physical activity because of their own perceived limitations.

Strategies for Overcoming Fears and Perceived Risks

Although fears and perceived risks might be unfounded, they're valid and real to those who experience them. As with other person-related barriers, education and insight are critical in

Figure 3.9 A range of opportunities allows participants with disabilities to engage in age-appropriate and meaningful physical activity.

helping individuals overcome these concerns. For some, information about what constitutes physical activity might be necessary. The old saying "no pain, no gain" might dissuade some people who believe that exercise, to be beneficial, must be high intensity, prolonged, and painful. Exercise and fitness practitioners could share recommended guidelines from organizations such as the American College of Sports Medicine (ACSM) and the Council on Physical Education for Children (COPEC) that offer recommendations for healthy and appropriate activity. Many professional organizations have resources describing the nature of physical activity and set guidelines for best practice. Practitioners might want to provide parents and children with the standards developed by the National Association of Sport and Physical Education (www.aahperd.org/naspe). This organization offers information regarding essential components of quality physical education programs, how programs should be developed and implemented, and the competency of practitioners involved in the programs. Practitioners working with adults with disabilities may recommend the National Center on Physical Activity and Disability (www.ncpad.org), which offers information and guidelines on many activities. Programs must be well planned, adhere to professional standards and guidelines, and consider individual differences and needs. Providing potential participants (or those guiding their physical activity decisions) with such material gives them a better understanding of the critically reviewed and professionally developed program guidelines and demonstrates that the practitioner is aware and knowledgeable about well-established standards in the field.

To further alleviate fears, participants should have the opportunity to observe and speak with others of similar abilities and concerns. Through dialogue and observation, they might find their fears to be based more on fiction and misinformation than on fact. They will learn that physical activity modifications and related accommodations can prevent injury, equalize participation, and promote a fun, exciting, and safe experience.

Entrenched Patterns of Inactivity

Many experts believe that past experiences contribute to present and future behavior. If an individual was physically active as a youngster, he or she is more likely to live a physically active lifestyle as an adult. Individuals who do not engage in any regular physical activity might be inactive simply out of habit. These entrenched behaviors remain influential on physical activity habits throughout the life span.

The Barrier of Inactivity Habits

As we have seen, many barriers influence physical activity choices and involvement. The inactivity that might result from context and person-related obstacles in turn becomes an additional barrier to participation. Despite known benefits of exercise, individuals with disabilities are more sedentary than the general population. Compared with adults with no disability, a smaller proportion of adults with a disability meet the national targets for physical activity, and a larger proportion are physically inactive (Centers for Disease Control and Prevention, 2007a). Despite increases in regular physical activity among Hispanics and people of other minority backgrounds, racial/ethnic disparities in physical activity remain evident (Centers for Disease Control and Prevention, 2007b). The type of disability is another factor influencing habitual physical activity levels among young people (Longmuir & Bar-Or, 2000). The population as a whole is at significant risk for inactivity and the associated health risks that go along with it (see the report of the surgeon general on physical activity and health at www.cdc.gov/nccdphp/sgr/sgr.htm).

Strategies for Overcoming Inactivity Habits

Just as there are many reasons for people being inactive, there are many ways to promote their adoption of and adherence to physical activity. Many of the strategies already discussed to overcome context-related barriers and those that speak to increasing individual knowledge and motivation can be used to change behavior and foster increased physical activity. In addition, practitioners can offer unique events to introduce potential participants to new activities, such as community run-walks or bicycle-wheelchair "fun rides." Local health and fitness clubs can identify groups through organizations and send out specialty mailings with advertisements, such as "exercise with a friend," "two for one," or "three free sessions" to try to help individuals overcome the inertia of inactivity. The extent of ways to educate and motivate individuals to become physically active is limited only by the creativity and commitment of the practitioner. Once participants become active, practitioners must continue efforts to provide enjoyable and accommodating programs so that all participants can continue to succeed.

THINK BACK

Think back to your own activity participation and to Brian White and the local fitness club.

1. What person-related barriers have you faced in your own exercise experiences?
2. Do you believe that person-related barriers might have prevented potential participants from joining Brian's program? If so, which barriers?
3. What steps should Brian take to overcome these barriers?

SUMMARY

Although barriers of different kinds can influence the inclusion of all individuals in physical activity programs, there are many ways to overcome such hurdles. The key to overcoming obstacles is a step-by-step approach of deconstructing traditional ways of knowing and doing and, more important, reconstructing a program where all are valued and respected.

Inclusive physical activity should be seen not as a method of programming but as an ongoing development of relationships and social networks for diverse individuals. Practitioners are responsible to consider both the context and the person in order to create accessible programs in which every participant is valued, respected, and empowered to meet his or her physical activity goals. Finally, people will not participate in physical activity programs if they do not know the programs exist, that they have a right to join, and that the activity is important for them. Educating individuals is essential to expanding their opportunities for inclusive physical activity.

What Do You Think?

1. Which barriers do you think are most limiting when it comes to inclusive physical activity? Why?
2. Do you believe the physical activity programs you know about or have experienced consider these barriers in the planning of the programs? Do you think they could? How?
3. Which barriers do you believe are the easiest to overcome? Why do you believe this?

What Would You Do?

Scenario 3.1

Maria and Juan are a happy young couple with a new baby boy, their first child. They are planning on having a big family. Little Juanito is a beautiful 11-month-old baby. He was born in April and will soon be having his first birthday. His family is very excited and is planning a big party for him. Maria recently visited her sister, Angelita, whom she had not seen since the birth of Juanito. Angelita has three children of her own and is helping Maria plan Juanito's birthday party. During the visit, Maria put little Juanito on a blanket on the floor to play with his cousins while she and Angelita talked. While they were talking, Angelita noticed that Juanito had not rolled over or moved from his place. She remembered when her children were that age they were all over the house and pulling up on the furniture. After they finished planning the party, Angelita asked Maria if Juanito was rolling over yet. Maria said no but that he did roll from his side to his back and seemed to be a very happy baby. Later, while driving home, Maria wondered if she should be concerned. Juanito had always been a happy baby and hardly ever cried. The only challenge they had ever had was a very long labor when he was born. But they had not had to return to the doctor since then. At the subsequent doctor's visit, the doctor suggested that Maria and Juan involve Juanito in a parent–child motor development program to expose the child to practitioners and movement-based experiences.

1. What possible context-related barriers are presented in Maria's situation?
2. What person-related barriers are present for Maria and Juanito?
3. What strategies might help Maria overcome these barriers?

Scenario 3.2

Marsha is a new recreational therapist who works at a live-in senior facility. This is the first time this facility has hired a recreational therapist. Most of the individuals who live at the facility are relatively independent, with some using assisted living and others 24-hour nursing care. Marsha is really excited because at her previous job for the city recreation program she worked with adults with developmental delays. Many of the programs were poorly attended because of a lack of transportation. She found this frustrating because she spent many hours preparing lessons and activities, and it was disappointing when only two or three people showed up. Marsha is really excited about her new job, knowing that transportation will not be an issue. Most of the activities take place on site in a nice new recreation room. She has also been provided with a facility van to take people off site to special events. She decided her first program for the residents would be to offer tai chi every day. But at the end of the first week, Marsha was sorely disappointed. Very few people attended the tai chi sessions. Transportation was not an issue, so what was the problem? Marsha scheduled a meeting with her boss to discuss her concerns. Assume the role of Marsha's boss.

1. What barriers might you identify with Marsha as potential reasons for the lack of attendance in the tai chi classes?
2. What suggestions would you give Marsha to confirm what the barriers are?
3. What strategies could you suggest to Marsha to help her overcome the barriers once confirmed?

PART II

Inclusive Physical Activity Program Planning and Implementation

Lifelong physical activity involvement is essential to the quality of life and health of all individuals. Promoting such involvement is the responsibility of all physical activity practitioners. With the basis for inclusive physical activity explained in part I, part II provides a systematic approach to planning and implementing appropriate programs for individuals of all abilities.

For inclusive settings to be successful, practitioners must have the necessary supports and skills that make inclusive programming possible. In chapter 4 we discuss the need for effective communication and a team approach for creating successful inclusive programs. Different models of consultation and several collaborative strategies are presented to assist team members in working collectively when offering inclusive programs.

Before any programming takes place, practitioners must consider the needs and interests of participants and the meaningfulness of the activities offered for each individual. Chapter 5 considers the focus of physical activity programming across the life span. Because initial assessment and ongoing evaluation are critical components of any effective program, this chapter also discusses the many purposes of assessment in inclusive physical activity. Issues and considerations related to assessment as well as insight into assessment strategies are presented.

A sequential process is offered in chapter 6 to help practitioners develop inclusive and age-appropriate programming. The practical approach described is then applied to three age groups: infants and toddlers, school-age children, and adults. Issues and strategies regarding access and accommodation are discussed for each age group.

Chapter 7 takes a functional approach to programming by examining factors related to the person, context, and task that influence movement skill and performance. Analysis of both tasks and movement performance is explained, and the process of creating opportunities for success is discussed. This is achieved through the functional approach to modifying movement experiences (FAMME) model, which offers a range of modifications that can be used to accommodate participants with varying skills. Emphasis is placed on participants' capabilities rather than limitations and the matching of skill to a particular movement situation.

CHAPTER 4

Teaming and Collaboration

RÉmy

LEARNING OUTCOMES

After completing this chapter, you should be able to

- define a person's frame of reference and understand how these vary across disciplines;
- discuss the elements of effective communication;
- describe the members of a professional team and their roles;
- explain the process of collaboration and the steps for effective problem solving;
- identify the benefits and barriers to consultation; and
- identify strategies for effective collaboration.

INCLUDING ALL INDIVIDUALS

Brooks Middle School, a brand new facility, has recently hired all its faculty and staff members. Emily Booth has been hired as the new physical education teacher, joining many other new teachers and professionals at the school. Emily is excited about her job and loves working with middle school children. She teaches six periods a day of coed physical education in classes that include children of wide-ranging levels of ability. Several of the students in her classes have individualized education programs (IEPs) along with a team of professionals who help plan their programs. Emily has never served on a collaborative educational team and is uncertain about her role in the process. Several team members have come into her classes to observe her students, including the physical therapist, occupational therapist, and adapted physical education teacher. They have come at different times, asking many questions about her curriculum, equipment, and the behavior of students in the class. Emily wants to meet with the adapted physical education specialist to question her about several of the students in class and get ideas for variations to the activities she's presenting. In fact, there's a particular student she's having trouble with, Maddy, who does not seem to want to participate in any of the activities. Emily is concerned she is not reaching this child; she is not sure if Maddy cannot do the activities, is not interested, or is having trouble adjusting to the class. An IEP meeting has been scheduled in two weeks to discuss Maddy's program.

Who will attend this meeting, and what are their roles? What is Emily's role within this group of professionals? She's about to become part of a collaborative team. Effective inclusive practice requires that professionals examine their own beliefs, as discussed in chapter 1, and work toward removing barriers and creating accessible inclusive settings for individuals of all abilities, as discussed in chapter 3. This process requires effective communication and collaborative practice. How will Emily become a contributing part of this team? What will she be able to share?

The need for a team approach to inclusive physical activity planning is clearly documented in the Individuals With Disabilities Education Act (IDEA). This federal law describes the need for educational teams to serve individuals from birth through their transition into adulthood in community-based physical activity programs. No one individual is expected to have the expertise necessary to instruct all individuals of varying abilities. The collaborative process allows for professionals across disciplines to come together in a creative process to design the best possible experiences for individuals with diverse abilities and needs (Cook & Friend, 2010; Winn & Blanton, 2005). However, merely being part of a professional planning team does not make the team effective. One of the key features of a collaborative team is that each member brings a unique perspective to the table. This perspective is known as the person's frame of reference. Frame of reference is based on individuals' previous experiences, beliefs, values, and training; this frame is the lens through which each individual views the world. These lenses shape an individual's view of others' abilities as well as their attitudes, as discussed in chapters 1 to 3.

The concept of frame of reference is analogous to the story of the three men who were blind and feeling an elephant for the first time. The first man held the tail and proclaimed that the elephant was like a rope. The second man felt the side and said that the elephant was like a wall. The third man tried to reach around the elephant's leg and said the elephant was like a tree trunk. Each of these men had a piece of information about the elephant but not the whole picture. They could choose to spend their time arguing over whose perspective was accurate, or they could respect and value each other's view and listen carefully, thereby gaining a better understanding of the elephant as a whole. The latter choice obviously would make them a more effective team (figure 4.1).

Figure 4.1 "Knowing in part may make a fine tale, but wisdom comes from seeing the whole." (Young, 1992, p. 36)

COLLABORATION AND CONSULTATION

Models of consultation and collaboration have been discussed extensively in the special education and health services literature. Consultation is typically defined as one professional assisting another professional to solve a problem for a third party. For example, a physical therapist tells a practitioner what activities to do with a client, or a physician tells an adapted physical education teacher of restrictions for a student's participation in certain types of physical activity. This dynamic often involves an unequal relationship among individuals, with the consultant serving as the "expert" (Coben, Thomas, Sattler, & Morsink, 1997). Although this type of consultation is important and can be critical at times, professional teams that work closely together to provide instruction to individuals with a variety of abilities often prefer a more collaborative style.

Collaboration Defined

Collaboration is ". . . a way to humanize the service delivery system. It improves the outcomes for children with special health needs and their families. Collaboration facilitates satisfying and effective relationships" (Bishop, Woll, & Arango, 1993, p. 11). This need for more collaborative relationships in the consultation process emerged in the 1980s, and the term "collaborative consultation" became prevalent in special education literature (Coben, Thomas, Sattler, & Morsink, 1997). Currently, collaboration has become a more general term to define a style or manner in which professionals interact (Cook & Friend, 2010).

Effective collaboration is based on several assumptions:

- That each individual engages in collaboration voluntarily
- That all parties have equal power and equal value

- That individuals agree on a common goal
- That all share in responsibility and decision making
- That resources and information are shared freely among participants
- That individual team members are equally accountable for outcomes

Effective collaboration recognizes that the input of several individuals allows for greater creativity regarding solutions and acknowledges the complexities of setting goals (Pugach & Johnson, 1995). Collaborative team members are reflective about their own personal practices and enjoy the social interactive process. They do not judge others but are open and receptive; they value the thoughts and ideas of others. Information brought by all professionals is equally valued and has equal status in addressing learners' or participants' individual needs (Friend & Cook, 2010). The collaborative approach recognizes the importance of each team member's role. For example, the general physical education teacher might be the consultant regarding what a student's behavior is like during active dynamic situations that classroom teachers might not see. In another instance, an individual with a disability might share perceptions on his or her needs and possible interventions for a fitness trainer. A collaborative approach acknowledges the complexities of setting goals, recognizes that each person in the process has valuable information to contribute, and values the input of several individuals because this allows for greater creativity in finding solutions.

Role Release

In addition to acknowledging that each member of the team has valuable and critical knowledge to contribute, collaborative members are also comfortable with role release. Role release means that team members are willing to share ideas from their knowledge base that are implemented by other team members. For example, a physical therapist might train a practitioner on stretching exercises for a participant to work on during an activity program; a speech pathologist might show an adapted physical educator speech and language goals to integrate into the physical education program. Expertise is thus shared across disciplines for improved programming and outcomes for participants.

Collaborative Team Process

In a collaborative process all individuals on the team benefit. Individual participants profit from the expertise of several individuals as well as their own critical input into the decision process. Team members gain greater knowledge through the process of sharing ideas with other members, which leads to greater professional expertise, satisfaction, and reduced isolation. The collective team process generally follows five steps (Bradley, 1994; Friend & Cook, 2010; Idol, Paolucci-Whitcomb, & Nevin, 1995; Pugach & Johnson, 1995):

1. **Needs identification.** For example, a student has trouble participating in physical education with his peers; or an adult has balance difficulties while engaging in a physical activity program. The first step in the process is to identify the cause of the problem and what needs to be done to solve it. Once the needs have been identified, the team begins to collect valuable information (step 2) to assist in the process of deciding how to address the problem. Depending on the age of the person, the setting, and the team members, needs might be identified by the individual participant, a single team member, or a combination of members.

2. **Data collection.** This step includes all kinds of resources, including a possible individualized assessment with both formal and informal procedures. These procedures might include standardized tests; observation; interviews with teachers or practitioners, parents, and participants; review of health records; and any other method that might provide insight into the needs of the individual. During this step, the team seeks to discover as much information as possible to determine the strengths and concerns for the individual. Once all

available information is gathered, the team discusses possible solutions (step 3). As much as possible, the participant is a part of this process. The individual and his or her family are important members of the team.

3. **Solution selection.** This step begins with a review of the data and involves the process of determining what intervention will best assist the individual in meeting his or her goals for successful participation. Only after a review of all the available information can the team begin to generate solutions. A short brainstorming session is a great way to start this process, and all ideas should be considered. Following the brainstorming session, ideas can be evaluated for effectiveness, adapted, and narrowed to determine the best solution possible. Solutions or interventions could be anything from changing the setting or equipment to adjusting instruction to working on specific skills. Possibilities for intervention are limited only by the creativity of the team. The data-collection and solution-selection steps involve the input of the entire team in an attempt to gain a complete picture of the individual.

4. **Implementation.** Once solutions have been selected, they are implemented. The implementation phase includes the initiation of services and the beginning of programming or changes. Implementation does not necessarily require the entire team. In fact, it might be one individual, or several, who implements the intervention. In a physical activity setting, the practitioner, general education teacher, adapted physical education teacher, instructional assistant, peer, or family member might be responsible for implementation. In many cases, a combination of individuals works together to provide a quality program.

5. **Evaluation.** This step is critical to the process. It's through continued data collection and evaluation that practitioners determine which interventions, strategies, or ideas are working. Data alone are useless, so it's up to the collaborative team to determine the meaningfulness and accuracy of the data collected. Data collection might include both formative (ongoing) and summative (final) assessment methods. See chapter 5 for a more extensive discussion of assessment methods. Documentation of data and evaluation is critical to determine the success of a program.

Documentation

Documentation is one of the most critical aspects of the collaboration process, partly because the practitioner is not always the one who implements the plan. For this reason, the practitioner must have all the necessary records for collecting or tracking progress. This information can be collected by the teacher, an assistant, a family member, the individual, the adapted physical educator, the community practitioner, or another team member, as long as the progress is documented in a systematic way. Documentation should be consistent with the goals and interventions determined by the team and should track progress. If no change occurs, the team can identify this early and reconvene to discuss alternatives. Simple methods of data collection include notes from daily observation, activity logs, systematic observations of behavior, checklists, and rubrics. We will discuss data collection further in chapter 5.

None of the above steps to effective collaboration can be accomplished unless effective positive relationships have been formed. For many professionals who are itinerant (travel from place to place) establishing relationships can be challenging because each environment has its own culture and climate. Itinerant professionals must be good at reading environments and communication signals to establish rapport, build relationships, and thus work collaboratively together to meet the needs of individuals within a variety of physical activity programs or settings.

In summary, the collaborative approach is a wonderful blend of professionals working for the best outcomes of the participant. The approach focuses on effective communication, equal value, equal status, role release, and respect for all team members in providing the most effective programming for individuals with disabilities. Because of the inclusive nature of the collaborative approach and its predominant use in special education literature, we highly recommend the collaborative approach to serving individuals of all abilities.

1. Think back to Emily's first IEP meeting with Maddy. What will be the process in identifying the needs for Maddy?
2. What documentation might the team use in this process?
3. What are some of the benefits of the team process for Maddy?
4. What are some of the challenges the team will face in this process?

TEAM MEMBERS

Now that we have discussed the collaborative process, we should consider the roles of the diverse team of individuals who collaborate to provide programming for individuals with disabilities. Such team members come from diverse disciplines, and this diversity helps them form a complete perspective. A team is defined as two or more individuals who form an interdependent, coordinated group that through good communication and clear procedures work toward a common goal, in this case providing quality physical activity programming for individuals with disabilities (Friend & Cook, 2010).

The members of a team are determined by the needs of a participant and the context in which he or she will be participating in physical activity. Team members of a school-based program might differ from those who serve in a sports program or community-based program. In any case, a combination of the following individuals might be involved: the student or participant, the parent or care provider, physical therapists, occupational therapists, music therapists, orientation and mobility specialists, recreational therapists, speech and language pathologists, special education teachers, administrators, psychologists, nurses or physician assistants, behavioral health workers, coaches, fitness trainers, community organization representatives, and adapted physical education specialists. Each of these individuals may play a role contributing to a holistic understanding of the participant. Roles are expected behaviors generally agreed on by members of the group. When all members of the team have a common understanding of expectations of members and each member understands his or her own role, teams are more productive and members are less likely to experience burnout (Brehm & Kassin, 1996; Edmonson & Thompson, 2001). In the following sections we briefly describe each of the individuals who might serve on a team along with an example of how he or she might interact with the physical activity practitioner.

Individuals

Of highest importance is the individual (participant) being served. The physical activity practitioner should address this person's desires and needs first. When possible, the participant should be a part of the program planning team. Whether this works well often depends on the age of the individual and the preferences of his or her parents or family members. In many cases, individuals know their needs better than anyone and can share them clearly and effectively. They can identify their own strengths and limitations and many times make their own adaptations to achieve success in a given situation. When working with adults, the physical activity practitioner should ask them what works best for them and what their desires and goals are in planning programs and interventions. When working with young children or participants with more limited abilities, the physical activity practitioner might need to

DID YOU KNOW?

The more information freely flows between team members, the more effective the team, and the greater the likelihood of goal attainment for the participant.

facilitate the process by identifying needs and goals and letting the participant respond to them along with identifying family preferences and desires.

Family Members

Family members usually know the most about the participant and see him or her on a daily basis. Parents or caregivers typically know the needs of the participant and often interact with all of the team professionals. In most cases, the parent or family member also knows the individual's family history and medical history. These members might have specific desires for the participant that should be addressed. For example, family members might want the physical activity practitioner to teach their child how to ride a bicycle as a lifetime recreational skill and for transportation later in life. Or they might want the individual to practice getting up from the floor and transferring in and out of a chair. In any programming, the desires of the individuals and their families should be paramount to instructional planning (as well as meeting educational standards and guidelines for individuals within public school physical education programs).

Adapted Physical Education Specialists or Adapted Physical Activity Practitioners

The adapted physical education specialist is responsible for physical education curriculum for individuals with disabilities who qualify for services within the public schools. This person should have teacher training in physical education, special education, and adapted physical education. Currently, several states require an adapted physical education (APE) specialist credential for teaching APE in the public schools. This credential usually requires university coursework in the area of adapted physical education and supervised student teaching experience. Other states require a teaching credential in physical education with an endorsement in APE. Many states with no credential or endorsement requirements use the adapted physical education national standards (APENS) exam as their requirement for adapted physical education specialists, and the Adapted Physical Activity Council (APAC) has developed a position statement on what is a highly qualified adapted physical education teacher (AAPAR, 2010).

American Alliance for Health, Physical Education, Recreation and Dance (AAHPERD), American Association for Physical Activity and Recreation Division: www.aahperd.org/aapar/careers/adapted-physical-education.cfm

In an examination of the roles of the adapted physical education specialist in the public schools, a national survey by Kelly and Gansneder (1998) found that 59 percent of adapted physical education teachers provided some form of indirect services. These indirect services were defined as " . . . itinerant or consultant . . . you provide information, assessment, or other assistance but do not teach the children directly. The actual physical education services are taught by another person" (p. 146).

The roles of the adapted physical educator within the public schools are diverse. They might teach independently of the general and special education teachers or in collaboration with them. Roles of the adapted physical educator include advocate, educator, courier, resource coordinator, and supporter or helper. These five roles have been identified by Lytle and Hutchinson (2004), but there are likely many other roles APE specialists play that have not been clearly defined or identified yet. Although APE specialists in the public schools are available as valuable resources for general and special educators, community college and university faculty who specialize in adapted physical activity can also be excellent sources for practitioners in the field. Most community colleges hire adapted physical activity instructors, and many university faculty members have a specialty in this area. These individuals can be excellent resources for community-based programs. Figure 4.2 shows the many roles that adapted physical education specialists play in the schools.

Adapted Physical Education National Standards: www.apens.org

Role of the Adapted Physical Educator

Advocate. An advocate is defined as one who pleads another's cause. APE teachers often serve as advocates for the students or individuals they work with. An example includes helping parents in times of transition as a student moves from one grade to another or one school to another. In this case the APE teacher is often the person who knows the student best and might have worked with the child for many years. APE teachers might also serve as advocates for students to facilitate inclusion or get services or programming within the community.

Educator. APE teachers often serve as educators. In this role they give information to others such as teachers, instructional assistants, and parents based on the training from their discipline. In the educator role, APE teachers share curriculum ideas, sample lesson plans, ideas for modifications, and equipment; they also demonstrate teaching episodes. They might assist an individual or an entire group. APE teachers often serve groups of teachers or parents through in-service trainings or conference presentations.

Courier. Couriers obtain information from one source and share it with another. This information is usually outside of their domain of expertise. An example of playing a courier role is getting medical information about an individual to share with a general physical education teacher about possible contraindications of an activity or obtaining behavioral information from the special education teacher to share with a classroom teacher to ensure interventions are consistent.

Resource coordinator. This role includes obtaining services or coordinating facilities. An example is providing information to parents about community programs and activities. Responsibilities could include scheduling to bring in outside organizations for assemblies such as disability dance troupes or wheelchair basketball teams. In this role, APE teachers need to work closely with custodial and secretarial staff for scheduling and planning of events.

Supporter or helper. This is the role that APE teachers often play when they're first working with a general physical education teacher or classroom teacher. In this role they establish rapport and help to maintain positive relationships with individuals they consult with. APE teachers give positive feedback, help with equipment, and assist general physical education teachers in any way necessary. In this role, APE teachers are often serving within the context of someone else's general physical education program. They might also assist with general education students and students on the APE caseload.

Figure 4.2 Five roles of the adapted physical educator as identified by Lytle and Hutchinson (2004).

Physical Therapists

Physical therapists (PTs) are medical health care professionals with scientific training in understanding the human body and how it functions in order to remediate dysfunction. The focus of the PT is on mobility, balance, posture, and the activities of daily living as they pertain to motor control and coordination of movement. Physical therapists are also trained in the use of environmental and assistive devices to facilitate function in daily living. A practitioner might consult with a PT in regard to specific positioning for optimal performance in an activity. PTs might also consult with practitioners about gross motor function, exercises, and activities to facilitate abilities following the termination of physical therapy. Termination of the PT's services might be based on the participant no longer needing therapy or on lack of medical coverage. In adult exercise programs, physical activity practitioners often pick up programming when therapy coverage ends. In such cases collaboration with the physical therapist and physician regarding needs and possible contraindications is critical for positive programming.

American Physical Therapy Association: www.apta.org

Occupational Therapists

Occupational therapists (OTs) are medical health care professionals who deal with the remediation of dysfunction. Their focus is on interventions for activities of daily living and stress adaptability (Pratt & Allen, 1989). OT training emphasizes sensory motor integration, activities of daily living, fine motor skills, positioning, assistive devices, and adapting behavior or equipment to help perform such tasks as eating, dressing, playing, and working. A practitioner might want to consult an OT about adapting the grip of an implement (e.g., racket, paddle, or golf club), suggestions for sensory diet activities to reduce stress, facilitating an individual's participation in physical activity, or using devices that might improve performance.

American Occupational Therapy Association: www.aota.org

Speech and Language Pathologists

Speech and language pathologists (SLPs) focus on the development of speech, language, and hearing. Physical education practitioners collaborate with speech pathologists on how to communicate with individuals. Goals and objectives among the two disciplines can often be easily integrated. For example, language is inherent in movement activities, and practitioners can easily integrate speech and language goals from the SLP into the motor programming. The SLP might also find it helpful to integrate gross motor goals during speech because motor activities are often motivating and for individuals of all ages. In some cases, the SLP and the adapted physical education practitioner might even present lessons or activities together, which can be particularly effective when working with young children in a play-based approach.

American Speech-Language-Hearing Association: www.asha.org

General Educators

General educators include teachers within the public school system who are not special education teachers, such as classroom teachers, elementary physical education specialists, or general physical education teachers. The general education teacher is often the one in the school setting who knows the child best. This teacher typically sees the participant every week day and has a good understanding of his or her learning style and strengths. The general education teacher is often familiar with how the participant interacts with peers in different settings, including the classroom, playground, lunch room, and perhaps elsewhere. This teacher also knows particular behaviors the participant might have and understands the curriculum being taught and how it is presented. This is important information in team planning and problem solving, such as when determining modifications or variations for instruction.

American Alliance for Health, Physical Education, Recreation and Dance: www.aahperd.org

Psychologists

Psychologists are frequently part of individualized education programming teams for students within the public school system and provide many services, including expertise in development, learning, counseling, and assessment. They serve on teams aimed at meeting the educational needs of students having difficulty in the school system, as well as on collaborative service delivery teams within the community. One of the roles of the psychologist on such teams is helping to assess the participant's achievement and abilities to allow for successful and educational planning. School psychologists also consult with teachers, parents, and other team members to help them address the development or behavior management of a child. School psychologists might also engage in district-wide work, such as serving on curriculum committees, planning and evaluating programs, and doing in-service training. They might also contribute to classroom education on emotional awareness, coping skills, social skills, and other topics.

American Psychological Association: www.apa.org

Behavioral Health Workers

Behavioral health care providers assist individuals and families with mental health issues and substance abuse recovery. They are frequently involved if an individual is experiencing depression, severe mood swings, behavioral problems, severe anxiety, sleep disturbances, severe agitation, or other mental health issues. Individuals of all abilities are at risk for mental health problems and health disparities. Feelings about self and others can be influenced by societal attitudes, lack of access or opportunities, or financial constraints. If an individual has mental health concerns, such health care providers play an important role in providing counseling, appropriate medications, or both.

Association for Behavioral Healthcare: www.mhsacm.org

Nurses and Physician Assistants

Nurses or physician assistants (PAs) are often helpful in providing necessary medical information for programming and in alerting practitioners and others of precautions that should be taken. Nurses might also contribute by explaining medical protocols for standard procedure for an individual with a disability or in an emergency. Individuals with severe allergies, medications, or other health concerns might have a nurse who is part of their individualized education program or individual home program. Most nurses and PAs are experienced with medications and their possible side-effects. They are also valuable connections to the medical community and sometimes a practitioner's best resource for medical information or in making medical referrals. In an infant program, a discharge nurse from a neonatal intensive care unit (NICU) might assist a family in connecting with early intervention services. For seniors, a community health care nurse might assist in caring for individuals who need daily assistance in the home.

American Nursing Association: www.nursingworld.org

Physicians

Other important players on the collaborative team might include general practitioners, neurologists, orthopedists, endocrinologists, or other specialists who work with participants within a physical activity program. Physicians are likely to serve as a referral source for community-based programs. They also provide information regarding restrictions to physical activity participation, and their medical records can supply important information about a participant's medical history. Although, because of their schedules, physicians might not be a part of typical program planning meetings, their information and expertise can be helpful to the team and should not be overlooked.

American Medical Association: www.ama-assn.org

Recreation Therapists

Recreation therapists (RTs) plan, organize, and direct recreational programs for individuals with disabilities. RTs are often excellent resources for community activities and programs for individuals of all abilities. Depending on the interests and needs of the participant, RT programs are typically for such activities as social interaction, games, aquatics, gardening, arts and crafts, and expressive arts. RTs work in many settings, including hospitals, rehabilitation centers, schools, community parks, recreational departments, and correctional institutions.

American Therapeutic Recreation Association: www.atra-online.com/index.cfm

Music Therapists

Music therapists are trained to use music to promote the physical, cognitive, psychological, and social needs of individuals of all abilities. They use the creative forms of singing, moving to, or listening to music to promote general health and well-being. Music therapists work in such settings as hospitals, community and mental health agencies, rehabilitation centers, day care facilities, nursing homes, and schools. Some practitioners collaborate with a music therapist to incorporate music into their physical activity programs. The presence of music enhances learning and motivation for many individuals.

American Music Therapy Association: www.musictherapy.org

Orientation and Mobility Specialists

Orientation and mobility (O&M) specialists provide one-on-one instruction to individuals with vision disabilities. Their role is to help individuals achieve independence and confidence in traveling in and through their environments. Mobility is the ability to travel from one place to another, and orientation is understanding one's position in space as it relates to other objects or people within the environment. O&M specialists might provide assessment, instruction, consultation and collaboration, family support, or in-service training. They can assist the physical activity practitioner in examining an environment's accessibility and helping to develop appropriate goals for participants.

Resources for O&M Specialists: www.orientationandmobility.org/misc.html

Fitness Practitioner

The fitness practitioner may serve in many capacities depending on their skills and job placement. Such jobs may include corporate fitness trainer, certified personal trainer, or group exercise instructor. Fitness practitioners may also serve as wellness coaches and advise on relaxation techniques, setting personal wellness goals, nutrition and weight management, and many other health priorities for individuals with varying abilities.

American College of Sports Medicine (ACSM): www.acsm.org

COLLABORATIVE TEAMS

- Have established group norms
- Promote the idea that we "sink or swim together"
- Develop and support goals together
- Share resources, ideas, and knowledge freely
- Have face-to-face interaction
- Share successes and recognize each other for positive work
- Hold each member accountable for the group process

Coaches

Coaches work closely with athletes of all abilities and types of settings. Typically, coaches work with individuals who perform physical activity in a competitive setting. Such elite athletes may participate in individual or team sports, Special Olympics, Paralympics, or other competitions. Coaches' roles may include fitness testing and screening; determining appropriate diet for optimum performance; motivational techniques; training regimens for on and off season; strategies to enhance performance; and instructional feedback for performance.

American Coaches Association: www.acasports.net/acasports.net/Welcome.html

Community Organization Representatives

Representatives from community organizations can be critical to effective teams for transition planning, understanding services, and other roles. Such organizations may include the Multiple Sclerosis Society, the Parkinson's Society, the Autism Society, early intervention programs, senior centers, regional centers that serve individuals with developmental "disabilities," or other community agency providers. These organizations provide important resources, programs, and supports for individuals of a variety of ages and abilities. It is important for all team members to be familiar with agencies and programs available in their geographic area. A list of resources and agencies can be found in appendix C.

In summary, effective teams are made up of two or more individuals who work together for the purpose of effective programming for an individual. Effective teams have clearly defined roles, respect for other members, social support, shared understanding of expected behaviors, and effective communication (Friend & Cook, 2010; Lytle & Bordin, 2001; Wiggins & Damore, 2006). To be an effective team member, one must continually practice these skills. For this reason, effective communication skills are discussed next. Here are examples of strategies a physical activity practitioner can use to help team members connect and stay connected.

- Call a local community college and ask for the coordinator of their adapted physical activity program.
- Ask for the names of the special education staff at the participant's school, including the APE, PT, OT, psychologist, and SLP.
- Make weekly or monthly calls to parents or family members of participants.
- E-mail or call physicians every six months to a year to check health records and receive updated information.
- Invite team members to present a workshop or lecture.
- Invite a team member to team or co-teach.
- Ask other team members to observe a program and make recommendations.
- Use worksheets to discuss issues or needs when difficult to find time to meet.
- Keep notes, minutes, or a communication log.
- Ask for feedback from team members regarding the practitioner's services.

THINK BACK

1. Which professional role might you play in your future career? Describe three key professionals and how they might help you in providing services to an individual.
2. Think back to Emily Booth's IEP meeting about Maddy. What team members might be present at Maddy's IEP meeting? Why do you think these members would be important to the team in getting a holistic picture of Maddy?

EFFECTIVE COMMUNICATION

Communication is the process of creating shared meaning and can be described as occurring "when someone attributes meaning to another person's words or actions" (Martin & Nakayama, 2000, p. 61). All professionals need effective communication skills for working with clients, co-workers, and their collaborative teams of other professionals, parents, and family members. Communication is a complex process involving many elements: listening, questioning, making statements, and using methods of nonverbal communication.

Listening

We will discuss listening first because it is the most critical aspect of communication and in establishing positive rapport with others. The two types of listening—passive and active—each serves an important purpose. The two types are often used together in a dialogue with another person. Passive listening involves listening without saying anything and is frequently used when the speaker needs to vent frustrations or explain something in detail. In this case the listener's job is to listen attentively without making comments. Three positive aspects of communication can result from passive listening. First, it allows the speaker to talk without interruption or interference from another's ideas or thoughts. Second, the process of talking about an issue can often reduce frustration (which is why we call it "venting"). Third, people sometimes find solutions to their own concerns through talking about them out loud.

Active (or reflective) listening is the process of sharing with the speaker that you have heard what he or she is saying and might involve paraphrasing, clarifying, questioning, or perception checking (Thomas, Correa, & Morsink, 2001). The listener should attend fully to what is being said and listen for the content and emotion of what is being shared. The listener can then paraphrase for the speaker what he or she has heard and try to correctly process the content of the interaction. Figure 4.3 illustrates the difference between ineffective and effective listening.

Regardless of whether passive or active listening is being employed, it is critical for the listener to enter the interaction with empathy (Covey, 1990). In other words, the listener should intend to fully understand the other person emotionally and intellectually without projecting his or her own ideas, thoughts, or feelings into what's being shared. This type of listening is a wonderful tool in gathering accurate information about another's perceptions, concerns, and ideas. Effective listening establishes rapport, shows concern and a desire to comprehend, and demonstrates accurate understanding.

We were given two ears and one mouth because it is twice as hard—and perhaps twice as important—to listen as it is to speak.

OR

Figure 4.3 Ineffective and effective listening.

Questioning

Another important skill for effective communication is questioning. How someone asks a question and the type of questions asked can influence an interaction positively or negatively. Questions are used to seek information, provide information, or clarify or confirm information. How a person gathers information is important because some questions can be perceived as intimidating. People should maintain professional equity in their interactions and not create a feeling of interrogation through the way in which questions are asked.

Questions that seek information are typically straightforward, such as, "What time should I meet you at the health club?" But questions that provide information can be intimidating, or irritating, particularly if they're stated in a way that suggests the other person should already know the information or if advice is being given (figure 4.4). Consider how you might feel if another professional said to you, "Didn't you call the physical therapist yet?" Such a question is not truly a question at all but a way of telling someone what (or how something) should have been done. Other examples include, "Don't you think her parents will be upset if we don't try the behavior strategies here that they are using at home?" and "His wife won't allow him to get in the pool without assistance, will she?" In the first example the person is really stating that she thinks the same behavior strategies should be used in the physical activity setting that are used at home. In the second example the person is saying that the wife does not let the husband get in the pool without assistance. Perhaps a better way to communicate this information would be to say, "Let's talk with the parents about what behavior strategies will work best in this setting. What do you think might work?" or "I believe his wife shared that she likes him to have an aid when getting in the pool. Perhaps we should talk with her about any concerns she might have with him getting in the pool by himself. What do you think?" In each example the question has been changed to a statement that is then followed up with a question that allows the other person to provide his or her thoughts. This shift in how information is relayed allows both individuals to share information freely without feeling intimidated or as if they should or should not have known or done something.

Figure 4.4 Questions can enhance or inhibit communication. How do you think this question affected communication?

Finally, questions are used to clarify information. Such questions are used frequently and can be helpful to ensure you're in agreement about expectations. For example, "You're going to bring the modified equipment next week?" or "Do you agree with me that Levia is ready for this activity?"

The most effective uses of questions are to seek information or clarify information. Questions used to advise or provide information should be used cautiously; the speaker should be clear about the intent of the question before asking it.

Questions can be categorized by whether they seek, provide, or clarify information. They can also be grouped by whether they are open or closed (table 4.1). A closed question requests a yes or no answer. An open question allows for elaboration and requests the responder to say

Table 4.1 Open Versus Closed Questions

Closed question	Open question
Does Jerry like physical education?	How does Jerry feel about physical education?
Can Jackie complete the mile run?	What is Jackie's fitness level?
Are you having trouble with balance?	What are your concerns about your balance?

more than just yes or no. Open questions are likely to promote more information (sometimes more than needed!). In general, questions should be phrased with purpose in mind. Closed questions are used when seeking quick, efficient information. Otherwise, people should give others a chance to express themselves more fully by asking open questions.

Making Statements

Statements are critical to effective communication and allow people to share ideas, thoughts, feelings, concerns, and perceptions. Statements can provide information, explain a process, give suggestions, convey direct commands, or indirectly request information. Statements that provide information are often descriptive in nature, describing an event, situation, or behavior (Friend & Cook, 2010). Descriptive statements are based on what's perceivable and usually do not include an evaluation of the event. Evaluative statements give the perceiver's take on what has been perceived. Compare the following two statements. Which is descriptive and which evaluative?

1. Maddy ran over, pushed Carolyn on the arm, and kicked the ball across the playground.
2. Maddy was mean to Carolyn and took the ball away from her.

The descriptive statement (1) gives details of what happened without assessing the behavior described. The evaluative statement (2) presents an opinion of what happened and does not describe the complete behavior. Clear and accurate descriptive observations and communication can be effective in problem-solving teaching and learning situations with other professionals. Removing the evaluative nature of an event allows people to be objective and open to the possible causes and solutions without passing judgment. For example, Maddy might have pushed Carolyn for many reasons, so jumping to the conclusion that the push was mean spirited might be premature.

Other types of statements explain a process or offer guidance to others. Teachers frequently use this form of communication when instructing individuals on how to complete a task or execute a skill. In this process the speaker typically describes the steps in detail and gives examples of what to do. For example, in a badminton class the teacher might describe the steps for completing an overhead clear and then demonstrate the skill for the class.

Other forms of statements are suggestions or direct commands. Suggestions are softer than commands, such as, "One idea is to reduce the weights for Susan" or "Maybe some stretches for the hamstrings would help Joey." Suggestions are meant to allow the listener the option of accepting or rejecting the idea. Commands are more forceful statements and suggest that the person being spoken to should do as he or she is told, such as, "Reduce the weights for Susan" or "Joey, stretch your hamstrings." Such statements do not intend to allow for alternatives and suggest that the one making them has authority. Effective teachers and other practitioners generally avoid stating commands.

Finally, statements sometimes request information. These statements are really questions and are generally spoken as an invitation for comments from another. They are indirect in nature and can help prevent the feeling of interrogation during a discussion or interview. "I wonder what the recreational therapist is doing with him" and "I'd like to know how they transferred him on the last field trip" are examples of statements that are inviting information. Such statements allow individuals to share freely as they choose. The speaker intentionally takes the risk of not getting the information desired. When receiving information is the primary goal, it is often best to ask questions directly rather than phrase them as statements.

Using Nonverbal Communication

We have all heard the expression "a picture is worth a thousand words." In fact, some people have suggested that up to 90 percent of communication occurs not through words but through nonverbal messages (Thomas, Correa, & Morsink, 2001). Nonverbal communication, which includes facial expression, posture, gestures, eye contact, proximity, and tone of voice, is a powerful mode of expression that people use at both conscious and subconscious levels.

You can tell a lot about what people are thinking or feeling by their facial expressions. Most of us have had someone give us "the look," meaning pay attention or quit doing whatever it is we are doing (figure 4.5). We have also witnessed the expressions of individuals attempting to perform a task that is difficult for them. Such a look that conveys so much—frustration, despair, self-consciousness, embarrassment, guilt, regret—is indeed worth the many words it would take people to try to describe the complexity of their feelings.

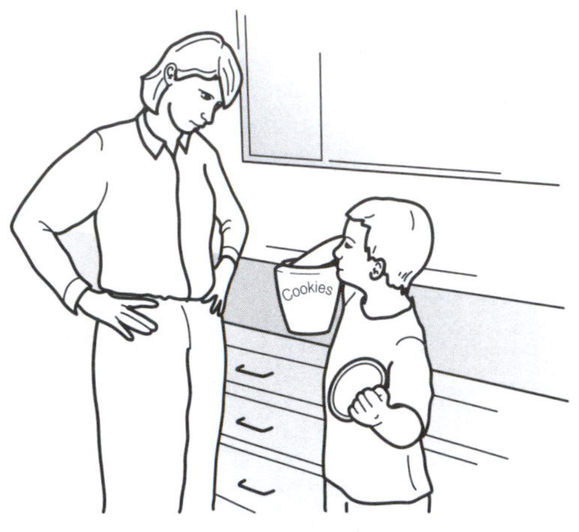

Figure 4.5 Body language can be much more efficient than words.

Posture can also tell us a lot about a person's feelings or attitude. During a meeting, when people are sitting with arms crossed against their chests, an observer might interpret that they are resistant or closed to the ideas being shared. Of course the observer could be mistaken—it could just be that the air in the room is too cold. Practitioners must be aware of these kinds of gestures and try to read them correctly based on the environment, the individuals, and the context.

Bear in mind that for individuals with disabilities, elements of communication might be altered. For example, a person with craniofacial muscular dystrophy might appear expressionless even when very happy; someone who has had a stroke might experience partial paralysis that affects facial expressions and voice tone. When working with individuals with disabilities, practitioners should be aware of possible variations in communication style and be sensi-

CULTURAL DIFFERENCES AND NONVERBAL COMMUNICATION

In North America, eye contact during communication sends the message that we are listening and paying attention. But in some Asian cultures too much eye contact is a sign of disrespect. In fact, gazing downward when speaking to a person in authority might show greater respect. Many cultures typically shake hands when meeting for the first time. This might be an inappropriate behavior for a male practitioner greeting a female participant of the Muslim faith, who may prefer not to shake hands. In another example, for a traditional Hmong family it may be considered impolite to touch a child on the head.

How close people are when they're talking is also a factor in communication. For example, in the Hispanic culture people tend to stand closer and touch more than they do in Asian cultures. An early intervention teacher might receive hugs when entering an Hispanic family's home and receive a head bow when entering an Asian family's home. Practitioners should be aware of an individual's comfort level in relation to proximity when interacting and should respect these differences. Often facial expression or other nonverbal behaviors will tell the practitioner if he or she has overstepped the boundaries. Keen observation skills are important to quality communication.

Although some nonverbal behaviors are generalized in certain cultures or settings, people are individuals. Just as we cannot say all people with a certain disability are the same, we cannot say that all people from a certain culture or region are the same. However, understanding cultural differences can help professionals be aware of their behaviors and avoid making assumptions about others' intentions based on misreading nonverbal interactions.

tive to how they might affect communication or interaction. They must strive to be in tune with the overall mood or tone of their participants without being oversensitive to the point of seeing messages in nonverbal communication when the messages are not there.

THINK BACK

1. How does the tone of voice and body language change the meaning of the words in the following statements?
   - "That family is really wonderful." (Spoken with a smile and positive tone while looking the person in the eye.)
   - "That family is really wonderful." (Spoken flatly with no enthusiasm while rolling the eyes.)
2. Emily Booth (from our chapter-opening scenario) is about to meet with her professional team members. Write two open-ended questions that she might ask at the meeting. Create two statements that would provide information to Emily if you were one of the team members.
3. As a friend of Emily, what suggestions would you give her to make sure that her body language in the meeting presented her as an open, interested, and willing team member?
4. Identify two elements of communication you would like to work on in your own professional interactions. How might these skills help you be a better communicator?

COLLABORATIVE TEAM PROCESS AND ISSUES

Teams are generally formed to assist in determining needs, writing individual goals, designing programs, and tracking progress. The members of the collaborative team are determined by the needs of the individual and family members. Desirable characteristics of effective team members include being open, caring, warm, understanding, positive, task oriented, enthusiastic, calm, flexible, and respectful of others' points of view (Kampwirth, 2003). Each member brings to the team his or her perspective and skills, which contributes to a holistic view of the child or individual. The team's purpose is to develop a shared framework, create a unified set of goals, engage in problem solving, and evaluate their effectiveness.

Many factors can influence the success of a team and its collaborative process. The team decision process, the quality of documentation, and the communication skills of team members all affect the team's effectiveness. In the following sections we discuss issues related to professional territory, benefits and barriers to collaboration, and strategies to enhance positive collaboration.

Professional Territory and Skills

Practitioners serving as itinerant consultants often work for a district, county, or special program. These professionals usually provide services to several locations. A survey of adapted physical education (APE) teachers in California showed that the range of sites served was from 1 to 30, with an average of 6 (Lytle & Johnson, 2000). Itinerant professionals, such as adapted physical educators, physical therapists, occupational therapists, and recreation therapists, usually have an office at a single site and serve individuals at that location or at several locations. Most general physical education teachers or physical activity professionals have their own gyms, rooms, and fields that make up their professional home. This space might be shared with a few others in their department or program. Itinerant consultants should keep this in mind when they enter another professional's space or territory. They are a guest in that environment, be it a family's house or a professional's office, and must be aware of expected behaviors and climate of each school or community environment. Depending on personalities, frequency of interaction, and other factors, it can take several weeks, months, or even years for consultants to establish rapport with teachers or professionals they collaborate with. The importance of establishing rapport, using effective communication, and being aware of the environment in which professionals work cannot be overstated.

Skills identified as necessary to be an effective consultant for physical activity are shown in table 4.2 (Lytle & Collier, 2002). Ideally, skills include good communication and listening, good people skills, strong content knowledge in general and adapted physical education, respect, and a sense of humor (Emes, Longmuir, & Downs, 2002; Horton & Brown, 1990; Knoff, McKenna, & Riser, 1991; Lytle & Collier, 2002). For many professionals, communication and interaction skills are learned on the job. However, many preservice training programs have integrated effective consultation training into their curriculum.

Collaboration can be a highly effective way to provide services for individuals of all abilities. First, collaborative consultation allows individuals to be educated with their peers or colleagues in a natural setting (Block, 2007; Lytle & Collier, 2002). Second, it can provide parents or caregivers with a sense of comfort, knowing they have a team for support and services. Third, it provides a holistic view of the individual. Fourth, it provides greater accountability for progress because all members are responsible for outcomes.

Table 4.2 Knowledge, Skills, and Attitudes of Effective Consultants in Adapted Physical Activity

Knowledge	Skills	Attitude
• Content in GPE/APE • Assessment • Writing goals, objectives • Program planning • IEP process • State or national standards • Special education laws • Task analysis • Motor and development skills • Knowledge about disability	• People skills • Can modify and adapt • Organizational skills • Problem solver • Communication skills • Big bag of tricks • Smile and be pleasant • Quick thinker • Punctual • Time management • Respect • See others' points of view • Adapt how you approach people • Physical skills • Attention to detail • Know where to find information • Perspective	• Disability awareness • Professionalism • Flexible • Self-motivated • Enthusiastic • Teamwork • Cooperative • Positive personality • Collaborative attitude • Be able to let things go and not bother you • Even tempered • Reflective • Approachable • Diplomatic • Trustworthy • Sense of humor

Adapted, by permission, from R. Lytle and D. Collier, 2002, "The consultation process: Adapted physical education specialists' perceptions," *Adapted Physical Activity Quarterly* 19: 261-279.

Fifth, all team members gain professionally by learning from each other, which reduces the possibility of professional isolation. Finally, collaborative consultation allows for creative problem solving (figure 4.6).

Along with the many benefits of the collaborative approach, some challenges exist. The two primary barriers to effective consultation are insufficient time and team member resistance to collaboration (Karge, McClure, & Patton, 1995; Lytle, 1999; Spencer, 2005). In fact, willingness to collaborate and incorporate new ideas and strategies has been linked with a strong knowledge base and ability to respond to the needs of individuals while also addressing a group (Brownell, Adams, Sindelar, & Waldron, 2006). The demands placed on professionals in all capacities are tremendous, and collaboration is often added on top of their typical responsibilities. It can be challenging for team members to find the time to meet for discussion. Public school adapted physical education teachers often find themselves contacting general educators during their prep period, lunch, recess, between classes, or after school. Communication frequently occurs via written notes, letters, documents, e-mails, and telephone calls. However, the most effective planning takes place when individuals have time to meet face to face, even for only 10 to 20 minutes. Most professionals relish the opportunity to talk with others and share ideas. However, time might be wasted on complaints, school or agency politics, stories, or other issues. It's important for professionals to listen and recognize this need. Collaborative team members might need to set aside a few minutes for informal discussion and then move to structured planning time. It is helpful if practitioners come to the meeting with upcoming curricular activities and related instruction plans. Then meeting time can be spent reviewing the curriculum and discussing possible modifications, adaptations, or how the material will be split if co-teaching or other collaborative teaching methods are used. The adapted physical educator then follows up by making any modifications to the curriculum or supplying needed materials. This model helps professionals be more efficient with their time.

Although some adapted physical educators or community practitioners might have flex time built into their schedules, a challenge in collaboration involves general educators or other professionals who have very tight schedules. Adapted educators must be flexible in finding ways to meet with others. Administrators and facility supervisors can assist instructors

Figure 4.6 Consultation assists teachers in changing instructional strategies that limit student participation and skill practice.

or service providers in finding time for consultation. When time becomes available, professionals must be well prepared and efficient in their use of precious minutes. There is never enough time for the kind of collaboration professionals desire (Friend & Cook, 2010).

Aside from time, the other major challenge for effective collaborative consultation is working with people who are resistant or lack proper understanding of physical activity curricula. As we have mentioned, practitioners must be able to share their curriculum and program focus with team members so they can collaborate on planning methods. For example, if a classroom teacher is not providing physical education or is only providing inappropriate activities, it can be very challenging for the adapted physical education teacher to brainstorm modifications. Consultants hear comments such as, "We don't have time for PE" or "We've been playing dodge ball and kickball." In such cases, the adapted physical education teacher has to both consult on how to modify the teacher's activities and provide some educating and curriculum ideas for the teacher—as well as supply in-service training (figure 4.6)! When team members do not appreciate the value of physical activity, consultation can be challenging. Regardless of the situation, professionals must first establish a trusting relationship and positive rapport before anything can be accomplished. Circumstances might require informing team members of the importance of physical activity and providing examples of how to create developmentally appropriate activities and programs. Physical activity practitioners might need to provide sample lessons and model instruction techniques for others. Regardless of the situation, team members have a responsibility to do whatever they can to work effectively to provide quality physical activity for all individuals.

Collaborative Connections

Confusion often exists about how adapted physical activity, physical therapy (PT), and occupational therapy (OT) interface. To what extent do they provide the same services? Although they are all based on the scientific foundation of human movement, these three fields are in fact quite different disciplines. One key element that makes adapted physical education very different from PT and OT is that physical education is a curriculum area that all children in the public schools must receive and is defined as a direct service under special education law IDEA. Although "adapted" physical education is not required for all children, physical education is required. Adapted physical education should be viewed as an academic content area, just as reading and math are content areas of education. On the other hand, PT and OT are considered related services under IDEA and are not required for all children. PT and OT are provided to students only if deemed "educationally necessary," which means if the child needs PT or OT services in order to participate or access the educational program. For example, some children might need OT services to help with modifications and adaptations for fine motor skills so they can complete assignments and

THINK BACK

Think of two teams or groups that you have worked with, one that was effective and one that was ineffective.

1. List the characteristics of each group.
2. What characteristics made the effective group a positive experience?
3. What is your frame of reference? What do you value in others and in yourself as team members? How might your values support or hinder your interactions with others?
4. Think back to Emily Booth. What information might she need about her role as a team member?

writing tasks on time. In another example, a child might need sensory integration training to help with focus and attention to tasks.

For adults, adapted physical activity can serve as a means to lifelong health and wellness with a focus on prevention, maintenance, and well-being. OT and PT are medical services that can be valuable resources for program planning and design within any physical activity program. Team members should recognize that these three disciplines are not interchangeable. Yes, they all deal with motor abilities, but each has a specific body of knowledge and expertise to assist in planning and programming for individuals with disabilities. These three disciplines, when collaborating, can provide the best possible services to all individuals.

COLLABORATIVE STRATEGIES FOR TEACHERS AND PRACTITIONERS

Many collaborative strategies exist for practitioners to use to help individuals with disabilities succeed in physical activity settings. We will discuss a few of these strategies here, including methods for creating time for communication, developing positive relationships, and implementing co-teaching techniques.

Strategies to Create Time

As we have mentioned, time is one of the primary challenges to effective collaborative teaming. For this reason, it is critical to have strategies to help create face-to-face meetings. The first and easiest strategy is to establish built-in meeting times. For example, establish that the first Friday of every month the team will meet at a designated time and place. This method is frequently used for faculty or staff meetings and can be effective for teams that regularly work together. However, team members often do not have similar schedules, so weekly meetings are not realistic. In such a case, it might be necessary to hold meetings at nontraditional times, such as Monday evenings or Thursday mornings before school. Community programs might also schedule meetings at nontraditional times, such as Saturday afternoons or late in the evening after a community program. Ideally, collaborative teams should meet monthly on a regular schedule—face to face, if possible. If face-to-face meetings cannot be worked out, another form of regular communication should be scheduled; communication is critical to collaboration. Each member should have all the information of the group so that planning is not fragmented. By using such methods as weekly e-mail, communication journals, phone messages, and 5- or 10-minute interactions or observations with individual team members, the group can be highly effective and efficient. Within the public school system, many districts have created release days to create time for teachers to meet. Within community-based programs, scheduling tends to be more flexible.

IDEAL MEETING SCHEDULE

- Entire team meets face to face at least every three months.
- Weekly e-mail updates on progress and questions are sent to all team members.
- Each member keeps a daily log of activity, interactions, and questions for team reference.
- Each member visits or observes other team members at least once a month. In some cases it might be necessary to observe or work as coteachers once or twice a week.

Strategies to Create Positive Relationships

Effective teaming requires positive rapport. This begins with effective communication skills and ensuring that other team members feel listened to and heard. Listening and reflecting on the other professionals' ideas or concerns can be extremely helpful. Finding things another team member is doing that are helpful and effective and commenting on them helps promote a positive relationship. This can be done verbally, via notes, or through writing a letter to the other team member's employer, commenting on how helpful their program is. Other ideas include the following:

- Honor each member's style of interaction.
- Acknowledge caseloads or class size and the demands that accompany this workload.
- Honor each member's teaching and management style.
- Invite others to visit your program.
- Bring snacks to share.
- Write frequent thank you notes.
- Invite families of other professionals to participate in special events, such as open house or other activities.
- Respect individual cultural and familial differences.

Co-Teaching

Co-teaching occurs when two professionals serve a diverse group of participants in a single setting (Friend, Cook, Hurley-Chamberlain, & Shamberger, 2010). Traditionally, co-teaching involves two instructors, but it could involve more. In a school-based physical education setting, co-teaching typically includes the general physical education teacher and the adapted physical education teacher working together to provide instruction to an entire class of diverse participants. In a community-based setting, two or more practitioners might work with a group of individuals in an activity program. Co-teaching provides many benefits to participants and practitioners, including the following:

1. Eliminates the need for participants to leave the program or facility for extra help
2. Allows for increased engaged time in physical activity
3. Ensures correlation of physical activity content for all learners
4. Allows all participants to benefit from the instruction of two teachers
5. Increases participant-teacher interaction
6. Prevents stigma of being pulled from activity for special help
7. Allows for development of social skills and interaction with peers
8. Promotes positive interactions and acceptance of all individuals
9. Allows for individualized support and modifications within a heterogeneous group
10. Provides for the sharing of ideas and resources to enhance the knowledge base for all team members involved in the program

In the following sections we will briefly discuss several styles of co-teaching, including one teaching, one observing; station instruction; parallel instruction; alternative teaching; one teaching, one assisting; and team teaching.

One Teaching, One Observing

In this instructional style one person is primarily responsible for the instruction, and the other is the observer. The role of the observer is generally determined by the co-teaching team and might include watching a single individual, a small group, or the group as a whole. The observer has the opportunity to watch for specific behaviors or skills. It is important to document observations with notes and coding forms (figure 4.7).

DID YOU KNOW?

By the year 2020 more than half of public school-age students in the United States will be from culturally and linguistically diverse backgrounds. Yet the majority of teachers and those in teacher preparation programs continue to be predominantly Caucasian and from the middle class (www.culturenmotion.org/).

Figure 4.7 Here one teacher is the facilitator and the other the recorder.

The observer might also assist individual participants as needed and move about the workspace to ensure success for every participant. The advantage of this approach is that it does not require a lot of joint planning time. However, care must be taken that no one person is feeling that he or she is carrying the burden. Both members of the instruction team may play either role. It is a good idea to alternate so that team members can appreciate each other's role and learn how perspectives and insights differ from different teaching perspectives. For example, in a community volleyball program one person might serve as the instructor for the lesson and the other roam around to provide cues, feedback, and assistance to aid in participant learning.

Figure 4.8 Stations support learning for individuals with disabilities.

Station Instruction

This approach allows for a variety of skills to be taught and for participants to break into smaller groups (figure 4.8). For example, in an elementary class, teachers might have motor stations for balance, locomotor skills, throwing, and catching. In a community-based setting, stations might be created for weight training, stretching, and aerobic activity. Co-instructors each take a station to assist participants with instruction. When it is not possible for an instructor to be at each station, some stations can be set up to review familiar skills. Participants work at these stations alone while instructors assist at the stations that include new skills. Volunteers, family members, university students, or cross-age peers are all good sources for station monitors. Be sure to train inexperienced staff before they supervise activities.

Parallel Instruction

In this approach co-teachers break the group in half and deliver the exact same content simultaneously. Co-teachers must plan lessons jointly. The main benefit of this approach is that instructors work with smaller groups. Obviously both instructors must know the content. How the group is divided depends on the purpose of the activity. Groups might be divided based on competitive levels or to create heterogeneous groups so that individuals can teach each other throughout the lesson. An example of this technique might occur during the beginning instruction phase of a new unit in which teachers want to provide feedback to students. The smaller groups allow for better observation and more feedback from a teacher.

Alternative Teaching

In this approach one instructor focuses on the larger group while another instructor works with a smaller group. The smaller group might work on completing an assessment of skills, preteaching content for the larger group activity, or practicing remedial skills. For example, in a physical education program, some students might participate in a large game of volleyball while a smaller group works on skill development. In a community-based program, some members might participate in a large-group water aerobics class while others complete an aquatic assessment of skills.

One Teaching, One Assisting

This method of co-teaching is similar to one instructor teaching and one observing, but here the second instructor moves around the space providing individualized assistance. In this method, the one instructing focuses on the group while the one assisting provides variations and individual feedback. In a group exercise program, the assisting instructor moves about the space providing corrections, motivation, positive feedback, variations, physical assistant, or other needs. For example, in a cardiac rehabilitation program, while one instructor provides group instruction another might be measuring blood pressure or heart rates. Or an assisting physical therapist might be helping an individual with the use of a walker or spotting with a gait belt.

Team Teaching

In a team-teaching environment both instructors are responsible for planning and implementing the program, just as in parallel instruction. However, during the actual lesson they take turns giving instruction, providing feedback, demonstrating, or facilitating. This differs from the one teaching and one observing approach in that each teacher or facilitator plays both roles during the activity. Each facilitator provides some instruction as well as moving about the instruction space to assist participants. In a community-based program, one teacher might instruct the group while the other helps an individual with modifications or physical assistance, as necessary; the teachers might then switch roles for the next phase of the lesson.

Although co-teaching can be time consuming, it is highly effective in enhancing instruction for diverse groups of participants. Regardless of which co-teaching method is employed, both individuals are responsible for the success of the class or program and the individuals within it. Which co-teaching method works best depends on the nature of the participants in the program and the content being taught.

Think back to Emily Booth, the new teacher at Brooks Middle School.

1. How might the adapted physical educator, physical therapist, or occupational therapist work toward developing a positive rapport with Emily?
2. What strategies might the team use to create an effective team environment that supports the individuals in Emily's program?

SUMMARY

Collaboration teams are made up of two or more individuals working toward a common goal. Each team member brings to the team a unique frame of reference, which comes from training, beliefs, and background. These varying frames of reference, or perspectives, allow for a holistic view of an individual as the team plans appropriate programming. Of primary importance to the teaming process are effective communication skills in order to create a common vision, determine appropriate goals, share ideas and resources, and problem-solve issues and needs. Team members must respect each other and value the diverse perspectives of others. Members of the team include the individual and family, as well as (possibly) the PT, OT, adapted physical educator, speech pathologist, general educator, psychologist, nurse, physician, or other activity leaders. Although there have been many models of consultation, the collaborative consultation model is the most current and desired model for professionals in educational and community settings. For effective collaboration, professionals must establish team norms and make time for effective planning and communication.

What Do You Think?

1. Think about your personal and professional history and your previous experience with individuals with disabilities. Describe your personal frame of reference. How might you interact with professionals in other disciplines?
2. Think of someone you respect and enjoy talking with. Referring to the types of communication described in this chapter, identify how this person uses communication effectively when talking with you.
3. What professionals from the team have you interacted with? Interview one of them about background, training, and experiences to better understand his or her frame of reference and how you might interact with this discipline in the future.

What Would You Do?

Scenario 4.1

1. Following is a dialogue between two professionals. Can you identify the purpose of the active communication the listener uses in each of her responses?

   Practitioner: I'm excited about working with Jackie in my program, but I'm nervous about being able to meet her needs. We've never had someone with her level of abilities before, and I'm a little worried about working with someone with autism (see appendix A).

   Listener (Response 1): So, are you saying you have some concerns about her participation?

   Practitioner: Yes, I'm afraid the program might be too difficult for her. I'm not sure how to modify all the activities. Some of them I'm sure will be no problem, like swimming and aerobics, but I have no clue about kickboxing and tennis.

   Listener (Response 2): You're concerned about how to adapt for kickboxing and tennis but feel pretty comfortable with swimming and aerobics?

   Practitioner: Yes, the individual activities will be fine, but I'm concerned about the partner activities. Jackie might get injured, and that could be a liability issue for the program.

Listener (Response 3): It seems as though you're very concerned about Jackie's safety during these activities. Is that right?

How did you do? Check your answers.

Response 1: Clarifying the content of what was shared

Response 2: Paraphrasing or summarizing what was said

Response 3: Perception checking of the emotion behind what was shared

2. Who might be on the team of individuals working with Jackie?
3. Describe the five steps to the decision process as it relates to Jackie's physical activity setting.
4. What types of collaborative strategies might be helpful in providing appropriate physical activity programming for Jackie?

Scenario 4.2

Bob has decided to begin a new exercise program at the community YMCA. He is committed to maintaining his fitness and abilities for as long as he can and has determined that, now that he has retired, the better physical condition he is in, the better he will be able to deal with his diagnosis of Parkinson's (see appendix A). Bob loves to play golf and has recently retired in Arizona to a home on the golf course so he can play regularly and enjoy the benefits of the great winter weather. In the summers, when it is really hot, he plans on staying at his cabin in the mountains of Oregon, not too far from where he worked for more than 30 years. There he enjoys fishing and walking. Bob has a new doctor at the Mayo clinic in Scottsdale and has been working with a PT. On Bob's first visit he met a trainer at the YMCA named Steve. Steve will be designing an individualized program for Bob.

1. What team members should Steve talk with as he begins to develop a program for Bob?
2. What questions would Steve want to ask each of these team members? Indicate whether each question is open or closed.

CHAPTER 5

Program Focus and Assessment

S. Kasser, courtesy of I.D.E.A.L.

LEARNING OUTCOMES

After completing this chapter, you should be able to

- describe how purposes of assessment differ across various inclusive physical activity contexts;
- explain the factors that influence the assessment process and discuss assessment strategies effective in providing meaningful assessment data;
- discuss the difference between formal and informal assessment approaches and implications for individuals with diverse ability levels;
- identify the focus of inclusive physical activity programming across the life span; and
- explain the connection between curriculum and assessment.

INCLUDING ALL INDIVIDUALS

Terrance just obtained a job teaching adapted physical education for Jackson County schools. In his new job he will serve as an itinerant teacher for several rural schools. He has just received his caseload and discovered he has students from preschool through high school. In his role he will be providing direct instruction to students and consulting with general education teachers and other professionals who might be collaborating on educational programming for certain students. Terrance is also teaching yoga two nights a week at a local recreation facility to earn extra money to help pay off his school loans. He's excited about his new job with the schools; he has recently reviewed the files on all his students and has visited the school sites he will be working in.

To create quality programs for each of the individuals he works with, Terrance will need skills in three key areas: (1) assessing individual strengths, (2) evaluating demands of a task or activity, and (3) understanding environmental variables and how they affect learning. Assessment, defined as the process of collecting information and then making decisions based on that information (Horvat, Block, & Kelly, 2007), usually includes two phases: measurement and evaluation. Measurement is the process of assigning a number to a characteristic (Burton & Miller, 1998). For example, if we measure someone's range of motion using a goniometer, we might find that her elbow flexion score is 90 degrees. In another case we might measure throwing accuracy to a target and get a score of 10. In each case, we end up with a number that represents a characteristic for the individual—in the first case flexibility and in the second case accuracy. However, these numbers are meaningless by themselves. During evaluation—the second and more important aspect of assessment (Burton & Miller, 1998)—the numbers derived from measurement are interpreted in context of the environment and the individual. The ability to see the big picture—all aspects of the individual, environment, and task and how they interact—is most critical to a meaningful evaluation.

Assessment is the cornerstone to effective instruction. In this chapter we provide an overview of assessment as it relates to individuals with disabilities. Our intention is to identify meaningful skills for individuals to learn based on their abilities, settings, interests, and future plans. Identifying what's critical, functional, and relevant for the individual is the first step in determining which skills to assess in order to promote positive health outcomes.

PURPOSES OF ASSESSMENT

Assessment is an integral part of effective physical activity instruction and must be incorporated into any quality program. It is an ongoing process that takes place before, during, and after programming and aids the practitioner in answering many important questions:

- What are the individual's current abilities?
- What activities are appropriate for this individual?

- What skills and abilities should be assessed for this individual?
- What are his or her interests now, and what might they be in the future?
- How effective is the program in meeting the needs of this individual?
- Is he or she benefiting from participating in this program?
- What new skills and abilities has he or she learned?
- How can instruction be enhanced for this individual?
- What skills and abilities has he or she learned through participating in this program?
- How has his or her quality of life been improved?

These are some of many possible questions asked during assessment. Physical activity practitioners must become competent and knowledgeable in the purposes and use of assessment. In the next section we briefly discuss several of the important reasons for assessment, including legal requirements, screening, support decisions, planning and instruction, progress, and sport classification (Burton & Miller, 1998; Choate & Evans, 1992; Horvat, Block, & Kelly, 2007).

Legal Requirements

The Individuals with Disabilities Education Act (IDEA) mandates assessment of individuals with disabilities from birth through 21 years of age. These requirements include "assessment to determine if there is a need for specialized educational services," to report progress on those receiving special services, and for reevaluation at least every three years.

Individuals with a suspected disability or who are at risk for a disability are entitled to have an assessment completed by their local special education program. However, just because someone has a disability or a risk for a disability does not necessarily mean he or she will receive services; the individual must also show a discrepancy in abilities that demonstrates a need for services. Anyone in the community or school can make a referral to the local education program for an assessment of an individual from birth through age 21. Once a referral has been made, the local education agency is obligated by law to follow through by informing the parents of the referral, obtaining parent or guardian permission, and completing a formal assessment to determine possible areas of need. At the completion of the assessment, an individual family service plan (IFSP) or an individualized education program (IEP) must be completed. No legal requirements for assessment exist for individuals older than 21. Assessment for adults is usually connected to a community-based program focusing on one of these areas: screening, setting decisions, planning and instruction, progress, or sport classification.

Screening

Screening is used primarily to determine if further evaluation is needed. In a school environment, students are generally screened as a group, which does not require parental permission. However, a child may not be pulled from his or her peers and given a test that no other student is given unless a parent (or other

THE IDEA CATEGORIES OF DISABILITIES

- Autism
- Deafness
- Deaf or blind
- Hearing impairment
- Mental retardation
- Multiple disabilities
- Orthopedic impairment
- Other health impairment
- Serious emotional disturbance
- Learning disability
- Speech or language impairment
- Traumatic brain injury
- Visual impairment, including blindness

caretaker) has first granted permission. For the process to be considered a screening, all students in the program must participate in the same activity. For example, in the past, middle school students were screened by the school nurse for scoliosis; each student was evaluated by the nurse to determine if a need existed for further testing. In physical education, screenings are often set up as stations including such areas as balance, eye–hand coordination, eye–foot coordination, and locomotor skills. Screening is typically designed as a pass-fail protocol. If a student is found to need individual testing, then parental permission is required; at this point the process becomes an individualized assessment.

Screening is also used for adults to determine if a particular program is appropriate. For instance, adults interested in joining an aquatic exercise class might be initially screened to determine their aquatic experience or what aquatic safety skills they possess. An initial screening might also be completed by a physical activity practitioner to determine if an existing medical condition, such as high blood pressure or cardiac problems, should be considered before an individual participates in certain exercises.

Support Decisions

When screening reveals that individuals need further assessment, the individuals are subsequently assessed to determine their areas of strength and areas of need; programmatic decisions are then based on this information. Through individual assessment, practitioners attempt to answer questions such as these: What support services might this individual need? How might the individual's needs best be met? How should programs be implemented? For example, a toddler who has motor delays might need physical therapy, occupational therapy, or adapted physical education. The interdisciplinary team must also decide (with the family) what, when, where, and how these services will be received. Services might be provided in the home, at an infant childcare center, or both. For a child in public schools, assessment decisions will determine if the child needs adapted physical education services and, if so, how and where these services will be provided. Some students might be assessed to require smaller group instruction rather than participating in a larger general physical education group. Students with disabilities can work together in these smaller groups to accomplish motor goals and social development. For an adult, support decisions are based on the individual's skills and interests as well as what programs are available in the community (figure 5.1). Such programs might include adult classes at the YMCA, community recreational classes, health club programs, or competitive sports programs. We will discuss programming and support decisions for physical activity programs in chapter 6.

Planning and Instruction

Once support decisions have been made, programming can begin. In any physical activity setting, it is important at the onset of programming to determine the current level of performance for the individual. Once current level of performance has been identified, the physical activity practitioner can plan the curriculum or program. Programs will vary depending on the age and interests of the participant, the professional standards and guidelines set forth by the organization or educational board, and the availability of the physical activity opportunities and resources in the community. For example, the National Standards for Physical Education state in standard 1, grade 2, "Demonstrate competency in motor skills and movement patterns . . . skips, hops, gallops, or slides using a mature pattern" (NASPE, 2004, pp. 15-16). Based on this standard, the focus of the curriculum should be on activities that help develop these skills. On the other hand, an adult who wants to work on personal fitness might not have a formal curriculum or document to guide the planning phase. In this case, the program depends entirely on the interest of the individual and which options are available. If programs are available, he or she might choose quad rugby, wheelchair basketball, a walking program, swimming, or weight training, depending on his or her interests and personal goals. More information on planning and programming is presented in chapter 6.

Figure 5.1 Decisions about physical activity should be based on the individual's skills and interests.

Progress

Once programming begins, assessment is critical to determine if the individual is benefiting from involvement. The evaluation of progress allows the practitioner to determine if the goals set for the individual are being met. Documentation of this process determines what the next steps should be. For example, an adapted physical education practitioner working with an infant might set a goal for the child to pull to a stand independently and maintain upright posture. The practitioner documents the activities and interventions being completed as well as the progress the child is making. This way, as soon as the child meets a goal a new one can be established. The evaluation of change over time is critical to the assessment process. The documentation of both the intervention and the progress informs the practitioner whether the instruction is effective or not. When a child is not making satisfactory progress, this is discovered early through the documentation, and the intervention can be changed to promote greater improvement. The same process is necessary for adults involved in physical activity programs or activities. It is always important to assess whether an exercise regime or activity program is benefiting a participant so that the program or protocol can be modified. For instance, in a walking program, documentation would include the steps or distance an individual walked each day. This information would show what progress occurred in strength and endurance over time.

Assessment is an ongoing process that should be embedded within instruction. It should be done continually, not only at the end of an activity or unit. Ideally, assessment should occur hourly, weekly, monthly, and yearly. During each moment of instruction, the practitioner is continually interacting with participants, observing and giving feedback, changing instruction to meet the needs of the learner, and adjusting to the ever-changing environment. On an hourly or daily basis the instructor reflects on the process—what's working, what's not working, and what needs to be done in the next session. Documentation of progress made toward goals and objectives should be done daily, monthly, quarterly, and annually. Annual reports give an overall picture of the individual's functional abilities in the movement context, including progress, new skills, behaviors, concerns, and goals for the future. Through a sustained dynamic interaction among the participant, task, practitioner, and environment, the participant acquires new skills.

Sport Classification

Practitioners use assessment to classify individuals for sport competitions. Sport classification, used to equalize competition, is often based on functional ability, medical evaluation, or both. For example, in Special Olympics, athletes are classified based on their age, gender, and skill level. In a 100-meter heat, participants might be between 8 to 10 years of age, all female, and have similar qualifying times. In wheelchair basketball (figure 5.2), a player classification system based on the location of the injury and functional ability (Davis, 2011) is used to equalize skill level among teams. This system classifies players by functional ability during shooting, passing, rebounding, pushing their wheelchair, and dribbling. Such functional elements as trunk stability, force, and balance are evaluated, which vary depending on the degree of injury to the spinal cord. Athletes are categorized by functional ability; point values assigned to each player on a team are totaled so that no team exceeds a certain number of points on the court at any one time. Typically, the sport organization responsible for governing the event is responsible for determining who and what will be used to determine classification and for maintaining records on athletes. Those who take part in the classification of athletes might include medical doctors, occupational therapists, physical therapists,

Figure 5.2 To ensure equitable competition, assessment is used to classify athletes so athletes of similar functional abilities are grouped together.

THINK BACK

Think back to Terrance, who works with individuals from birth through adulthood. How might you help Terrance answer these questions?

1. Terrance's neighbor has a daughter, Julia, who is 19 months old and having trouble learning to walk. What can Terrance do to assist his neighbor? How might assessment be used to assist Julia in learning to walk?
2. Terrance has just started teaching his yoga class. Most participants are between ages 30 and 60. What purpose might assessment provide for Terrance in this setting?
3. Terrance is working with a student at the high school who is interested in wheelchair racing. How might Terrance use assessment with this student?

or others who have completed specialized training. This assessment for sport classification ensures that competition is equitable and challenging for all. For more information on sport classification, visit these websites:

International Wheelchair Basketball Federation: www.iwbf.org

International Paralympics Committee: www.paralympic.org

Deaf World Games: www.ciss.org

CP Sport (sports for people with cerebral palsy): www.cpsport.org

Special Olympics: www.specialolympics.org

ASSESSMENT CONSIDERATIONS

For practitioners to obtain the most complete and accurate picture of an individual's level of performance or functioning, several questions must be answered. What factors need to be considered when selecting the best evaluation instrument? What type of assessment will provide the most useful information? How do we ensure the information gathered is accurate? What factors might influence assessment data?

General Test Characteristics

To make the assessment process as meaningful as possible, practitioners should always select the most appropriate instrument for gathering performance data. When choosing an evaluative instrument, tests should be examined based on characteristics that render the test as either suitable or unsuitable for the particular situation. Important assessment tool characteristics include validity, reliability, objectivity, and norms (Horvat, Block, & Kelly, 2007).

1. **Is the test appropriate for the purpose?** Some instruments are developed for the sole purpose of screening and do not provide the comprehensive information necessary for support decisions or programming decisions. Other tests are developed specifically for fitness. A practitioner would not want to use a fitness test to evaluate motor development or a test designed for 3- to 10-year-olds for a high school student. Knowing the purpose of the assessment is critical to test selection.

2. **Is the test reliable and valid for the individual and performance being assessed?** Because assessment provides the foundation for justifying and making important decisions regarding physical activity involvement, practitioners must know that these decisions are based on information they can trust. The test must be examined for validity, and external factors that affect reliability must be analyzed. Test validity and reliability are usually discussed in the introductory chapters of any quality standardized assessment tool and should be reviewed before the tool is chosen. However, the validity of test results might be influenced by several factors both intrinsic and extrinsic to the individual. Person-related factors (intrinsic factors) include such aspects as the participant's mood, level of motivation, fatigue (figure 5.3), anxiety about the assessment, medication, attention span, native language, understanding the directions, and cultural relevancy of items on the test (i.e., do test items reflect the individual's normative cultural motor patterns).

Validity asks, Does the test truly measure what it says it measures?

Reliability asks, Are measurements consistent? Would you get the same results if you performed the same test twice under like conditions?

Objectivity asks, Would two different instructors get the same results if measuring the same child or group of people?

Among extrinsic factors that can affect test results are modifications to standardized test instructions, the setting in which the test is administered, and the communication style used to convey instructions. For example, a test might require that directions are given in a

Figure 5.3 Clearly this teacher will not get the best performance from this child on this particular day. What person-related factors will influence the validity of this assessment?

certain way, using exact language. The individual might be able to perform the task but does not understand the language of the test protocol. If the physical activity practitioner changes the language to help the student understand the directions, this change affects the validity of the test results. Many other extrinsic factors exist beyond those we have mentioned that can affect assessment results. Although no test or test situation is perfect, practitioners must try to ensure that the information they are gathering best represents the individual's performance abilities by considering the nature of the assessment, the individual performing, and the setting in which the assessment is conducted.

3. **Does the test compare against normative data?** If the results of the test are compared against normative data, practitioners must look closely at the population used to create such norms. Are the norms based on age, gender, disability, ethnicity, or some other criteria? How many individuals were used to create the norms, and when were these norms created? The score of the individual being assessed must be compared to appropriately matched samples. Also, it should be noted that normative data is based on an average, so individuals in the original sample scored both above and below that particular number. Typically, the larger the sample, the better the data will be for comparison.

4. **Is the test sensitive enough to detect changes in performance and discriminate among individuals?** Many tests are available for many different purposes, and not all tests have the same ability to detect variations in performance. The ability of a test to discriminate between small variations in performance is critical to test selection. Skills, or components of skills, must be broken down into measurable parts small enough to determine a score. For example, table 5.1 compares two test items for the overhand throw. Clearly, sample 2 provides much more information and allows for distinguishing among variations in performance among individuals as well as measuring changes in performance within an individual over time. In sample 1, many participants can pass this test, and differences in performance cannot be distinguished.

5. **Is the assessment or test safe for the participant?** Safety is always a concern when working with people in a movement context. Basic safety recommendations apply when planning and implementing a motor assessment:

Table 5.1 Two Test Items for the Overhand Throw

Sample 1: Overhand throw		Sample 2: Overhand throw with softball	
Throws a softball forward	Y N	Steps with opposition	Y N
		Elbow back	Y N
		Downward arc in preparation for throw	Y N
		Follow-through toward target	Y N
		Transfer of weight	Y N
		Hip rotation	Y N
		Distance ________	Y N

- Select a testing instrument that's appropriate, valid, and reliable for the individual you're testing.
- Review medical history with the family or individual before completing the assessment. Check for medical concerns or activities that are contraindicative for the individual.
- Ensure equipment is safe for the individual to use based on his or her ability.
- If the individual fatigues easily, break the assessment into multiple sessions.
- Start with activities that provide success and gradually work to more challenging tasks.
- Never put participants in situations that could be detrimental to their health or well-being. This sounds like common sense, but mistakes are made. For example, when using a standardized test protocol that requires specific guidelines, a novice assessor might be so concerned about precisely following the protocol that he or she fails to consider possible consequences to the participant.

Assessment Strategies for Obtaining Meaningful Data

Practitioners use several assessment strategies to obtain useful information. A three-pronged approach to effective assessment considers these facets: the administration of the assessment, the practitioner's skill in implementing the assessment, and the participant's ability to execute the tasks of the assessment. Table 5.2 lists many of the considerations in conducting assessments.

From an administration standpoint, practitioners should choose assessment tools based on how well the instruments match the purpose for which they are intended. Instruments developed for specific ages and groups should be used for those groups. Many low-cost, easy-to-administer assessments are available that can provide important information. Practitioners might also choose to create observation checklists or rubrics that supply valuable data specific to the information they desire. Examples of informal instruments are discussed later in this chapter, and sample rubrics are presented in figures 5.6 and 5.11. Many physical education texts also provide checklist examples, criteria for exercises or skills, and tools for

Table 5.2 Assessment Considerations in Selection of Tools

Administration considerations	Practitioner considerations	Participant considerations
• Ease of administration • Cost • Time • Individual vs. group • Purpose of assessment • Relationship of test content to teaching and learning environment • Age range • Population • Norm referenced • Criterion referenced • Standardized	• Skills • Knowledge and experience with tool • Knowledge of student • Knowledge of context and learning environment • Curriculum knowledge	• Age • Time of day • General health • Medication • Interest • Motivational level • Learning style • Comprehension • Previous experience • Native language • Culturally relevant

DID YOU KNOW?

A standardized motor test involves a set of motor activities that require a response. This response elicits a numerical representation or measurement.

evaluation (Best-Martini & Botenhagen-DiGenova, 2003; Horvat, Block, & Kelly, 2007; Graham, Holt-Hale, & Parker, 2010; Kelly, Wessel, Dummer, & Sampson, 2010).

Considerations related more to the practitioner also require thoughtful assessment planning. Practitioners should review assessment instruments thoroughly at the outset and understand the tool's intent, how to use the tool, and how to interpret the measurement data. Next, to ensure that the assessment process is appropriate, practitioners must understand the participants' needs and the context in which they will perform the tests. Finally, and most important, the practitioner must know which skills and activities are most meaningful for each participant and focus assessment on these priorities. In chapter 6 we present guidelines for identifying program priorities for individuals in inclusive physical activity programs.

The third part of the process of obtaining accurate, reliable assessment data pertains to the participant and his or her ability to accommodate individual differences in the assessment process. For instance, some individuals might show smaller gains or increments in improvements over time than anticipated. In rare cases, skills might actually decline; for example, after an eight-week fitness program, a participant might do fewer sit-ups than he or she did before completing the program. However, in such cases, the practitioner might be assessing more than just an improvement in performance; perhaps he or she is testing for the level of independence gained or a reduction in prompts needed by the participant to complete the task. Because of the variability in performance of participants, practitioners should assess performance on multiple occasions rather than rely on a single test session. Many factors—motivation, fatigue, blood sugar level—can result in fluctuations in performance levels. Table 5.3 identifies participant variables that might influence assessment outcomes and suggests strategies for practitioners to follow to obtain reliable and valid assessment results.

Table 5.3 Assessment Strategies Related to Participant Variables

Participant-related consideration	Assessment strategy
Small improvements in performance	Levels of prompting/independence gained
Unfamiliarity with tester or test items	Familiarization period
Optimal movement pattern nonexistent	Practitioner-made rubric
High variability in performance	Multiple assessment sessions Observe decreased variability pattern
Distractibility	Removal of distractions
Motivation	Peer support/verbal encouragement
Medication	Scheduling of assessment
Attention span	Multiple assessment sessions
Individual disposition	Determine motivators from parents or teachers
Learning style preference	Use most appropriate learning style (e.g., visual, kinesthetic, musical, and the like)

Formal and Informal Assessment Tools

A formal assessment tool is designed to yield the same results regardless of who is administering it (assuming the protocol is followed). Many people are familiar with the scholastic aptitude test (SAT) and the graduate requirement exam (GRE) and have experienced taking standardized tests at some point during their education. These tests are designed with precise directions and specifications that allow for consistency across administrators. All standardized tests are formal tests. In many cases, a standardized test might be administered to determine eligibility for special education services within a public school system.

Informal assessment tools are designed to evaluate progress or performance but do not adhere to the strict guidelines of a formal test. Examples include checklists, observations, questionnaires, interviews, rating scales, and teacher-made tests. Informal assessments can be extremely valuable for program planning and ongoing evaluation. In some cases, a teacher might elicit a more accurate performance from a student in a natural setting than when following a protocol (figure 5.4). Standardization used in formal tests often does not allow for the playful nature of individuals and might not always elicit the best possible performance.

Informal assessment allows instructors to create tools specific to the curriculum and environment in which they teach and to incorporate more meaningful or functional skills or tasks. In assessing an individual, it is often necessary to combine formal and informal methods to get a complete picture. We will discuss methods of informal (authentic) assessment later in this chapter.

Figure 5.4 Informal observation of children in their natural environment can elicit a more reliable performance than a standardized test.

Norm-Referenced and Criterion-Referenced Tests

Many assessment instruments are available to document performance, each serving its own purpose. Some assessment tools, known as norm-referenced tests, are used to compare individuals to their peers. Normative data comes from the product measurement of a particular skill, such as the number of sit-ups in 20 seconds. From a large sample of individuals, statistics are applied to determine averages. However, it must be noted that the "average" statistic for that measurement came from a whole range of scores from individuals. In a third-grade class, are all children reading at a third-grade level? Are they all computing math at a third-grade level? Are they all writing at a third-grade level? Would they all have the same motor skill level? Even within the domain of motor skills, some individuals will be good at balancing and others will excel at eye–hand coordination skills. While norm-referenced tests often are scored based on the product or outcome of a skill, such as the number of sit-ups done in 30 seconds, other types of assessment tools might look at the process of the skill or how it is performed, such as how someone catches a ball. For example, are the arms bent and relaxed in ready position? Is the ball caught and controlled with the hands? Although norm-referenced tests can be very helpful in determining how one learner compares to a group, most norm-referenced tests are not based on individuals with disabilities. This can make the use of a norm-referenced test inappropriate, depending on who is being tested and the purpose of the assessment. In many cases, a criterion-referenced test or another procedure, such as an authentic assessment method, might be more appropriate.

A criterion-referenced test is an example of a process assessment. These tests are used to compare an individual against predetermined criteria. Table 5.4 shows an example of criteria for galloping from the Test of Gross Motor Development 2 (Ulrich, 2000). In this example, the process of the performance is most important, not the product.

Table 5.4 Test of Gross Motor Development 2: Sample Criteria for the Gallop

Skill	Performance criteria
Gallop	1. Arms are bent and lifted to waist level at takeoff. 2. A step forward with the lead foot is followed by a step with the trailing foot to a position adjacent to or behind the lead foot. 3. For a brief moment both feet are off the floor. 4. A rhythmic pattern is maintained for four consecutive gallops.

From *Test of Gross Motor Development-Second Edition (TGMD-2)* (p. 2; Table 3.4), by D.A. Ulrich, 2000, Austin, TX: PRO-ED, Inc. Copyright 2000 by PRO-ED, Inc. Adapted with permission.

In another example, the Brockport Physical Fitness Test (table 5.5) uses a criterion reference for minimum and maximum heart rates for aerobic functioning. In each case, a performance standard is set for the individual to meet (Winnick & Short, 1999).

Table 5.5 Brockport Physical Fitness Test—Minimum and Maximum 10-Second Heart Rate Values

Aerobic functioning	Minimum	Maximum
General	23	30
Quadriplegic (C6-C8) Resting HR <65 Resting HR ≥65	 14 (Resting HR + 20)/6	 17 (Resting HR + 30)/6
Arm-only exercise	22	28

Reprinted from J.P. Winnick and F.X. Short, 1999, *The Brockport physical fitness test manual* (Champaign, IL: Human Kinetics), 78. By permission of J.P. Winnick.

Considerations for individuals with disabilities may also exist with criterion-referenced tests. Note that what's mechanically efficient for one person might not be the most efficient movement for another. For example, someone with spastic cerebral palsy (see appendix A) might find that the best way to throw for distance is to throw over the shoulder and backward. Another individual might find stepping with the opposite foot, using trunk rotation, and following through in the direction of the target to be most effective. Always recognize individual variability in performance. The challenge for the reflective practitioner is to find out what works best for each individual and help him or her develop these skills to optimal capacity. In many cases, traditional premade standardized tests are not appropriate. In such cases, authentic assessment methods can be an appropriate alternative.

Authentic Assessment

Authentic assessment has many advantages over formal or standardized methods of assessment, primarily in that authentic assessment connects assessment to curriculum (Mintah, 2003; Smith, 1997b). Many standardized tests include content that has little relation to the actual curriculum. For this reason it can be challenging to write goals and objectives for a student's IEP or activity program based on formal assessment results. For example, a learner might be asked to balance on one foot as part of a standardized test. The child might have some difficulty with this static balance task, but might have no trouble with dynamic balance activities, such as galloping or skipping, and can use these in dynamic physical activity. Authentic assessment techniques allow teachers to evaluate students on an ongoing basis in ways that connect to the curriculum and standards. Although reliability and validity of authentic assessment methods might be lower, they still provide valuable information about a learner. Physical activity teachers can improve reliability and validity by ensuring the tasks align with the curriculum. According to Joyner and McManis, "If the assessment is not related to the content taught in class and the way that it was taught in class, the assessment will not provide a true indication of student ability" (1997, p. 39). Quality authentic assessment methods have several components, including the following (Block, Lieberman, & Connor-Kuntz, 1998; Lieberman & Houston-Wilson, 2009; Lund, 1997; Mintah, 2003):

- Tasks are based on real-world settings.
- Tasks require higher-level thinking and application.
- The criteria for performance are presented in advance.
- The assessment is part of the curriculum and embedded in the instruction.
- Teachers and learners work together in the process, supporting each other and providing feedback.
- Learners often perform work publicly.
- Learners demonstrate skills in a variety of situations.
- An evaluation of the process is included, as well as the product of learning.

Authentic assessment is defined as evaluation of student performance in natural, real-life situations (Block, Lieberman, & Connor-Kuntz, 1998; Choate & Evans, 1992; Melograno, 1994; Mintah, 2003).

Many types of authentic assessment methods exist, including task sheets, systematic observation, written essays, journals (figure 5.5), interviews, exhibitions or performances, and portfolios (Lund, 1997; Mintah, 2003; Pike & Salend, 1995; Smith, 1997b). Again, the most important component of any authentic assessment tool used is that it reflects the standards and outcomes or IEP goals and objectives to be reached by the individual learner. One way to ensure the standards or objectives are being met is by using rubrics.

Rubrics can be developed for any type of authentic assessment and should reflect the outcomes of the program. Outcomes are based on designing down from the standards—to the program, to the course, to the unit, to the lesson (Hopple & Graham, 1995; Lieberman & Houston-Wilson, 2009). Although standards are appropriate for many students, how they are tailored and how the associated benchmarks

Figure 5.5 Journals can be a valuable tool in assessing student understanding.

are developed determines if they are inclusive of all children. Benchmarks are typically written to focus on a predetermined movement form and might exclude some students from achieving the desired criteria by virtue of their ability differences. Inclusive benchmarks incorporate the criteria necessary to attain the goal of the skill while allowing learners opportunities to meet the benchmark in different ways (Johnson, Kasser, & Nichols, 2002). Figure 5.6 shows a national standard for physical education, an IEP objective, and an inclusive rubric for throwing.

1. Remember Terrance from the chapter-opening scenario? What test characteristics should Terrance consider when selecting tools for individuals within his program?
2. How might Terrance use both formal and informal tools to assess his students?
3. In working with individuals with diverse abilities, how might Terrance use norm-referenced, criterion-referenced, and authentic assessment methods to evaluate participants in his many programs?

Throwing Competency Rubric—Grades 3 & 4: NASPE Standard 1

Standard 1—Demonstrates competency in many movement forms and proficiency in a few movement forms.

Standard 1 benchmark—Throwing with appropriate form, controlling accuracy and force.

Sample objective from an IEP—By [Date here] Joe will demonstrate an overhand throw by orienting his wheelchair sideways to the target, moving his trunk forward with his throw, and following through toward the target in four out of five trials, as observed and recorded by his teacher.

Rubric for Scoring

Needs work: Meets some or all of the criteria in 1A or 1B

Competent: Meets all of the criteria in 1A or 1B, all of the criteria in two other assessments, and some of the criteria in the remaining assessment

Exceeds standard: Meets all of the criteria in 1A or 1B and all of the criteria in the remaining assessments

Assessment 1: (Form A)

Student demonstrates

- A preparatory motion of the throwing arm (arm brought back to imitate throw) Yes No
- Body orientation appropriate for optimal release of the ball Yes No

- A forward weight shift toward target Yes No
- A follow-through beyond the release of the ball Yes No

Assessment 1: (Form B)

Student demonstrates

- A downward arc of the throwing arm to initiate the windup Yes No
- Rotation of hip and shoulder to point where nondominant side faces target Yes No
- Elbow up and back Yes No
- Weight transferred by stepping with opposite foot Yes No
- A follow-through beyond point of release diagonally across body Yes No

Assessment 2: (Spatial Accuracy)

Student demonstrates

- Ability to hit a stationary target (2 square feet, or .18 square meters) from a distance of ________ feet/meters Yes No
- Ability to hit a stationary target (2 square feet, or .18 square meters) from a distance of ________ feet/meters Yes No

Assessment 3: (Spatial and Temporal Accuracy)

Student demonstrates

- Ability to throw an object to a moving target so that the object is catchable (moving target is no more than ________ feet/meters away) Yes No

Assessment 4: (Force)

Student demonstrates

- Ability to throw ball with appropriate force so that it is catchable from a distance of ________ feet/meters Yes No
- Ability to throw ball with appropriate force so that it is catchable from a distance of ________ feet/meters Yes No

Figure 5.6 Example of related standard, objective, and inclusive rubric for the overhand throw.

Reprinted, by permission, from *The Journal of Physical Education, Recreation and Dance,* April 2002, p. 45. JOPERD is a publication of the American Alliance for Health, Physical Education, Recreation and Dance, 1900 Association Dr., Reston, VA 20191.

ASSESSMENT ACROSS THE LIFE SPAN: WHAT ARE WE LOOKING FOR?

Assessment is important to any inclusive physical activity program, and knowing where to direct assessment efforts is critical. As we mentioned earlier, assessment should not involve every skill or activity possible. This would be too cumbersome for even the most efficient practitioner. Assessment should focus on the skills and activities most meaningful for participants in terms of their age, physical activity opportunities available, and possible future physical activity involvement. At different times across the life span, practitioners will focus on various aspects of movement. Table 5.6 lists the skills and abilities often focused on and assessed in physical activity programs for individuals across the life span.

Although in this chapter we discuss general trends for evaluation and assessment across the life span, assessment priorities are not entirely exclusive to one particular period. For example, reflexes are generally examined during infancy, but they might also be assessed later in life in relation to neurological concerns. The same is true for walking. An individual's ability to walk might be reevaluated following a head injury or stoke. Likewise, many adolescents and adults participate in the same activities, and the assessments approach might be similar.

Table 5.6 Focus of Programming Across the Life Span

Infants and toddlers	Early childhood (preschool)	Elementary school	Adolescents	Adults
• Spontaneous movements • Reflexes • Motor milestones	• Fundamental motor skills • Orientation skills • Play participation • Locomotor • Object control • Water readiness	• Locomotor skills • Nonlocomotor skills • Object control skills • Movement concepts • Rhythms and dance • Aquatics • Fitness • Leisure activities	• Sport-related skills • Fitness • Leisure activities • Aquatics • Activities of daily living	• Leisure activity • Fitness • Activities of daily living • Aquatics • Sport skills

In addition to the identified movement skills and activities listed in table 5.6, assessment might also include gathering information on communication skills, social skills, on-task behavior, and other behaviors. Practitioners should consider the related aspects to physical activity involvement that might need to be addressed and developed for successful participation. A practitioner might also need to assess the settings in which inclusive physical activity programs might exist. These environmental assessments or surveys might focus on the accessibility of the site, or they might be directed toward particular activities to determine which skills or tasks must be taught so that participants can more successfully access the program activity. The focus of physical activity participation and related assessment priorities for individuals across the life span are described in the following sections. Separating information by age groups is convenient for organizational purposes, but the ultimate decision about the focus of a program is based not on age but on the current needs and abilities of individuals in their current settings as well as the skills they will need in future settings.

Infants and Toddlers

Individuals who work with infants and toddlers in the motor domain must work with a cross-disciplinary team of professionals and the family to provide appropriate assessment and programming for the infant or toddler. An occupational or physical therapist often provides motor assessment and programming for early intervention teams. However, the adapted physical educator is often called on to serve infants and toddlers as part of their teaching caseload (Cowden, Sayers, & Torrey, 1998; Cowden & Eason, 1991). Physical and occupational therapists along with the adapted physical education specialist work collaboratively with the rest of the early intervention team to provide the best possible evaluation and programming for the infant and his or her family. The focus of assessment and programming at this stage in life is on spontaneous movement, reflexes and reactions, and motor milestones (figure 5.7).

Spontaneous movements are movements that appear to serve no purpose, such as reciprocal kicking and arm movements. However, these movements are quite similar to patterns used later in life and might really be quite purposeful. For example, research shows that infantile supine (on the back) kicking is a rhythmical and coordinated movement similar to upright walking (Thelen, 1995; Thelen, 1985; Ulrich & Ulrich, 1995). Thus these early movements tell the practitioner something about the child's future potential as a mover.

Reflexes and reactions are involuntary movements often observable in infants. The persistence or absence of reflexes outside of their general developmental time period can be a sign of neurological concerns. In such instances, reflexes are often seen across the life span (table 5.7). For example, the retention of the symmetrical tonic neck reflex might inhibit an individual's ability to tuck the head to the chest to perform a forward roll, or the startle reflex might affect the ability to focus in a gym where there are many sudden loud noises.

Stewart Cohen/Digital Vision

Figure 5.7 Early physical activity programs focus on the acquisition of motor milestones.

For the developing infant, reflexes tend to disappear shortly before voluntary motor patterns begin. Research suggests a strong connection between reflexes and voluntary movement patterns. By changing environmental conditions, the persistence of reflexes and an earlier onset of a motor pattern can be influenced. For example, in one study, infants' stepping reflex was elicited daily for the first eight weeks of life. This practice actually increased the stepping reflex, and these infants began showing the signs of walking earlier (Zelazo, Zelazo, & Kolb, 1972a, 1972b).

Finally, motor milestones are typically voluntary motor behaviors observed in infants and toddlers. Although individuals might vary as to when they reach these motor milestones, they generally follow the same sequence (e.g., lifting the chin when lying on the stomach, lifting the chest when lying on the stomach, rolling over, sitting, standing with help, creeping (stomach up), standing alone, and walking (Haywood & Getchell, 2009).

Individuals who work with infants and toddlers need a strong educational background in motor development to understand how reflexes and reactions can influence motor behavior throughout life. The Hawaii Early Learning Profile is an excellent user-friendly developmental checklist for evaluating motor performance in infants and toddlers. This tool also provides curriculum to assist in the development of skills and ideas for parents as they interact and play with their children. For a more complete list of formal tools, see appendix D.

When assessing infants and toddlers, we need to understand what motor skills are important as well as the context in which the child is developing; that is, we need to see

Table 5.7 **Infantile Reflexes and Reactions**

Reflex/ reaction	Starting position (if important)	Stimulus	Response	Time	Warning signs
PRIMITIVE REFLEXES					
Asymmetrical tonic neck reflex	Supine	Turn head to one side	Same-side arm and leg extend	Prenatal to 4 months	Persistence after 6 months
Symmetrical tonic neck reflex	Supported sitting	Extend head and neck; flex head and neck	Arms extend, legs flex; arms flex, legs extend	6 to 7 months	
Doll eye		Flex head	Eyes look up	Prenatal to 2 weeks	Persistence after first days of life
Palmar grasping		Touch palm with finger or object	Hand closes tightly around object	Prenatal to 4 months	Persistence after 1 year; asymmetrical reflex
Moro	Supine	Shake head, as by tapping pillow	Arms and legs extend, fingers spread, then arms and legs flex	Prenatal to 3 months	Presence after 6 months; asymmetrical reflex
Sucking		Touch face above or below lips	Sucking motion begins	Birth to 3 months	
Babinski		Stroke sole of foot from heel to toes	Toes extend	Birth to 4 months	Persistence after 6 months
Searching or rooting		Touch cheek with smooth object	Head turns to side stimulated	Birth to 1 year	Absence of reflex; persistence after 1 year
Palmar-mandibular (Babkin)		Apply pressure to both palms	Mouth opens, eyes close, head flexes	1 to 3 months	
Plantar grasping		Stroke ball of foot	Toes contract around object stroking foot	Birth to 12 months	
Startle	Supine	Tap abdomen or startle infant	Arms and legs flex	7 to 12 months	
POSTURAL REACTIONS					
Derotative righting	Supine	Turn legs and pelvis to other side	Trunk and head follow rotation	From 4 months	

Reflex/ reaction	Starting position (if important)	Stimulus	Response	Time	Warning signs
POSTURAL REACTIONS *(continued)*					
	Supine	Turn head sideways	Body follows head in rotation	From 4 months	
Labyrinthine righting reflex	Supported upright	Tilt infant	Head moves to stay upright	2 to 12 months	
Pull-up	Sitting upright, held by 1 or 2 hands	Tip infant backward or forward	Arms flex	3 to 12 months	
Parachute	Held upright	Lower infant toward ground rapidly	Legs extend	From 4 months	
	Held upright	Tilt forward	Arms extend	From 7 months	
	Held upright	Tilt sideways	Arms extend	From 6 months	
	Held upright	Tilt backwards	Arms extend	From 9 months	
LOCOMOTOR REFLEXES					
Crawling	Prone	Apply pressure to sole of one foot or both feet alternately	Crawling pattern in arms and legs	Birth to 4 months	
Stepping	Held upright	Place infant on flat surface	Walking pattern in legs	Birth to 5 months	
Swimming	Prone	Place infant in or over water	Swimming movement of arms and legs	11 days to 5 months	

Reprinted, by permission, from K. Haywood and N. Getchell, 2009, *Life span motor development,* 5th ed. (Champaign, IL: Human Kinetics), 96-97.

the big picture. Infants and toddlers do not function in isolation but within the context of their family. For this reason, assessment at this level focuses on the entire family. What are the family's strengths, and how is the family and environment supporting the growth and development of the infant or toddler? Are there areas in which the family needs support? Here are some questions that might be asked:

- What is the child's medical and health history?
- What activities does the family like to do with the child?
- What support services are in place for childcare, medical care, and so on?
- What are the family's perceived needs?
- What are the family's perceived strengths?
- What are the family's goals for their infant or toddler?
- What types of playgroups or parent support groups are available?

- How does the infant or toddler interact with the primary caregiver?
- How does the infant or toddler interact with others?

Answers to these questions can provide insight into the strengths and needs of the family and child. Appendix D provides a more complete list of assessment tools for infants and toddlers.

In addition to formal tests that help determine an infant's or toddler's current motor abilities, many informal ways of gathering information help provide a more holistic picture of the child (figure 5.8). These might include interviews with the parents or caregiver, informal observations, questionnaires, or checklists of skills or activities. For example, here are questions that might be asked of the parent during a home visit and informal observation:

1. Can you tell me about your son Trent?
2. What kinds of things does Trent enjoy doing with you or other members of the family?
3. What are Trent's strengths?
4. Can you share a little bit of information about Trent's siblings?
5. How does Trent move about the house or play space?
6. What are your concerns for Trent?
7. What does a typical day for Trent look like?
8. What would you like to see Trent doing a year from now?
9. What kinds of things do you like to do as a family?

Figure 5.8 An informal interview can provide valuable information about a child and his or her family.

Such questions elicit information not garnered through the standardized test instrument, such as what the child likes and dislikes, how he or she interacts with others, and what the family's goals are. This information is just as critical to the overall assessment as information gathered through using the standard tools and will assist in determining outcomes for the individual family service plan. Combining formal and informal data gives the practitioner the best assessment information for planning.

Terrance just learned that he will be working with three toddlers who attend a center-based special education program two days per week. He will be seeing them once a week at the facility.

1. What will be the focus of Terrance's assessment with these toddlers?
2. What types of information will Terrance want to gather from the center before beginning his programming?
3. What information might he want to gather from the parents of these children?

Preschool to High School

Although it is important to understand the context and general program of activities for any age group, such understanding is just a foundation for the more important issue of knowing how to assess the skills an individual has and needs in order to participate in a particular setting or program. To be successful in program planning, practitioners must be able to assess not only a person's capabilities but also the tasks and environment. As children grow older and leave home for school-based programs, the focus of their physical activity shifts toward the development of playground skills and fundamental motor skills (figure 5.9).

For preschoolers, the general content areas include locomotor skills, orientation skills, object control skills, play participation skills, and equipment skills (Wessel & Zittel, 1995; Sanders, 2002). The Active Start national standards for birth to five provide guidelines for programmers (NASPE, 2009). Table 5.8 provides a sample for program goals, objectives, and learning outcomes for the young child. Although not all children can meet every program objective in the same way, they can all meet the learning outcomes. For example, examine the first learning outcome in table 5.8: To demonstrate selected fundamental locomotor skills and incorporate them in play and rhythmic activities at school and at home. A child who uses a wheelchair for mobility might not hop or gallop but can complete locomotion by pushing his or her wheelchair in various patterns and directions independently and can play a game of moving and stopping with music, which would clearly meet this learning outcome.

Felix Mizioznikov/fotolia.com

Figure 5.9 Gross motor playground skills are important for development.

Assessment for the preschool child should focus on the acquisition of the skills listed in the program focus. One frequently used method for assessing young children is the transdisciplinary play-based assessment (Linder, 2008). This method does not compare a child to his or her peers but rather allows for the assessment of skills to take place in a natural play setting (figure 5.10). In a traditional assessment approach, each discipline evaluates the child individually; in the transdisciplinary play-based approach, one person serves as the play facilitator, and all areas are assessed simultaneously. Members of the transdisciplinary team make recommendations for toys, materials, and activities to elicit desired skills. The play facilitator works with the parent and child to follow the child's lead while respecting the child's desires and wishes. This allows the team to observe the child's learning style, skills, and activity preferences. A play-based approach includes the following benefits:

- Assessment takes place in a natural setting.
- More flexibility is allowed in the testing setting.
- The focus is on the use of toys and play activities, which are a child's natural mode of learning.
- Fewer professionals interact with the child.
- It allows for the use of modeling behaviors or activities.

Table 5.8 Preschool Program Focus

Program goals and content area	Program objectives	Learning outcomes
Locomotor skills	• Roll • Crawl or creep • Walk • Run • Jump down • Jump over • Hop • Gallop • Rhythmic patterns • Wheel	To demonstrate selected fundamental locomotor skills and incorporate them in play and rhythmic activities at school and at home.
Orientation skills	• Ascend stairs • Descend stairs • Climb up a ladder • Climb down a ladder • Walk on a balance beam • Move in pathways, levels, and directions • Forward roll • Log roll • Spatial awareness • Body awareness • Imitative/expressive movements	To demonstrate selected body management and spatial awareness necessary for participating in play at school and in-home activities.
Object control skills	• Track object visually • Reach • Push object • Roll a ball (underhand) • Throw a ball (underhand) • Bounce a ball (dribble) • Kick a ball • Strike a ball • Throw a ball (overhand) • Catch a ball	To demonstrate selected fundamental object control skills and enhance eye–hand and eye–foot coordination necessary to participate in more complex game activities at school and home.
Play participation and equipment skills	• Hang from a bar • Pull an object • Ride in wagon • Ride a tricycle or bicycle • Swing on a swing • Slide down a slide • Travel on a scooter board • Parachute play	To demonstrate selected play and movement skills necessary to participate in activity settings alone and with others at school and at home.

Adapted from J. Wessel and L. Zittel, 1995, *Smart start* (Austin, TX: PRO-ED, Inc.), 14. By permission of L. Zittel.

- Cross-disciplinary interaction is allowed.
- A holistic view of the child is taken.
- Various disciplines are allowed in order to understand how specific areas interface with other disciplines in determining goals for the child.

In addition to the use of formal tools such as the Brigance or Peabody, or the use of a transdisciplinary play-based approach, additional informal procedures supplement content and provide a more complete picture of the child. Informal assessments also provide for daily documentation of progress over time. Such informal methods might include anecdotal records, checklists, rating scales, work samples, videos, or rubrics. One such example is a developmental checklist for particular skills. Table 5.9 shows a preschool checklist for the skills of jump over, hop, gallop, and rhythmic patterns (Wessel & Zittel, 1995).

Checklists such as these might be developed by the teacher or found in many quality predeveloped curriculums. Figure 5.11 provides another example of a teacher-made rubric for the skill of riding a tricycle. Using this type of informal tool can supplement the team assessment and document progress.

Comstock

Figure 5.10 Critical information can be gathered through a play-based approach.

As a child progresses from preschool to elementary school, the physical activity program focus shifts to movement concepts and skill themes (Graham, Holt-Hale, & Parker, 2010). Movement concepts and skill themes serve as the movement alphabet to make up the skills we use to interact in more complex activities, such as small-group games, dance, aquatics, and sports. Movement concepts include spatial awareness, effort, and relationships. Skill themes include locomotor skills, manipulative skills, and nonmanipulative skills. In chapter 8 we provide a complete summary of skill themes and movement concepts. Figure 5.12 shows a sample progression of skill focus from elementary school to high school and adulthood.

The individual skills emphasized in public school physical activity programs might be assessed and evaluated in several ways. Often, formal tests are used to determine initial needs, to compare students to a population, to determine individual goals and objectives, and to evaluate progress. Formal tests used in the area of physical activity in the public schools vary significantly. Appendix D provides an extensive list of tools used to evaluate motor skills for individuals from preschool through high school.

Deciding which tool is most appropriate for an individual depends on several questions:

- Why are you assessing the student?
- What skills do you want to evaluate?
- What is the curriculum of the physical education program?
- What are the individual's needs during a testing situation?
- What skills are required in a particular setting?
- What skills will this student need in the future for lifetime physical activity?
- What skills and abilities are important to the family and individual?

Table 5.9 Record of Progress

Child ______________________________

Jump over 2 out of 3 times Date ______________	Hop 2 out of 3 times Date ______________	Gallop 2 out of 3 times Date ______________	Rhythmic patterns 2 out of 3 times Date ______________
___ Jump forward, 2-foot takeoff	___ Hop forward, push off on foot, land on same foot 3 or more times	___ Step forward lead foot, step with rear foot near heel of lead foot	___ Clap or move (stamp, step, tap) 8 consecutive beats; even, moderate tempo
___ Jump forward 12 inches (.3 m), 2-foot takeoff and landing	___ Repeat on other foot 3 or more times	___ Period of nonsupport (hop) as rear foot nears lead foot, 3 or more times	___ Move (run, walk, hop) 8 consecutive beats; even, fast tempo
___ Jump forward 24 inches (.6 m), 2-foot takeoff and landing, maintain balance	___ Hop forward on 1 foot, slight forward lean, 5 feet (1.5 m)	___ Gallop forward, 1 foot leading, 5 times	___ Clap or move (stamp, step, tap) 8 consecutive measures of uneven rhythm; moderate tempo
___ Prepare to jump forward, knees bent about 90 degrees, arms behind body, takeoff angle 45 degrees	___ Repeat on other foot, 5 feet (1.5 m)	___ Repeat with other foot leading, 5 times	___ Move (gallop, skip, slide) 8 consecutive measures of uneven rhythm; fast tempo
___ Arms thrust forward, legs extended at takeoff, arms lower on landing, knees bent	___ Hop on either foot, elbows bent at waist level, 10 feet (3 m)	___ Gallop forward 10 feet (3 m), either foot leading	___ Clap or move (stamp, step, tap) 3 consecutive measures, accenting first beat of each measure; moderate tempo
___ Jump forward 30 inches (.7 m), 2-foot takeoff and landing, feet contact ahead of body	___ Lift both arms forward with hop, push off	___ Arms bent at sides, lift arms upward with weight transfer to lead foot	___ Move (locomotor) 6 consecutive measures, accenting the first beat of each measure; moderate tempo
	___ Nonsupporting leg bent, foot does not drag	___ Rear knee bent, foot does not drag	___ Move (locomotor) 6 consecutive measures, accenting the first and second beat; moderate tempo

Rubric: Tricycle Riding for Preschoolers

Check each item that the child can do.

Ridor

- ☐ Sits on tricycle or in wagon with assistance
- ☐ Enjoys riding while another person pushes

Starter

- ☐ Needs assistance to mount tricycle
- ☐ Can sit on the tricycle and put feet on the pedals with assistance

Mover

- ☐ Gets on and off of trike with minimal assistance
- ☐ Attempts to pedal with assistance
- ☐ Propels self with feet on the ground

Pedaler

- ☐ Gets on and off trike independently
- ☐ Pedals independently
- ☐ Propels self forward without turning

Traveler

- ☐ Gets on and off trike independently
- ☐ Pedals around obstacles
- ☐ Stops independently

Figure 5.11 Rubrics can be informal tools that supplement formal assessment instruments.

Some of these questions, as well as others that might come up as a result of the assessment process, might not be answerable through formal tests.

Standard assessment methods will not provide a complete picture of a child's ability; in some cases, such methods are not appropriate at all. When this is the situation, informal data collection and authentic assessment methods should serve as the primary means of gathering information, or at least as a supplement to formal testing. Many elements can be evaluated through informal measures such as parental interviews, checklists, coding sheets, and observations. Elements of the physical activity environment that can be observed and documented or tallied include time on task, opportunities to respond, peer interactions, appropriate behavior, and successful attempts, just to name a few. Figure 5.13 provides an example of a documentation sheet for the opportunity to respond. This tool could be used to determine if a student had ample opportunities to engage in physical activity within a particular setting, such as the game setting in figure 5.14.

As the child grows and progresses from preschool to elementary school to middle school and into high school,

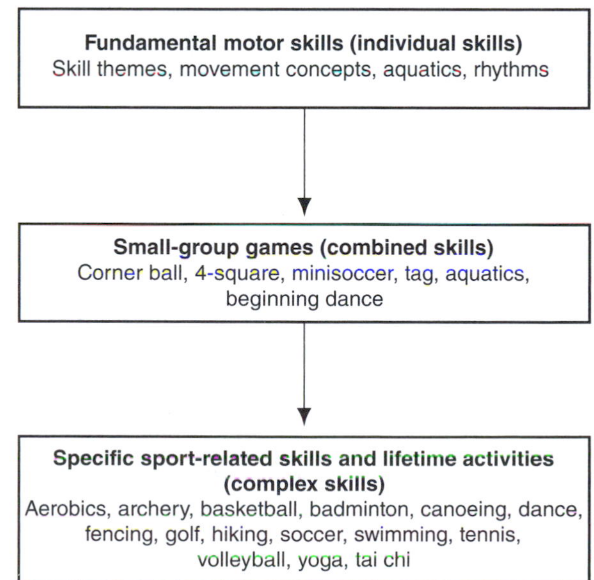

Figure 5.12 A sample progression of skills from elementary school to high school and adulthood.

Opportunity to Respond Coding Form

Date ______________________________

Lesson ______________________________

Time of day ______________________________

Activity or skill ______________________________

Each time the targeted student has an opportunity to engage in the activity (e.g., strike the ball, make a play), place a tally in the box provided.

Student 1	Student 2	Student 3

Questions to ask

1. Did students have relatively equitable opportunities to respond during the lesson?
2. Did students have a high frequency of responses during the lesson?

Figure 5.13 Sample coding form to use to determine if a student had ample opportunities to engage in physical activity within a particular setting.

individual skills are combined into simple physical activities, more complex skills, and lifetime activities. The focus of the program at each grade level should be determined based on the national standards for physical education (NASPE), state standards and guidelines, district or school guidelines, and parent and learner interests and needs. Regardless of the grade level a student is in, the curriculum should be adapted to meet the needs of all learners (as described in chapter 7). As students enter high school, the focus of their programs should be meaningful to them as individuals and should focus on lifelong physical activity participation (figure 5.15) and fitness as well as functional skills. The focus shifts toward how students will be physically active as adults. In the next section we discuss adult programs and assessment in detail. This same content applies to high school students as they prepare to transition into the adult world.

Figure 5.14 Seeing skills in the context of a game can be critical to the assessment process.

Figure 5.15 Activities must be meaningful to the participant and focus on lifetime activities.

THINK BACK

1. How might Terrance's focus on physical activity be the same or different for his elementary students compared to his high school students?
2. How might Terrance use both formal and informal procedures to assess a student? Can you provide an example of each?
3. What might be some of the advantages of the transdisciplinary play-based approach to assessment over other standardized tools for Terrance's preschoolers?
4. Terrance would like to create a rubric for tennis. Can you help him design a rubric for the forehand to use with students of all abilities?

Bold Stock/age fotostock

Figure 5.16 Adult activities should be meaningful and may focus on improving skills, social interactions, or contact through physical activity to enhance quality of life.

Adults

Physical activity programs for adults can focus on several goals, including maintaining strength; cardiovascular endurance; flexibility; neuromotor training (coordination, agility, balance, gait, and proprioceptive training); functional performance for activities of daily living; enhancing social interactions and contact through physical activity programs; developing skills for leisure or recreational pursuits; or providing sport opportunities either for recreation or competition (figure 5.16) (ACSM, 2011; Durstine, Moore, Painter, & Roberts, 2009). Assessment at this stage should focus on the skills and exercises that directly relate to and facilitate individual functional goals and physical activity participation choices.

Assessment is an important aspect of exercise programming for at least three reasons: It establishes the participant's current level or functional ability; it provides the basis for individualized goals and safe, beneficial exercises; and it allows participants and practitioners to gauge progress. Physical fitness or exercise programs should include all aspects of fitness: flexibility, strength, and cardiovascular endurance. Developing and maintaining sufficient levels of muscular strength, flexibility, and endurance are essential to enhancing independent living skills, preventing disuse atrophy, and avoiding acute or chronic injury. As such, assessment is important before starting any training to determine needed adaptations and techniques and appropriate training regimes. In addition, a physician's referral regarding any limitations or needed considerations is typically prudent before designing and assessing participants for any program. Table 5.10 displays some common tests for these fitness components.

Table 5.10 Common Fitness Assessments

Test name	Description	Age
Passive and active range of motion	Flexibility	Adult
Manual muscle test	Strength	Adult
Hand-held dynamometer	Strength	Elementary to adult
Repetition maximum weights	Strength	High school to adult
Isokinetic testing	Strength	High school to adult
Submaximal and maximal HR tests	Cardiovascular endurance	High school to adult
Arm crank and wheelchair ergometry	Cardiovascular endurance	Middle school to adult
Gait speed, distance	Neuromuscular	Adult
Goniometry	Flexibility	Adult
Sit to stand	Balance and symmetry	Adult
AAHPERD functional fitness test for older adults		Adult

Organizations such as the American College of Sports Medicine (ACSM) offer guidelines in exercise testing and evaluation as well as recommendations for frequency, intensity, and duration for the typical population (2011). Some assessment instruments or testing protocols might not be suitable for all individuals with disabilities. Before any fitness testing takes place, the practitioner must review the individual's medical history to determine the safety of conducting the test. Complete understanding of conditions for which exercise testing is contraindicated (e.g., blood pressure problems, heart conditions, diabetes, and so on) is necessary. The practitioner should also be aware and knowledgeable of the signs and symptoms of exercise intolerance and when an exercise test should be terminated. In addition, the practitioner must know the individual's history and current use of medications and the effects of medications on exercise.

Activities that facilitate balance and mobility might also be important for some individuals as they endeavor to maintain independence and competency in functional everyday tasks. Several clinical instruments allow baseline data from which to later assess progress. Table 5.11 includes several tools for measuring balance and mobility.

Table 5.11 Common Tests of Mobility and Balance

Test name	Description	Age
Berg balance scale	Balance evaluation	Adult
Functional reach test	Activities of daily living	Adult
Tinetti balance	Balance evaluation	Adult
Timed get-up-and-go test	Speed and agility	Adult
Gait abnormality rating scale	Walking gait performance	Adult

Many scales and instruments are also available to assess functioning in various activities of daily living (e.g., stair climbing, dressing, and so on) that involve balance and coordination components (figure 5.17). Practitioners without experience in administering these tools might elect to assess these activities through observation. Care must be taken when evaluating results and making decisions based on information that might be unreliable or not measured using set criteria and sensitive measurement scales.

S. Kasser, courtesy of I.D.E.A.L.

Figure 5.17 Balance is critical to the functional ability of many adults.

Activity participation of adults might also involve sport-specific or leisure-related experiences (table 5.12). Assessment of the prerequisite skills and performance of these individuals is necessary for programming or training efforts to improve performance. Much of this assessment is conducted within the context of the sport or activity, and practitioners use their experience and observational skills or self-design assessment scales to obtain the needed information. Assessment would include fitness and balance aspects and activity-specific movement skills as well as the use of personal equipment, such as mobility aids and wheelchairs, and activity-specific equipment, such as the monoski or other modified devices.

As is true for younger participants, the goal of any physical activity program for adults and older adults is continued involvement in a physically active lifestyle and the ability to perform daily functional skills. Whether the focus is increased independence, skill development for recreational pursuits, or

Table 5.12 Sport and Leisure Activities

Individual	Dual	Team
• Bowling • Archery • Golf • Skiing • Billiards • Skating • Track and field • Weightlifting • Aquatics • Walking • Aerobics • Hiking • Biking	• Table tennis • Tennis • Badminton • Fencing • Dance • Bocce • Horseshoes	• Basketball • Volleyball • Hockey • Soccer • Softball • Quad rugby

*This table includes many of the sport and leisure activities in which adults participate. It is not intended to be comprehensive—only to offer examples of activities.

enhanced performance for competitive sport involvement, accurate assessment data must be gathered for optimal programming to ensue. Assessment of progress is also critical to determine if goals have been achieved or if present activity plans or training regimes need to be further modified. This assessment information—supplemented through continual communication with individual participants and others in the support network—provides the foundation for these decisions.

1. What types of skills might Terrance be looking for in the preschool children in his program?
2. How might Terrance determine if a child in his program is getting plenty of playing time to improve his or her skills?
3. What might be important areas to assess in Terrance's yoga class for adults? How might Terrance assess these areas?

SUMMARY

Assessment is a multifaceted approach to collecting information about an individual's performance and abilities. It is an ongoing process inseparable from programming and critical to any effective program. Several of the functions of assessment include legal obligations, screening, support decisions, planning and instruction, progress, and testing for sport classifications. Assessment is an inherent part of all effective programs and instrumental in planning for individual family service plans, individualized education programs, individual transition plans, and adult physical activity programs. The selection of the most appropriate tools for data collection is critical to the assessment process, so practitioners must consider specific test characteristics before choosing which tools to use. Both formal and informal procedures are important in the assessment process to gain a complete picture of an individual's abilities. In examination of an individual, the focus of programs and assessment might change across the life span, but it is always important to determine what is most important to and for the individual learner. Not every person needs to be evaluated on every skill; rather, those skills that are functional and appropriate for them in a given setting and in future settings should be tested. In this chapter we have supplied a general overview of assessment and program focus; in chapter 6 we expand on this information by providing details on issues related to preparing and planning for inclusive physical activity programs. Then, in chapter 7, we help you better understand considerations regarding the needs of individuals and how to make appropriate modifications based on their capabilities.

What Do You Think?

1. Identify two standardized tools available in your profession for assessing individuals' movement abilities.
2. Think of someone you interact with through volunteer hours or your job and design an informal tool to help you understand this person's movement abilities.
3. Using the same individual, what assessment considerations would you need to make based on the individual, the environment, and the tasks?

What Would You Do?

Scenario 5.1

Beth is working with adults in an individualized community-based exercise program. A new participant, Ann, has just joined her program. Ann has a spinal cord injury at T-8. She uses a manual wheelchair for mobility and is very active in sports for individuals with disabilities. She competes in wheelchair basketball and wants to train for a marathon.

1. What are the possible purposes of assessment for Ann?
2. How might Beth assess Ann's abilities?
3. What skills would Beth want to evaluate with Ann?
4. What questions would be important to ask Ann during the assessment process?

Scenario 5.2

Francisco is 11 years old and has just entered Erica's adapted physical education program. He also attends Ms. Frank's fifth-grade class as well as special education services. Francisco was diagnosed at birth with severe cerebral palsy and uses a wheelchair for mobility. His potential intellectual abilities are unknown because his ability to communicate is very limited. He communicates with his facial expressions and has some head control. His chair is manually operated, and his instructional assistant pushes him to his class and other services. The speech-language pathologist is working to find a functional means of communication for Francisco. Francisco also receives regular physical therapy.

1. What types of tests are appropriate for evaluating Francisco's abilities?
2. How would you go about assessing Francisco? What methods would you use?
3. What is an appropriate program focus for Francisco?

CHAPTER 6

Preparing and Planning Inclusive Physical Activity Programs

© Jeff Greenberg/age fotostock

LEARNING OUTCOMES

After completing this chapter, you should be able to

- discuss the steps for creating inclusive physical activity programs;
- describe the referral process for an individual who might need physical education support from birth through 21 years of age;
- explain how youth and adults with disabilities can access physical activity programs involving sports, recreational, and fitness activities;
- provide examples of physical activity goals, objectives, and benchmarks for an individual of any age; and
- apply the steps to planning an inclusive program to your particular field of study.

INCLUDING ALL INDIVIDUALS

Beth and Tom are the parents of Jackson, an 11-year-old diagnosed with Down syndrome shortly after birth. The family received early intervention services when Jackson was an infant, which then continued as he went on to an integrated preschool from three to four years of age. At five he entered the local general education school, where he received support services for full inclusion in physical education. Jackson has lived in the same neighborhood since he was a baby and is currently in the fifth grade at Marimont Elementary School. He loves his teacher, and his neighbor and best friend Sean is in physical education class with him. Jackson has been very involved in sports because his parents are avid outdoors people who go camping, hiking, and cycling every weekend that the weather permits. Jackson has recently become involved in Special Olympics and enjoys competing in track and swimming. He has also played in the local community soccer league since he was seven. Tom and Beth are considering moving closer to Tom's mother, who's beginning to need assistance because of arthritis. However, a move would mean going to a neighboring community and changing schools for Jackson. Beth has contacted the school district and is waiting to hear about the possible transfer. She is concerned because she has heard that Jackson might not be placed in the general sixth-grade physical education class. She wonders what the referral process will be like if they change districts and how long it will take. The idea of this change raises many questions for her about Jackson's education. What will the middle school be like? How will the transition to high school go? Will Jackson be able to make new friends?

The road toward inclusive physical activity is founded on a commitment to the philosophy of inclusion as well as knowledge of how all participants can gain access to and become meaningfully involved in physical activity opportunities. Although Jackson has been involved in physical activity programs from an early age, what procedures are in place to ensure his continued involvement in general physical education? If you were his new physical education teacher, what steps would you take to provide Jackson with the best program?

Physical activity practitioners need to know the process through which all individuals enter into physical activity, how those involved find support and guidance, and how practitioners responsible for the programs are held accountable. Although legal requirements and the personnel involved might differ across settings and programs, the process of prioritizing goals, ensuring best practice, providing support, and making accommodations is the same for all individuals regardless of age or context. In this chapter we begin with an overview of the steps involved in inclusive physical activity programming; we then provide insight on how these steps are followed for infants and toddlers, school-age children, and both young and older adults.

A PRACTICAL APPROACH TO INCLUSIVE PHYSICAL ACTIVITY PROGRAMMING

Inclusive physical activity involves a sequence of steps that practitioners must take to ensure equal access and optimal programming for everyone. Figure 6.1 shows the process of developing and implementing inclusive and individualized physical activity. The process involves five steps necessary to break down the barriers to inclusive physical activity, as discussed in chapter 3. The process integrates collaboration and network skills, discussed in chapter 4, and appropriate and meaningful assessment, described in chapter 5, that lead to appropriate planning and programming.

This process includes two phases. The first is the *preparation* phase, which consists of three steps:

1. Ensuring access
2. Establishing support networks
3. Promoting positive physical activity environments

The second phase is the *planning and implementing* phase, which includes two more steps:

4. Planning for individualized instruction
5. Assessing success

Although this process might appear to be linear, there's continual reevaluation and flow between the preparation phase and the planning phase. Figure 6.1 illustrates this flow and the need for ongoing reflection involved in the planning process. The process involves the three Rs of reflective practice, as discussed in chapter 2: ready, rethink, and retry (see figure 2.5). All good practitioners reflect on each step of the process and make changes throughout each phase.

Ensuring Access

The first step toward offering an inclusive physical activity program is creating and ensuring access for all potential participants. The physical activity practitioner must advocate on behalf of participants. For some youngsters, this entails determining who qualifies for services and how to obtain increased support. For instance, in a school-based setting, a student might become eligible to receive support and services associated with physical education if, by law, this child is identified as having a disability. In addition, the student must qualify for these supports and services by meeting appropriate assessment and state-determined performance criteria. For youngsters in non-school-based settings or adults in the community, access means increasing avenues for entry into physical activity programs and assisting them in overcoming barriers they might face.

As we discussed in chapter 3, access also involves educating participants regarding the benefits of physical activity, the opportunities available to them, and informing them of their rights related to accessing physical activity programs. A physical education teacher should seek out students with disabilities in the school who might not yet be assigned a physical education class or inquire if all students in the school are indeed receiving physical education. The teacher might need to discuss with students and parents the requirements of physical education and help them understand the benefits of meaningful participation. Likewise, a fitness practitioner might explore programs at the facility that currently include individuals with differing capabilities. If these programs are limited, more programming opportunities must be developed; the public must then be made aware that these new programs exist and that individuals of all abilities are welcome. Spreading the word about new programs might involve open houses or invitations for people to come tour the facility and hear about the programs available. Presentations could also be provided to particular community groups regarding the benefits of physical activity and how people can become more active. It is also a good idea to tell local organizations or community agencies about the program, emphasizing that everyone is invited to participate.

Of course such efforts might be unsuccessful if administrators, supervisors, and other persons significantly involved with potential participants are not also educated about inclusive programming. School administrators should be supplied information about the legal rights and responsibilities of their school regarding physical education for children

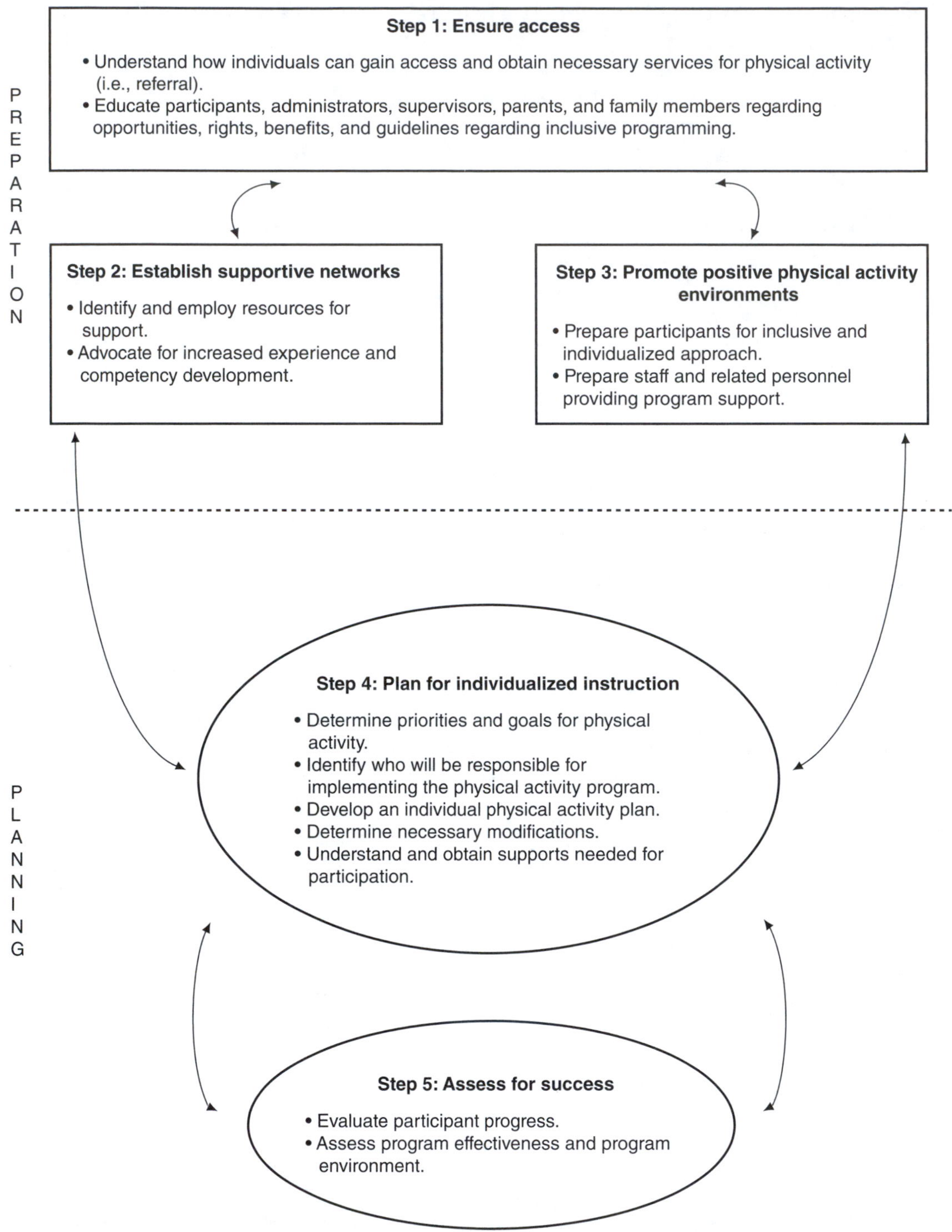

Figure 6.1 Developing and implementing inclusive physical activity programs involves many important steps.

with identified disabilities; they should also understand how children with physical activity needs are referred and supported. Directors of community recreation centers or health clubs and appropriate medical professionals should be informed about the variety of programs available in the community. Whatever the situation, the program facilitator should commit to include all individuals and support them by opening the doors and welcoming them into the program.

Establishing Support Networks

Once a commitment to creating and increasing access is made, the next step is to identify and establish networks of individuals who might offer support to the physical activity practitioner. As mentioned in chapter 4, collaborative teams are critical to the success of any program. Certain individuals might offer valuable insight and information regarding medical information and physical activity recommendations or contraindications for particular participants. They might also provide information about adaptations, instructional strategies, and behavioral practices that have been effective in other contexts.

Support networks are invaluable because physical activity professionals must advocate not only for participants but for themselves as well. The success of inclusive practices rests with the knowledge and skills professionals have regarding effective strategies and insights for individualized programming. Practitioners must advocate for increased support and training to this end. They might ask to observe other inclusive programs or professionals effective at implementing inclusive activities, to attend conferences and workshops, or to complete courses focusing on inclusive physical activity. Through collaborative and supportive networks, practitioners can gain the insights, knowledge, and skills to become adept and confident in developing and implementing effective inclusive physical activity programs.

DID YOU KNOW ?

The National Dissemination Center for Children with Disabilities has information for teachers, administrators, and parents on disability definitions, laws, IEPs (individualized education programs), access, supports, accommodations, assistive technology, and a plethora of other topics related to individuals with disabilities. Visit http://nichcy.org.

Promoting Positive Physical Activity Environments

Regardless of how committed a practitioner is to including all individuals, the overall success of the program depends largely on the attitudes of all those involved. Thus the next step in the process is promoting positive physical activity environments by preparing everyone involved for the inclusive and individualized approach. Participants with disabilities, as well as the staff and related personnel who support them, must be informed of the philosophy underlying the program and understand the capabilities and needs of all participants.

Preparing Participants

Preparing potential participants with disabilities involves increasing their knowledge about the activity setting and gaining their confidence that the program can meet their needs. Raising participants' comfort levels before they begin the program eases their transition into the program. Here are suggestions to assist with this process.

- Distribute written material describing the mission statement, philosophy, and program or activity.
- Invite potential participants to visit the program to observe and ask questions.
- Provide a video of the program for potential participants to watch at home.
- Provide contact numbers of staff members for obtaining additional information.
- Provide contact numbers of current participants in the program for information sharing.
- Schedule a visit with a program staff member or teacher.
- Offer one day of participation as a visitor.

Preparation of participants also involves those individuals who are already in the program. Several strategies can help these individuals become familiar with the wide range of participants who might join them and the array of methods and materials that might be employed to promote everyone's involvement and success. These individuals should feel comfortable and confident that their program can be improved through the diversity of experiences and abilities new participants bring.

When the practitioner leads by example, establishes an atmosphere of acceptance and equity, and employs an inclusive style from the start, program participants will be more positive and accepting. In this way, participants become committed to the success of the program or activity and have a vested interest in the success of all those involved. This can happen only if all participants are made aware of the range of abilities existing within the program, provided an explanation regarding why accommodations and modifications are necessary, and given opportunities for ideas and strategies to further promote success and enjoyment of all those involved.

Prepare Support Personnel

The staff that supports individuals within the program must understand the program's philosophy and goals. Support members should know the range of abilities of individuals who might join the program and the supports necessary for these participants to have success. Such supports might include the use of assistive devices, variations in instruction or activities, or the assistance of another person. Support personnel must be clear on their roles and expectations in supporting participants and knowledgeable about the activities or modifications in which they will be involved. Those providing support must be continually supported themselves. Open lines of communication should be emphasized before the program starts and continue throughout the support staff's involvement in the program.

Planning for Individualized Instruction

Once participants and support personnel involved in inclusive programs are prepared for the program's onset, the process shifts from program preparation to program planning. At this point, the program participants become the primary focus, with the goal being to individualize instruction. The following steps facilitate individualized instruction.

- **Determine priorities and goals for all program participants.** Priorities for a toddler might be on balance and mobility so the child can move across a grassy playground to play with friends. A middle school student might be interested in participating in a general physical education cooperative games unit with classmates, whereas an older adult might want to participate in an aerobics or yoga class at a local fitness center. In each case, program priorities are participant-based, and goals are meaningful to the individual. As discussed in chapter 5, many factors must be considered when developing the focus of an individual's program and assessing skills and capabilities to determine appropriate goals. Most important to consider are the skills the individual needs to participate in physical activities and to execute functional tasks at present and in the future. Of course, the activity interests of the individual and his or her family are also considered when setting goals and priorities.

- **Determine who is responsible for teaching the physical activity program.** The next step of planning focuses on who will teach participants the skills they need to participate in the physical activities that have been identified. In some cases, the program instructor might have the knowledge and skills required to teach all participants at all ability levels. In other cases, practitioners might need the assistance of trained professionals to modify activities to accommodate individual differences. Although some programs might involve previously organized large groups and prestructured programming, in some cases it might be necessary to offer alternative activities in small-group settings. Whether these activities are supervised by the program instructor or by an adapted physical activity practitioner, decisions regarding an individual's activity program must be made with inclusion in mind.

- **Develop an individual physical activity plan.** Once priorities have been determined, an individualized physical activity plan is developed. These plans take into account the priorities and goals identified as well as the professional standards and guidelines set forth by the profession. For school-age children, an individualized education program is developed based on physical education standards. These standards relate to lifelong physical activity participation and might be achieved in many ways. For the fitness professional, guidelines and practices have been established by health and fitness organizations (see appendix C). Some sport organizations have also established rules and regulations to guide coaches in the training and sport skill development of their athletes.

- **Determine necessary modifications.** We have discussed the what and where of individualized physical activity programming. Now we turn to the how. As discussed in chapter 1, what a person is capable of achieving does not depend solely on his or her abilities but also on the task being attempted and the context. Based on the concept of capability shifting discussed in chapter 1, modification strategies can be directed toward the task or the context to promote success. Strategies to modify the context include changes in instruction, organization, or procedures. Modifications in the type of equipment used and the physical setting might further promote inclusive physical activity. For students with disabilities, curricular or program tasks might be modified as well. In chapter 7 we discuss the breadth of modifications possible when developing inclusive physical activity plans and key considerations in determining the appropriateness of such changes.
- **Understand and obtain supports needed for participation.** Given the range of abilities and needs of participants in inclusive programs, no one person can be expected to have all the expertise and skills necessary to provide an individualized and effective program for every participant. Thus it is important to identify who will provide support to the participant (if support is necessary), what supports are best to provide, and what degree of support is needed. The goal is to promote independence and increased competence of each participant regardless of age or ability. Practitioners should know that in some cases providing unnecessary support can have a negative effect on the participant's interaction with others in the program or lead to increased dependence and learned helplessness.

Assessing Success of Inclusive Efforts

In inclusive physical activity, program assessment and evaluation are just as important as program planning. Those who organize and implement programs must be accountable for what they do, and evaluation of participant progress is essential to this end. Some of the issues discussed in chapter 5 regarding assessment for individuals with disabilities must be carefully considered to ensure that evaluation information is accurate and meaningful. However, accountability goes beyond measuring to what extent a particular individual has reached his or her goals. Inclusive programs intend that all participants reach their potential. These programs implement continued reevaluation of the program environment, which includes the attitudes of others and the effectiveness of modifications and accommodations being employed. As discussed in chapter 2, practitioners must continually employ the 3 Rs. They must *ready* their own practice and the influence it has on the people involved. They must *rethink* practices they have just implemented. They must *retry* new methods that include and accommodate all participants in their programs.

INCLUSIVE PHYSICAL ACTIVITY FOR INFANTS AND TODDLERS: PREPARATION AND PLANNING

The benefits of early physical activity for infants and toddlers are well accepted and, in fact, led to the passage of legislation mandating services for infants and toddlers who might be at risk for delays (P.L. 99-457) (figure 6.2). Physical activity contributes significantly to a child's early development in all aspects of learning, including cognitive, social–emotional, language, and fine and gross motor development. With proper supports, all infants and toddlers can participate in meaningful physical activity to help them develop into physically active and healthy children.

Photodisc

Figure 6.2 Infants with suspected or documented delays can qualify for early intervention programs that involve movement activities.

Ensuring Access

Many infants and toddlers have ample opportunities to be physically active, such as playing with mobiles in their crib or reaching for toys while lying on the floor. Infants might also participate with their mothers or fathers in structured group programs such as infant massage class, "baby and me" swim class, or a parent–infant exercise class. Toddlers often have chances to play with other children through parent-organized playgroups or community programs. Much of this activity occurs in informal or loosely organized settings such as at home, at community parks or recreation centers, or in neighborhood backyards. For some children, opportunities are wide and diverse, but other young children might not have occasions to play with others or to participate in infant and toddler programs because of the barriers they and their parents experience. As we discussed in chapter 3, such barriers as time, transportation, cost, or a parent's own physical activity habits or beliefs can influence how much physical activity infants and toddlers get.

Unfortunately, access issues often surface for infants and toddlers with disabilities. These children have less impromptu opportunities or invitations to join in play and physical activity. In addition, many infants and toddlers born prematurely or with significant disabilities are medically fragile in the early months and not ready to participate in physical activity programs. However, research reveals that the earlier a child with suspected delays receives intervention, the less likely he or she will encounter delays later in life (Ramey & Ramey, 2004). Knowledge of the increased benefits of early intervention coupled with the awareness that decreased opportunities exist for these children have led to legislation promoting physical activity involvement for this age group. Early intervention services are mandated by the Individuals with Disabilities Education Act (IDEA) (NICHCY, National Dissemination Center for Children with Disabilities, 1998). Any infant or toddler from 0 to 36 months of age who has an identifiable disability or is at risk for delays might be eligible for early intervention services (see appendix B for eligibility criteria). School districts, county programs, regional centers, or local public or private agencies might provide supports and services. The services would relate to any areas of suspected delay and might include communication, physical, cognitive, social or emotional development, or adaptive behavior (self-help skills).

Infants who qualify for services are generally identified through the local education area's child-find procedures. These child-find procedures provide information to parents via the following methods:

- Contact through neonatal intensive care units
- Local parent support organizations
- Community health and developmental screening
- Local pediatricians or other public health providers
- Public service announcements

Once a child is identified and referred, the early intervention program is required to contact the family to determine if they would like an evaluation. If the parents decide they want early intervention services, they give written permission for an early intervention team to begin an assessment of family and child needs.

Establishing Support Networks

Many parents find support and guidance during playgroups or activity sessions, during which information about development, observed behavior, and future expectations is freely shared and discussed. But such opportunities often do not occur for parents of infants or toddlers with disabilities because parents are not yet connected to other parents of children who have similar disabilities and needs. For these parents, the early intervention team can provide several supports, including infant and toddler parent support groups, parent networks, a resource library for information on development and disabilities, toy lending, and other direct intervention services.

On completion of assessments, the early intervention team meets with the parents to develop a service plan for the family. This team might include special educators, speech and language pathologists and audiologists, health care providers, therapists, adapted physical educators, social workers or psychologists, and others who might provide services to the infant and family. A designated service coordinator or case manager typically coordinates these individuals and all services.

The service coordinator can be any individual on the team and is generally the person the family feels most comfortable with and who has the skills to carry out the plan. This person is responsible for making contact with the family and should be knowledgeable about early intervention regulations, community services, parent support groups, family resource centers, recreational programs, childcare services, respite care, and community medical and financial assistance programs.

Promoting Positive Physical Activity Environments

Infants are naturally active learners, and much of their initial learning comes through movement experiences. For example, infants learn about cause and effect by pushing the buttons on a pop-up toy; they learn about gravity by pushing their bowl off the table; and they begin to roll over while reaching for something that intrigues them. For infants, positive physical activity means setting up an environment that is safe and encourages interaction and exploration through self-initiated and facilitated play. The importance of parent–child interaction to promote development is well documented (Spiker, Boyce, & Boyce, 2002), and the safer and more comfortable a child feels, the more likely he or she is to explore and learn. However, for the parent of a child with a significant difference in ability, this interaction might be even more critical because the parent might need to assist the infant in exploring their world. Although most children follow a similar developmental sequence from rolling to creeping to walking, the pace at which these skills develop varies significantly. Some children might even skip a particular skill altogether. Variations in ability and the way in which children participate in play or activity should be accepted and encouraged. For parents of children with disabilities, it is critical to have a supportive environment in which to relax and play with their child. Sharing information with other parents, initiating playgroups, and inviting parents and children over for a visit are all ways to create positive environments for infants and toddlers. Professionals help create positive environments by providing support to parents for the excellent parenting they are doing, helping parents with ideas for homemade toys, demonstrating how to set up a play environment, or showing how to integrate motor development activities into everyday activities (e.g., assisting a toddler to stand while holding onto the coffee table to play with a toy, or having the child stand on one foot while the parent removes each shoe).

Planning for Individualized Instruction

For an infant or toddler who might be at risk of a developmental delay or who has an identifiable disability, early intervention is beneficial. The early intervention team, along with the parents, discusses and develops an individualized family service plan (IFSP) as outlined in the IDEA. The IFSP is a written document that explains the strengths and needs of the family, services to be provided, and when and how these services will be implemented (figure 6.3). For infants and toddlers, the IFSP includes written objectives for the child in each area of need. These objectives are called outcomes. During the IFSP meeting, the early intervention personnel share the results of their assessments and evaluations, and together with the parents determine appropriate outcomes for the child based on child and family needs. The parents' desires are very important to this process, and outcomes should be written in the words of the parents as much as possible. For example, if parents say they would like to see their child roll over or crawl, then the outcome is written with that in mind. Figure 6.4 is an example of an IFSP developed for a toddler.

Required Information for the IFSP

- Statement of the family's resources, priorities, and concerns
- Statement of the infant's or toddler's present level of functioning
- Expected outcomes for the infant and family, including criteria, procedures, and time lines
- Statement of services needed to meet the needs of the family and infant, including frequency, duration, and method of delivering services
- Date of initiation of services
- Identification of the service coordinator
- Transition plan for preschool when the child turns two years, six months

Figure 6.3 The IFSP requires information to be included on the form.

INDIVIDUALS WHO MIGHT SERVE ON THE IFSP TEAM

- Parent or guardian
- Early intervention teacher
- Physical therapist
- Adapted physical education specialist
- Occupational therapist
- Pediatric nurse
- Psychologist
- Speech pathologist

Services for infants and toddlers should be provided "to the maximum extent appropriate" in the natural setting. This might be at home, at a childcare facility, or in a school program. The setting should be where the family feels most comfortable receiving services and where the child naturally interacts with his or her environment. Ideally, serving children at home allows professionals to provide families with intervention ideas and suggestions that match their environment (e.g., demonstrating for a family in their living room how to assist a toddler with pulling up to standing at the couch). Implementing services at home also makes it more likely that parents can help their children practice on a daily basis independent of professionals (figure 6.5).

Northeast Region—Individualized Family Service Plan (IFSP)

Child's name Francisco Juarez

DOB 6-01-12 IFSP date 5-24-13

Child-Related Family Concerns, Priorities, and Resources
(To be included only with the concurrence of the family)

Strong family support and extended family. Grandparents live in the home with the family and assist with childcare.

Family Outcome Statement(s)

Family would like to see Francisco walking and standing independently.

Child's Strengths and Present Level of Development

Comments: Francisco is a wonderful and happy boy. He smiles and engages with others easily. He enjoys music and toys and is starting to babble.

Vision: Screened by vision specialist. No concerns.

Hearing: Screened by audiologist. No concerns.

Source of information: Hawaii Early Learning Profile, observation, parent interview

Physical (fine and gross motor): Rolls in either direction. Pushes up on one hand when on stomach. Can pivot stomach. Can sit unsupported. Protective extension to right but not left.

Cognitive: Throws and drops objects. Listens to speech attentively. Rolls to get a toy. Looks at pictures in a book when named and turns to find a sound. Likes to play "Peek-a-boo."

Communication: Babbles single consonants such as "ba." Says "dada" and "mama" and waves goodbye.

Social or emotional: Shows likes and dislikes for people or objects. Prefers mother to meet his needs. Cooperates in play and smiles frequently.

Self-help skills (eating, dressing, bathing, and the like): Enjoys putting toys in his mouth. He can feed himself a cracker with his right hand and drink from a cup with assistance. Takes a nap each day for about an hour and a half.

Health status: Francisco is in good health. He was six weeks premature at birth but has made consistent gains in all areas since he has been home from the hospital.

Current physician: Dr. Joy

Medications/equipment: No medications or equipment at this time.

Figure 6.4 Sample page from an IFSP showing current level of performance for a toddler with developmental delays involved in an inclusive physical activity program.

Figure 6.5 Serving children at home allows professionals to provide families with intervention ideas and suggestions that match their environment.

Although there is no legal requirement of a written document for children without identified disabilities, individualizing activity goals and needed supports remains important. For instance, parents often decide which activities their children should participate in, who should be present to offer support and guidance, and which behaviors or skills they desire for their children to achieve (e.g., social skills, sharing, communication, dressing, motor skills). How each family goes about planning for their child's development varies significantly, but some activities include the following:

- Read infant or toddler books and magazines on development.
- Talk with family members and friends.
- Seek out parent–toddler playgroups.
- Talk with other parents about their experiences.
- Complete background checks on childcare providers and check necessary credentials.
- Interview other parents who have attended a particular facility before placing the child.
- Consult with physician during well-baby check-ups.

Anyone who has grown up with younger brothers and sisters, infant cousins, or nieces and nephews has seen firsthand the natural developmental progression of infants and toddlers. However, for many new parents their first-born child is their first chance to watch the developmental process unfold. Many new parents have common goals for their children, which are often based on a sequence of skills that include rolling over, sitting up, crawling, standing, and taking their first steps. All children, regardless of their ability level, need adult guidance and a supportive environment for optimal physical activity development.

Assessing the Success of Inclusive Efforts

Assessing the success of inclusion for infants and toddlers includes examining the extent to which children can participate in their natural environment. This might be at home with family, in a playgroup with peers, or among other people or objects. For most children, this examination is an informal process, a type of authentic assessment, that takes place through well-baby check-ups, photographs, videos, and baby books containing dates, times, and locations of such events as the first step, first word, or first solid food. Families of children with disabilities might use these same methods to document growth and development in the natural environment. However, if the child is receiving early intervention services under the IDEA, they will also have additional documentation through the IFSP process, as described earlier.

IFSP meetings and documentation are required every six months to review progress and determine new outcomes as the previous ones are met. An IFSP meeting can also be held at any time that parents or other team members think it is necessary. Along with an evaluation of skills, parents and professionals can assess a toddler in how well he or she interacts with peers in a play setting.

As a toddler nears school age, many families begin to assess and explore preschool placements. This time is an important transition for many families and children because it is their first school experience. Parents and childcare providers often choose to tour the facility as they prepare for this important transition. Some parents visit the school with their children and help them get familiar with the new environment before school starts. Children with disabilities that have an IFSP are required to have a formal transition planning meeting as they get ready for preschool. This meeting is required by the IDEA to occur by the time the child is 2 years and 9 months old. The purpose of the transition meeting is to discuss a reevaluation of the child to determine if intervention services will continue to be needed. The discussion also involves if and where the child will receive preschool programming and which and how special education services will be implemented. The same multidisciplinary team of individuals who implemented the IFSP completes the transition plan, along with the individuals who will be working with the child in his or her next placement (e.g., the preschool teacher and any other new faces). During this transition phase the child is oriented to the new environment.

Regardless of an infant's or toddler's abilities, keeping records of changes that occur over time is a good idea for parents or caretakers. Families will appreciate looking back at pictures, videos, or notes recording the child's development. Plus, through such documentation professionals can help parents understand and appreciate the incredible growth their child is making.

Think back to Beth and Tom as new parents and their experience with Jackson.

1. How might they have been referred for early intervention services?
2. What types of services might they have needed for Jackson?
3. What types of programs or activities would have been appropriate for Jackson as an infant and toddler?
4. What is an IFSP? Based on what you know about Jackson and his family, what kind of information might have been included on Jackson's IFSP?

INCLUSIVE PHYSICAL ACTIVITY FOR SCHOOL-AGE CHILDREN: PREPARATION AND PLANNING

Many benefits to inclusive physical education environments exist for school-age children. First, inclusive environments allow children to be educated in their home school in their natural environment. Children who go to their neighborhood schools have the opportunity to become friends with their peers and are more likely to be involved in class birthday parties, local field trips, and community events. Second, all students are provided with an opportunity to value and respect individual differences; they grow up appreciating their own skills and valuing the unique skills and abilities of others. The children of today are the future parents of children with disabilities tomorrow, and mutual respect for one another is critical. In regard to physical activity, research shows that including students with disabilities does not have a negative effect on peers without disabilities, especially in cases in which students have mild disabilities (Obrusnikova, Block, & Válková, 2003; Vogler,

Koranda, & Romance, 2000) and when modifications of activities are not too severe and do not change the nature of the game (Block, 2007; Kalyvas & Reid, 2003). Overall, students with disabilities can be successfully included in physical education when proper support is available (Block & Obrusnikova, 2007).

Ensuring Access

As with toddlers, many children of school age have opportunities for unstructured physical activity involvement. Unlike their younger counterparts, however, their involvement tends to be in more organized and structured settings. School-age children typically have physical education classes scheduled for various amounts of time within their school week. In addition, many youngsters have opportunities to participate in after-school physical activity sessions, recess, and sport programs. Although access to physical activity programs such as recreation leagues and physical education classes is usually not an issue for most children, these programs are often less inclusive of children with significantly different abilities. As such, the children who do participate in them have little opportunity to experience and interact with peers with disabilities. As described earlier, an inclusive program is one in which individualized and accommodating instruction exists for everyone, and a range of individual abilities offers a far richer experience for all those involved.

DID YOU KNOW?

All children with identified disabilities are required by the Individuals with Disabilities Education Act to have physical education instruction to the same extent that their peers are provided with physical education.

For children with disabilities, access to inclusive physical activity programs is not easy. Children who previously were involved in an early intervention motor program through an IFSP will either exit out of the program at age three if services are no longer needed or transition into another individualized movement program through their school. Some children who did not receive early intervention services as infants or toddlers might also need support and services as they grow older because many educational concerns and physical needs are not revealed until a child ages. School districts have procedures and guidelines for public school-age children who might need referral for special education services, including physical education. Most students with variations in ability may be provided instruction within the general physical education class with or without modifications. However, if a child's motor or behavioral concerns are great enough, the general physical education teacher might need additional support services within the class to teach the child effectively. All teachers of physical education programs should feel supported and know that special education services are available in these settings for children who qualify and need additional assistance (figure 6.6).

The referral process for a child who needs assistance in physical education or other educational classes usually begins with a student study team (SST), also known as a child study team (CST). The SST is a team of individuals from the school that serves to assist teachers with modifications to help a child succeed in the general education program. The makeup of the student study team might vary, but their primary role is to serve as a support team for general education teachers, including physical education. A screening form (figure 6.7) is often helpful in the initial data collection process to assist in determining the needs of the learner.

The purpose of the SST is to assist teachers in resolving challenges they might be having with students in their teaching and learning environments. The role of the SST is to generate ideas and solutions to create more successful learning experiences for the child. These suggestions are then implemented and documented by the physical education teacher. If the SST suggestions were unproductive in creating a more positive learning environment for this student, the child may then be referred to special education services for further assessment and evaluation.

The special education process usually begins with a written referral notice (figure 6.8) (although a referral may be verbal) that describes current concerns and what has been

Eligibility Categories

1. Mental retardation
2. Hearing impairment, including deafness
3. Speech or language impairment
4. Visual impairment, including blindness
5. Serious emotional disturbance
6. Orthopedic impairment
7. Autism
8. Traumatic brain injury
9. Other health impairment
10. Learning disability
11. Deaf blindness
12. Multiple disabilities

Figure 6.6 Special education services are available for students in the categories listed in section 1401 of the *Individuals with Disabilities Education Act*, as amended by the *Individuals with Disabilities Education Improvement Act of 2004*.

attempted in the past. An assessment plan is then designed to determine the areas that need to be tested, which might be any area of suspected concern, such as hearing, vision, motor development, cognitive skills, perceptual motor learning, or behavior. The written plan is then taken to the parents for permission. Consent from the parents or guardians to assess must be obtained before any evaluations are conducted. Once the parents give permission for assessment, the areas of concern are evaluated. However, if the parents do not want their child assessed, this request must be respected, and the assessment may not be conducted. Individuals who may assess a child include the psychologist, special education teacher, physical therapist, occupational therapist, adapted physical education teacher, speech pathologist, nurse, or other personnel. Following the assessments, an individualized education program (IEP) meeting is scheduled at a time convenient for the parents. Each individual who completed testing with the child shares a written report with the parents and IEP team members.

INDIVIDUALS WHO MIGHT SERVE ON THE STUDENT STUDY TEAM

- Classroom teachers
- Principal
- Special education teachers
- Counselor or psychologist
- Related service personnel

Unlike physical education programs in the public schools, no formal guidelines exist for ensuring children with disabilities access to community-based recreation programs, intramural programs, or public sports programs. Students, however, may not be denied access based on section 504 of the Rehabilitation Act and the Americans with Disabilities Act legislation.

Physical activity practitioners need to be aware of these laws and provide programs that

- meet the needs and abilities of all individuals within their community,
- offer programs that follow a philosophy of inclusion, and
- provide a diverse offering of activities.

Adapted Physical Education
Preschool Motor Screening Form

Name of child______________________________ Date ________________

DOB______________________________ Age _________

Evaluator _________________________________

Please indicate with a Y for yes or an N for no, for each of the following items based on your experience with the child.

General motor skills

____ Stands on one foot momentarily

____ Walks on tiptoes

____ Walks up stairs alternating feet

____ Walks down stairs alternating feet with one hand held

____ Runs well without falling and can change speed

____ Jumps off the floor with both feet

____ Attempts to hop on one foot

____ Walks on a balance board on the ground with one hand held

____ Catches a playground ball that is bounced into arms

____ Throws a beanbag overhand in a forward direction

____ Pedals a tricycle

____ Climbs a short ladder to go down a slide

____ Balances on a swing to be pushed

Other observations

____ Child chooses to watch when others are playing.

____ Child bumps into objects or others in their environment.

____ Child has a need to touch everything around him or her.

____ Child is able to follow simple directions with others.

____ Child seems overstimulated by sounds, touch, or other sensory stimuli.

Favorite activities include:

Comments or concerns:

Figure 6.7 A sample screening form might include these specific skills appropriate for youngsters at this age.

Referral to SST for Adapted P.E. Grades 2 and 3

Each person requesting an assessment or screening for adapted PE should fill out this checklist. If the student does not demonstrate difficulties in many areas and does not really stand out compared to peers, a referral for assessment is not appropriate.

Student observed ______________________ Age _____ Grade _____ Date ___________

School ____________________________ Classroom teacher _________________________

Person making referral_____________________________

Potential DIS condition _____________________________ Enrolled in special education Y N

Playground skills

- ☐ Will jump long rope independently
- ☐ Can hit moving tetherball
- ☐ Will walk forward and backward heel, toe 10 feet (3 m) on playground line

Social-emotional

- ☐ Plays well with peers
- ☐ Follows playground rules
- ☐ Participates in group activities

Object manipulation

- ☐ Bounces ball four times with one hand (dribble)
- ☐ Catches playground ball from 15 feet (4.5 m) with hands only (no trapping)
- ☐ Kicks playground ball rolled from 15 feet (4.5 m)
- ☐ Can throw bean bag overhand approximately 15 feet (4.5 m)

Physical fitness

- ☐ Performs standing long jump for approximately 30 inches (.7 m) (forward arm swing and balance on landing)
- ☐ Can do eight curl-ups in 30 seconds
- ☐ Can touch toes with legs extended while sitting on floor

Other observations or reasons for referral:

Recommendations of SST:

- ☐ Refer to APE teacher for assessment
- ☐ Classroom or PE teacher to provide minimal modifications in general PE and return to SST if problems continue

_____________________________________ ____________________

SST chairperson Date

Figure 6.8 Sample referral form. The special education process usually begins with a written referral notice.

MEMBERS OF THE IEP TEAM AS REQUIRED BY THE IDEA

- Parents or legal guardians of the child
- At least one general education teacher
- At least one special education teacher or at least one special education provider
- A representative of the local education agency
- An individual to interpret the instructional implications of evaluation results who might be a member of the team described previously
- At the discretion of a parent, legal guardian, or agency, other individuals who have knowledge or special expertise regarding the child, including related services personnel, as appropriate
- The child (when appropriate)

Establishing Supportive Networks

The physical educator can find support and guidance from many other individuals. The parents or guardians of the child are most important to communicate with and can usually provide helpful insight. Family members know the child best and have information regarding the child's likes and dislikes, medical history, natural physical activity rhythms, and what the child responds to best. Physical educators might also network with other teachers within the school or district, educators from sessions at professional conferences or workshops, related service personnel (such as physical and occupational therapists and school psychologists), and other professionals within the school.

A physical activity practitioner working to develop and implement inclusive programs in the community needs to establish ongoing communication with the participants themselves, of course, and also with their family members, medical personnel, human service or agency personnel, and even community resource and volunteer organizations. Regardless of whether an individual is planning programs within the public schools or community, no practitioner should function in isolation. Planning for inclusive physical activity programs requires positive collaboration from many professionals. No one should feel alone in the process.

Promoting Positive Physical Activity Environments

Critical to the success of inclusive efforts is a welcoming and accepting atmosphere. Preparing peers and support personnel for inclusion of children with disabilities results in a positive physical activity environment.

Preparing Peers

Successful efforts to include children with disabilities in physical activity programs depends heavily on peer acceptance (Block, 2007). If a child's disability is not understood and accepted by classmates, peers might view the child negatively and be reluctant to accept any accommodations he or she might need (Wilson & Lieberman, 2000). Several strategies can be used to increase peer awareness of the wide range of abilities existing within a program (Lieberman & Houston-Wilson, 2009). Figure 6.9 provides some examples of ability awareness activities. As mentioned earlier, in any awareness activity or simulation, the focus should be on the new skills to be learned and how the environment can support this learning through modification. The focus should never be on the deficits or difficulties of individual learners.

Ability Awareness Activities

- Invite guest athletes with disabilities to speak in class.
- Watch videos on disability sports.
- Explore the Internet for disability sport information and competitions.
- Participate in an activity while simulating a disability, such as using a wheelchair while playing basketball or doing parachute activities.
- Participate in a disability sport such as goalball or beep baseball.
- Play a game without talking, using only hand signs to communicate. (Teams create their own communication system.)
- Hold a class discussion about modifications for individual differences.
- Discuss ways that students can work with each other in the class.

Figure 6.9 Ability awareness activities prepare peers for inclusion of others with disabilities.

In any learning environment or activity, including ability awareness activities, time should be spent at the close of the lesson discussing what occurred. This can be done in many ways, including group discussion, individual journals, or role-playing experiences. Whatever method is selected, the instructor must promote and model positive communication skills and effective listening and assist participants in processing their learning; participants should be encouraged to talk about any difficulties they experience.

Most important, the physical educator, right from the start, can foster increased awareness and acceptance of individual differences through adopting an instructional approach that is individualized for everyone, including those with high ability. For example, in a basketball program, participants might be given the choice to work at several areas, such as a skill-development station, two-on-two half-court minigames, a full-court modified game, or a traditional competitive game. In this way they can select the practice area that best meets their needs, abilities, and interests. In an inclusive program, modifications are viewed as common practice and used for all individuals in the program, not just for those with low abilities or perceived to be in need of modifications. Enhancing peer awareness of needed modifications also shows how individuals can participate in activities in many ways. Peers can more fully understand the need for activity modifications by experiencing the modifications themselves. For example, peers might take turns using a wheelchair during a game of tag or in a tennis match with minor rule modifications. Regardless of the activity variation, peers must realize and appreciate that modifications do not give individuals an unfair advantage. Emphasize to them that modifications are used to allow students increased participation and a chance to achieve success equal to others. Participants also see that modifications used during activities in fact make a game more challenging and exciting for everyone involved. When all participants in the program agree to this practice, a positive and accepting environment exists for everyone. These principles hold true whether planning for a physical education classroom or teaching in a community recreation program.

In school physical education programs, students of all abilities are placed in classes together, but in community sport programs children might be placed based on age and skill level. For example, in Special Olympics students compete based on age and skill classifications, as occurs in most competitive recreational sports programs. However, as any coach knows, even when children are classified by age and ability there remains wide variation in the skills of particular children and even within an individual child across different skills. By using an inclusive approach in all programs, all children can succeed.

Preparing Support Personnel

Along with peers, other individuals who will potentially offer support to participants with disabilities must be prepped for inclusive programming. Such support might be provided by instructional assistants, peer tutors, or community volunteers, many of whom likely have no formal training or experience in this realm. This being the case, it is critical that support personnel be given guidance by those responsible for the participant's physical activity program. In physical education, there is sometimes a misunderstanding about who provides support personnel with this guidance. General physical educators might assume that special educators inform support staff about their role and responsibilities, whereas special education teachers might believe that the physical educator is offering this guidance. As a result, support personnel staff members are sometimes at a loss regarding how to facilitate a learner's participation within the class. For learners to benefit from inclusive physical education programming, collaborative communication among all team members must occur. Training of support personnel should involve information pertaining to the individual learner with whom they will be working as well as methods in which they might assist this individual within the program (Giangreco & Doyle, 2004). This training can be achieved through staff in-service meetings, conferences, disability awareness workshops, and site visitations to other inclusive programs. Several resources are available that might further assist support personnel in their roles as facilitators of inclusive physical activity programs (see appendixes A and C). Block (2007) offers suggestions on information to share with support personnel:

- The philosophy of the physical activity program and general outcomes of physical education for all students (e.g., NASPE standards, program goals)
- General information about the support person's role and the expectations associated with this role
- Detailed information about the learner, the learner's goals, specific concerns, health issues, and safety procedures that might be related
- Suggestions and guidance regarding modifications that might be necessary and alternative activities to use when activities are deemed inappropriate or unsafe

Taking the time to prepare supporting individuals benefits everyone involved in the program. Many times, support personnel not only assist learners with significant disabilities but also help with the instruction of the class or work with small groups as they interact and learn together. In essence, support personnel offer helping hands, allowing practitioners to teach all learners more effectively and successfully.

Planning for Individualized Instruction

After ensuring access, establishing networks, and promoting a positive environment, it is time to plan for individualized instruction. In an inclusive setting, learners with significant disabilities might need an individual program plan. In a school setting, this process of planning is required by the IDEA for students with identified disabilities and results in the development of an individualized education program (IEP). An IEP documents the what, where, and how of the child's physical activity plan (figure 6.10). The planning process should also include transition plans and planning for participation in recreation and sport programs.

Developing an Individualized Education Program

The development process and foundation for the IEP begins with several questions:

- What skills do individual students require for success in present and future physical activity experiences?

Key Elements of the IEP as Required by IDEA 2004 [Part B, Section, 300.320]

(a) ***General.*** As used in this part, the term individualized education program or IEP means a written statement for each child with a disability that is developed, reviewed, and revised in a meeting in accordance with §§300.320 through 300.324, and that must include—

(1) A statement of the child's present levels of academic achievement and functional performance, including—

(i) How the child's disability affects the child's involvement and progress in the general education curriculum (i.e., the same curriculum as for nondisabled children); or

(ii) For preschool children, as appropriate, how the disability affects the child's participation in appropriate activities;

(2)(i) A statement of measurable annual goals, including academic and functional goals designed to—

(A) Meet the child's needs that result from the child's disability to enable the child to be involved in and make progress in the general education curriculum; and

(B) Meet each of the child's other educational needs that result from the child's disability;

(ii) For children with disabilities who take alternate assessments aligned to alternate achievement standards, a description of benchmarks or short-term objectives;

(3) A description of—

(i) How the child's progress toward meeting the annual goals described in paragraph (2) of this section will be measured; and

(ii) When periodic reports on the progress the child is making toward meeting the annual goals (such as through the use of quarterly or other periodic reports, concurrent with the issuance of report cards) will be provided;

(4) A statement of the special education and related services and supplementary aids and services, based on peer-reviewed research to the extent practicable, to be provided to the child, or on behalf of the child, and a statement of the program modifications or supports for school personnel that will be provided to enable the child—

(i) To advance appropriately toward attaining the annual goals;

(ii) To be involved in and make progress in the general education curriculum in accordance with paragraph (a)(1) of this section, and to participate in extracurricular and other nonacademic activities; and

(iii) To be educated and participate with other children with disabilities and nondisabled children in the activities described in this section;

(5) An explanation of the extent, if any, to which the child will not participate with nondisabled children in the regular class and in the activities described in paragraph (a)(4) of this section;

(6)(i) A statement of any individual appropriate accommodations that are necessary to measure the academic achievement and functional performance of the child on state and district-wide assessments consistent with §612(a)(16) of the act; and

(ii) If the IEP team determines that the child must take an alternate assessment instead of a particular regular state or district-wide assessment of student achievement, a statement of why—

(A) The child cannot participate in the regular assessment; and

(B) The particular alternate assessment selected is appropriate for the child; and

(7) The projected date for the beginning of the services and modifications described in paragraph (a)(4) of this section, and the anticipated frequency, location, and duration of those services and modifications.

Figure 6.10 The IEP is a legal binding document between the student's family and the school district.

- What are the goals, objectives, and benchmarks of the plan?
- Who will teach these skills?
- What modifications will be helpful for individuals with disabilities?
- What supports are needed for students within this setting?

What skills do individual students require for success in present and future physical activity experiences?

For a child with a significant difference in ability, some activities might be more meaningful than others. Priorities for programming should be based on the child's strengths, needs, age, both the child's and parents' interests, as well as future goals for the child outside of school with their family and in the community.

Developmentally appropriate curriculum is generally based on national and state standards for physical education and guidelines for community sports and recreation programs. For the young child, programming typically includes the development of skill themes and movement concepts that will gradually be combined into individual, dual, or team sports, as well as skills in aquatics, rhythms, and dance. The physical educator must consider which skills are appropriate for a child with a significant disability in the program and which skills will lead to appropriate and meaningful participation in the future. At the elementary level, this approach appears to coincide with the skill development considered appropriate for other children the same age and the kinds of activities they participate in to develop these skills. As students grow older and enter secondary school, their program needs to begin to shift focus to lifetime activities. What will the student participate in outside of school and after graduation? What kinds of activities does the community provide? What does the environment support? Are there recreational programs such as dance, martial arts, team sports, or swimming available? Are there health clubs? If so, what programs do they offer? Is the environment conducive to cycling, mountain biking, rock climbing, or hiking? As a student grows older, it is critical that the physical activity program promote development of skills that support lifelong physical activity. At this level, there might be a greater divergence between the routinely offered curriculum and the nature of the activities that are more meaningful for students with significant disabilities. Although the physical education program might involve units in team sports such as soccer or flag football, these activities might not be appropriate for every student based on individual preferences, likelihood of future participation in the community or postgraduation, and the like. It is necessary to consider the skills and activities most important for the individual student rather than considering involvement in all the activities available in that program. This decision is made by the general physical educator, adapted physical educator, parents, and other team members, all of whom contribute information and work together to decide the most meaningful focus for the student's physical activity program.

What are the goals, objectives, and benchmarks of the plan?

Practitioners should have goals and objectives for individuals within their programs. These can be written in a variety of ways; in physical activity programs they are written in three areas or domains of behavior: the cognitive, affective, and psychomotor domains. According to experts in the field, these are the appropriate categories for objectives. The cognitive domain includes thinking skills, memory, analysis, and synthesis of information. For example, remembering the rules of a game, analyzing a movement sequence, and creating an original game are all cognitive goals. The affective domain focuses on feelings about oneself, others, and movement. Examples of the affective domain include how someone feels after participating in an activity, how he or she interacts with others during a competitive or cooperative activity, and how he or she internalizes feelings about a movement after performing a task, such as hitting the sweet spot on a tennis racket. Finally, the psychomotor domain relates to the movement itself. The performance of a skill might be based on the process or how the skill is performed or the product or outcome of the movement.

Goals generally focus on a broad category, such as improved eye–hand coordination, understanding strategies for basketball, or improved positive interactions with peers. The goals written for any student should relate to the general physical education curriculum and to his or her interests and desires for activity and fitness after graduation from high school.

Objectives are very specific and relate to a goal. A well-written objective includes the following elements:

- Behavior: What observable skill or task will be performed?
- Condition: How will this task be performed? Equipment and environment should be considered.
- Criteria: How is it determined that the skill has been mastered? What are the criteria for success?

Benchmarks, or short-term objectives, are subcomponents of an objective. Recent revisions to the IDEA 97 require that special education services report progress to parents at the same frequency as general education programs. This generally means quarterly or triannual reporting for grades or IEP objectives. A well-written benchmark includes the same elements as an objective, considering the behavior, the condition, and the criteria. Also included is the date by which the benchmark will be accomplished. Figure 6.11 illustrates sample goals, objectives, and benchmarks.

Although specific objectives and benchmarks are required to be documented for children who have an IEP, all learners within a program should have goals and objectives. Although the IEP process is more formalized, and the multidisciplinary team decides the goals and objectives together with the parent or guardian and child, goals and objectives should be developed for each individual within any program and be documented through such means as journals, portfolios, and student files. These goals should be determined based on curriculum standards and by the student in combination with the teacher and the parents or guardian. Parents can play an important role in helping practitioners identify physical activity goals that support family activities and discover what is available in the community. Figure 6.12 is a sample physical activity survey that can be given to parents or guardians to solicit input on physical activity programming for their child.

Who will teach these skills?

Most students will receive physical education by the general physical educator working within the school. For students with disabilities, several options exist regarding who will facilitate their physical education. According to the IDEA, students with disabilities should be educated to the maximum extent appropriate with students who do not have disability labels or in the least restrictive environment (LRE). This principle allows some children with mild disabilities to be taught by the general physical educator within the general physical education program, but it also accepts that other students with identified disabilities receive their physical education from a physical activity professional in segregated or more isolated settings. Such practice often translates into noninclusive programs within the public school system. Although inclusion of students with disabilities into general physical education is not always achieved, for many reasons, an inclusive philosophy should be applied to all situations through which children receive their physical education program. Regardless of who teaches these students, an inclusive approach is imperative. Physical education for public school children can be facilitated by the general physical educator, the general physical education teacher with support from an adapted physical educator, or the adapted physical education specialist alone. Physical education can be offered in many settings, but the ultimate goal is an educational experience that best serves the child within an inclusive program. The decision of where and how a student with a difference in ability is to receive physical education ultimately rests with the IEP team that serves the child. If a child has an identified disability that qualifies for special education services, the child will have an IEP. In the following section we discuss the range of inclusive practices for individualized physical activity programming for school-age children.

Sample Goals, Objectives, and Benchmarks

Goal: Bobby will increase his knowledge of the skills for softball.

Objective: Bobby will identify the four critical elements of the overhand throw with 100% accuracy.

Benchmarks:

By ______________, Bobby will identify one critical element of the overhand throw with 100% accuracy.

By ______________, Bobby will identify two critical elements of the overhand throw with 100% accuracy.

By ______________, Bobby will identify three critical elements of the overhand throw with 100% accuracy.

Goal: Maria will develop positive social skills for game play during physical education.

Objective: Maria will demonstrate positive social interaction with peers by giving at least two high-fives to peers during game play in four out of five games.

Benchmarks:

By ______________, Maria will demonstrate positive social interaction with peers by giving at least one high-five to her peers during game play in one game.

By ______________, Maria will demonstrate positive social interaction with peers by giving at least two high-fives to her peers during game play in two out of five games.

By ______________, Maria will demonstrate positive social interaction with peers by giving at least two high-fives to her peers during game play in three out of five games.

Goal: Ming will improve her upper-body strength.

Objective: Ming will decrease her time for pushing the length of the basketball court in her sport chair by three seconds in four out of five trials.

Benchmarks:

By ______________, Ming will decrease her time for pushing the length of the basketball court in her sport chair by one second in four out of five trials.

By ______________, Ming will decrease her time for pushing the length of the basketball court in her sport chair by two seconds in four out of five trials.

By ______________, Ming will decrease her time for pushing the length of the basketball court in her sport chair by three seconds in two out of five trials.

Figure 6.11 Can you identify the domain for each objective as well as the behavior, condition, and criteria?

Welcome to Physical Education!

Physical education can be an important part of your life. Being physically active can help you live healthier, avoid disease, participate in fun activities, and even help you feel better about yourself. In physical education this year we'll provide you with many challenging activities you can do to stay physically active and have fun.

Over our semester together I want to make sure that you get the opportunity to develop skills and participate in activities that are meaningful to you. To give you input on what we do in physical education this semester, fill out the following survey and review it with a parent or guardian before handing it in. Also make sure to have your parent or guardian complete and sign the back before handing it in for credit. Thank you!

1. What physical activities do you participate in after school or on weekends (sports, skating, walking, bowling, and so on)? ______________________________

   ____
2. What other physical activities, games, and sports do you enjoy participating in?

   ____
3. Can you think of some physical activities, games, or sports that you would like to try but haven't? ______________________________
4. What games, sports, or physical activities would you like to participate in during your semester in physical education? ______________________________

   ____

Note to parents and guardians: To help in the development of the activities your child will be participating in, please answer the following questions and sign the bottom of this form. Thank you!

1. As a family, what physical activities do you participate in or encourage your child to participate in? ______________________________
2. Are there any activities, games, or skills that you'd like to see your child participate in or develop through physical education? ______________________________

   ____
3. Any other comments? ______________________________

   ____

Parent Signature ______________________________ Date ______________

Student Signature ______________________________

Return this survey by September 15th for full credit.

Figure 6.12 A physical activity survey given to parents or guardians to gain input on physical activity programming for a child.

Created by S. Hannigan-Downs and B. Fitzgerald, 2002. By permission of S. Hannigan-Downs.

- **Full-time general physical educator within general physical education (GPE).** Ideally, general physical education taught by a GPE teacher would be the most inclusive setting. Students of all ability levels participate with their age-appropriate peers with necessary modifications and support in order to be successful. For instance, a child might use a different piece of equipment or have a slight change in rules while participating in an activity. These more simple modifications might be implemented quite easily with the child not requiring any specialized services. The GPE teacher might ask other personnel (e.g., other physical educators, adapted physical education teacher, physical therapist, occupational therapist, recreation therapist) for ideas on how to create an inclusive environment for all students. All students at all ability levels should be provided successful experiences and be challenged to improve their skills.
- **Full-time general physical educator with adapted physical educator support within general physical education.** Adapted physical education (APE) is a service, not a placement. This means that adapted physical education services can be provided in a range of contexts, one of which is the general physical education class. Adapted physical education is taught by an adapted physical education specialist. In many states, an APE specialist credential or an endorsement in APE is required to teach in this area. These individuals are trained in how to make the curriculum accessible to all individuals, regardless of ability. In this case, the APE teacher works alongside the GPE educator within the general physical education program. The APE professional can either assist the general educator more broadly with the ongoing activity or work directly with an individual child needing support within this program.
- **Part-time general physical educator within GPE and part-time adapted physical educator within specialized PE.** APE services might also be provided within more than one context, or a student might receive more than one type of physical education. For example, a student might be included within the GPE class with modifications two times a week and receive adapted physical education by an APE specialist within a more specialized physical education context three times a week. Within the context of individualized physical education, programming should be inclusive in nature. It is the teacher's responsibility to ensure that a philosophy of inclusion prevails within the context of any physical education setting. Again, all students must have access to physical activity and the opportunity to be valued, respected, and successful members of the class.

One way to promote appreciation for diverse learners in this environment is through the inclusion of students from the GPE program. This may involve inviting students from the GPE program to serve as peer tutors or to participate alongside students with disabilities as team members or player coaches. Regardless of who participates in the specially designed physical education program, the program should meet the needs of all learners at all levels of ability.

Although it is not the best practice, specially designed physical education is sometimes taught by a special education teacher. In specially designed physical education, the special education teacher is responsible for students' academic education plans and teaches the physical education curriculum just as he or she would any other subject area. This scenario is analogous to an elementary classroom teacher being responsible for teaching physical education rather than an elementary physical education specialist. If a student is in a separate special education class and does not leave the special education class to go to general physical education, then that teacher is responsible for teaching the student's physical education. Even in this situation an inclusive approach should be followed, and students without disabilities may be invited to participate.

What modifications will be helpful for individuals with disabilities?

Practitioners employ many modifications to individualize activities for students. One way that programs are tailored to meet the needs of participants is by modifying the task that is to be completed. For example, in a modified kickball game a participant who uses a wheelchair because of limited leg strength might be required to throw the ball rather than kick it. Or this same participant might practice sitting back in his or her wheelchair to strengthen the back muscles while others in the class do sit-ups on a mat for abdominal strengthening (figure 6.13). In each example, the task is altered to include all participants by allowing them to practice appropriate and meaningful skills or exercises. Another focus for modifications is related to the context. This might involve changes to instruction procedures, such as teaching style, type and amount of feedback, and sequencing of activities. The organization of the activity might also be modified. For some participants, the distribution and duration of activities might need to be changed, whereas for others the way in which participants are grouped might promote greater participation. The physical setting is another strategy for individualizing activity. Equipment modifications are commonly used to include participants with disabilities. For instance, a student with less developed eye–hand coordination might be more successful in a softball game when using a lighter bat and bigger ball. For others, the size of the space they are using might influence performance and need to be modified. In chapter 7 we look closely at activity modification and strategies effective for including students with disabilities into physical education.

What supports are needed for individuals within this setting?

One of the guiding principles underlying inclusive physical activity is that individuals with disabilities should participate together within physical activity programs. Within a school setting, the goal is for students with disabilities to be taught by the general physical educator within the GPE program. To achieve this end, a range of support strategies might be used. Decisions regarding who will provide support, what type of support will be most effective, and how often support is necessary must be made by the individualized education program team. They base their decisions on several factors, including the expertise of the general physical educator for modifying activities, the nature of the activities in which the student

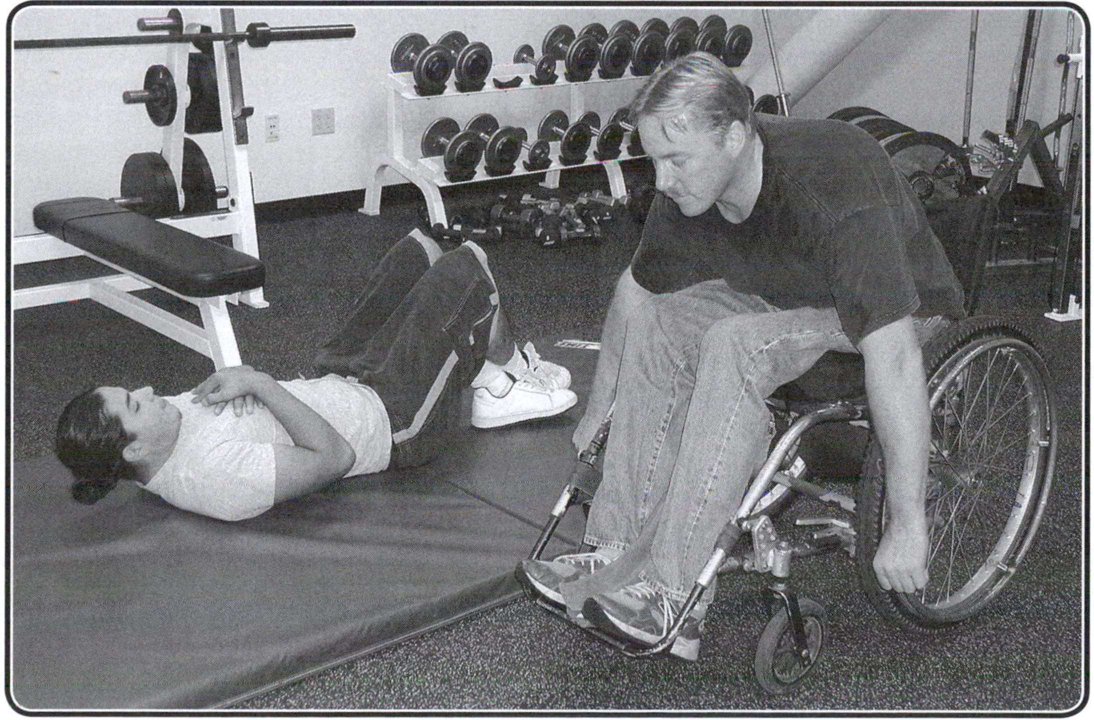

Photo courtesy of R. Lytle.

Figure 6.13 Fitness activities can be individualized to meet varying capabilities and needs. One student might do sit-ups to work on abdominal strength while another does sit-backs in his wheelchair to work on back strength.

will participate, and the grade level of the class in general. Block and Krebs (1992) proposed a continuum of support that begins with no support needed by the participant to progressively more support provided as necessary (figure 6.14). In each case support should be provided as necessary while taking care not to *oversupport* or automatically revert to the maximum level of support possible. Not all participants with disabilities need much assistance; giving them more than they need can lead to increased dependence on the part of the participant and less interaction with peers. Again, many participants can likely benefit from some form of support within the class, even participants with higher skills.

Support Levels

Level 1: No support needed

1.1 Student can make necessary modifications on his or her own.

1.2 GPE teacher feels comfortable working with student.

Level 2: APE consultation

2.1 No extra assistance is needed.

2.2 Peer tutor watches out for student.

2.3 Peer tutor assists student.

2.4 Paraprofessional assists student.

Level 3: APE direct service in GPE one or two times per week

3.1 Peer tutor watches out for student.

3.2 Peer tutor assists student.

3.3 Paraprofessional assists student.

Level 4: Part-time APE and part-time GPE

4.1 Flexible schedule with reverse mainstreaming.

4.2 Fixed schedule with reverse mainstreaming.

Level 5: Reverse mainstreaming in special school

5.1 Students from special school go to general school for GPE.

5.2 Students without disabilities go to special school for GPE.

5.3 Students with and without disabilities meet in community for recreation training.

Figure 6.14 There are many ways of providing support to create successful inclusive learning environments for all individuals.

Reprinted, by permission, from M.E. Block and P.L. Krebs, 1992, "An alternative to least restrictive environments: A continuum of support to regular physical education," *Adapted Physical Activity Quarterly* 9: 97-113.

Transition

In general, transition planning means preparing individuals to make a change from one environment to another. Transitions occur frequently in the lives of children as they move from one grade level to the next and then on to college or into the community. For individuals with disabilities, transition planning meetings are required by federal law at specific times. These times include during the transition from an infant–toddler program into preschool and during the move from high school to college or into the community.

The transition from high school to the community can be challenging for any individual because this is the transition into adulthood. Many questions related to an individual's physical activity habits and skills must be answered at this time, including the following:

- Will the individual participate in a community college or university physical activity program?
- Where will the individual live? What physical activity options are available in that community?
- What physical activity skills does the individual have? What skills will he or she need?
- How independent is this individual in his or her physical activity?
- What programs will be accessible for this individual?
- What transportation services will he or she need?
- What medical services does he or she have?
- What family or social supports does the individual have for help with physical activity goals?
- What types of recreational and leisure activities does he or she enjoy?

Because there are so many issues and questions that need to be addressed for a successful transition, the law requires that for individuals with identified disabilities, the transition process begin at age 14. Of course an earlier, rather than later, consideration of transitional demands is a good idea for any child. By planning early, the necessary skills can be taught and programs and services identified before students graduate and move on. The transition planning team for students with identified needs is made up of the same individuals as the IEP team. However, as the student gets older, and agencies and services are identified outside of the school system that will support the student, representatives from those agencies are invited to be a part of the team. During the initial transition plan is a good time to identify an action plan. An action plan should include what needs to be done, who will address that need, and when this will be accomplished (table 6.1). An action plan helps identify who is responsible for what; the plan should be revisited (along with the IEP documentation) at each meeting to track progress.

Whether a student has a formal transition plan or not, practitioners must consider the kinds of physical activity and recreational programs that will be available to the student after graduation. How will the student maintain physical fitness for daily living, health, and stress reduction? Programs that students might access include the YMCA, community recreation programs, or park districts, fitness clubs, and community college classes. The school's adapted physical educator along with the general physical educator, therapists, and parents can be excellent resources during the transition process and might be able to assist with information, community outreach, and program coordination. The adapted physical education specialist knows what activity programs are available in the community as well as what sport organizations might be of interest to the student. These physical education professionals can provide questionnaires to the parents or guardian and the student regarding what the student needs and desires relating to physical activity. Physical education professionals can also serve as a community liaison, contacting directors of recreation and physical activity programs in the community. For example, they might contact a local health club to determine how accessible the club is and what types of programs and activities they offer. They might also discuss the club's willingness to provide scholarships for students with physical activity needs during their senior year as an incentive for them to

Table 6.1 Sample Action Plan

Outcome or need	Steps to meet the need	Who is responsible?	When will this be done?	Date to be completed	Follow-up
What activities are available in the community?	Visit or call community, recreational, and physical activity programs.	Adapted physical educator and regional center worker	September/ October	By next IEP meeting in November all information should be gathered.	Evaluate all information at the next IEP meeting and set a new action plan with specific community-based goals for the following year. Specific goals and objectives will be determined at the IEP meeting and written up as part of the IEP.
What communication skills are needed to participate?	Consult with speech pathologist.	Speech pathologist			
How will the individual get there?	Explore public transportation programs. Check on family support.	Special education teacher			
What support services are available?	Talk with regional center and family members.	Psychologist			
What support services will Joe need to participate in the physical activity programs?	Talk with regional center and family members.	Psychologist APE			
What skills does Joe already have that will allow him to be successful?	Talk with physical activity teachers/APE/ PT and review reports at next meeting.	PT/APE/GPE			
What skills will Joe need to learn to be successful and independent?	This will be identified after the physical activity programs are determined.	Team discussion following data collection			

continue to participate in fitness club activities after graduation. Practitioners might begin community programming for physical education during the student's junior and senior years of high school. For example, the adapted physical education specialist might take students off campus to participate in aerobics classes, swim class, rock climbing, or other community-based activities, depending on the student's interest and abilities and what programs are offered. Of course these experiences should be inclusive and involve students with a range of abilities.

Physical Activity Participation in Recreation and Sport Programs

In the preceding section we focused mainly on inclusive efforts within school-based physical education programs, but the questions that should be asked and decisions that need to be made follow a similar sequence for community-based programs as well. Children interested in participating in a recreation or sport program should first be interested in the activity; the activity should also be meaningful for the child. Although some of these opportunities might be within a general recreation or sport program offered by a general practitioner, others might be more specialized and offered by physical activity practitioners with more experience and knowledge in modifying for individual differences. Similar to specialized school physical education programs, these specialized recreational or sport activities might be less inclusive than general programs. Although this might be common, inclusive specialized sport programs do exist. For instance, Special Olympics offers unified sport skill development and competition in which athletes with and without identified disabilities participate on the same team. Once activity preferences and opportunities have been identified, modifications and supports might be necessary for optimal involvement.

Assessing Success of Inclusive Efforts

Determining the extent to which a program is successful for each participant is critical for program effectiveness and an integral part of inclusive reflective practice. Practitioners must assess by the minute, day, week, month, quarter, and year the extent to which their instruction is meeting the needs of their learners. Practitioners accomplish assessment in several ways, including through the use of

- observations,
- check sheets,
- journals,
- portfolios,
- formal standardized assessments,
- informal teacher-made tests related to physical and cognitive skills,
- group projects,
- reevaluation of goals and objectives,
- video-recording of skills, and
- rubrics.

Refer to chapter 5 for examples of these kinds of assessments.

The documentation process helps participants set goals and watch their progress unfold in a meaningful and tangible way. Good records also provide an ongoing feedback loop between the practitioner and participant to see their development and progress. For participants, this feedback lets them know how they are doing and allows them to check their goals against their progress. For the practitioner, documentation provides valuable information about whether specific teaching strategies and methods are working so that modifications can be made if necessary. Good documentation also allows practitioners to evaluate progress toward goals and educational standards. For most learners, the methods of assessment previously listed are used to determine quarterly and semester grading as well as end-of-the-year reports to parents. Learners with disabilities might also have their goals and objectives identified on the IEP. For the purpose of meeting federal guidelines as mandated by the IDEA 97, these goals and objectives must be evaluated at least annually with progress reporting matching that of any other child within the general education program. Details about assessment methods and techniques were covered in chapter 5.

Think back to Jackson once again. Assume you were his high school physical education teacher.

1. Who might also be a part of Jackson's multidisciplinary IEP team with you?
2. Why would Jackson be required to have an IEP?
3. What types of goals and objectives would you write for him?
4. How might you prepare your students to foster a supportive inclusive environment for diverse learners in your class?
5. What activities might Jackson be involved in after he graduated from high school? How would you prepare him for these activities?

INCLUSIVE PHYSICAL ACTIVITY FOR ADULTS: PREPARATION AND PLANNING

It is well documented that physical activity is important for overall health and well-being for all individuals, including younger and older adults (U.S. Department of Health and Human Services, 2000). The many benefits of this involvement include increased energy, greater flexibility and strength, reduced risk of cardiovascular disease, maintenance of general mobility and functional independence, decreased stress and depression, and improved metabolism. Whether an individual is involved in exercise programs, sport participation, or recreational pursuits, the right amount of physical activity can maintain health and improve quality of life. All individuals, regardless of their abilities, need access to and programming for physical activity throughout their life span.

Ensuring Access

Many of the barriers discussed in chapter 3 limit the physical activity involvement of some adults. Although some strategies presented in that chapter might promote increased adoption of physical activity by some individuals, for others with significant disabilities access to physical activity is much more challenging. Access to programs for these adults often depends on what the community has to offer. Some opportunities might include community recreation programs; physical activity clinics or labs within a hospital, university, or community college setting; or programs, events, or teams offered through specialized sport organizations. Many programs exist to benefit adults with significant disabilities. These adult programs are entirely voluntary for the participants, who often hear about them through medical professionals, other participants, or resource materials distributed to local or regional agencies and organizations. For instance, individuals with disabilities interested in exercising might find that the local YMCA offers aquatic exercise classes; those wanting to learn to ski might hear about special ski programs through state organizations geared to adapted physical activity programming. In addition to the exercise or fitness setting, many programs also exist for elite athletes who compete in world-class events, such as goalball, water skiing, or track and field, to name a few. These elite athletes generally participate via a sport organization or governing body that oversees

DID YOU KNOW?

The definition of disability for adults in the United States is often based on the inability to engage in gainful work activity because of a medically determinable physical or mental disability that has lasted for no less than 12 months.

training and competitions. Some examples include Paralympics, Special Olympics, United States Association for Blind Athletes, United States Cerebral Palsy Athletic Association, and the Les Autres Games (see appendix C for complete list of associations).

Establishing Supportive Networks

A physical activity practitioner working to develop and implement inclusive programs in a community should establish ongoing communication not only with potential participants but also with medical personnel, family members, human service or agency personnel, and even community resources such as transportation services and volunteer organizations. In most cases, obtaining a medical history and consent before having participants begin a program can start this process of communication and collaboration and establish links among professionals who might support the practitioner when individualizing physical activity programs. (See appendix E for a sample medical history and referral form.) Networks could also include individuals who come with participants to a program to assist or simply to get more information about participating. For practitioners interested in providing recreational or sport programs, networking with others who might support them in their efforts to promote better programming or training for interested individuals is effective. These practitioners might find that other coaches and recreation leaders have valuable information and strategies to share.

Although a team approach to programming is not always mandated by law for adults as it is for students in a public school system, it is still considered best practice. The more practitioners communicate with participants and others, the more likely the practitioner is to attain a holistic view of the participant and be better able to plan programming to improve daily living, functional skills, enjoyment, and independence.

Promoting Positive Physical Activity Environments

Participants' involvement in an inclusive program depends largely on their comfort level. Adults interested in joining a physical activity program or facility might first need some questions answered. Informational brochures, visits, and direct communication with staff and other participants help at this stage. The program staff also has an obligation to ensure that new participants are welcomed and accepted into the program by others already involved. This can be accomplished in three ways: (1) by ensuring that adequate equipment and resources are available so that already established programs are not interrupted, (2) by offering similar support and benefits to all members so no one is perceived as getting special treatment or inequitable services, and (3) by giving all participants the opportunity for feedback and suggestions about how the program or activity might run more smoothly and inclusively. Again, education and information sharing are essential to fostering acceptance of individuals with disabilities, even in community-based fitness programs or recreational or sport activities.

Planning for Individualized Instruction

As with other age groups, program planning for adults begins with determining priorities and the focus of the program. For an adult in an activity program, priorities are determined by his or her interests, needs, future activity pursuits, and nature of activities of daily living. This information is then used to establish the focus of the program, desired goals, and the amount of time needed to achieve these goals.

Safety and well-being are critical within the context of any activity program. As mentioned earlier, practitioners offering community-based activity programs must have participants obtain medical consent or physician approval before they start in the program. Any limitations or concerns should be documented and kept in the participant's file. Recommendations for specific activities might also be offered. The program file should include a medical history, the participant's priorities and desires within the program, the exercises or activities of the individualized plan, and a daily record of activity and progress notes.

An individualized exercise plan based on personal goals and needs is developed for most adults in community-based exercise programs (figure 6.15). For adults who receive services from regional centers, an individual program plan (IPP) is provided. Although no specific individualized plan is developed for individuals involved in sport programs, training regimes might be tailored to meet individual goals, needs, and functional abilities. Coaches work together with participants to achieve this end.

Photo courtesy of S. Kasser, photographer T. Bolduc.

Figure 6.15 Individualized exercise programs are developed with the participant's interests, goals, and capabilities in mind.

Assessing Success of Inclusive Efforts

Unlike physical activity programs for children in schools, physical activity programs for adults are not legally obligated to conduct program or participant evaluation. Nevertheless, assessment of participant success and program effectiveness is just as important for adults as for young people. Daily exercise logs or records can be used to determine if exercise goals are being met or if participants are making progress toward achieving their goals. Program staff might also solicit participant feedback regarding program aspects such as facility appropriateness, equipment availability, support, and staff assistance.

Let's consider Jackson once more as he transitions into adulthood.

1. What type of physical activity programs might Jackson be involved in as an adult?
2. How would he find out about these programs?
3. What might be the focus or priority areas in this program?
4. What would you use to assess if Jackson is making progress in his physical activity program?

SUMMARY

Although team members, settings, and program goals vary across the life span in planning for inclusive programs, the steps to the process remain the same. Physical activity practitioners must carefully and purposefully plan and evaluate the process of inclusive physical activity on a regular basis to ensure access, establish supportive networks, promote positive environments, plan for individualized instruction, and assess success. It is through the continued reflective process and implementation of the 3 Rs—ready, rethink, retry—that practitioners can promote success for every participant in the program.

What Do You Think?

1. Consider your future professional career and the setting in which it will take place. How might the process (steps) for inclusive physical activity programs apply to your setting?
2. What kinds of supportive networks are available in your community for infants with disabilities? For children? For adults?
3. How might you design an awareness training program for your setting?
4. How might you evaluate the success of inclusive programming in your setting?
5. Infant–toddler programs require an IFSP, and school-age children have an IEP. If you were going to write an individualized program for an adult, what would you consider as important information to include in this documentation? How might you gather this information?

What Would You Do?

Scenario 6.1

Judy is a teacher at Little Tikes preschool program. As the coordinator of the program, she has recently met with a family in the community who has twins who will be starting the program the following year. The parents have asked Judy to attend a transition planning meeting for their children, Jason and Julie, who were both born five weeks premature. Jason has some visual problems, and Julie shows some delays in general development. Judy is a little concerned about meeting the needs of Julie and Jason but is committed to making this a positive preschool program for them. Judy is knowledgeable about general development and appropriate curriculum, but she wonders how to make adaptations for the twins. She has never attended an IFSP or IEP and is curious what is involved in this process.

Imagine you are a member of the IFSP team. Answer the following questions for Judy.

1. Who will be at the meeting for Jason and Julie?
2. What will take place at this meeting?
3. What supports are available for Judy in planning for Julie and Jason?
4. How might she best prepare the environment for Julie and Jason's transition?

Scenario 6.2

You are a personal trainer at your local fitness facility. You have been informed that you will have a new participant next week who has made an appointment for an initial orientation and program design. The following week, you arrive to meet Sam, your new participant. On meeting with him you discover that he is blind because of complications caused by diabetes. As you talk with him, you discuss his fitness goals and needs. You learn he is interested in a spinning class as well as general weight training.

1. How will you go about finding support networks for yourself in providing appropriate programming for Sam?
2. What strategies might you use to ensure that Sam feels welcome within your facility?
3. What information might you need in planning for Sam's programming?
4. How might you go about determining the success of Sam's program?

CHAPTER 7

A Functional Approach to Modifying Movement Experiences

L. Lieberman, courtesy of Camp Abilities.

LEARNING OUTCOMES

After completing this chapter, you should be able to

- describe how person-related changes and task and context modifications can facilitate skill and activity performance;
- provide examples of contextual and task modifications for individuals with disabilities;
- apply modification strategies to activity programs for individuals of varying ages and capabilities; and
- describe the functional components model and its application to inclusive physical activity programming.

INCLUDING ALL INDIVIDUALS

Karen Morgan, a new physical education teacher at Marsh Elementary School, has 18 children in her kindergarten class, including one child with a cognitive difference, Sara. Sara is generally good natured but often does not follow the rules of the class. This has become a problem for Karen, especially when they go outside for physical education because Sara does not want to come back inside. Sara also wanders away from the blacktop area where the class is playing and refuses to get off the swings. Karen wants to make sure all students in her class are successful. She plans on discussing her concerns at Sara's next individualized education program (IEP) meeting, but in the meantime she is determined to find a way to keep Sara involved during physical education. She has tried to plan fun activities for the children and has been working with them on bouncing and catching playground balls with partners. All the children are actively involved except Sara.

In chapter 6 we presented the sequence of steps necessary to include all individuals in physical activity programming. These steps highlighted the need to prioritize goals and secure necessary supports when preparing and planning for inclusive practice. Once the focus of the program has been determined and the program practitioner has been identified, efforts shift to modifying the physical activity program for participants with disabilities. Effectively involving all individuals in physical activity requires good problem-solving skills on the part of the practitioner. He or she must be able to assess the situation and determine how and what could be changed to foster increased participation and success for each individual involved. In this chapter we help guide practitioners through this process and suggest methods to make activities inclusive for everyone through a functional approach to modifying movement experiences (FAMME).

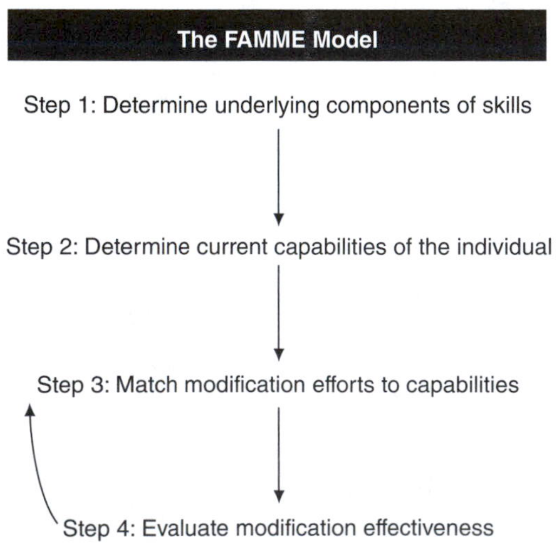

Figure 7.1 The four steps leading to inclusive physical activity programming.

The FAMME model provides a conceptual framework for accommodating all individuals within a physical activity program. The four-step process helps practitioners consider the range of possible modifications to promote success for all participants (figure 7.1). The feature stressed in the FAMME model is matching modifications to ability differences in efforts to provide optimal challenges and task completion for every participant in the program. An optimal challenge is a task goal that allows success while presenting a challenging experience to foster continued skill progress for the participant, regardless of skill level. The purpose of the FAMME model is to achieve this optimal point for all participants by matching their capabilities to the task and context during movement activities. In doing so, the practitioner considers all factors that contribute to a movement skill or task outcome: what the individual can do, how the setting should be constructed, and which goal or task the individual is attempting to accomplish.

In chapter 6 we also detailed how to individualize the planning process and determine meaningful goals and activities for all participants. In this chapter we take this further by looking at individualized activity plans and determining how skills and activities can be modified for differences in abilities. First we describe the process of matching modifications to the capabilities and needs of participants. Then we present the possible modifications that might be employed as they relate to the individual, setting, and task. Last we discuss our insights regarding the process of evaluating the appropriateness and effectiveness of chosen modifications.

STEP 1: DETERMINING UNDERLYING COMPONENTS OF SKILLS

The first step in providing inclusive physical activity is understanding the foundation for performing the skill or activity. Although all skills vary in terms of their intended use and the movements necessary to carry them out, many have similar underlying functional components or requirements, including

- Strength
- Flexibility/range of motion
- Balance/postural control
- Coordination (eye–hand, eye–foot, body)
- Speed/agility
- Endurance
- Concept understanding
- Self-responsibility/self-control
- Attention
- Sensory perception

These components are prerequisites for any individual attempting to execute the movement activity or skill. For instance, kicking a ball to a stationary target involves eye–foot coordination, balance, leg strength, task understanding, and other related factors. Running to catch a disk requires eye–hand coordination, balance, task understanding, speed, leg strength, and flexibility. Many of the same components underlie many tasks but have different degrees of importance or influence depending on the goal being attempted. Throwing a ball to a stationary target requires strength, balance, and coordination. When the target is farther away or moving, a greater degree of all three of these skills is required. Thus the first step toward providing optimal challenges is to assess the task and identify the underlying components needed to perform the skill. Although these skill components relate to the performance of most skills, practitioners should also be aware of other performance-related factors that can affect task completion and success, including levels of motivation, fatigue, and energy.

THINK BACK

1. Think back to Karen Morgan's kindergarten class. What are the underlying skill components necessary to participate in the activity she has selected for her students (bouncing and catching playground balls with partners)?
2. Based on the list of skill components, what might be some of the challenging areas for Sara given what little you know about her?

STEP 2: DETERMINING CURRENT CAPABILITIES OF PARTICIPANTS

The next step in providing inclusive physical activity involves identifying participant capabilities. When considering modifications, practitioners focus on capabilities of participants rather than general characteristics associated with a label or category (e.g., athlete, learning disabled, autistic). Modifications should directly relate to and be based on current capabilities necessary to participate in the activity and perform the task. As indicated in figure 7.2, several person-related factors can affect an individual's capability to execute the various components underlying a physical activity. For example, obvious differences in capabilities exist because of differences in age. A seven-year-old child might be considerably less strong than a high school student. Most adults have a greater capacity to understand complex concepts and strategies than children have. Other factors, such as a medical condition, might also influence functional capabilities. An adult with joint pain and swelling caused by an injury or arthritis might have limited range of motion compared to another individual, such as an adult jazz dancer. An athlete with increased muscle tone caused by cerebral palsy might have differences in balance compared to other members on his or her team. Experience, genetics, and motor ability also can influence the functional capabilities of physical activity participants. As discussed in chapter 2, practitioners must understand that an individual's capabilities are not permanent but are a function of the person, task, and context. A person's capabilities are subject to change with practice and modifications.

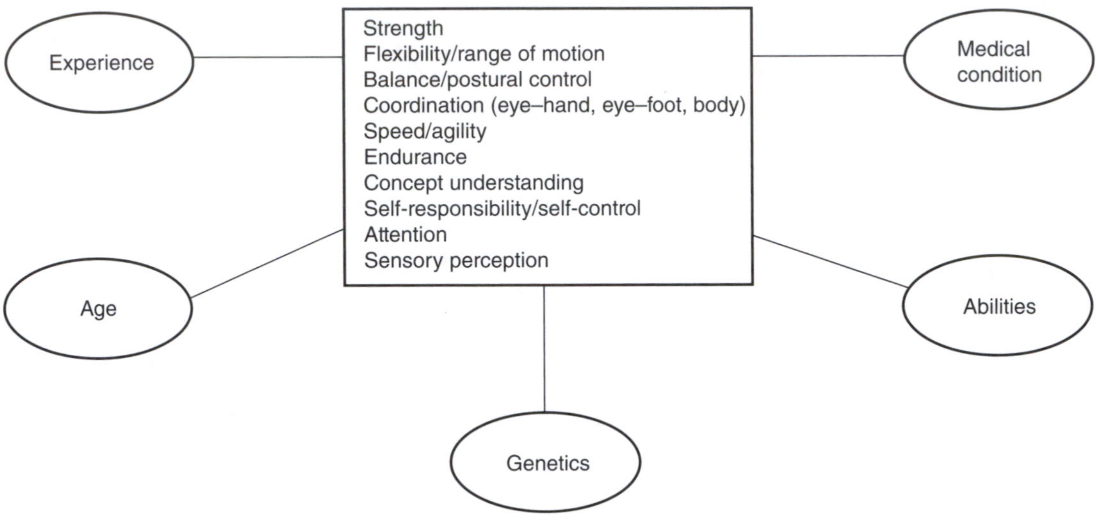

Figure 7.2 Many person-related factors affect components underlying movement skills.

DID YOU KNOW?

When we talk about a person's abilities and capabilities, we're talking about two different things.

- Motor abilities—stable, enduring traits, largely genetically determined, that serve as determinants of a person's *achievement potential* for the performance of specific skills. Such abilities include perceptual motor abilities and physical proficiency abilities.
- Capabilities—characteristics of individuals that are subject to change as a result of practice and that underlie skilled performance of a task.

Source: Magill, R.A. 2010. *Motor learning and control: Concepts and applications.* New York: McGraw-Hill Companies, Inc.

Many factors influence an individual's capability in the different skill components underlying performance. Two individuals might have very different factors that contribute to similar movement capabilities. For instance, a ninth-grader might have increased flexibility because stretching is a regular part of her fitness program, whereas another ninth-grader with Down syn-

THINK BACK

1. Based on your personal history, which factors have influenced your capabilities in the skill components?
2. Imagine you are Sara in Karen Morgan's kindergarten class. Which factors do you think might be influencing your capabilities as a kindergartner? How might you perform in each of the prerequisite components underlying various activities?

drome might have increased flexibility caused by genetics. An adult in an exercise class might demonstrate decreased body awareness because of sensory perception differences caused by multiple sclerosis, whereas another adult in the class might have poor kinesthetic awareness because of limited experience. Remember that practitioners focus on capabilities when making modifications for inclusive participation, and that many factors influence the capabilities that a person brings to a movement situation. For example, an adult who has decreased body awareness caused by some neurologic condition might need to use mirrors for visual feedback on limb position. Likewise, an adult with limited movement experiences might also benefit from instructional strategies that incorporate visual feedback. Regardless of the cause for capability differences, the strategies and modifications to promote success might be similar.

STEP 3: MATCHING MODIFICATION EFFORTS TO CAPABILITIES

Once a participant's capabilities have been identified, the next step is to direct modifications specifically to the underlying prerequisite skill components. As we described in chapter 2, the capability of an individual, and thus his or her performance, can change as a result of changes within the person over time, changes to the context within which tasks are performed, and changes to the tasks themselves (figure 7.3). This being the case, modifications can be made in some or all of these areas. Table 7.1 lists examples of how changes in person, context, or task can affect performance.

To ensure success for some participants, practitioners might need to incorporate a range of modifications. For the success of others, minor modifications to either the task or the context might be enough to provide an optimal challenge. Table 7.2 shows an example of matching modifications to functional differences in the skill of throwing. In the left column are some of the underlying skill components for throwing. On the right are possible modifications related to the person, context, or task that might be employed to ensure an optimal challenge for all participants.

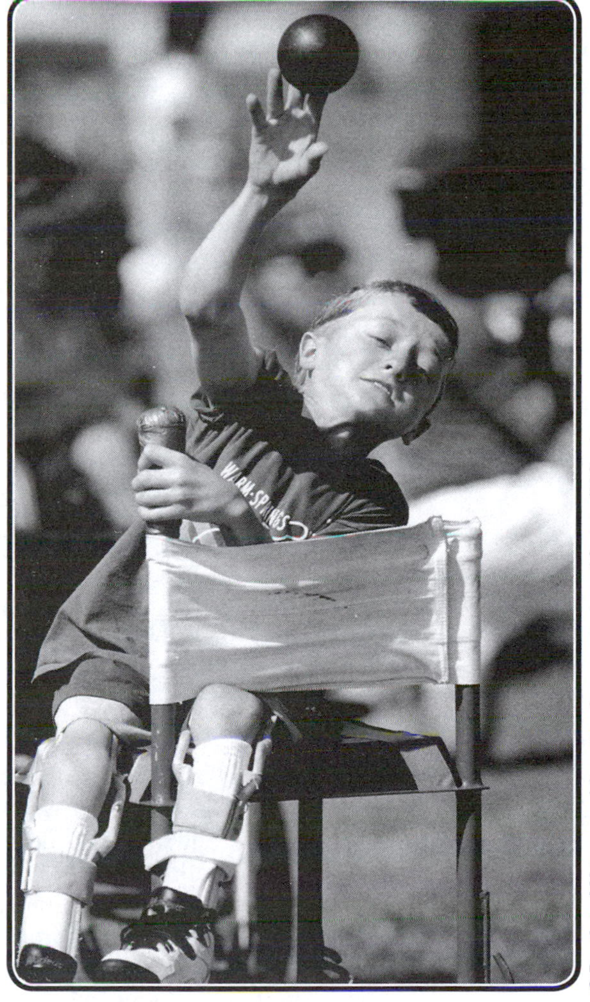

Figure 7.3 Matching modifications such as body positioning and shot weight to participant capabilities can increase this youngster's performance.

Table 7.1 Examples of Changes in Person, Context, or Task and the Influence on Performance

Factor	Example
Person over time	Increase in strength for older adult after an individualized resistance exercise program
Changes in context	Increase in mobility for an individual who uses a wheelchair in a game of flag football by playing on a hard surface rather than on the grass
Changes in task	Increase in success of dribbling a basketball by dribbling with two hands simultaneously rather than with only one

Table 7.2 Possible Modifications for Throwing

Capability difference	Person	Context	Task
Strength	Resistance exercises	Increase or decrease target distance	Throw, roll, or push ball off a ramp or table
Range of motion	Specific stretches	Closer or farther target Smaller or larger ball Use of throwing extension	Throwing underhand instead of overhand throw
Coordination	Brain integration activities	Larger or smaller target Stationary or moving target	Throw or roll ball
Concept understanding	Preteach concepts or cues Focus on one cue at a time	Verbal cue Auditory cue Tactile cue or physical prompt	Break skill down into smaller tasks or increase complexity and strategy use in game
Balance	Balance training activities	Decrease or increase target distance Increase base of support with wall, chair, or walker Decrease base of support	Throw seated in chair Roll ball with two hands Throw off one foot or into the air

This table provides only examples of capability differences with accompanying person, context, and task modifications.

Person-Centered Changes

One way to increase a person's skill performance is to directly influence his or her physical, cognitive, emotional, or behavioral capabilities. For example, as an individual changes in strength or flexibility, his or her capability to execute or complete the same task also changes; a task that was once difficult might now be easier to accomplish. Person-related factors such as alertness, attention, understanding, and motivation can also influence the realization of the task goal. Some of these changes might be a function of physical training or continued practice and learning. Other strategies related to the individual also might directly alter performance. For instance, medication to reduce increased muscle tone might increase range of motion, ultimately improving functional movement and performance. Although these person-related changes are not necessarily considered modifications, they do affect the performance of the individual and are viable strategies for capability shifting, as described in chapter 1. However, these types of strategies are often guided by the individual and his or her medical provider rather than by the physical activity practitioner. The practitioner should, however, be informed of any strategies being employed, such as medication, that might affect performance. The practitioner is responsible for making changes within the task and context to create opportunities for optimal challenge and success that consider person-related factors and promote, when possible, person-related changes.

Modifying the Task

Creating modifications to a task is one way to provide inclusive programming for participants with a wide range of capability levels. Modifications can be created through several approaches, including closed to open skill progressions, skill extensions, skill switching, and individualized goal setting.

Closed to Open Skill Progression

Practitioners often employ general guidelines when designing activity sessions. One popular practice is to have participants practice closed skills before attempting them in an open environment. Closed skills are skills performed in a stable or predictable environment in which performance demands do not change during the execution of a skill. The participant decides when to begin the action. For example, hitting a ball off a batting tee is a closed skill. The ball does not move during the time the participant decides to swing and when the swing is taken. On the other end of the continuum are open skills, which are attempted in dynamic, unpredictable contexts. The participant must respond to the action of an object, to the changing environment, or to both. Batting a pitched ball is an example of an open skill. In this case, the participant responds to when the pitch is delivered and the flight of the ball after it is thrown. Depending on the type of pitch, the batter might need to adjust while the ball is in motion.

Although a progression from closed to open skills is effective in many situations, the move might be too quick for some participants and thus not create an optimal challenge at a given capability level. An important consideration in a progression from closed to open skills is whether aspects of the context that determine the movement vary from one attempt to the next (Gentile, 2000). For example, climbing a stationary ladder with rungs spaced evenly throughout has no variability across practice. However, changing the spacing between rungs on a ladder so that participants practice climbing with different step lengths more closely simulates the variety of climbing structures found on the playground. With this kind of intertrial variability, a progression from closed to open skills can be expanded. Practitioners can offer increased practice for participants with differences in capabilities by progressing practice slowly before asking participants to perform skills in more complex and dynamic real-world settings.

The same strategy can be applied to other open skills, such as hitting a pitched ball, returning a serve in tennis, or catching a pass in football. By increasing the number of steps in the progression and offering increased practice at these stages, tasks are matched to individual capability and readiness levels, thereby achieving more inclusive programming.

Skill Extensions

The ability of practitioners to break a movement task down and sequence it appropriately can significantly influence meaningful activity participation and skill improvement. Practitioners often use progressions of tasks to sequentially lead participants from beginning levels to more advanced levels of a skill. Progressions are developed through a series of extension tasks (Rink, 2005). Practitioners start at a less complex point and gradually increase the complexity or difficulty. Many aspects of a movement task can be modified to change its level of difficulty. Figure 7.4 presents common methods for developing task progressions.

Extending traditional progressions or skill hierarchies has been suggested as an effective method for accommodating participants of diverse skill levels (Block, 2007). By including more simple tasks in the progression, participants once unable to access the task can now participate. Similarly, extending the progression to include more complex tasks provides others with more developed skill abilities increased challenges and opportunities to develop

Common Extension Strategies

Breaking a skill down into parts

Example: Practice just the rope swing in jumping rope.

Changing symmetry of movement across limbs

Example: Practice the breaststroke before the front crawl stroke.

Changing the complexity of the movement pattern

Example: Practice juggling using a cascade pattern rather than a column pattern.

Adding or decreasing base of support for balance

Example: Practice the yoga pose of balancing tree on both feet rather than just one.

Combining two skills

Example: Practice dribbling and then practice dribbling with a layup.

Figure 7.4 Extension strategies help practitioners lead participants from beginning levels to more advanced skill levels.

Adapted from Rink 1998.

their skills even further. For example, with an extended skill progression for catching, as shown in the following list, a student with decreased eye–hand coordination can access the activity by having the ball bounced to her (figure 7.5), while another learner proficient in eye–hand coordination can participate in catching by having the ball thrown to her.

- Looks at the ball placed on lap or tray
- Touches ball placed on lap or tray with one hand or head stick
- Touches ball placed on lap or tray with one or two hands
- Touches ball rolled to optimal position at midline
- Catches ball rolled to optimal position
- Touches ball swung on rope to optimal position
- Catches ball swung on rope to optimal position
- Catches ball swung on rope to side
- Touches with one hand a slowly tossed ball from 5' away to optimal position
- Touches with two hands a slowly tossed ball from 5' away to optimal position
- Catches with two hands a slowly tossed ball from 5' away to optimal position
- Catches with two hands a slowly tossed ball from 10' away to optimal position
- Moves body to optimal position to contact a slowly tossed ball from 10' away to either side
- Moves and touches with one hand a slowly tossed ball from 10' away to either side
- Moves and catches with two hands a slowly tossed ball from 10' away to either side
- Moves and catches with one hand a slowly tossed ball from 10' away to either side
- Moves in a specific pattern to catch a ball thrown from a moving passer 20' away

Similar progressions can be developed for the range of skills used in movement activities. These skill extensions can work for youngsters or participants of any age working individually at stations or playing in games and sport activities. For instance, participants involved in a

Figure 7.5 This youngster's capability to catch is improved by extending the skill to have the ball bounced to her.

team handball activity involving throwing and catching to move a ball toward an opponent's goal can use catching from a throw, a bounce, or a roll to achieve the game's objective.

Skill Switching

Another strategy for modifying a task involves the concept of skill switching, in which skills that have similar functional outcomes or intended purposes are grouped together and can be used interchangeably (Balan & Davis, 1993; Davis & Broadhead, 2007) (table 7.3). Throwing, striking, and kicking are grouped together as object propulsion skills because the purpose of each skill is the projection of an object away from the body using a limb or piece of equipment. An activity requiring participants to propel an object, such as kicking a pitched ball in a kickball game, might allow some players to kick the ball while others collect and throw the ball out into the field. Similarly, object-reception skills of catching, trapping, and blocking are grouped together because they all involve stopping and securing a moving object and can be interchanged to increase participation of individuals with disabilities. A youngster with limited arm strength who uses an electric wheelchair can demonstrate effective pass reception in a flag football game by moving his or her body and wheelchair to the optimal location at the correct time. This player, while wearing a Velcro vest, ensures completion of the pass by moving to allow the pass to contact and stick to the Velcro vest. Others in the game might catch the pass with two hands for a completed play. In each case, skills with a similar functional purpose are performed together. The practitioner must consider the meaning that task goals or skills have for participants and how skill switching can offer increased participation and benefit.

Individualized Goal Setting

Although the strategies just discussed can increase physical activity participation, practitioners need to remember that the basis for all movement opportunities is the meaning or importance the experience has for each participant. Individuals entering physical activity programs come with widely diverse needs and interests, likes and dislikes, and desires.

Table 7.3 General Task Categories

Task category	Functional goal	Criteria for success	Skills needed
Locomotion on land	Translating from point A to point B	Efficiency, velocity, distance, spatial accuracy, temporal accuracy, accuracy of movement form	Rolling, crawling, creeping, tumbling, cruising, walking, running, hopping, sliding, galloping, skipping, climbing, jumping
Locomotion in water	Translating from point A to point B	Efficiency, velocity, distance, spatial accuracy, temporal accuracy, accuracy of movement form	Dog paddle, human stroke, breast stroke, side stroke, butterfly, jumping, diving
Object propulsion	The projection of an object away from the body with the use of a limb or piece of equipment	Velocity, distance, spatial accuracy, temporal accuracy, efficiency	Throwing, kicking, striking, volleying, rolling, heading, shooting, dribbling
Object reception	The act of stopping, securing, or impeding a moving object with the use of the body, body parts, or piece of equipment	Efficiency, spatial accuracy, temporal accuracy	Catching, trapping, tackling, blocking

What is meaningful and appropriate for one person to participate in and achieve must also be individually considered. Individualized goal setting is critical to successful inclusive programming. Thus the overall focus of the program and reason for participation play important roles in inclusive physical activity. For instance, an adult who regularly uses a wheelchair might participate in aquatic activity to work on range of motion and weight bearing, whereas others in the class may perform aerobic exercise to increase endurance. Practitioners must value the input of individual participants in determining program focus and goal setting. Otherwise, when what is being offered is required of all participants with no regard to individual needs and interests, lack of motivation and effort typically result. The meaningfulness of an activity is the key to motivation, adherence, and continued physical activity.

Activity objectives can be modified to emphasize the link between the point at which participants are currently performing and the point at which they hope to perform. Although overall goals and standards might be similar, learning or participation objectives will likely need to vary to align individually with the uniqueness of each person. For example, the goal for some participants might be to achieve a smoother, more efficient movement form, whereas for others it might be to achieve a set number of repetitions. If physical fitness, for instance, is an objective of the physical activity program, developing realistic and individually designed goals and outcomes is critical. While some participants are doing sit-ups on a mat to increase abdominal strength, for example, other participants who use wheelchairs can be doing their sit-ups in their chairs to increase back extensor strength. In both cases, increasing muscular strength of the trunk is the goal, but which muscles are targeted depends on individual needs.

Program focus and activity objectives can be tailored to meet the needs of a range of participants and provide the foundation for inclusive physical activity programming that is important and meaningful.

Modifying the Context

Altering the context is another way to accommodate all individuals. By structuring a physical activity environment that appreciates and respects individual differences and maximizes person-related variables, the practitioner can optimize individual performance. In chapter 6 we discussed the importance of promoting positive attitudes and preparing participants and support personnel. Practitioners must then make a series of decisions regarding what participants will do, how participation can be facilitated, and in what ways the setting should be modified. Several critical considerations must be examined to optimize the learning and performance environment. Rink (2005) identifies three instructional functions as responsibilities of the practitioner in the practitioner–participant relationship: presenting activities, organizing and managing the instructional setting, and selecting instructional strategies.

DID YOU KNOW?

Research has shown that the way practitioners organize and structure the environment affects how participants value achievement, how they process and attend to information, and how they think about themselves and their performance. Establishing a motivational climate promotes motor skill performance and influences participants' perceived physical competence.

Presenting Activities

An important competency for practitioners to develop is the ability to present activities and tasks to participants in a manner that motivates them and promotes skill development. Environments that ensure maximum participation through effective instruction tend to engage participants and increase capabilities. Practitioners can employ several strategies and procedures to meet the needs of their program's participants.

One consideration when presenting task and performance information to participants involves how this information is communicated. Verbal instruction is the most common method of communication with participants and can be modified to meet diverse participant capabilities. For some participants, the length of the instruction might need to be modified. For instance, individuals with shorter attention spans might not be able to sit and listen as lengthy instructions are given. These learners might benefit from shorter instructions and specific performance details shared over time as they practice. Limiting the number of steps given in the instructions and using familiar words might also elicit clearer understanding for some participants. Verbal cues are often effective in conveying critical aspects of the task without overwhelming participants with more lengthy instructions. Effective cues are critical to the task, brief, and organized (Rink, 2005). Cues can also be tailored to participants' capability levels by the language used, number of words used in the cue, and the focus of the cue. For instance, participants with differences in concept understanding might be told to "Keep elbow high! Step opposite! Put hand out and snap wrist!" when learning to throw overhand, whereas others might benefit from a more simple "step and throw" cue.

For some participants, it is enough to verbally share the details of the activity. For others, demonstrations to supplement verbal cues are effective. Always consider the participant and the content of the information when modifying demonstrations. The proximity of participants to the demonstration can be adapted to increase effectiveness. Participants with differences in vision or high levels of distractibility might move closer to the demonstrator for increased focus. Practitioners can also consider whether key points need to be highlighted before the demonstration and if demonstrations and verbal instructions should be presented simultaneously or separately. For some participants with differences in concept understanding and attention, knowing what to selectively look for in the demonstration might be helpful. Or a participant who is deaf, for instance, might not be able to adequately receive all instructions relayed through an interpreter and watch the movements of a demonstration at the same time. For others with differences in cognitive capabilities, repeating the demonstration several times might be necessary.

Media materials can also help practitioners convey important instruction information. Pictures, charts, video clips, and other visual aids can engage participants in several ways.

Figure 7.6 Physically guiding this young boy through the draw and release of the arrow might convey important skill information.

These materials can be used to reinforce and repeat details previously shared in verbal instructions or demonstrations. They might also work to motivate participants who enjoy and are reinforced by brightly colored pictures or videos depicting others involved in movement skills. As with other communication strategies, the appropriateness of media approaches for participants should be considered on a case-by-case basis.

For some participants, physical guidance through a desired movement might be necessary to convey information (figure 7.6). For example, a practitioner might stand behind a participant learning to putt a golf ball and help hold the club and strike the ball. By manually guiding the participant through the task, the practitioner enhances concept understanding and provides important tactile cues for increased sensory perception and body awareness. Although physical guidance might be effective in improving concept understanding and skill capability, practitioners also need to help participants become as independent as possible. With this in mind, the extent and frequency of physical assistance should gradually diminish over time. Physical guidance might be replaced with physical prompts in which the practitioner helps only to initiate the movement, and then the participant completes the task. Eventually, gestures and verbal cues might be enough to elicit task performance. Through this process, participants do not become overly dependent on the practitioner and begin to rely on natural cues and less intrusive prompts to participate in the activity.

Organizing and Managing the Instructional Setting

When designing physical activity experiences, practitioners make decisions on how best to organize the setting and the activity plans to promote all objectives being achieved. Certain modifications in organization can result in greater inclusion of participants in the programs. These modifications might involve organization of participants, time, space, individual positioning, or equipment.

Group Size and Grouping Techniques

Practitioners must consider the optimal number of participants who can work together and still achieve individual outcomes through practice. In some situations, participants might work individually or in partners; at other times small or large groups might be best. Ideal group size depends on several factors, including the nature of the activity, length of down time for participants, and the attentional focus and capacity of participants. Some participants who are more easily distracted might need to work in smaller groups with increased guidance for their skills to improve. Larger groups might also increase waiting and not provide enough active involvement to maintain attention and on-task behavior.

Another consideration is how to group participants. Best practice has moved from participants choosing their own groups (lower-skilled players are often chosen last) to practitioners creating groups of mixed ability. In the latter case, groups are devised so that each group has a continuum of ability levels, thereby equalizing competition or practice. The rationale behind this strategy is that less-skilled players will learn from the more-skilled ones and can be matched or paired against each other in the game. Although less-skilled players might sometimes learn from higher-skilled peers, there is often unequal active participation in the game, and skill development occurs less for those who need it the most. Rink (2005) suggests that heterogeneous or mixed ability grouping might work well for peer teaching or collaborative learning situations but that grouping by ability level might offer individualized and optimal challenge for all involved. Practitioners can offer a continuum of options or different levels of play. One group might have a high level of competitiveness, another a more recreational level, and another a level geared toward skill development. With guidance from the practitioner, participants can then choose the level of participation they prefer.

Time Considerations

Time management can also be modified to create more inclusive and dynamic capability shifting of participants. Time management relates to scheduling physical activity sessions as well as monitoring the duration and pace of practice. The time of day that participants engage in physical activity might significantly influence their performance and learning process. Practitioners should try to determine the best time for participants to be active and then arrange activities around this time. For individuals who fatigue more easily than others, physical activity sessions might be offered early in the day. On the other hand, some participants, such as those with medication schedules, might gain more from sessions offered later in the day, when medication effects have peaked. Participants and others from the support network or IEP team should offer input to help practitioners make scheduling decisions.

How long participants practice a task can also be modified to help optimize skill development. Some individuals might need additional sessions to achieve a desired physical activity outcome, whereas others might attain personal goals in fewer sessions. Within a particular session, some participants can remain engaged in an activity and continue practicing for longer periods of time. Others might tire or become off task within a relatively short time. Practitioners must observe and assess whether participants are engaged and ensure that practice is productive. The length of the activity session can be altered depending on how engaged participants are. There should also be options available for participants who need to change activities more quickly to remain active and on task. It is important, however, to ensure that participants have enough time to practice for skill improvement before transitioning from the task. Clear participation expectations and reinforcements, as well as prompts, are useful for some individuals with differences in attention and self-responsibility. Regardless of the duration of the task practice, transitions between activities are also critical to effective management. The length of time between tasks and expectations during this time can be modified to meet individual needs. Some participants might need time to rest or receive additional instruction, whereas others might need to quickly begin the next activity to remain involved and less distracted. Also, some participants might need a signal that a transition is about to occur. This pretransition cue can prompt them to finish their last practice attempt and prepare themselves for a change rather than being surprised by sudden shifts in expectations. Again, decisions regarding length and type of transition should be individualized, based on each participant's capabilities.

Physical Activity Space

How physical activity space is used and organized can contribute to the inclusion of all individuals. Defining the practice area is an important first step in accommodating individual needs and differences. The type of surface on which practice occurs might affect some participants' capabilities. For instance, a flat surface might allow for increased performance for individuals with balance or mobility differences. Although the size of an activity area is often dictated by the nature of the activity or skill, defining the area in which participants practice can also help keep learners on task and close by for further instruction and feedback. Cones or brightly colored markers can accentuate boundaries for individuals with differences in vision, attention, or understanding. Dividing the practice area is another way to accommodate differences. By breaking up the practice space, practitioners can adjust the amount of total space available, thereby altering task demands. For instance, reducing space for some participants engaged in group activity might result in reducing the force or speed needed and lead to greater success. On the other hand, allowing more space for activity might require greater movement and lead to increased fitness levels. Participants who are more easily distracted might also need a smaller space partitioned off to stay focused. Mats, markers, poly spots, or hoops can be used to define personal space or a practice area.

The size of the practice area can also be manipulated to suit participants' needs. Some individuals might require reduced space or boundaries in some activities so that force or speed is modified. For example, reducing the boundaries in a tag game for a participant with a difference in speed might increase the player's success at tagging others. Conversely, other participants with differences in balance, for instance, might need a larger space in which to move during certain movement games. Decreasing or increasing the distance to a target or moving players farther from or closer to a net or basket changes the force needed by these players to achieve success. In all cases, if learning outcomes are to be achieved, modifying spaces to match the type of activity and the needs of participants must be thought through before activity begins.

Individual Positioning

The formation of participants within the physical activity space should also be considered. Many different group formations are used in physical activity settings, including squads, lines, circles, and scattered formations. Scattered formations are preferred by those who do not like wasting time getting into set formations, but scattered formations are also beneficial as they allow less observation of others, including those with less developed skills. Lines and circle formations can place participants with disabilities in the spotlight, showcasing their differences in skill. Regardless of which group formation is used in program activities, each individual's position within the formation should be considered. If squads or lines are used, practitioners should ensure that all participants can see and hear instruction. This might require some individuals being moved in closer to the practitioner. Some participants, especially those with differences in attention, might need to face away from others and away from equipment to prevent being distracted. Some participants with differences in self-control might also need to be in closer proximity to the practitioner for increased guidance and instruction. Positioning participants in the best place to obtain needed instructions, observe demonstrations, and avoid distractions contributes to an inclusive and effective learning environment.

Figure 7.7 Throwing a club rather than a ball and adding stability to this young girl's wheelchair increases her activity participation and chance of success.

Equipment

Practitioners should consider each piece of equipment and how it is used to support a participant's current functional level and help him or her achieve desired goals (figure 7.7). By establishing a task goal and providing equipment choices for learners, practitioners can more easily accommodate differing capabilities within the same activity (Davis & Broadhead, 2007). As an example of taking advantage of equipment choices, a participant with differences in coordination might choose a larger ball when involved in a catching activity with a peer, whereas others in the group might use smaller balls as they practice, and learners with increased capability in eye–hand coordination might elect to throw and catch irregular shaped balls to remain challenged. Targets can also be raised or lowered and distances to targets increased or decreased to provide optimal challenges for participants with different levels of skill. Table 7.4 shows a list of equipment characteristics that can be modified for differences in participant capabilities.

Table 7.4 Equipment Characteristics

Weight	Lighter	⟷	Heavier
Size	Smaller	⟷	Larger
Shape	Regular	⟷	Irregular
Height	Lower	⟷	Higher
Speed	Slower	⟷	Faster
Distance	Closer	⟷	Farther
Sound	Soft	⟷	Noisy
Color	Pale	⟷	Bright
Trajectory	Medium level	⟷	High or low level
Direction	Forward	⟷	Backward and sideways (right and left)
Surface contact	Increased	⟷	Decreased
Surface or texture	Level or smooth	⟷	Rough or uneven
Length	Shorter	⟷	Longer
Resiliency	Less	⟷	More

Another modification strategy to consider is using a different piece of equipment for the intended task rather than the piece typically used. For example, someone with differing eye–hand coordination involved in a modified softball game might choose to use a large-headed racket rather than a bat to strike a pitched ball. Another possibility is to add a piece of equipment to assist in task completion. For instance, an adult with decreased range of motion and strength involved in a bowling league might elect to use a bowling ramp instead of a two-handed approach. Increasing the amount of equipment used in an activity can also provide increased opportunities to respond and allow for faster improvement. For example, adding additional balls in a target throwing game for young children allows for increased contact with the balls and prevents dominant players from controlling the activity. Remember, though, that increasing the amount of equipment likely also increases the attention demands on participants. Practitioners must determine if participants can handle this increased level of difficulty and ensure the safety of all participants involved in the activity.

Equipment decisions pertain not only to context modifications but also to task progressions, as discussed earlier. Changes in equipment used might allow participants to achieve additional steps in the sequence that they otherwise would not attain. For instance, Suzi might be able to kick a small stationary ball to a stationary partner quite accurately. But she might not be as successful with this size of ball if the task were more complex. For instance, she might need a larger ball to pass accurately from a dribble to a peer who is also moving down the field.

Practitioners must also assess how equipment choices affect participant behavior and performance. Although some participants might benefit from colored markers and cones, others might be easily distracted by these visual cues. Practitioners should have the equipment they intend to use ready and attempt to eliminate distractions caused by equipment when modifying for inclusive programming.

Selecting Instructional Strategies

Effective practitioners develop appropriate content and skill progressions and think carefully about how to organize physical activity sessions. Such practitioners are also actively engaged in how practice and learning proceed. They are always considering what style of instruction is best, how skills should be taught, which activity procedures need to be modified, and how to give feedback to best meet individual needs and capabilities.

Instructional Styles

One decision practitioners need to make is how to best deliver instruction content for a particular group of individuals. They want to select a style that is most appropriate for the content being taught, the objectives of the lesson, and the abilities of the participants. This decision-making process determines the responsibilities of the practitioner and participants. Table 7.5 shows a spectrum of instructional styles as developed by Mosston and Ashworth (2002). The instructional style can be considered on a continuum from more practitioner-directed styles to more participant-discovery approaches. The strategy chosen for a group

Table 7.5 Continuum of Teaching Styles

	Instructional style	Description
Teacher directed ↑	Command	Purpose: To learn a task accurately within a short time. Teacher makes all decisions and directs all learning.
	Practice	Purpose: To provide the learner with time to work individually and privately. Teacher provides individual feedback.
	Reciprocal	Purpose: To work with a partner. Partners provide feedback to each other based on criteria set by the teacher or practitioner.
	Self-check	Purpose: To learn to do a task and check one's own work. Criteria for self-check is determined by the teacher or practitioner.
	Inclusion	Purpose: To learn to select one's own level of a task to perform and check one's own work.
	Guided discovery	Purpose: To discover a concept or answer through a sequence of questions presented by the teacher.
	Convergent discovery	Purpose: To discover a solution to a problem, clarify an issue, or arrive at a conclusion by using logical procedures and critical thinking skills.
	Divergent production	Purpose: To discover multiple answers to a single question.
	Individual program—learner's design	Purpose: To provide the learner with the opportunity to design, develop, and perform a series of tasks organized into a personal program.
	Learner-initiated	Purpose: To provide learners an opportunity to self-initiate the design, implementation, and evaluation of their own learning.
↓ Participant directed	Self-teaching	Purpose: To engage in lifelong learning based on complete self-direction. No teacher or practitioner involved.

Adapted from Mosston and Ashworth 2002.

or individual can be selected based on how much practitioner direction is necessary to ensure participant learning. A participant who has more difficulty with concept understanding or self-responsibility might benefit from the command style, in which the task and all performance decisions are made by the practitioner. The participant's role, in this style, is to follow and perform the task as described. Conversely, a guided discovery style invites participants to engage in problem solving and critical thinking as they seek to meet desired outcomes; this method might work best for participants who are more independent and responsible.

Although multiple instructional methods might be employed to accommodate differences in participant abilities and needs, practitioners working with groups might find it difficult to use multiple styles that are effective for everyone involved. They might need to switch styles throughout an activity session or use a style that is most appropriate for the group and then employ different approaches selectively with individuals during practice. For instance, a practitioner might determine that the self-check style is best for a group of fourth-graders involved in a tumbling lesson. As the learners are practicing, he or she might find a command style most effective when working with a child who needs additional support for concept understanding.

When working with individuals with disabilities, the inclusion style might facilitate the most appropriate programming. The inclusion style involves an approach that incorporates multiple levels of performance within the same task. Instead of a single standard that some will achieve and others will not, the task design allows for all participants to be included by offering choices regarding the degree of difficulty and individual goals. Figure 7.8 shows how changing the task design can foster inclusion rather than exclusion. Instead of holding the rope parallel to the floor for all individuals to jump over, the rope is slanted, thereby allowing participants to access the activity and succeed at different levels. Participants decide at which level they would like to enter the task and how the task will be subsequently attempted. For example, they can repeat the same level of difficulty or choose a more difficult or less difficult level. This same approach can be applied to many activities, such as those involving nets, targets, or goals. This style has important implications for inclusive programming. It implies that the practitioner philosophically embraces the concept of

Figure 7.8 A horizontal rope allows youngsters only one choice of height to jump over the rope. The slanted rope (pictured here) allows many choices of height for the youngsters to select from.

inclusion and the idea that legitimate options must be created for successful programming. The practitioner acknowledges the range of capabilities participants bring to any physical activity setting and is creative in ensuring that each individual is offered meaningful and beneficial experiences.

Whole–Part Practice

Some participants perform best when practicing a skill in its entirety. For other participants, task complexity can be reduced by having them practice and develop competency in parts of the task before practicing the whole movement skill together. For instance, a participant with coordination differences might begin practicing a delivery of a bowling ball from the line before combining the two-step approach with the delivery. This strategy can also be used to teach participants with differences in concept understanding more complex dance routines in which small sequences of steps are taught before other steps or movements are added and the routine is performed as a whole. Even when breaking a skill into parts, participants should have an idea of what the whole skill looks and feels like before practicing its parts. This whole–part approach is not recommended when tasks are relatively easy or have a natural flow or continuous motion to them, such as the golf swing. In these cases, the entire skill should be practiced and other modification strategies employed as needed.

Activity Procedures

The level of involvement and degree of success experienced by participants in an activity can be manipulated by modifying the rules of play. Rules are designed to facilitate the way in which skills are performed and participants interact. By changing the rules, practitioners can increase or decrease the challenge for participants. For instance, a child who moves more slowly than his or her peers in a tag game can be allowed two tags instead of one before being "caught." An adult with proficient eye–hand coordination and accuracy might be allowed to shoot only from outside the key, whereas others can shoot from inside or outside.

More inclusive programming can also be achieved by modifying the roles and responsibilities a participant has in an activity. Individuals can choose positions in which they might experience greater success than in other roles. For example, a player with limited mobility might perform effectively as a pitcher in a softball game compared to how he or she might perform as an outfielder (figure 7.9). A player with less developed balance and speed might choose to serve as the team's goalie in a soccer game rather than play offense. Although matching roles to participant capabilities might be effective, practitioners should not narrow participant options. Some participants might prefer to participate in several positions on the team and need additional skill development and modification to succeed in these roles. Responsibilities within an activity can further facilitate inclusive programming. Although some players in a basketball game might play person-to-person defense, others might be more successful in a zone defense in which they can guard a particular area of the court. Roles and responsibilities can be individualized for each participant, even when involved in the same activity, and these roles can change throughout play as needed to ensure meaningful involvement and success.

DID YOU KNOW?

The United States Tennis Association has established game play for individuals who use wheelchairs. The rules are the same as for stand-up tennis, but the player using a wheelchair is allowed two bounces of the ball. In this way, a player using a wheelchair can play against another player who is standing.

Providing Feedback

An essential aspect of instruction is providing participants with meaningful information about their performance. Feedback helps participants focus on the task at hand and stay motivated to continue practicing. Although reinforcers such as music, free time, and other rewards might help externally motivate some participants, specific and contingent feedback can be modified to increase motivation and promote skill improvement. Individuals can benefit from feedback that considers the task goal, the abilities of the participant, and the context in which the skill is performed. The type of feedback offered can be tailored to accommodate individual differences. For instance, beginners with differences in concept understanding might be given more corrective feedback or information on how to correct errors rather than just evaluative or descriptive feedback on what they did. Here are examples of different kinds of feedback:

- On your next throw, point to the target when you let go of the ball. (corrective)
- I like the way you stepped with your opposite foot on that throw. (evaluative)
- You snapped your wrist on that forehand shot. (descriptive)

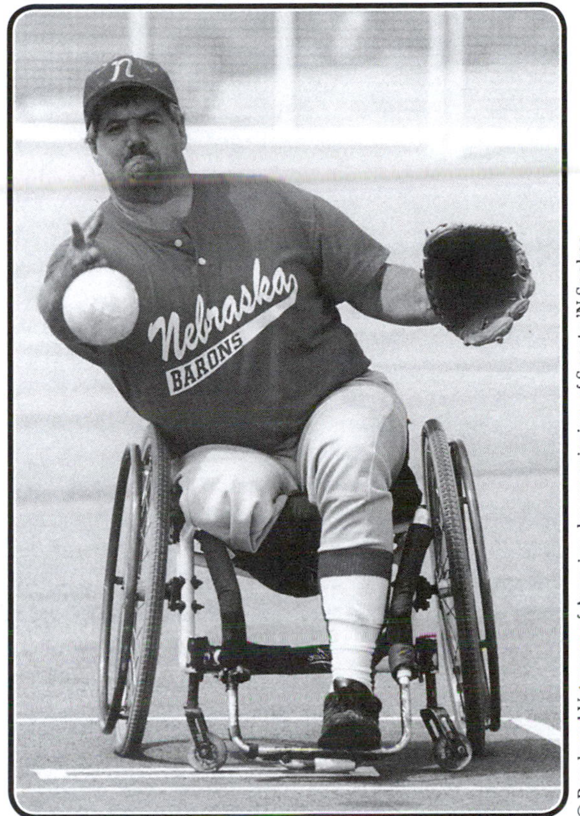

Figure 7.9 Certain responsibilities within a game or activity might provide greater activity involvement and yield more success than other positions.

The amount of feedback also plays a key role in improvement. Too much information might overwhelm participants with differences in attention capacity; others respond best to extremely detailed feedback. Prioritizing feedback information and connecting feedback to cues used during task presentation might reduce the total amount of feedback and help participants focus on the most critical aspects of the skill. Using consistent feedback-related cues might also benefit participants with differences in cognitive understanding or attention. The timing of feedback can also affect learning. Feedback given immediately after performance might be best for participants with shorter attention spans or decreased on-task behavior, whereas some participants might engage in self-assessment and receive instructor feedback a bit later. The schedule of feedback can also differ to accommodate individual differences. Participants who seem initially less motivated can receive more feedback early on in practice sessions and less information as they progress in skill and desire. Regardless of what feedback decisions are made, practitioners should note that too much feedback can result in participant dependence on the feedback. To foster increased independence, feedback should be given only when needed and be gradually reduced over time.

THINK BACK

1. How might Karen Morgan create both open- and closed-skill challenges in her skill practice for the children on bouncing and catching?
2. What skill extensions might she use to foster success for Sara and others in the group?
3. If you were Karen, what organizational strategies might you employ to keep Sara on task and participating with the group?

STEP 4: EVALUATING MODIFICATION EFFECTIVENESS

The last step in the FAMME model encourages practitioners to evaluate the appropriateness and potential effectiveness of modifications being considered. We discussed the specifics of assessing success in chapter 5. In this section, we provide further guidelines for determining if modifications are appropriate.

Modifications should be chosen that have a positive effect on all involved—the participants for whom modifications are made, other participants in the program, and the practitioner facilitating the activity. The main objective of reflecting on and selectively choosing the most effective modifications is to promote optimal challenges, positive attitudes, and acceptance. Modifications that are too hard or too easy or that create negative feelings and resentment toward the individualization process should be reassessed. The following questions provide practitioners guidance when considering modifications. If the practitioner can answer yes to each of these questions, the modifications are likely appropriate and effective in promoting a positive environment for all involved.

1. **Is the modification age-appropriate?** When making changes to activities, make sure the modified activities are age-appropriate. For example, a junior high school student with less developed eye–hand coordination might need a lighter and slower piece of equipment when practicing striking to be successful. Having the learner hit a beach ball into the air several consecutive times is less age-appropriate than using the beach ball within the context of a modified volleyball game. The modified game is more likely to be valued by peers and looked on as a similar-age activity. In fact, many other learners might want to use this same modification to increase their success rate. This same principle holds true for participants of all ages. The modification should allow for greater success and still be viewed as appropriate for all participants of a similar age.

2. **Is the modification functionally appropriate?** Modifications should be chosen that have the potential for increasing physical activity participation at present and in the future. For example, promoting a participant's success while bowling by having him or her move closer to the pins might not be as effective as using bumpers or a bowling ramp, which are available and allowed in community bowling facilities. Or, having someone practice serving a volleyball over a lowered net might provide success but fail to promote the participant's involvement in a recreation league or community-based game of volleyball, which requires a specific net height. Instead, having the participant move closer and practice serving over a higher net might lead to more inclusive involvement later on.

3. **Does the modification allow the participant to be as independent as possible?** Modifications should increase success but not at the expense of active involvement of the participant. In the past, a participant using a wheelchair in a recreational or school softball game might have been pushed by a teammate to reach first base before the throw. But this modification does not provide for independence and individual accomplishment. Alternative modifications that would allow for greater independence and skill development for all involved might include changing the distance needed to travel to first base or requiring the outfield to throw two or more times before making a play on the batter. Modifications should always allow the participant the greatest possible amount of independence. However, changing rules for some participants might or might not be appropriate given the activity or context. More competitive leagues, for instance, might not allow such rule changes, whereas schoolyard play might. The level of independent participation must be considered in light of the varying contexts.

4. **Does the modification ensure maximum participation of the participant?** Sometimes it is necessary to identify particular positions on a team that might be a better match for a participant's functional capabilities. For instance, a softball player might find more success pitching than playing shortstop. However, in such a case, the practitioner must ensure that the game is designed to provide the pitcher with ample skill development, opportunities to interact in the game, and reasonable success at that position. This would be true for any individual playing at this position.

5. **Does the modification avoid singling out or spotlighting high- or low-ability participants?** Design activities to allow for a variety of ability levels. For example, if participants are running in class for cardiovascular development, have them start at different places in the gym and run in a circle. In this way no one will be in the front or back of the group, and runners can go at their own pace without being spotlighted. In another example, having students throw to targets lined up on the same wall and then move back as they successfully hit the

target eventually results in the most skilled participant being farthest away and the lowest skilled learner being closest to the wall for all others to notice. An easy way to prevent this is to have all participants throw at targets placed at varying distances in several locations. Participants might be required to move around to three or four targets of their choice, allowing for more movement and challenge for all involved without spotlighting any one individual. Some activities, such as relays and obstacle courses, do not always lend themselves to inclusive practice and equal opportunity. Thoughtful decisions on activities and how to organize them are critical to ensure that no participants feel put on display for others to view.

6. **Does the modification allow for optimal challenge for everyone in the activity?** Most important, practitioners must be cognizant of the level of participation of all individuals in the activity. Modifications should focus on raising the skill performance of those for whom modifications are deemed necessary. Equality is not achieved by reducing the skill level of others in the activity. For example, in a game of tag, a participant who has difficulty tagging others can be given a reaching implement, such as a foam tube, or boundaries can be reduced for runners rather than having peers walk so they can be more easily tagged. Having participants walk so they can be more easily tagged may lead to resentment or boredom among participants.

7. **Is safe participation ensured for all participants once the modification is implemented?** No matter which modification strategy is chosen, the practitioner must ensure the safety of all participants. Adapted equipment should be stored away when not in use; practitioners should teach and practice rules and safety procedures for any program.

Practitioners must consider these questions and decide which modification is best; as the activity unfolds, they must also determine whether additional modifications or changes are necessary. As mentioned in chapter 2, the 3R process of *ready, rethink, retry* can promote success and enjoyment for all participants and definitely applies when modifying for inclusive physical activity programming.

THINK BACK

1. What are four methods of presenting information discussed in this chapter?
2. What are four of the organizational management considerations when presenting an activity? How might Karen Morgan alter some of these to help Sara achieve more success in her physical education class?
3. Based on Karen's class, think of some modifications for the activities she is doing. Apply each of the seven questions just discussed to determine if your modifications are appropriate.

APPLYING THE FAMME MODEL

Once the four steps of the FAMME model are understood, the process can be applied to any individual in any physical activity context. Tables 7.6 and 7.7 provide an in-depth look at how the model can be used to support the involvement of participants in two different activities. In the examples presented, notice how modifications are connected directly to the capability differences of the participant in relation to the underlying components necessary to achieve the task goal. The practitioner might choose from many possible modifications to achieve the desired outcome; his or her decision should be based on the evaluation criteria we have discussed.

Case Study of Jason

Jason is an eight-year-old boy who enjoys physical education. He is at age level in his academics and has good social and communication skills. He also gets along well with his peers. His balance and agility are less developed because of his cerebral palsy. The class is involved in a tag game, and Jason is chosen to be the player who tags others. Table 7.6 is an example of the FAMME model applied to Jason's capabilities and the underlying components required to play the game of tag.

Table 7.6 Applying the FAMME model to Jason

Underlying components of tagging	Jason's functional differences	Modifications
Concept understanding	X	None needed
Balance	Balance	Ensure surface is flat Choose to gallop (Jason) Decrease speed and use reaching extension
Coordination	X	None needed
Speed/agility	Speed/agility	Decrease size of area Use reaching extension
Sensory perception	X	None needed
Strength (legs)	X	None needed
Endurance	X	None needed
Flexibility	X	None needed
Attention	X	None needed
Self-control	X	None needed

Case Study of Laura

Laura is a 35-year-old woman beginning a fitness program involving resistance exercise. She is articulate and insightful. Although her range of motion is good, she has muscular weakness in her legs and some difficulty with balance and body awareness caused by symptoms associated with multiple sclerosis. Table 7.7 is an example of the FAMME model applied to Laura's capabilities and the underlying components required for resistance exercises.

SUMMARY

Modifying activities to meet the needs of individuals with disabilities is critical to the success of any physical activity program. The FAMME model provides logical steps to the process of making modifications, including determining the underlying components of a skill or activity; determining the capabilities of the individual; matching any modifications to the capabilities of the individual; and evaluating the effectiveness of the modifications selected. In every instructional situation the practitioner must be able to evaluate the dynamic interplay of the person, task, and environment and make a meaningful match that optimizes success and independence among participants.

Table 7.7 Applying the FAMME Model: Laura

Underlying components of weightlifting	Laura's functional	Modifications
Concept understanding	X	None needed
Balance	Balance	Ensure surface is flat Use hand-held weights bilaterally Perform sitting versus standing
Coordination	X	None needed
Sensory perception	Body awareness	Use mirror for visual feedback Provide tactile cues or manual guidance Offer verbal cues and metaphors
Strength (legs)	Strength	Move limb horizontally in antigravity plane Use elastic bands versus weights
Range of motion	X	None needed
Speed/agility	X	None needed
Endurance	X	None needed
Flexibility	X	None needed
Self-control	X	None needed

What Do You Think?

1. Choose a skill that you have performed many times. What underlying components are important when performing this skill?
2. Consider a recent movement experience you have had. What modifications could be made within that experience for another participant with differences in balance? How about differences in eye–hand coordination?
3. In your view, are any of the ways to assess the effectiveness of modifications more important than others? Why or why not?

What Would You Do?

Now that you have seen the FAMME model applied in two situations, can you use the model for the following individuals?

Scenario 7.1

Joanne is a sophomore in high school. She loves shopping and socializing with her friends and is trying out to be a song leader for next year. She is a good student and has recently won an award at the county fair for her artwork. She likes physical education well enough but despises team sports. Recently her class finished a unit on dance that she enjoyed very much, but her class will be entering a unit on soccer starting next week. Joanne has asthma that can be aggravated by exercise, and many team sports and fitness activities cause stress for her. She does not like activities in which others depend on her or in which her performance is spotlighted. She prefers individual activities and does not like most ball games.

Scenario 7.2

Francis is a physical activity director at his local YMCA and has an adult participant, Jack, in one of his programs who is having behavior problems. Jack cannot seem to stand still during basketball sessions and is often "out of control," as Francis puts it. If things do not go his way, Jack yells at other participants in the group, and several times he has thrown the ball in anger. Francis is afraid Jack is going to accidentally hurt someone if he does not get his behavior under control. Francis is frustrated with Jack and has tried talking with him and has also written notes to the staff of the group home where Jack lives. Unfortunately, the problems continue. Complete the FAMME model for Jack.

Underlying components of soccer	Joanne's functional differences	Modifications of soccer

Underlying components of basketball	Jack's functional differences	Modifications of basketball

PART III

Application of Inclusive Practices

Part III includes five chapters that describe direct application of the programming strategies and FAMME model presented in part II. Each chapter describes movement skills or physical activities for individuals across the life span and shows how differences in capacity can be matched with modifications to increase skill performance and success for all participants. Examples of modifications are presented for movement skills (chapter 8), games and sports (chapter 9), health-related fitness activities (chapter 10), aquatics (chapter 11), and outdoor pursuits (chapter 12).

CHAPTER 8

Movement Skills and Concepts

LEARNING OUTCOMES

After completing this chapter, you should be able to

- explain that skills can be considered as a sequence of critical elements;
- discuss the link between critical elements of a task and functional components; and
- apply the FAMME model to movement skills and concepts when modifying for individual differences.

INCLUDING ALL INDIVIDUALS

Janet is a second-grader in Tony Gallant's physical education class at Homer Elementary School. She is a friendly child who enjoys physical activity and participating with her peers. Her academic skills are at age level in all subjects except for math, but these skills are emerging. Janet uses a wheelchair because of paralysis of her legs from spina bifida but has good wheelchair mobility and control. Her class is just about to begin a unit on throwing and catching. Tony understands from the supportive network he has established that Janet will need some modifications to activities because of her functional capabilities and present level of performance. Tony is a new instructor with little experience teaching children with disabilities. He very much wants Janet to succeed and hopes to see her progress in performing the fundamental movement skills and concepts covered in his second-grade class.

Tony is clearly interested in ensuring that Janet is provided with a meaningful and optimal physical education program. If you were Tony, what is the first thing you would need to know about the skill of catching before making modifications for Janet? What modifications to this skill might help her the most?

In chapter 7, we presented the process for modifying tasks to meet individual capabilities. In this chapter we take the next step by practically applying the functional approach to modifying movement experiences (FAMME) model to fundamental motor skills and concepts. We also deal with prioritizing modification efforts by connecting aspects of tasks to functional capabilities of individuals when performing a skill. All practitioners should strive to create variations for fundamental movement skills and concepts that set a foundation for competence and enjoyment in lifelong physical activity.

OVERVIEW OF MOVEMENT SKILLS AND CONCEPTS

Individuals of all abilities require early movement experiences in which they practice and refine basic skills and concepts. Instruction that accommodates individual functional differences in capabilities results in well-learned basic skills that prepare participants for acquiring more advanced skills. Many participants who lack fundamental skills exhibit ineffective movements when they try to progress to more advanced play and sport activities. Also, movement skill performance can improve or regress over time depending on such factors as practice, health status, and age.

Fundamental movement skills include locomotor and nonlocomotor movements as well as manipulative skills (table 8.1). These skills are the precursors for many advanced activities, and mastering them promotes successful participation in sports and other leisure activities. For example, playing offense in a game of basketball involves dodging and running skills as well as catching and dribbling skills. Golf involves striking, walking, and

DID YOU KNOW?

Qualitative analysis is the systematic observation and appraisal of movement quality in order to provide effective solutions to improve performance. The qualitative analysis process involves four steps: preparation, observation, evaluation and diagnosis, and intervention.

Table 8.1 Movement Skills and Concepts

Skills (What we do)	**Locomotor Skills** (Traveling)	Crawling Walking Running Jumping Hopping Skipping Sliding Leaping Galloping Pushing or rolling (wheelchair) Chasing, fleeing, dodging
	Nonlocomotor Skills (Performed in a relatively stationary location)	Balancing Turning Pulling/pushing Twisting Bending Rocking Swinging Collapsing Falling Stretching Reaching
	Manipulative Skills (Object receipt and propulsion)	Stopping Trapping Pushing Rolling Catching Throwing Kicking Dribbling Volleying Striking
Concepts (How we do it)	**Spatial awareness** (Where the body moves)	**Location**: Personal or self space, general space **Direction**: Up, down, forward, backward, right, left, clockwise, counterclockwise **Levels**: High, medium, low **Pathways**: Straight, curved, zigzag **Extensions**: Near and far
	Effort (How the body moves)	**Time**: Fast, slow **Force**: Strong, light **Flow**: Bound (stiff), free (flowing)
	Relationships (Who or what the body moves with)	**Body parts**: Round, narrow, wide, twisted, straight **Other objects or people**: Over, under, around, near, far, along, through, meeting, parting **With others**: Leading, following, meeting, parting, mirroring, matching, alone, partners, group

From Graham et al. 2010; Pangrazi 2007.

twisting. Participants need to understand how to use their bodies to execute these skills effectively and how to adjust the skill to changing contexts and situations in a variety of activities.

PREREQUISITE KNOWLEDGE OF TASK ELEMENTS

Before practitioners can modify tasks for individual differences in capability, they must know their participants' abilities and understand the task they want to modify. They should know the task's purpose, the movement patterns and techniques involved, and the common sources of error. For example, a practitioner who knows that kicking a ball for distance involves weight shifting onto the opposite foot, forward trunk movement, and eyes maintained on the ball throughout contact can more effectively teach cues, make modifications, and provide appropriate feedback for error correction.

A good understanding of a task includes knowing the task's critical elements or features, which are the aspects of a task necessary for effective results (Knudson & Morrison, 2002). These aspects are the observable features of performance that practitioners often use to offer meaningful instructional cues or points of emphasis to their participants. They are also the basis of analysis and assessment of the participant's performance. Table 8.2 presents an example of the critical elements for the overhand throw and illustrates instructional cues associated with each element. According to Knudson and Morrison (1996), critical features of skills are identified based on the effectiveness in achieving the movement goal, the efficiency of effort, and safety of the performer. Practitioners' abilities to identify and understand the critical features of skills come from experience in observation and professional development via the literature in the field. For individuals with differences in capability, these task elements can also provide direction for modification efforts. Through understanding the sequence of critical elements for a given task and acknowledging that a range of effective movement exists across individuals with differences in movement capabilities, practitioners can prioritize which elements are most crucial to successful performance and which elements need to be modified (figure 8.1). For instance, a student with differing ability in coordination might execute the critical elements of striking quite well except for optimal contact of the ball. By focusing on this element, the practitioner might be better able to determine necessary modifications and thus provide a successful experience. Given the movement form and outcome observed, the height of the ball or the participant's orientation to the batting tee might need to be modified to allow more accurate contact.

Table 8.2 Critical Features and Sample Cues for the Overhand Throw

Critical feature	Sample cue
Target location	Keep your eyes on the target.
Angle of release	Throw flat or throw up an incline.
Relaxation	Relax your upper body.
Leg drive and opposition	Step with the opposite foot.
Body orientation	Turn your side toward the target.
Strong throwing position	Align the arm with your shoulders.
Sequential coordination	Uncoil the body.
Inward rotation of the arm (follow-through)	Roll the arm and wrist at release.

Adapted with permission from *The Journal of Physical Education, Recreation and Dance,* August 1996, pg. 33. JOPERD is a publication of the American Alliance for Health, Physical Education, Recreation and Dance, 1900 Association Dr., Reston, VA 20191.

L. Lieberman, courtesy of Camp Abilities.

Figure 8.1 Practitioners can provide effective modifications to a task once critical elements and associated cues have been identified.

THINK BACK

Think back to Janet in Tony Gallant's class described at the beginning of the chapter.

1. What are the critical elements for catching?
2. How might these elements for catching be the same or different for Janet or one of her peers?

CRITICAL ELEMENTS AND DIFFERENCES IN MOVEMENT CAPABILITIES

Even when the critical elements for a task have been identified, some of the task's features might not be readily observed in individuals with differences in movement capabilities. For example, a participant who uses a wheelchair might be unable to step with the opposite foot when throwing overhand, or someone with increased muscle tone in his or her legs who uses crutches for balance might have difficulty demonstrating rhythmic movement while galloping. Practitioners must understand the critical elements of a skill, but they must also know how individual differences affect these critical elements. Only then can they have realistic expectations of movement skill performance for individual participants. The practitioner should also understand the influence of specific elements on skill outcome. For example, a participant using a wheelchair who is unable to step with the opposite foot during a throw can be instructed to move his or her trunk in a forward motion and use trunk rotation to increase force. In this way, the critical element of stepping with the opposite foot is replaced with trunk motion to achieve a similar performance outcome (figure 8.2).

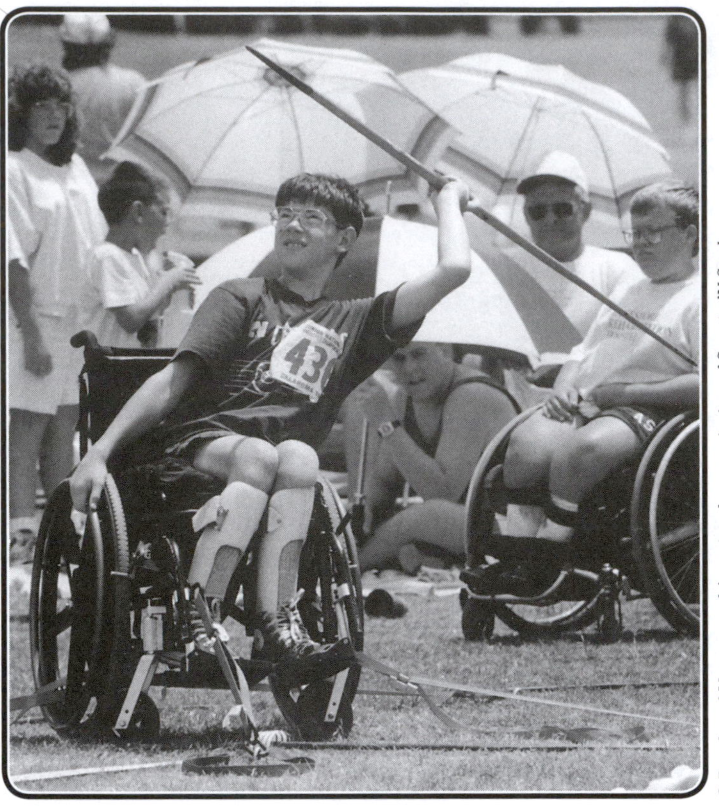

Figure 8.2 Teaching an athlete who uses a wheelchair to shift his weight and move his trunk forward during throwing leads to skill improvement and success.

After identifying critical features and variations of tasks for individual participants, the next step is making modifications that promote success of the key elements. As discussed in chapter 7, variations based on the task and context can be employed to meet the needs of participants with functional differences in movement capabilities. Here are considerations for practitioners when modifying a task:

1. How can instruction be modified to provide successful opportunities for all participants involved in the activity? Can concepts such as flow, force, time, or levels be altered to provide optimal challenges? How will the size of the object used, the number of people involved in the task, and the organization of space affect the participants?
2. Does the modified task elicit a participant's best performance? How does the practitioner's understanding of the functional capabilities of participants and the critical elements of a task lead to successful performance?
3. Does the modified task assess the psychomotor, cognitive, or affective content it was designed to assess? Are the goals and meaningful involvement of participants still being realized?

Think back to Janet's involvement in Tony Gallant's catching unit.

1. Which critical elements might need modifications?
2. From what you learned in chapter 7, which modifications might you want to try?

MODIFICATION OF FUNDAMENTAL MOVEMENT SKILLS AND CONCEPTS

Most often, teaching fundamental movements and concepts involves individual skill practice leading toward partner and small-group activity. For example, students in a physical education class might be working on skipping within a general space or practicing their dribbling and kicking with a partner in a designated space. Regardless of the task, instructors should provide choices and modifications to meet individual needs and provide optimal challenges.

As discussed in chapter 7, modifications can be made to the task or the context that might include instructional, organizational, or equipment variations. Because of the focus on skill practice and refinement typical of teaching fundamental skills and concepts, these modifications can be implemented more easily than might be possible when teaching more advanced games and sport skills. For instance, a task can be presented in such a way to give choices regarding movement form. A practitioner might ask students to balance on three parts of their body. Because the participants' actions do not directly relate or depend on others in the group, they can choose which body parts they want to balance on. In another case, an instructor could use task cards to foster skill development. He or she might ask participants to kick a ball toward a target a set number of times. Although the task of kicking the ball to the target remains the same for all participants, changes to the directions could involve an increase or decrease in the number of times players are asked to hit the target or the distance they kick from. Again, practice incorporates multiple targets with participants working independently within the group, thereby allowing individualized goals. The nature of practice at this level also allows more choice in the equipment participants use. Through making a range of equipment available, practitioners help participants get more comfortable and achieve more success in performance outcomes. For instance, students involved in volleying activities could choose from balloons, beach balls, volleyball trainer balls, or regulation volleyballs when practicing the skill.

As we have discussed, individualizing fundamental movements and skills requires an understanding of the critical elements of the skill and an awareness of task sequences that progress participants toward more advanced skills. Participants can practice activities in many ways. Table 8.3 identifies several aspects that can be manipulated to present a range of task practice conditions from simple to more complex.

Table 8.3 Common Progressions of Fundamental Movement Skills and Concept Practice

Simple	Complex
Closed skill	Open skill
Individual	Partner to small group
Single skill or concept	Combined skill or concept
Cooperative	Competitive
Offense	Defense

A task can by be modified by controlling the environment in which the task takes place. As we discussed in chapter 7, one way to modify a task is to make it either a closed or open skill. For example, someone shooting a basketball from the free-throw line is at the simpler end of the continuum because of the fixed nature of the environment in which the skill is performed (figure 8.3). Someone shooting a jump shot in basketball while being defended is an open skill and thus more difficult.

A task can also be modified by controlling how many individuals are involved at one time. It is typically easier to perform a task alone than with a partner, and partner activities are usually easier than small-group activities. Once a participant can execute a task alone, the complexity of the task can be increased by adding a partner to the activity. For example, when a youngster is first learning to overhand strike, it is easier to practice striking a balloon alone. The task's difficulty is increased when two peers practice striking the balloon back and forth.

Another way to modify tasks is to have individuals participate in cooperative environments before competitive ones. In a cooperative activity, players work together toward a common goal. Such activities can encourage participants to be more accepting of others with abilities different from theirs. Cooperative activities also allow players to practice skills without the threat of being embarrassed or pressured if they execute the skill less

Photo courtesy of David Punia.

Figure 8.3 Practice in a closed context is an effective strategy for skill development. The context can later be shifted to an open environment by adding more participants and gamelike play.

skillfully. Cooperative learning activities work best in small groups. For example, a practitioner could have individuals participate in an activity in which groups of three work on throwing and catching skills.

In competitive activities, a good way to modify a task is by teaching offense movements before adding defense movements. In general, players need to feel comfortable with their offensive techniques before they are ready to perform with defensive opponents. Adding a defender to a task adds a new level of complexity for them, so instructors must time this choice well. Participant frustration is almost a given if a defender is added to an activity too early in skill practice. In such cases, their progress toward gaining the skill abruptly halts and performance diminishes. Once players are being defended, they tend to stop attending to proper mechanics and focus on the defender instead.

Finally, tasks can be modified through a combination of movement concepts (figure 8.4). Movement concepts can be manipulated to help participants with fundamental movement patterns or sport-specific movements. Movement concepts encompass three areas: spatial awareness (where the body moves), effort (how the body moves), and relationships (moving with people or objects). Spatial awareness involves location (personal space, general space), direction (up or down, forward or backward, right or left, clockwise or counterclockwise), levels (low, middle, high), pathways (straight, curved, zigzag), and extensions (large or small, far or near). Effort involves time (fast or slow), force (strong or light), and flow (bound or free). Relationships involve body parts (round, narrow, wide, twisted), other objects or people (over or under, near or far, along or through, meeting or partnering), and interaction with others (leading or following, mirroring or matching, solo, partners, groups). For example, someone learning to slide could also be taught directions. The practitioner could have participants slide while moving in a pathway. The participant could then choose to slide in a zigzag, curved, or straight pathway.

THINK BACK

Think again of Janet in Tony Gallant's class.

1. Tony needs some variations for his class to progress their catching skills. Can you give Tony 10 ideas for progression in catching skills using closed to open variations?
2. Using the movement concepts, how many variations for the skill of catching can you think of?

Figure 8.4 Movement concepts can be combined by having participants moving in general space and in different pathways.

EXAMPLES OF PRACTICE

By understanding task elements and considering simple to complex progressions in movement skills and concepts, practitioners can modify any activity to create optimal challenges for their participants with disabilities. Another way to examine skills and their possible modifications is by looking at the general task categories as described by Balan and Davis (1993). This classification system (first touched on in chapter 7) provides a meaningful framework for looking at modifications across skills.

DID YOU KNOW ?

The ecological task analysis model proposed by Balan and Davis (1993) encourages practitioners to think outside the box by varying equipment, allowing movement options, and encouraging and acknowledging student choice. This kind of innovation yields enjoyment and success.

Locomotion on Land

To move successfully on land, individuals need to acquire several locomotor and nonlocomotor skills, including walking, running, hopping, skipping, galloping, turning, twisting, rolling, balancing, and stretching. For example, skipping is a difficult skill that involves balance and rhythm. If a participant has difficulty with balance, he or she can hold onto an object (e.g., hand or bar) to maintain balance while performing the skipping movement. A practitioner can then observe if he or she is skipping correctly. The participant might have the rhythm necessary to perform the skill but might lack the necessary balance. If the practitioner is attempting to assess the ability of this participant to skip, it is important for the performance context to measure what was intended. Through having the participant perform the skipping skill while holding a hand, the balance element is reduced, and the practitioner can observe if the child can indeed skip. Table 8.4 shows an example of modifications for jumping based on variations in capabilities. Table 8.5 lists modifications to locomotor activities to help participants succeed in locomotor skills on land.

Table 8.4 Modifications for Jumping

Capability difference	Modification
Balance	Hold peer's hand during jump. Perform jump next to wall and touch wall during jump.
Coordination	Slow jumping down. Practice without arm action at first.
Strength	Jump down incline mat or off slight rise.
Flexibility	Shorten distance or height required to jump.
Endurance	Allow rest in between multiple or sequential jumps. Alternate jumping with walking or slow locomotor movement.
Concept understanding	Use visual cues (such as footprints or poly spots). Employ counting sequence or verbal cues for critical features.
Speed and agility	Increase distance between landing spots. Reduce angles or need to change directions if jumping sequentially.
Attention	Perform jump in direction away from others. Reduce equipment students are jumping over and around.
Self-responsibility	Require limited number of jumps before providing reinforcers or choices.
Sensory perception	Use tactile demonstration. Provide sound cue for jump direction or landing.

L. Lieberman, courtesy of Camp Abilities.

Figure 8.5 The skill of rolling in a game of goalball can be modified by changing the size and weight of the ball or varying the distance to the opponent's goal line.

Object Propulsion

Object propulsion involves an object moving away from the body after contact with a body part or with another object or implement. To propel objects successfully, participants must be able to perform such skills as throwing, kicking, punting, dribbling, volleying, striking, or rolling.

There are many ways to modify skills that involve object propulsion. Table 8.5 lists modifications for individuals with disabilities when performing these skills. For example, in a rolling task, practitioners must understand the factors that affect the outcome of the roll. Factors such as the size, weight, and shape of the ball as well as the size and angle of the roll toward a target or goal line can be manipulated to promote success for participants of all ability levels (figure 8.5). For example, to increase the complexity of a throwing task, practitioners might reduce the size of the target and increase the distance to the target. Table 8.5 also lists possible equipment modifications that can be used for other object propulsion skills.

Table 8.5 Modifications for Capability Differences in Locomotor, Object Propulsion, and Object-Reception Skills

	Easy ◄———► Difficult		
LOCOMOTOR			
Space and speed	Slowly within large space and individually	Slowly within large space with others moving slowly	Fast within small space with others moving fast
Surface	Decline surface Smooth and flat	Horizontal surface Smooth and uneven	Incline surface Uneven and hilly
OBJECT PROPULSION			
Distance	Very close	Near	Far
Ball size	Large	Medium	Small
Ball color and background color	Yellow and black	Blue and white	Yellow and white
Ball shape	Round	Oblong	Irregular
Ball movement	Stationary	Moving slowly	Moving rapidly
Angle of trajectory	Horizontal	30- to 35-degree arc	45-degree arc
Net	Lowered net	Slanted net	Regulation net
Weight of implement or object	Light	Medium	Heavy
OBJECT RECEPTION			
Reception location	Body midline	Preferred side	Nonpreferred side
Ball type	Balloons or beach balls	Oversize trainers	Regulation ball
Contact area	Large	Medium	Small

Reprinted, by permission, from G. Morris and J. Stiehl, 1999, *Changing kids' games* (Champaign, IL: Human Kinetics), 37.

Object Reception

Object reception involves taking in an object coming toward the body. Participants need to acquire several skills—timing, catching, trapping, blocking—before they can successfully receive a variety of objects.

Table 8.5 lists modifications to accommodate individuals with disabilities when performing object reception tasks, such as catching skills. For instance, changing the angle of a tossed

Think back again to Janet in Tony Gallant's class.

1. Referring to table 8.6, what types of modifications in equipment might Tony use for catching tasks?
2. What variations to the locomotor skills might Tony make for Janet in his class when teaching, galloping, skipping, sliding, and jumping?

ball can help someone catch more effectively. Using a glove may also improve success at catching because it reduces the grasping component during the catch. Table 8.5 identifies other types of equipment to modify when helping participants practice receiving objects. Table 8.6 lists modifications for catching based on capability differences.

Table 8.6 Modifications for Catching

Capability difference	Modification
Balance	Catch while seated in chair. Tossed ball comes to midline of body.
Coordination	Use larger ball. Use balloon or light foam ball that moves slowly. Tossed ball comes to or near midline of body.
Strength	Use light-weight ball.
Flexibility	Tossed ball comes to midline of body. Use light-weight or foam ball. Use larger ball to limit joint movement.
Concept understanding	Use physical guidance or verbal cues.
Attention	Limit number of balls being thrown in area.
Self-responsibility	Require limited number of catches before providing reinforcers or choices.
Sensory perception	Use tactile demonstration or physical guidance. Provide sound cue in ball and timing of catch.

Note: Differences in speed, agility, and endurance are not critical to successful catching.

SUMMARY

Accommodating for individual differences in the performance of fundamental movement skills requires a thorough knowledge of the critical elements of the task coupled with an understanding of the skill progressions necessary to foster skill development. Practitioners can become more insightful about which aspects of tasks participants might have difficulty with and which modifications would be most effective for increasing ability. Modifications to the critical elements of a skill can also increase the challenge for participants once they have gained competence in a skill. The ability of a practitioner to use modifications wisely and to accommodate for individual differences helps participants develop and refine the basic skills and concepts they need to build a foundation for continued involvement and success in physical activity.

What Do You Think?

1. How might you vary the movement skills for participants with differences in strength, endurance, or attention?
2. Identify the critical features and sample cues for a skill. How might these be modified?
3. What are the four ways that skills can be modified as discussed in this chapter? Using the same skill you used in question 2, modify the skill in each of the four ways.

What Would You Do?

Scenario 8.1

Frank works for the local basketball league coaching 7- and 8-year-old boys. Frank has been coaching for three years. In his program he tries to provide all the boys with many minutes of game time as he develops their basic skills of dribbling, passing, catching, shooting, and establishing court position. In his first practice Frank started with introductions and a name game to help the boys get to know each other. Then he ran the boys through a few activities to assess their skill levels. During the activities, one boy (an eight-year-old named Devon) seemed to be frequently off-task and had a hard time paying attention during the discussion of expectations of the boys and the practice schedules. After the practice, Devon's mom came up to Frank and said how happy she was to see Devon getting involved in basketball. She shared that Devon loved the sport and frequently spent time at home in the driveway shooting baskets, "just shooting, and shooting, and shooting." She also shared that he had been diagnosed with attention deficit and hyperactivity disorder (ADHD) and that he took medication to help him focus. However, at times he still had difficulty. Devon's mom felt that the benefits and skill development learned through participation on a team sport would be excellent for Devon. She hoped that Frank would accommodate Devon's learning ability and help him succeed.

1. What questions might Frank want to ask Devon's mom before working with him?
2. Dribbling is one of the basic skills of basketball. How might Frank make variations in dribbling to simplify or increase the complexity of the skill for Devon and others?
3. What modifications might Frank want to consider for Devon when planning his practices?

Scenario 8.2

Shanna Jones, an elementary physical education teacher, has been teaching for six years and loves her job. This year her new fifth-grade class has 25 students with diverse abilities. One girl, Sarah, has muscular dystrophy and uses a power wheelchair. In her six years as a teacher, Shanna has not had many students who used wheelchairs. She has heard of muscular dystrophy but knows little about it. She recently received a notice for an IEP meeting regarding Sarah. She saw on the notice that the nurse, physical therapist, occupational therapist, adapted physical education teacher, and classroom teacher would all be there. Shanna was looking forward to the meeting and knew from previous experience that the team of individuals would provide helpful information. She was about to start a unit on balance activities and pyramids and was wondering what types of modifications she might make.

1. What functional capabilities might Sarah have?
2. How might these influence her ability to perform the skill themes and movement concepts in Shanna's class?
3. What are the functional components required for balance and pyramid activities?
4. What types of modifications might Shanna make in her units to ensure success for Sarah?

CHAPTER 9

Play, Games, and Sport

LEARNING OUTCOMES

After completing this chapter, you should be able to

- describe the benefits and purpose of play;
- explain the difference between play and games;
- diagram a game or sport's elements and apply the principles of the FAMME model to make variations in games to meet the needs of all individuals; and
- define sport and its relation to play and games.

INCLUDING ALL INDIVIDUALS

Jim Nasium teaches six periods a day of physical education at Blair High School in Vermont and also coaches basketball. During the fall semester he will be presenting new units to several of his classes, including cooperative games, badminton, basketball, paddleball, volleyball, and team handball. In addition, he teaches an elective physical education class in lifetime and leisure activities that includes cross-country skiing, in-line skating, bowling, and golf. This semester he will be working with several students transitioning from middle school who have been receiving special education services. Blair High has no adapted physical education sections, so these students will be integrated into Jim's program. Jim has been teaching traditional games and sports for five years and is trying to come up with some new ideas for changing his activities to meet the needs of the increasingly diverse students in his classes. In addition to the possible needs of the students from special education, his lifetime leisure class has students with extremely diverse abilities and far-different sport participation backgrounds.

How will Jim include the new students in his program? How might he change the current activities and games within his program so that all participants have an equal opportunity for optimal challenge and success? Jim is considering the functional approach to modifying movement experiences (FAMME) model (discussed in chapter 7) and wondering how he might apply the model to the games, sports, and lifetime activities within his program. He knows that play, games, and sport have critical roles in learning, retaining skills and knowledge, and promoting quality of life.

In this chapter we discuss the relations between play and games and sport and how to understand the components of games and sport. We then apply the FAMME model to the game components to illustrate how to create optimal challenges and success for individuals of all abilities.

PLAY

In an often-cited definition, Dutch historian Johann Huizinga (1955) calls play a free activity that is different from ordinary work-a-day life. Although characterized as not serious and unrelated to material gain, play involves the participant "intensely and utterly." Huizinga also identified social groupings and order, make-believe, disguise, and secrecy as qualities of the play world.

The outcome of all playful interaction is uncertain and contains social, personal, and physical risks. Play is tacitly goal directed without requiring formal or technical rules. Rules in this sense are probabilistic and involve social consensus. Play is pleasurable, done for its own sake, with little thought about consequences. Why this is so, and how play can be beneficially incorporated into our lives to improve our health and functioning, specifically within instructional settings, is the focus of this chapter.

In Latin, *homo* means man and *ludens* means player.

Play is a fascinating and universal human phenomenon described and defined in many ways. Play has been called a means of exploration, assimilation, imagination, symbolism, relaxation, recreation, stress reduction, affect regulation, intrinsic motivation, recapitulation, proximal development, autotelia and paratelia, catharsis, expressing positive emotion, exhausting surplus energy, performing, practicing, and learning. Play has been characterized as paradoxical, reversive, transgressive, both orderly and disorderly, and containing contradictions between the real and unreal. Amidst so many differing views, what can we make of this behavior that is so often taken for granted (Lytle, 1999)?

In this case, definitions are not very helpful in understanding the power and potential of play. With over 50 dictionary definitions of this ubiquitous word, its complexity, importance, and benefits for humans is only hinted at (figure 9.1). One way to understand what play entails is through recognition of the natural human characteristics of playfulness.

Figure 9.1 Play is critical to the learning and development of all individuals. How is this child experiencing the world through his senses and play?

Human action–oriented playfulness involves cognitive, social, and physical spontaneity, humor, personal empowerment, and manifest joy (Lytle, 1999). Of all the primates, humans are the most creative and playful. *Homo ludens* is the term that describes human players with this enduring characterization embedded in our genetic structure. The reason for play to be built into our genes has baffled social and behavioral scientists for centuries, and theories—often contradictory—have been proposed dating back to the ancient Greek philosophers. What is obvious is that play is important for all humans of all ages and abilities.

Many questions remain regarding the role of play in human life. Investigators are only recently realizing the intricate, complex, and reciprocal connections among human neurology, emotions, play, reasoning, and learning. The individual's somatic–cognitive system relies on the innate union of play and emotions and feelings. This is important because it is now known that emotions, through their significant impact, are necessary for meaningful retention in learning. For example, cognitive and somatic images from a person's life experiences are the groundwork for learning, deciding, and reasoning. These images can come from the external sensory apparatus for touch, taste, sight, hearing, and smelling and also through the "hidden" senses of the kinesthetic (e.g., muscle and joint awareness) and vestibular systems (e.g., balance). Through playful manipulation of these current and remembered images, play aids in the learning process and is critical for beneficial development and health. For example, if someone moves rhythmically, and the beat and graceful motion feels good, then that individual will retain the movement pattern better than if the movement was ordinary and less emotionally engaging. Through its spontaneity, novelty, and absorbing qualities, play allows for change, creativity, and cognitive flexibility, as well as personal, social, and physical skill development. This is true for infants exploring their stimulus-rich world, adolescents giggling and moving freely, and older men and women who employ more cerebral playfulness through language, joking, and creative thinking. The role of play in the human experience is critical to overall health and functioning.

DID YOU KNOW ?

The somatic–cognitive system is the interaction between the mind and body and their influence on each other.

1. How are play and learning connected?
2. What's the importance of play in the acquisition of cognitive, social, and motor development?
3. Why are emotions and play important in Jim Nasium's classes? Why might emotions and play be important as he begins to think of ways to modify his current games and sports?

GAMES AND SPORT

Games and sport involve players and foundational elements of play, yet they differ from play in that they have rules and predictable outcomes based on a goal to win. Thus games and sport, sometimes called "contests," require playful competition and involve a game structure built around physical skill, strategy, or chance either singularly or in combination, as seen in figure 9.2. Moving from the spontaneous nature of play to the competitive elements found in games and sport, an important point must be emphasized. Although games mix the natural and beneficial qualities of playfulness with the learning and personal growth potential of competition, competition can be beneficial only if participants have a chance of succeeding.

Sport derives from the playful but competitive character of the human being. Although all sports are games, sport is more than just a competitive game. Sport is a microcosm of

Figure 9.2 Sport and contests involve competition. Competition can be beneficial only if participants have a chance of succeeding.

societal beliefs and values joined with cultural and community ritual, celebration, and festival. One of the important roles of games and sport is to provide an enjoyable, meaningful challenge and the possibility of success for all participants.

Sport games can be categorized in several ways based on how they are played and their basic game structure. The most common categories are invasion games, court games, field-oriented scoring games, and target games (Almond, 1986).

- **Invasion games.** Invasion games, such as soccer, basketball, or lacrosse, involve such skills as running, chasing, fleeing, dodging, catching, and throwing. They include both offensive and defensive elements and off-the-ball and on-the-ball movements. Players must invade the other team's territory to score.
- **Court games.** Court games such as tennis, volleyball, and badminton involve skills including striking with an implement, running, turning, twisting, balancing, jumping, and volleying. Court games also involve both off-the-ball and on-the-ball movements and offensive or defensive maneuvers, such as setting up to attack and defending or creating space. Court games can be either divided (tennis) or shared (racquetball).
- **Field-oriented scoring games.** Field-oriented scoring games such as baseball, softball, and cricket involve many of the same sport-specific skills found in invasion and net games. These skills include striking with an implement, running, throwing, catching, turning, twisting, and fleeing. Field-oriented scoring games also involve offensive strategies such as getting on base and advancing to the next base, as well as defensive strategies such as preventing scoring.
- **Target games.** Target games include activities such as golf, bowling, darts, and croquet. The sport-specific skills involved in these games include striking with an implement, walking, rolling, twisting, turning, throwing, and transferring weight. Target games require propelling an object with accuracy. They involve strategies such as ways to reduce the number of strokes or hits, knocking an opponent away, and hitting or rolling a ball with spin.

Regardless of how a game is categorized, every game has core elements in common: equipment, players, movement patterns, organization, and rules. By looking at the core elements of games and the purpose for playing a game we can determine how to make modifications based on the functional capabilities of participants of any age or ability. Of primary importance in all games or sports is for all participants to be fully engaged in the process and attain a degree of success. Figure 9.3 lists general guidelines for creating success. In the rest of this chapter we describe game elements and how to apply them to a game or sport activity.

Educational Purpose of Games

Games are played for many reasons. Too often teachers and practitioners select games based on what "seems like fun" or what they are familiar with from their past experience, which is often institutionalized, highly publicized versions of sports. These reasons for game choices run counter to a specific learning purpose. Although all learning should be fun and engaging, enjoyment should not be the sole purpose for playing a game. Before beginning any game activity, practitioners should determine the educational purpose(s), also called the activity's goals or objectives (figure 9.4). There are many purposes and associated benefits for games, as shown in table 9.1.

Once a practitioner has determined the educational purpose for playing a game, he or she selects an appropriate activity. For example, if he or she wants to develop communication skills, a cooperative game that requires groups to problem-solve might be a good choice. Because most activities, games, or sports can be modified to meet a desired purpose, one is limited only by the imagination. However, when modifying games and sports it helps to understand the elements of games and how they can be manipulated to meet set objectives.

General Guidelines for Successful Activities and Games

- Everyone is active all the time (no waiting!).
- Everyone has an opportunity to be successful.
- Avoid elimination games. If there's an element of elimination, rotate players back into the game or into another activity or have them complete a task or skill practice and then rotate back in. This activity should be fun and allow for skill development with no down time for anyone.
- Use creative ways to get into groups. Here are some examples:
  - Birthdays or birth months
  - Names, letters, numbers
  - Playing a game such as Hug, Hug; People to People; or Secret Hand Shake
  - Shoe types, shoelace style, and number of eyelets
  - Favorite TV show, TV character, candy bar, season, and vacation spot
  - Each person is given a card. If a deck of cards is used, groups can then be formed by suits, color, or numbers. Stickers can also be used in this way.
- Don't be afraid to change the rules.

Figure 9.3 Guidelines to help plan and facilitate games and activities.

Figure 9.4 What do you think the purpose of this activity is?

Table 9.1 Purposes of Games

Purpose	Benefits
Physical skills	Increased select skills or combination of skills such as throwing, catching, kicking, volleying, skipping, galloping, and jumping
Social and psychological dynamics	Improved peer interactions, communication skills, cooperation, self-concept, and body image; increased self-esteem and self-worth; stress reduction
Fitness	Increased muscular strength and endurance, cardiovascular development, flexibility, body composition
Cognitive skills	Increased problem-solving skills, content knowledge, etiquette; history of game and sport; strategy development; appreciation of lifetime activity

Elements of Games and Sport

All games and sports have elements that shape the nature of the game. These elements include equipment, players, movement patterns, organization, and rules (Lytle, 1989).

- **Equipment.** Not all games require equipment, but many do. The equipment for any game includes the size, type, number, and locations of items apart from the participant. For example, the equipment required for a tennis match includes rackets, tennis balls, and a net. To play tag one might use no equipment or use cones to mark the playing area or an object for tagging such as a beanbag, yarn ball, or foam noodle.
- **Players.** The participants of a game are generally specified, including the number of players and whether the game is played individually, with another person, or in a small or large group. Specifications also include who these players are (e.g., men, women, children, individuals who use wheelchairs). In soccer, 10 players form each team, and two teams play against each other to make up a match. Competitive or professional players are often classified by gender, age, and ability. Such is the case with the Special Olympics, Paralympics, Olympic Games, and many professional organized sports. However, in most classroom and community programs individuals of mixed abilities participate in the same programs based on a designated curriculum or on their interest in the activity.
- **Movement patterns.** Movement patterns include all of the skills required for a particular game or sport as well as the movement concepts related to those skills. For example, the game of baseball requires throwing, catching, striking, running, sliding, and walking. In addition, these skills might be performed in different ways, including variations in direction, level, or pathway. In baseball, examples include running straight to the bases, moving sideways to field a grounder, or running backward and jumping up high to catch a fly ball. Movement skills and concepts are listed in chapter 8. All physical activities, from walking down the street to playing ice hockey, are made up of combinations of movements.
- **Organization.** The organization of a game or sport refers to the parameters and dynamics of the playing space. For example, volleyball is played on a court 59 feet (18 m) by 29.6 feet (9 m) and divided in half by a net 7 feet 11-5/8 inches (~2.4 m) for men and 7 feet 4-1/8 inches (~2.25 m) for women. However, in sitting volleyball the court is 32.8 feet (10 m) by 19.6 feet (6 m), and the net is 3.8 feet (1.15 m) (for men's division). Each game or sport has traditional guidelines for the playing area, but nothing precludes a practitioner from combining traditional spaces or dynamically changing areas during the game, depending on the game's rules.
- **Rules.** The rules structure the game and set the parameters for play. Over the years, games have been modified in many ways using similar elements. For example, the game of golf has been modified to be played with a disc, turning the activity into a game of disc golf.

The rules, followed by the game organization, movement patterns, and then players and equipment, follow an order and relative hierarchy of importance so that any given element could affect a preceding element. This is most clearly seen when rules, game organization, or movement patterns are altered, because equipment and players would also be changed. For example, if the rules of a traditional game of softball are changed to double-diamond baseball, then the organization, movement patterns, players, and equipment all must change. (Double-diamond baseball uses a large space in which two fields are positioned back to back, and batters can choose to hit either toward the field in front or into the field behind them; after hitting the ball, they can run to either field's first base. All the field space is used, and there are no boundaries.)

1. What are the differences between play and games or sport?
2. Before beginning an activity, why is determining the purpose of playing a game the most important decision? What are some of the purposes Jim Nasium might have for playing games in his programs?
3. Can you explain to Jim the game elements as a possible framework for making modifications?

MODIFYING GAMES AND SPORTS

All activities, games, and sports can be diagrammed into the game elements of purpose, equipment, players, movement patterns, organization, and rules. The purpose of the game and the functional capabilities of the participants dictate how the practitioner sets up the game and the rules enforced. We will use the game of 4-square as an example of how to diagram a game or sport, how the game elements can be changed, and how the functional components can be applied to games. Table 9.2 shows the diagram of a game of 4-square.

Table 9.2 Diagram of the Traditional Game of 4-Square

Game elements
Purpose: Eye–hand coordination
Equipment: Playground ball
Players: Four with no specific criteria; one person in each square
Movement patterns: Striking, sliding
Organization: 8-by-8-foot (2.4 × 2.4 m) box divided into four squares.
Rules 1. One person in each square. 2. Players can hit the ball in the air or off one bounce. 3. Players can hit to any square other than their own. 4. A fair hit will bounce in an opponent's square. 5. A ball hitting a line is considered in play. Note: A determination of "fair hit" will also be declared (e.g., contact time with ball, spins, use of body parts).

Determining the Functional Components of a Game or Sport

The general elements for a game of 4-square are shown in table 9.2. As mentioned earlier, any of these elements can be changed to increase success for individuals involved. The variations a practitioner employs should follow the guidelines described in chapter 7. Variations should allow for optimal performance by all participants based on the FAMME model (i.e., matching the functional capabilities of participants with the functional components of the activity). For example, the game of 4-square requires the prerequisite skill components shown in figure 9.5. As you can see by the placement of the X on each continuum, some components are more important in a traditional game of 4-square than others. However, the degree of importance of each component relative to 4-square might change as game modifications are made. This allows the practitioner to match the activity to the capabilities of the participants to create optimal challenges.

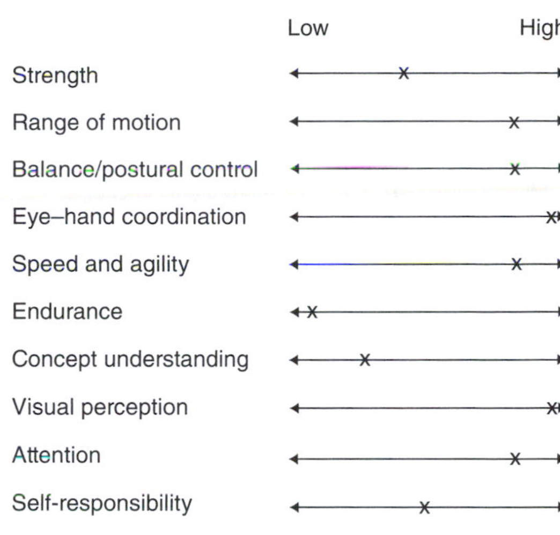

Figure 9.5 Relative importance of skill components in a traditional game of 4-square.

QUESTIONS TO ASK WHEN MAKING MODIFICATIONS

- Do the modifications meet the purpose for playing the activity?
- Is the modification age-appropriate?
- Is the modification functionally appropriate?
- Does the modification allow participants to be as independent as possible?
- Does the modification allow for maximum participation?
- Does the activity prevent singling out or spotlighting individuals?
- Does the variation promote optimal challenges for all individuals?
- Is the variation safe?

Functional Components Game Wheel

Based on what they know about the relative concentration of functional skills for a given game, practitioners can make variations in game elements to accommodate all ability levels, thereby creating optimal challenges for all involved. Figure 9.6 illustrates the functional components game wheel, which includes the five game elements and the functional skill components based on the FAMME model. The components on the outside of the wheel are not exhaustive. For example, changing the environment might be something you would do because of a particular functional component need. If strength was a concern for a participant in a wheelchair, you might move play to a gym floor instead of grass to allow for ease of movement. This could be considered a change in the rules. The wheel can be turned and the various game elements can align with different skill components to indicate a possible game modification. Once the skill components for an activity and the current functional capabilities of the participants have been identified, modifications can be made to match the participant and the activity.

A more detailed look at the application of the functional components game wheel is shown in table 9.3 for the game of 4-square. Included are the functional components needed to play the game, sample game elements to be modified, and examples of possible variations. This illustrates how select game elements relate best to given functional components.

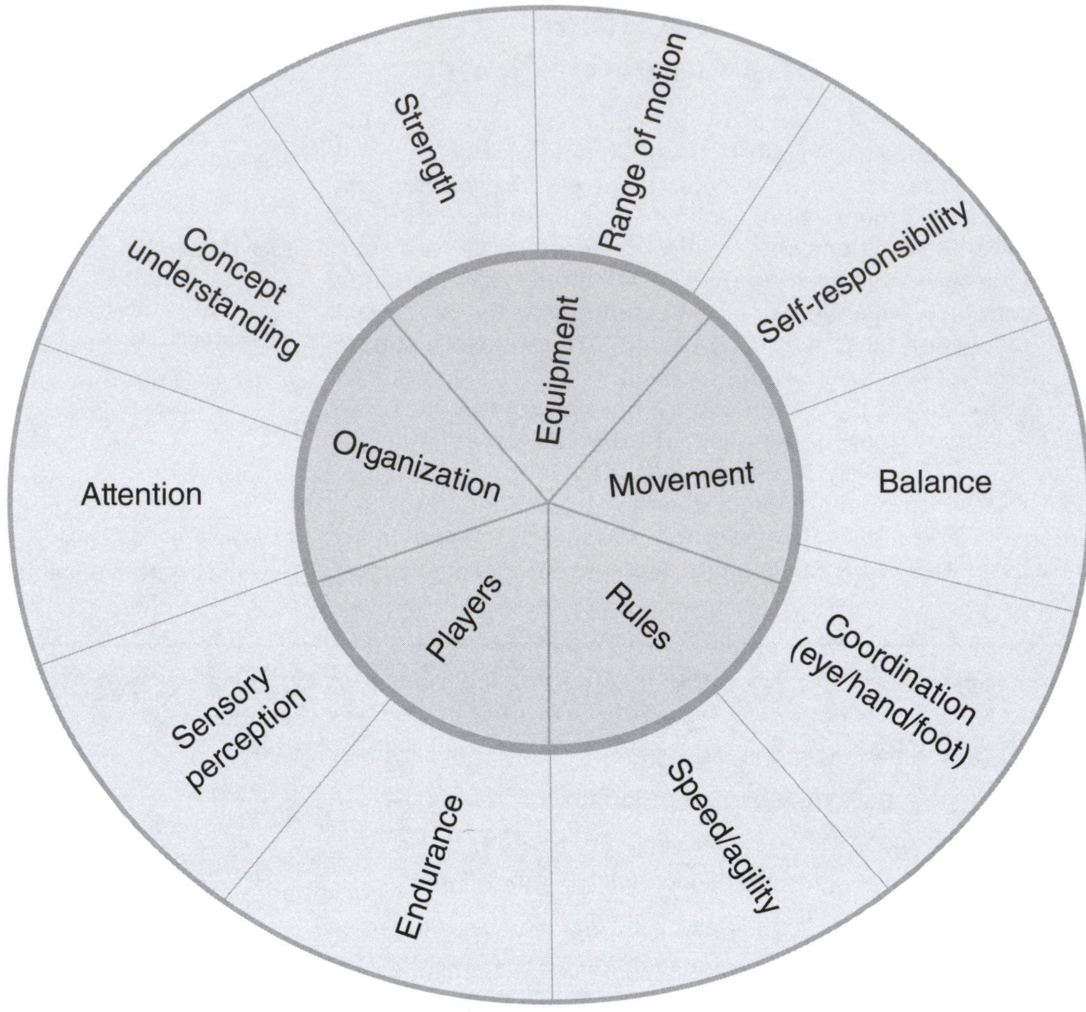

Figure 9.6 The functional components game wheel based on the FAMME model.

As you can see in table 9.3, a game element can be changed to influence several functional components. This is true for any game or sport. For example, in the 4-square game just described, changing the equipment might be beneficial for variations in strength, range of motion, balance, eye–hand coordination, speed, agility, and visual perception. As discussed earlier under organizational elements, the volleyball court size or net height is changed in competitive volleyball depending on gender and if players are standing or sitting. In goalball (figure 9.7), all players must wear blindfolds to equalize the playing field and allow

THINK BACK

1. Select any game or sport that Jim Nasium will be teaching and identify for him the functional components required for the activity and their relative importance (similar to the example in figure 9.5).
2. What variations based on the games elements might Jim make for this activity?

Table 9.3 Capability Differences, Game Elements, and Variation Possibilities for the Game of 4-Square

Capability differences	Game element	Variation possibilities
Strength	Equipment	Use lighter or heavier balls.
	Organization	Increase or decrease spaces.
	Rules	Catch or hit from rolling to multiple bounces to no bounces.
Range of motion	Organization	Increase or decrease space.
	Equipment	Increase or decrease size of ball or the use of an extension.
	Players	Use partners in square.
Balance and posture control	Equipment	Increase or decrease base of support with the use of a chair, walker, or wall.
	Movements	Play sitting on the ground or in a chair.
Eye–hand coordination	Equipment	Increase or decrease size of ball. Use extensions (e.g., rackets, hockey sticks).
	Movement	Touch and push; catch and throw; strike and volley.
Speed and agility	Equipment	Increase or decrease size or weight of equipment.
	Organization	Increase or decrease size of playing space or change shape of space.
	Players	Increase or decrease the number of players.
Endurance	Rules	Rotate out for rest if fatigued.
	Organization	Team members or partners rotate after each hit.
Concept understanding	Organization	Increase or decrease the number of squares.
	Rules	Increase or decrease the number of rules.
	Players	Use partners or teams.
Sensory perception	Equipment	Increase or decrease the size of the equipment. Use equipment with sound or a bell.
	Movements	Rolling, catching, striking, or use extensions.
	Organization	Increase or decrease the playing area.
Attention	Organization	Play 2-square.
	Rules	Play for short time period then rotate.
	Players	Decrease number of players.
Self-responsibility	Rules	Increase time of activity.

for fair competition. Players are provided with blindfolds regardless of their visual acuity. Competitions may be divided by men, women, adults, or children to create equitable teams for meets. However, in recreational play teams are often mixed. Variations, in both games and sports, are designed to create optimal challenges and successful experiences for all.

Figure 9.7 Goalball is designed for individuals with differing visual abilities but can be an exciting and dynamic sport played by all.

SUMMARY

Play is important for the health and well-being of humans at all ages. By extension, playful games and sports can be employed by all individuals to gain knowledge and skills and to reinforce previous learning. However, given the competitive structure of games and sports, caution must be used. Only when players have a chance of being successful or winning are games and sports positive experiences. Through analyzing participants' functional skills, elements of any game or sport can be modified to meet purposeful educational outcomes. The nature of these modifications is limited only by the practitioner's imagination. Well-crafted games can enhance the enjoyment, challenge, engagement, and learning for individuals of any age.

What Do You Think?

1. Using the game elements form, diagram a traditional sport you have played. Now examine this sport and create variations based on the functional components (e.g., variations in strength, flexibility, endurance).
2. Look at table 8.5 in the previous chapter. Examine each of the variations listed in the table. What functional components might each variation support? What game elements could each variation relate to?
3. Determine a purpose for playing a game. Now make up a new game of your own using the games element model.

Game Elements Form

Game elements	Possible variations
Purpose	
Equipment	
Players	
Movement patterns	
Organization	
Rules	

What Would You Do?

Scenario 9.1

One of the students in Jim's classes next year is Jason, a great kid who loves sports and is an avid football fan. Jason uses a wheelchair and has spina bifida; he also has a shunt in his head. Jason has not missed a Monday night football game in five years, a fact he's very proud of. He is also a pretty good student and maintains a B average. During middle school he dealt with a few bouts of depression, as many students do in dealing with puberty, girls, school dances, and social pressures. He gets along well with his peers and has a dog named Hank that is his best friend. Extremely interested in competitive sports and coaching, Jason hopes to help with the school's football team; his dream is to be an assistant coach by his senior year. Jason also attends a wheelchair sports camp every summer and enjoys water skiing, football, and basketball. Jim is looking forward to working with Jason but knows very little about spina bifida and is concerned about Jason's safety in class.

1. Based on what you know about Jason and what you know about spina bifida from appendix A, what might be Jason's functional capabilities?
2. If Jason is enrolled in Jim's general physical education class, what modifications will need to be made for the activities Jim will be teaching?

Scenario 9.2

Valeri Parker, a fourth-grade teacher, loves working with her students in movement experiences and takes her class for physical education three times per week. This year she has two students with disabilities in her class. One young girl, Marta, was diagnosed with fetal alcohol syndrome when she was born. She is a bright young girl but has some general overall delays in her development. She loves to play outside and enjoys the swings most of all. Diego is from Mexico and speaks very little English; he is a bit shy but seems to be getting more comfortable as he gets to know the classroom and other children. There are several other students who speak Spanish in Valeri's class, and she has some conversational skills in Spanish herself. Diego, who was diagnosed with fragile X at birth, loves music and running and enjoys follow-the-leader type games. Valeri is interested in working on cooperation skills in her physical education classes. (She has the following equipment available: 3 playground balls, 5 jump ropes, 4 foam noodles, 20 beanbags, 20 carpet squares, 3 beach balls, 3 foam balls, 2 plastic bats, a large parachute, and several cones.)

1. What functional abilities might Marta and Diego have? How might these abilities relate to other students in the class?
2. Using the game elements model as a guide, create a game (or change a game you are familiar with) for Valeri to use in her physical education class that will teach cooperation and communication skills. Check your activity by answering the Questions to Ask When Making Modifications. Also, does the activity meet the guidelines for success?

CHAPTER 10

Health-Related Fitness and Conditioning

Photo courtesy of David Punia.

LEARNING OUTCOMES

After completing this chapter, you should be able to

- explain the connection between physical fitness and health for all individuals;
- name the key components of physical fitness and exercise programs;
- describe general modifications to the principles of fitness conditioning; and
- apply exercise prescription strategies to fitness programming for individuals with disabilities.

INCLUDING ALL INDIVIDUALS

FitnessFirst is the local health and fitness club for the community of Lowden. Sandra Smith has just started as the new director of fitness programming at the club this past June. She has come to the facility with extensive expertise in fitness programming and a desire to increase the number and types of programs offered. This last week, Ricardo has come to the club interested in becoming a member. Ricardo is 43 years old and has some muscular weakness and fatigue caused by multiple sclerosis. Ricardo's physician recommended that he begin exercising to remain healthy and maintain his independence and capabilities. Ricardo and Sandra set up an appointment to begin planning his program. Wanting to set up the most beneficial program for Ricardo, Sandra wonders what his goals should be. What should his fitness program consist of? What will she need to know about modifying exercises given Ricardo's differences in strength and endurance?

Sandra is well aware of the importance and benefits of adopting an active lifestyle. She also understands the link between being physically active and living a quality life. She knows that quality of life is a multidimensional and complex evaluation of life experience that involves general health and functioning. Quality of life also typically includes two other factors: self-esteem and sense of personal well-being.

Convincing evidence supports the idea that exercise is important to overall health and well-being for all individuals. These benefits are varied and include both physical and psychosocial outcomes. According to the Surgeon General's Report (U.S. Department of Health and Human Services [USDHHS], 2000), the physical benefits include increased muscular strength, flexibility, cardiovascular endurance, and weight reduction. Physical activity also reduces the risk of heart disease and such chronic conditions as hypertension, diabetes, osteoporosis, and degenerative joint disease. Physical activity goes beyond these physical benefits to further enhance quality of life, promoting psychological well-being. Exercise enhances general mood, reduces feelings of depression and isolation, and increases self-esteem.

All of this considered, it is easy to see that exercise benefits contribute significantly to quality of life and that people of all ages and abilities can benefit from regular physical activity. Unfortunately, despite the known benefits of physical activity, most people in the United States do not exercise regularly in a way that fosters increased health and wellness. Furthermore, compared to people without disabilities, individuals with significant disabilities have higher rates of chronic conditions and lower rates of recommended health behaviors, including physical activity (USDHHS, 2000). Involving individuals in appropriate and well-designed physical fitness programs is critical to helping them make physical activity and fitness a regular part of their lives.

DID YOU KNOW?

According to Healthy People 2010, 29 percent of people with "disabilities" and 23 percent of people without disabilities reported no leisure-time physical activity.

PHYSICAL FITNESS GOALS

People have many different reasons for exercising. For some, participation in fitness activities provides the health-related benefits we have described. The primary health-related fitness goals are to lower the risk of developing health problems and preventable disease and to avoid premature death. A person can be well even if he or she has differences in movement capabilities, whether these are caused by a particular experience or factors such as cerebral palsy, injury to the spinal cord and paralysis, or advanced age (figure 10.1). Disabilities are not considered illnesses or deficiencies. Regardless of ability level, age, or level of experience, exercise benefits can lead to wellness.

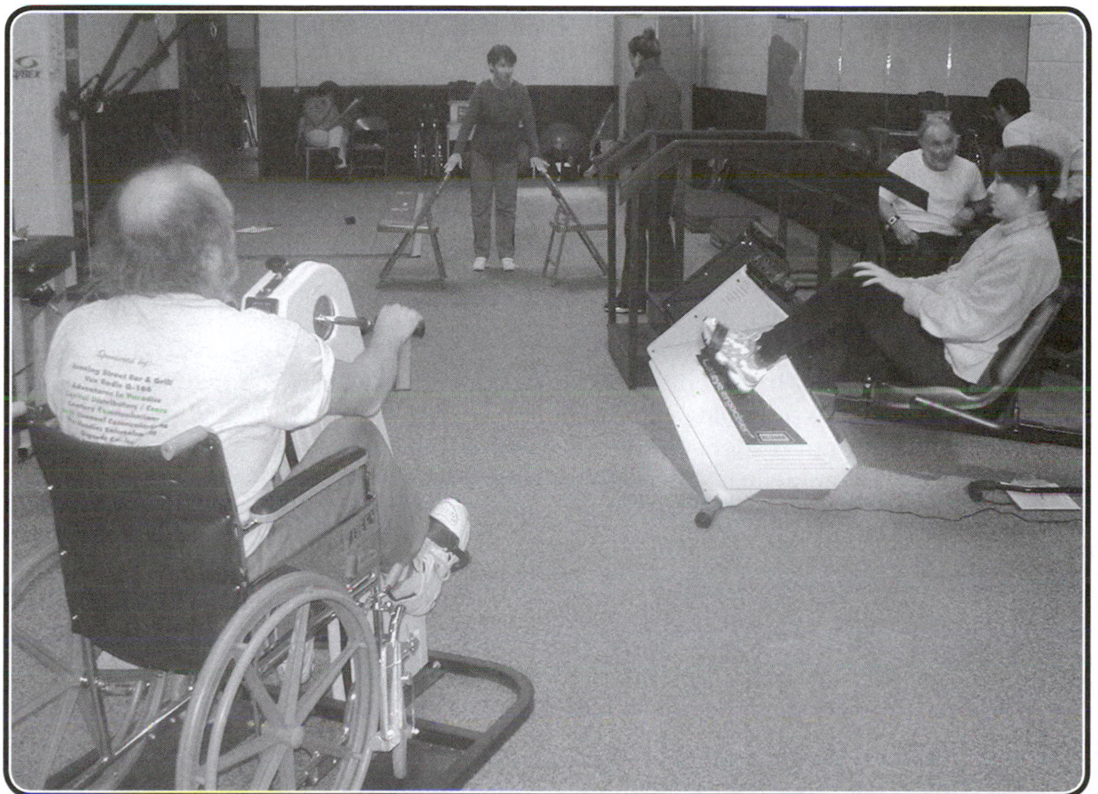

T. Bolduc, courtesy of I.D.E.A.L.

Figure 10.1 Individuals of diverse abilities with different goals for exercising can each benefit from exercising for wellness.

For some people with disabilities, fitness improvement is related more to efficiently conducting and completing activities of daily living. Improvements in strength, flexibility, and balance can increase the functional competence and level of independence in such tasks as cleaning, dressing, and preparing meals. For others, fitness might be based on the desire to achieve greater levels of sport performance and achievement. Athletes who incorporate fitness and conditioning activities into their sport-specific training do so with the hope of increased success. Increases in strength, flexibility, and endurance can result in increased speed, power, and overall performance in sport activities.

IMPLICATIONS FOR PHYSICAL ACTIVITY PRACTITIONERS

Physical activity practitioners agree on the importance and need for physical fitness, but not all practitioners have the complete knowledge and skills needed to include all individuals in fitness activities and programs. Many physical activity practitioners are familiar with developing programs for most people, but including individuals with disabilities and modifying programs to achieve meaningful fitness outcomes can present significant challenges for some. To include participants with disabilities into their fitness or exercise programs, practitioners must consider the type of fitness activity, the capabilities of the participant, and the context in which fitness activities take place. We recommend the following guidelines for practitioners considering inclusive fitness activities:

- **Increase knowledge regarding the foundation of fitness programming.** Practitioners should know the components of fitness and the general training principles associated with fitness development. They should understand the considerations for exercise prescription (how often, how much, which activity best meets the participant's goals) and keep abreast of the evolving recommendations for health and fitness forwarded by professional organizations such as the American College of Sports Medicine (www.acsm.org), the President's Council on Physical Fitness and Sport (www.fitness.gov), and other professional organizations with guiding standards for practice.

- **Understand exercise implications for individuals with disabilities.** Practitioners must know which activities and exercises are meaningful and appropriate for participants with disabilities considering their present activity status and desired fitness outcomes. In addition to understanding which goals and activities are recommended for their participants, practitioners should also know the exercise implications and activity contraindications for these individuals with disabilities. For example, although most individuals with disabilities display similar physiological responses to exercise, some (e.g., people with spinal cord injuries) might not respond in the same way regarding heart rate response and heat dissipation. General guidelines are available from disability sport organizations and sport programs (appendix C). Other publications, such as Durstine, Moore, Painter, & Roberts' (2009) *ACSM's Exercise Management for People with Chronic Diseases and Disabilities*, are available to educate practitioners and participants with disabilities on exercise implications and considerations.

- **Assess participants' readiness to exercise.** Before participants begin any fitness program, practitioners should complete a health screening or appraisal (figure 10.2). Assessing the exercise readiness of all participants is critical to ensuring a safe program. Participants (and those closely associated with them) should be educated about the nature of fitness development, the specifics of the program, and the implications or inherent risks associated with exercising. It is common practice for practitioners to obtain informed consent from those potential exercisers indicating they are fully aware of the benefits and risks involved and are choosing to engage in the program. Next, practitioners should obtain a medical release form from a physician who knows the participant's medical history, current health status, and state of readiness to exercise. Within this health appraisal, practitioners should assess the current fitness status of the individual. Baseline fitness data provides information about exercises that might be contraindicated and gives insight regarding program direction and possible exercise and modifications.

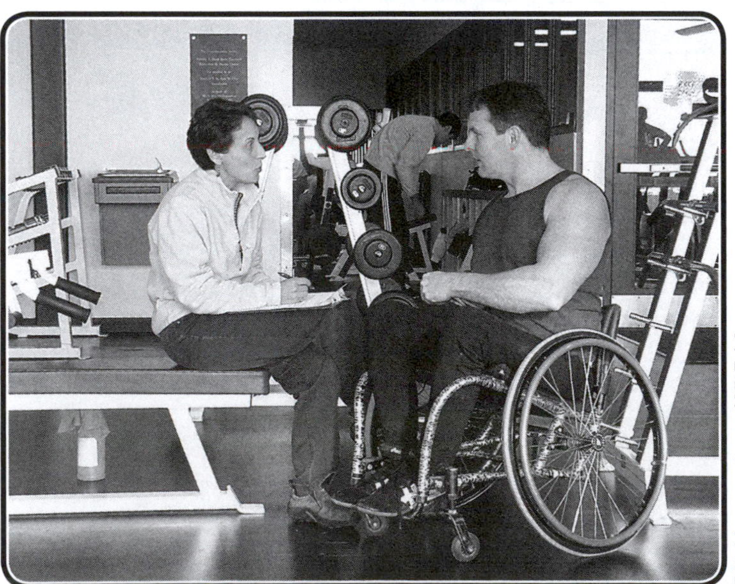

T. Bolduc, courtesy of I.D.E.A.L.

Figure 10.2 Practitioners must obtain important personal and medical information from participants (or others in the participant's support network) to ensure safe and appropriate exercise programming.

- **Help participants set realistic and appropriate fitness goals.** Once the practitioner has a basic understanding of fitness programming for individuals with disabilities and knowledge of a participant's readiness to exercise, identifying realistic and meaningful fitness goals is the next step. For instance, the goal of one participant in a physical education class might be to perform a correct stretch without bouncing; another participant's goal might be to perform a new stretch or exercise. An adult exercising in a fitness center may want to increase the time spent walking on a treadmill, while another participant may want to increase speed and percent grade on a treadmill. Practitioners must know how to assist participants in identifying outcomes that are attainable within the parameters of the exercise program so that participants remain motivated and adhere to their physical activity program. Goals that are unreasonable considering the participant's current exercise level and abilities or that are unattainable in the given period of time designated serve only to frustrate and disappoint participants, sometimes causing them to drop out of the program.

THINK BACK

Think back to Sandra Smith and Ricardo at the FitnessFirst Health Club.

1. Sandra has a strong foundation in fitness and knows her field well. What are the three other implications for programming she must consider in designing a program for Ricardo?
2. What information might Sandra want to gather?
3. How might she go about setting appropriate goals for Ricardo? What should these goals focus on?

TRAINING PRINCIPLES

For participants in exercise programs to meet their fitness goals, practitioners need to consider training principles known to elicit fitness improvement. These principles help practitioners guide participants on how the program or exercise sessions should be developed and progressed. An understanding of the concepts of exercise science has served as the foundation for these principles of exercise conditioning. The principles define a range of recommendations regarding the appropriate quantity and mode of exercise that can safely lead participants toward personal fitness goals. These guidelines define the frequency, intensity, type, and progression of the exercise program.

- **Overload and progression.** Overload refers to the load or amount of resistance placed on the body (or body system). Over time, the body adapts and becomes accustomed to the load and resistance placed on it so that eventually no additional benefit takes place. For continued fitness gains to occur, the load or amount of stress placed on the body or system must increase. The progression of this overload is a critical factor in how effective training regimes are in promoting fitness goals. Practitioners must understand how to progress overload for maximal benefit and safety.
- **The FITT principle.** The FITT (frequency, intensity, time, type) principle is used to describe how exercise training should be planned to promote maximum benefit for participants. For any participant involved, practitioners must consider how often the exercise or activity should be performed (frequency) and how hard the exercise should be (intensity). Other factors such as the duration of the activity (time) and the mode (type) of activity must be considered in terms of improving a particular component of fitness. The progressive overload of these variables can and does differ depending on which component of fitness is targeted. In the next section we describe these fitness components and how the FITT principle applies to each.

COMPONENTS OF FITNESS AND STRATEGIES FOR INCLUSIVE PROGRAMMING

A comprehensive and well-rounded approach to fitness includes exercises that develop flexibility, muscular strength, muscular endurance, and cardiorespiratory fitness. Although personal fitness goals and individual capabilities will influence which one of these areas is emphasized, each of them is important for overall health and well-being. Inclusive fitness programming involves integrating knowledge of the general principles of exercise training and participant needs with the skills and competency required for modifying exercise plans. To meet the needs of participants with disabilities, individualization of exercise programs must involve decisions about the appropriateness of fitness activities, tailoring of exercise principles, and adaptation of exercise techniques.

Flexibility Training

An important component of fitness is flexibility, which involves the ability of a joint and the muscles and tendons surrounding it to move freely through a full range of motion (ROM). Optimal flexibility allows a joint to move efficiently. Although some individuals with disabilities might not have full range of motion, they should have enough movement of the joint to perform functional tasks. For instance, someone with increased muscle tone caused by spasticity might not be able to flex fully at the hip, but he or she should do flexibility exercises to maintain functional range of motion and the ability to climb stairs safely. The importance of flexibility cannot be overlooked when developing an individualized fitness program; integration of stretching exercises should become regular practice.

Flexibility and range of motion is affected by several factors. Limitations might be caused by the structure of the joint and properties of the connective tissue (e.g., adhesions, scar tissue, or contractures), or they might derive from neuromuscular influences, such as spasticity. Other influences on flexibility include genetics, age, gender, temperature, pain, and balance of opposing muscle groups (ACSM, 2011).

Static stretching, the most common flexibility-training method, involves lengthening a muscle group and maintaining a stretched position for a set period of time. Bouncing movements or ballistic stretching is usually not recommended for general fitness programming. Although flexibility exercises can help maintain or improve range of motion, flexibility can be improved only up to a point. Table 10.1 outlines the training principles applied to flexibility.

Table 10.1 Training Principles Applied to Flexibility

Training variable	General recommendation
Frequency	Before and after each exercise session or activity; minimum 3 days per week
Intensity	To subjective sensation of tension—not past point of pain
Time	10-30 seconds for flexibility (not warm-up); 2 or 3 repetitions each
Type	Static stretch of major muscle groups Dynamic stretching for sport performance
Overload	Slight increase in intensity and stretch point; increasing number of repetitions and increasing frequency
Progression	Begin slow and easy moving into stretch; major core muscles first, then to extremities and smaller muscle groups

Modifications for Flexibility Training

During flexibility training, the frequency of a stretching program might be gradually increased to daily sessions, especially for people with joint-limiting conditions such as contractures, spasticity, or arthritis. The intensity of the stretch can be modified by increasing or decreasing the degree of stretch, holding a static stretch for a longer or shorter time, or increasing or decreasing the number of repetitions (figure 10.3). For individuals with spasticity, a more rhythmic and reciprocal shortening and lengthening of the muscle might be most effective for promoting relaxation and more optimal lengthening of the muscle. The number of repetitions might also be gradually increased, especially if the stretch is held for shorter durations. Along with making variations to the FITT principles, modifications can also be made based on underlying functional differences, as described in chapter 7. Table 10.2 shows modifications for stretching based on variations in the functional capabilities.

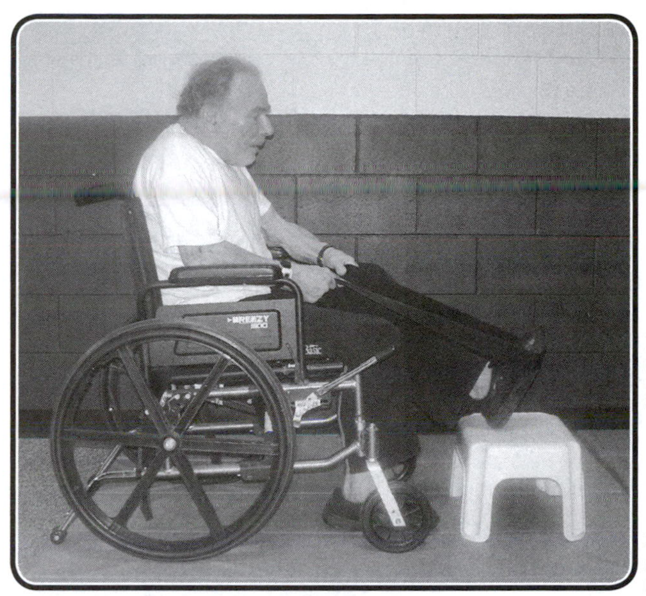

T. Bolduc, courtesy of I.D.E.A.L.

Figure 10.3 The intensity and duration of a stretch can be increased through the use of assistive straps.

Table 10.2 Modifications for Flexibility Training

Capability difference	Modification
Balance	Perform stretch sitting or lying down. Hold wall while standing or use wall for trunk support while sitting on mat.
Coordination	Use mirror for visual feedback. Verbal feedback from others for body or limb position. Manual guidance for appropriate position or movement.
Strength	Self-assist movement of limb or joint with other limb or hand. Obtain assistance from another participant.
Flexibility	Use strap or stable structure to self-assist in stretch. Position body to allow gravity to assist stretch. Obtain assistance from another participant for passive stretch. Use proprioceptive neuromuscular facilitation (PNF) technique if trained and knowledgeable.
Endurance	Require fewer repetitions.
Concept understanding	Use manual guidance. Incorporate visuals such as pictures. Employ peer model and support.
Attention	Count to specific number for stretch completion. Establish stretching routine.
Sensory perception	Use verbal feedback for technique.
Self-responsibility	Use recording form for monitoring and reinforcing.

Note: Difference in speed and agility are not critical to successful stretching.

Consider Ricardo from Sandra's FitnessFirst program. Using appendix A and what you know about flexibility, answer the following questions.

1. What might be the focus of Ricardo's program related to stretching?
2. Using the FITT principle, how would you develop a stretching program for Ricardo?
3. What special considerations or modifications might you want to make for Ricardo?

Muscular Strength and Endurance: Resistance Training

Two important aspects of health-related fitness are muscular strength and muscular endurance. Muscular strength is the ability of a muscle or group of muscles to exert maximal force against resistance. Muscular endurance is the ability of a muscle or group of muscles to exert force against submaximal resistance over a period of time. Increases in each of these areas are important to maintain strong and dense bones, prevent chronic back problems, prevent muscle injury, and, for some people, to increase or maintain function and independence.

An individual's muscular strength and endurance might be influenced by deconditioning, neuromuscular factors such as motor unit recruitment, lack of reciprocal inhibition and spasticity, or progressive muscular conditions (ACSM, 2011). Muscular strength and endurance is commonly developed through resistance training involving manual resistance (e.g., push-ups), free weights (using dumbbells or cuff weights), resistance bands or pulleys, and exercise machines. Practitioners and participants must employ proper safety measures when doing resistance training exercises. Table 10.3 illustrates the application of the FITT principle to resistance training.

Table 10.3 Training Principles Applied to Muscular Strength and Endurance

Training variable	General recommendation
Frequency	3 to 4 times per week with 1 day of rest between sessions
Intensity	Light to moderate, 40-70% projected maximal effort
Time	3-5 sets of 3-7 repetitions for strength; 12-20 for endurance
Type	Body weight, single-joint to multijoint activities, resistance exercises
Overload	For strength, slowly increase level of resistance to greater level. For endurance, increase the number of repetitions or time of repetition or decrease rest interval between activities.
Progression	Progress slowly to avoid injury.

Modifications for Resistance Training

Although overload through progressive resistance exercise is often recommended, participants with progressive neuromuscular conditions might have fitness goals geared more toward maintaining strength rather than increasing it. Not only can the FITT principles be modified, increased rest between sets or sessions might further reduce overload and possible fatigue or loss of muscle function. Frequency of resistance exercise sessions can be manipulated based on participant needs and goals. Increasing frequency beyond the two or three days per week typically recommended should involve either alternating muscle groups or high- and low-intensity sessions so muscle groups are not overfatigued. For most people, two or three days a week are sufficient regardless of capability or condition. Individualization of resistance exercise can be achieved more readily by altering the variables of intensity and duration. By manipulating the number of repetitions, sets, load, and recovery time, the training load can be modified for different individuals. For instance, beginners or individuals with muscular weakness should train with low or easier training loads by decreasing resistance and increasing repetitions (figure 10.4). Typical recovery periods of two to four minutes can also be modified, depending on goals and capabilities. Shorter periods of exercise might be used to promote endurance, whereas longer recovery times might be appropriate for individuals for whom fatigue is an issue. Because the potential for injury increases with increasing workloads, practitioners must always consider ability differences and take care not to progress participants too quickly or overload them inappropriately. See table 10.4 for modifications for muscular strength and endurance training based on functional differences.

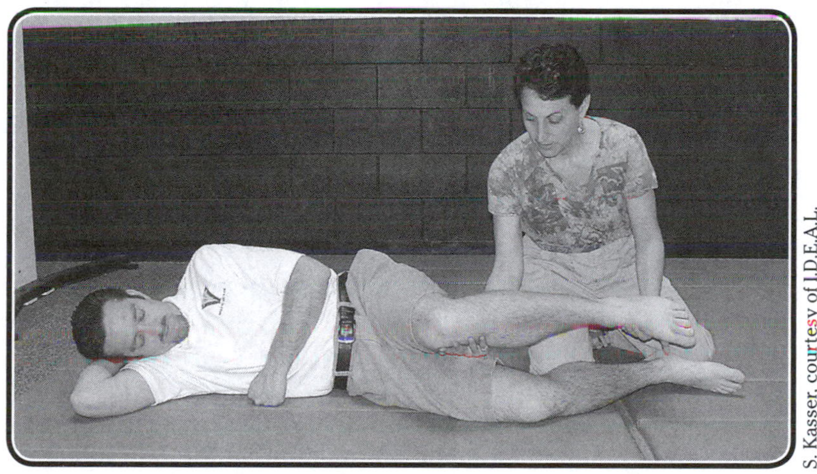

S. Kasser, courtesy of I.D.E.A.L.

Figure 10.4 Having a participant move a limb in an antigravity plane of motion can reduce the resistance or load and help maintain or improve muscular strength.

THINK BACK

Let's return to Ricardo again. Using appendix A and what you know about strength training, answer the following questions regarding Ricardo's strength-training program.

1. What might be the focus of Ricardo's program related to strength training?
2. Using the FITT principle, how would you develop a strength-training program for Ricardo?
3. What special considerations or modifications might you make for Ricardo's strength-training program?

Table 10.4 Modifications for Muscular Strength and Endurance Training

Capability difference	Modification
Balance	Perform exercise sitting. Perform exercise bilaterally (free weight in each hand). Use exercise machines.
Coordination	Use resistance machines that stabilize and require set movement. Use some single-joint exercises to reduce task complexity. Perform unilateral exercise. Use free weights if appropriate to ease control of movement.
Strength	Perform exercise in anti-gravity plane (horizontal movement). Perform in aquatic environment. Use different forms of resistance depending on strength level (gravity, band, or free weight). Employ eccentric contractions as well as concentric contractions.
Flexibility	Strengthen through available range. Strengthen for balance between muscle pairs.
Endurance	Do multijoint versus single-joint exercise, fewer repetitions. Sequence exercises so muscle group isn't fatigued (alternate between upper-and lower-body exercise, agonist and antagonist).
Concept understanding	Use manual guidance. Offer visuals such as pictures. Have peer model and support. Sequence to perform in set routine and easy order (head to toe).
Attention	Count to guide speed of movement (1-2 for concentric; 1-2-3-4 for eccentric). Establish circuit.
Sensory perception	Provide physical guidance, verbal feedback, or mirrors for technique.
Self-responsibility	Use recording form for monitoring and reinforcing.

Note: Differences in speed and agility are not critical to successful strengthening and endurance.

Cardiorespiratory Fitness

Cardiorespiratory, or aerobic, fitness, often considered one of the more important aspects of health-related fitness, is a measure of the heart's ability to pump oxygen-rich blood to the rest of the body. Cardiorespiratory fitness also involves the ability to adjust to and recover from physical activity. Practitioners are well aware that aerobic fitness is crucial for reducing the risk of coronary heart disease, high blood pressure, obesity, diabetes, and other chronic conditions. It also helps maintain functional capabilities, independence, emotional well-being, and life satisfaction.

"The first wealth is health."
—Ralph Waldo Emerson

Practitioners involved in developing fitness programs for individuals with disabilities must be aware of factors that might influence the physiological systems that support aerobic exercise. For instance, some individuals with paralysis caused by a spinal cord injury or multiple sclerosis might have difficulty with cardiorespiratory fitness because of dysfunction of the autonomic nervous system (Durstine, Moore, Painter, & Roberts, 2009). Differences in cardiorespiratory fitness might also be caused by decreased ability to use large muscle movements during activity because of joint pain, muscle weakness, or difficulty in muscle recruitment. Differences in temperature regulation and muscular fatigue might also limit aerobic exercise capacity (Durstine, Moore, Painter, & Roberts, 2009).

People develop and improve cardiorespiratory fitness through engaging in activities that require moving large muscle masses over prolonged periods of time. Swimming, bicycling, jogging, and aerobic dancing are common fitness activities that promote aerobic capacity. The training might involve continuous activity or short bouts of intermittent aerobic activity accumulated over time. Ways to apply the FITT principles to cardiorespiratory fitness are shown in table 10.5.

Table 10.5 Training Principles Applied to Cardiorespiratory Fitness

Training variable	General recommendation
Frequency	3-5 times per week
Intensity	55-90% maximal heart rate (dependent on baseline fitness)
Time	15-60 minutes total (can be accumulated over time)
Type	Walking, jogging, running, dancing, or fitness activities
Overload	Increase speed, time, or tempo.
Progression	Progress slowly in design.

Modifications for Cardiorespiratory Fitness Training

Like the other fitness components, aerobic capacity can be enhanced through gradual overload. To achieve benefit, people should train three to five days per week, regardless of capability. Exercising fewer than three days a week might be meaningful for someone who is extremely deconditioned or unmotivated, but exercise sessions should progress to at least three days for training benefits to occur. Resting between sessions might be necessary for individuals with progressive conditions or fatigue. Lower intensity bouts are also useful to start or for those with excessive fatigue or circulatory problems, heart disease, or history of stroke. Although heart rate and perceived exertion are useful measures for assessing intensity, practitioners should be aware of factors that might render these evaluative methods inappropriate, such as autonomic nervous system differences or certain prescribed medications. Duration of aerobic training can also be manipulated to accommodate individual differences. A participant who is deconditioned might begin with shorter bouts of exercise and gradually increase over time (figure 10.5). Or he or she might begin with an interval training method before progressing to a continuous protocol. Table 10.6 lists other modifications for individual differences in cardiorespiratory fitness based on functional capabilities.

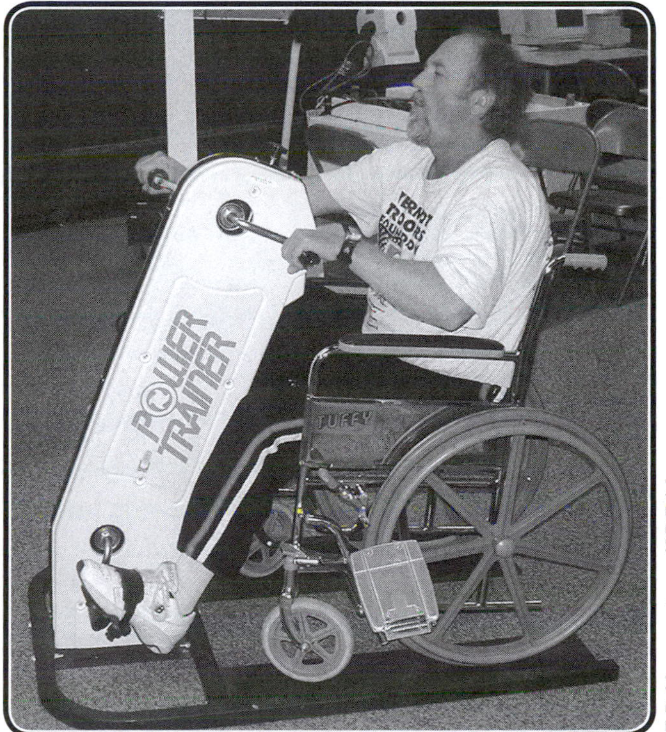

T. Bolduc, courtesy of I.D.E.A.L.

Figure 10.5 Short bouts of aerobic exercise might be appropriate for participants with decreased cardiorespiratory fitness or muscular endurance.

Table 10.6 Modifications for Cardiorespiratory Fitness Training

Capability difference	Modification
Balance	Use stationary or recumbent bike rather than running, or use hand supports on treadmill. Arm ergometer
Coordination	Move in any manner to music for a continuous period of time.
Strength	Use upper body versus lower body or vice versa depending on upper- or lower-extremity strength differences. Offer variations in speed, distance, or rest periods.
Flexibility	Perform through available range; use less resistance (aquatic versus land).
Endurance	Use interval versus continuous training.
Speed	Modify time or distance.
Concept understanding	Use peer to serve as pacer, task sheet, or pictures.
Attention	Employ intervals. Develop aerobic circuit. Use fitness stations.
Sensory perception	Use step test versus mile (1.6 km) run for individual with visual differences; use sighted guide for individuals with low sight.
Self-responsibility	Use recording form to monitor progress and reinforce. Employ peer support for engagement.

Let's think back once more to Ricardo. Using appendix A and what you know about cardiorespiratory fitness training, answer the following questions:

1. What might be the focus of Ricardo's program related to cardiorespiratory development?
2. Using the FITT principles, how would you develop a cardiovascular training program for Ricardo?
3. What special considerations or modifications might you make for Ricardo's cardiorespiratory program?

HEALTH-RELATED FITNESS ACTIVITIES

So far in this chapter we have focused on components and principles related to traditional fitness programs that involve specific exercises and fitness tasks. Do not take this to mean that the only valuable method for fitness improvement is through resistance training, running, or stretching exercises. Individuals of all ability levels have benefited from health-related activities such as aquatic activities (see chapter 11), walking, dancing, and outdoor activities such as hiking, skiing, and snowshoeing (see chapter 12 for outdoor pursuits). In fact, within the past 20 years widespread interest has developed in many alternative forms of fitness enhancement, such as spinning, yoga, and tai chi.

Spinning

Spinning is an indoor aerobic conditioning program using stationary exercise bikes (figure 10.6). Spinning is performed in a group setting and led by an instructor. The benefits of spinning include aerobic conditioning and endurance and increased leg strength. There is less potential for injury or trauma to joints in spinning than in other activities, and this activity might be more motivating for those who appreciate feedback and guidance from others. Spinning also helps people stay in shape during times when cycling outside is not convenient. See table 10.7 for modifications for spinning.

Figure 10.6 Spinning is one option for maintaining health-related fitness.

Table 10.7 Modifications for Spinning

Capability difference	Modification
Strength	Reduce resistance on flywheel.
Balance and posture control	Use recumbent bike.
Concept understanding	Increase verbal cues and feedback.
Attention	Have spinning partner close by.
Endurance	Use shorter bouts or intermittent bouts.
Coordination	Reduce frequency of cadence or pedaling.

Note: The table offers examples of modifications for some of the capability differences that might exist. See table 10.6 for other modification possibilities.

Yoga

Yoga has attracted the attention of people of all ages and ability levels. Nearly all yoga styles are rooted in hatha yoga, a physical discipline that focuses on developing control of the body through various poses. All yoga styles seek to balance the mind, body, and spirit, but they go about it in various ways. Styles might differ in how poses are performed or where attention is focused (e.g., on mastering and holding a posture, on breathing, or on the flow of movement). For instance, Ashtanga yoga emphasizes power and stamina and can be quite physically demanding, whereas Kripalu yoga emphasizes breathing, relaxation, and inner awareness. There are at least 11 popular forms of yoga, and no one style is necessarily better or worse than another. Practitioners thinking of adding yoga to their activity program should find a style that meets participants' needs, focus, and capabilities. See table 10.8 for yoga modifications.

Table 10.8 Modifications for Yoga

Capability difference	Modification
Strength	Choose appropriate style. Practice with one limb or side of body separately. Reduce intensity or space of pose.
Balance and posture control	Widen base of support or open stance more. Hold on to a chair or wall.
Concept understanding	Increase verbal cues and feedback. Offer physical guidance.
Attention	Offer short cues.
Endurance	Reduce time pose is held. Practice few postures.
Coordination	Practice components with a single limb.

Note: The table offers examples of modifications for some of the differences in capability that might exist. See table 10.6 for other modification possibilities.

Tai Chi

The origins of tai chi go back many hundreds of years, but the activity has seen increased popularity over the last decade or so. Many people of all ages, including older adults and individuals with disabilities, use tai chi as a means of exercise. Tai chi can best be described as a moving form of yoga and meditation combined. Originally derived from martial arts, the slow graceful movements of tai chi are designed to focus the mind and breathing through a complex series of maneuvers.

The benefits of tai chi include relaxation, reduced stress, and improved motor control, balance, and flexibility. There are several styles of tai chi, but the Yang style is the most practiced. This style is made up of two substyles: the long form, which has 128 or so separate postures, and the short form. Both forms consist of a number of moves or postures, each joined by a transition or link. Each movement might be very short or made up of a complex sequence of submoves. Although each is an individual definitive element to the form, they flow continually into each other and are not practiced separately. Table 10.9 lists modifications for tai chi.

SUMMARY

The principles of fitness conditioning provide the minimum level of exercise necessary for training benefits to occur. Most of the recommendations related to the training principles and guidelines, however, came out of research involving adults without significant differences

Table 10.9 Modifications for Tai Chi

Capability difference	Modification
Strength	Practice with one limb or side of body separately. Reduce intensity or space of sequence.
Balance and posture control	Hold on to partner or chair. Perform some elements seated. Increase width of stance.
Concept understanding	Provide physical guidance.
Attention	Provide simple cues and concurrent demonstration.
Endurance	Choose short form. Practice subsequences.
Coordination	Slow sequence further.

Note: The table offers examples of modifications for some of the differences in capability that might exist. See table 10.6 for other modification possibilities.

1. Considering Ricardo's goals, what other fitness activities might you plan for him? Why these particular activities?
2. If Ricardo were to participate in spinning, what strategies or modifications might you use to facilitate his success?

in abilities and medical status. Exercise programs should be individualized by considering general principles in relation to information about the participant obtained through assessment and screening. Both the participant's personal goals and health status should be taken into account when planning exercise protocols. It is also important to modify the FITT principle based on age, functional differences, and movement capabilities. Whether the goal is to improve performance in a sport or activity or enhance a participant's ability to improve mobility or perform activities of daily living more independently, practitioners can manipulate the frequency, intensity, and duration of exercise programs to assist each participant in achieving personal goals. Recommendations for exercise should be continually monitored to ensure that participants' programs remain appropriate and safe. Ongoing modifications should be made based on how participants respond to their program and to accommodate any changes in health status or capability.

What Do You Think?

Now that you have learned more about creating inclusive fitness programs, how would you answer these questions about developing Ricardo's exercise program?

1. What might be Ricardo's overall goals related to his personal wellness?
2. How might Sandra Smith create a balanced program of strength, flexibility, and endurance for Ricardo? Try designing a complete exercise program for Ricardo yourself.
3. What barriers might affect Ricardo's progress in his program? How would you help Ricardo overcome these barriers?

What Would You Do?

Scenario 10.1

Marissa is 28 years old and lives with a roommate. During college she studied communications and competed on the volleyball team. Over the winter break of her junior year, she was in a serious car accident when she hit black ice on the road. During the accident she sustained a traumatic brain injury that left her in a coma for a week. After leaving the hospital, Marissa spent five months in rehabilitation, where she relearned how to talk and walk. As a result of her injury, she now has trouble with short-term memory. In addition, her right side is weaker and has some muscle contractures. She can walk with assistance or by using a walker for short distances, but she uses a wheelchair to get around town. She still enjoys physical activity, including water activities and weight training.

1. What kind of program would you design for Marissa?
2. How might Marissa's injury have affected her strength, flexibility, and endurance?
3. What modifications might you want to use in designing a program for her?

Scenario 10.2

Jason teaches seventh grade at Johnson Junior High School. As part of the requirements for seventh grade, all students must be given physical fitness testing. These scores are then reported to the state. Jason uses the Fitnessgram, which includes the following tasks: the pacer or one-mile (1.6 km) walk–run; percent body fat or body mass index; curl-up test; trunk lift; push-up, modified pull-up, or flexed arm hang; sit-and-reach or shoulder stretch.

This year Jason has several students from the middle school sport teams, a few students with limited skill proficiency in most activities, two students with severe obesity, and one with spina bifida who uses a wheelchair.

1. How might Jason develop fitness goals for his students?
2. What types of activities might be appropriate for his class?
3. How might Jason make adaptations in fitness activities in preparing his students to take the Fitnessgram?

CHAPTER 11

Aquatics

Esther M. Ortiz-Stuhr and Luis Columna

LEARNING OUTCOMES

After completing this chapter, you should be able to

- describe general teaching modifications when prescribing activities for individuals with different ability levels;
- apply teaching progressions when providing aquatic activities to individuals with different ability levels; and
- apply the FAMME model to aquatic skills when modifying for individual differences.

INCLUDING ALL INDIVIDUALS

Michael and Jake are a pair of 11-year-old twins who are extremely smart and funny. Their mother, Jenna, has been taking them every Friday to a swimming program at a local YMCA for the past few years. According to Jenna, they love this program because it allows them to participate in fun activities and socialize with other children. They also look forward to seeing the teacher, Mr. Robert, who every Friday receives them with a big smile. Mr. Robert has several years of experience teaching swimming to children with various levels of abilities. However, he has grown particularly fond of the twins because, he says, "they brighten my day." Michael and Jake have weakness in their upper and lower extremities. Both are overweight and, over the past few years, both have lost significant body strength. The two require the use of wheelchairs to move about. It is also sometimes difficult to understand them because of speech differences. At the age of three, Michael and Jake were both diagnosed with muscular dystrophy. According to Jenna, this was sad news for her family because she had lost an uncle with the same health condition.

If you were Mr. Robert, what activities would you teach Michael and Jake in an aquatic environment? What modifications would you need to make for the boys to be successful in aquatic environments? What help and support might be necessary for Michael and Jake's family?

Aquatics can be considered an important gateway into inclusive physical activity. Whether swimming for fitness or participating in aquatic sports or recreational activities, the water opens many doors for participants across the life span. For those with disabilities, the water is often considered the "great equalizer" because temperature, buoyancy, and adapted equipment increase movement capabilities, enjoyment, and success. In this chapter, we will apply the FAMME model to a range of aquatic activities.

OVERVIEW OF AQUATIC SKILLS

Aquatics can offer essential physical activity and be an important lifetime recreational skill for everyone. The water is one of the most beneficial environments for individuals of all ages and abilities (Columna, 2011). For example, the buoyancy of water can help develop strength while allowing for maximum mobility for an individual with limited strength or balance (Yilmaz, Yanardag, Birkan, & Bumin, 2004). Aquatic experiences give individuals with sensory differences a variety of opportunities that help them improve their well-being throughout their life span (Auxter, Pyfer, Zittel, Roth, & Huettig, 2009). Involving people with disabilities in appropriately designed and implemented aquatic activity may introduce these individuals to all the benefits and joys that physical activity can bring (figure 11.1).

Several organizations such as the YMCA, the American Red Cross, and the American Association for Physical Activity and Recreation (AAPAR) have provided opportunities and access to aquatics programs, not only for school-age children but for populations across the life span (Lepore, Gayle, & Stevens, 2007). These organizations believe that every individual, no matter his or her age or ability level, has the right to health, wellness, and quality of life that aquatic environments can provide. These organizations thus offer various credentials

peppi18/fotolia

Figure 11.1 Individuals of all ages and ability levels can participate and enjoy the water.

for aquatics instructors as well as programs serving individuals with varying abilities. Just as important, they have collaborated with other constituent groups in advocating for the rights of individuals with disabilities regarding their participation in aquatic environments.

As discussed in chapter 7, the FAMME model matches modifications to ability differences in an effort to provide optimal challenges and task completion for every participant in a program. When applying the FAMME model to aquatic environments, instructors must demonstrate creativity and forethought. Lepore, Gayle, and Stevens (2007) describe the modifiable components of an aquatics program to include instruction, equipment, strategies, strokes, swim skills, games, recreational skills, and water safety skills. To identify the appropriate adaptations that promote successful participation in aquatic environments, instructors must consider the individual differences of the participant, the complexity of the task, and the existing environmental factors, which can be accomplished by conducting assessment procedures in each of these areas (Columna, 2011).

DID YOU KNOW ?

Swimming consistently ranks as one of the more popular recreational activities in the United States.

WATER COMPETENCE

The ultimate goal of a developmentally appropriate aquatics program is to provide individuals with the skills they need to enjoy different aquatic environments across their life span. Langendorfer and Bruya (1995) called this concept "water competence." Water competence requires individuals to demonstrate proficiency in a variety of aquatic skills. In other words, all individuals are expected to learn how to swim and be able to use what they have learned in a variety of aquatic settings, such as canoeing, kayaking, boating, diving, and water games.

Langendorfer and Bruya introduced the water competence model (figure 11.2) as a way to understand the many opportunities aquatic settings can offer. For example, if a person develops appreciation for aquatic environments, he or she might participate in aquatic sporting events or in a variety of recreational aquatic opportunities.

Providing a variety of satisfying aquatic opportunities to individuals with disabilities helps to expand choices for a lifetime of physical activity. For a person to enjoy the different opportunities that are presented in the water competence model, swimming might be a prerequisite, although swimming is not the only way that people can enjoy the water. For example, individuals with disabilities who are unable to swim or access the water for a variety of reasons can still enjoy floating on an inner tube while vacationing with their family (figure 11.3).

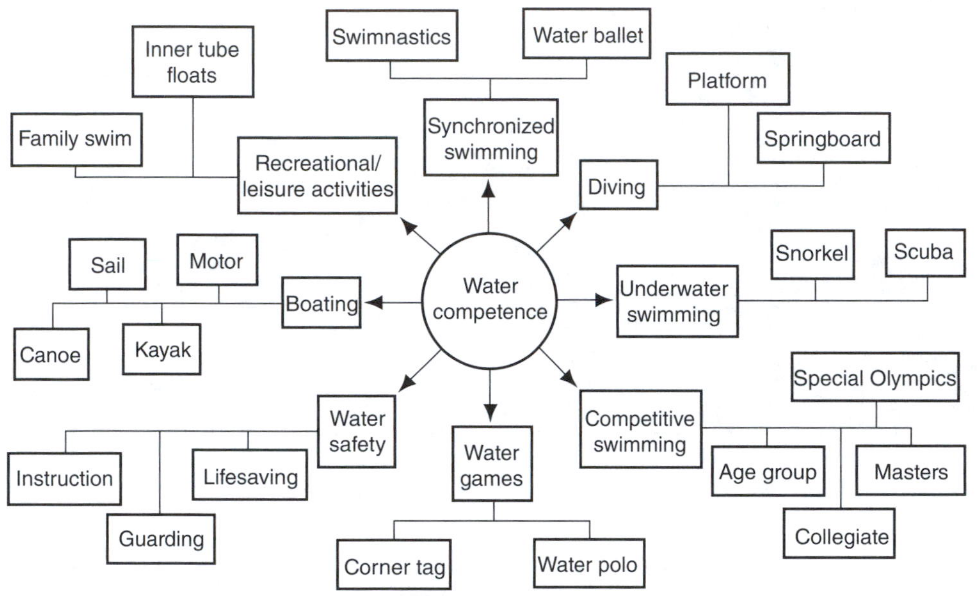

Figure 11.2 The water competence model.

Reprinted, by permission, from S.J. Langendorfer and L.D. Bruya, 1995, *Aquatic readiness: Developing water competence in young children* (Champaign, IL: Human Kinetics), 3.

© Kevin Tietz | Dreamstime.com

Figure 11.3 Floating on inner tubes offers many people the chance to relax and enjoy the water with family and friends.

1. Considering the water competence model, do you believe Michael and Jake can become water competent? Why or why not?
2. In what ways do you think the twins could use their water competence to participate in inclusive aquatic activity?

IMPLICATIONS FOR AQUATIC ACTIVITY PRACTITIONERS

The role of the aquatics instructor is to teach individuals skills that will allow them to enjoy and be safe in and around aquatic environments. In doing so, participants can have fun and take part in aquatic activities that promote health and maintain functional abilities across the life span. A quality aquatics program includes information regarding rules (e.g., safety), instruction in a variety of swimming strokes, and opportunities to explore different recreational activities. We recommend the following guidelines when considering inclusive aquatic activities:

- **An aquatics program should provide participants with knowledge and skills that will allow them to participate in activities safely.** This includes introducing them to safety rules, appropriate use of equipment, and various swimming techniques. According to Columna (2011), when instructors assess the present level of performance of individuals with disabilities in aquatic environments, they should include the cognitive domain to determine what the individual knows about aquatic environments. In other words, instructors can assess knowledge of rules and appropriate equipment and can ask participants to verbally and physically demonstrate different swimming strokes.
- **Along with teaching rules and safety, participants should be familiarized with the aquatic settings and recreational opportunities that they might access.** If we take another look at Langendorfer and Bruya's water competence model (figure 11.2), we see that participants may learn to swim, but they may also learn basic skills for underwater swimming, competitive swimming, synchronized swimming, water games, or sailing. For individuals with greater functional ability, serving as an instructor, lifeguard assistant, or lifeguard might also be options.
- **To be water competent, individuals should be taught fundamental aquatic readiness skills (figure 11.4).** In other words, before trying to teach a participant different swimming strokes, the instructor must not only teach basic aquatic skills but also ensure that the individual is behaviorally and internally ready to learn them. This readiness should be assessed for several reasons. First, participants' attitudes toward physical activity—including aquatics—can determine how motivated they are to be physically active. Second, participants must interact with other participants, which—depending on their ability—can involve many other affective factors (Columna, 2011).
- **As we have mentioned, when trying to apply the FAMME model in aquatic environments, one of the first things to consider are factors related to the individual participant.** These considerations include knowing the present level of performance of the participant (what he or she can do), the particular aquatic interests of the participant, and any aquatic experience the participant has had. For instance, does the individual feel comfortable in the water? Is he or she afraid of waves? Has he or she been exposed to a pool, lake, river, or ocean? It might be that the individual has had experience with a body of water that has influenced his or her comfort level in similar water.

DID YOU KNOW ?

Angela Madsen, founder and director of the California Adaptive Rowing Program, was the first individual with a "disability" to row across two oceans, collecting a host of records in the process.

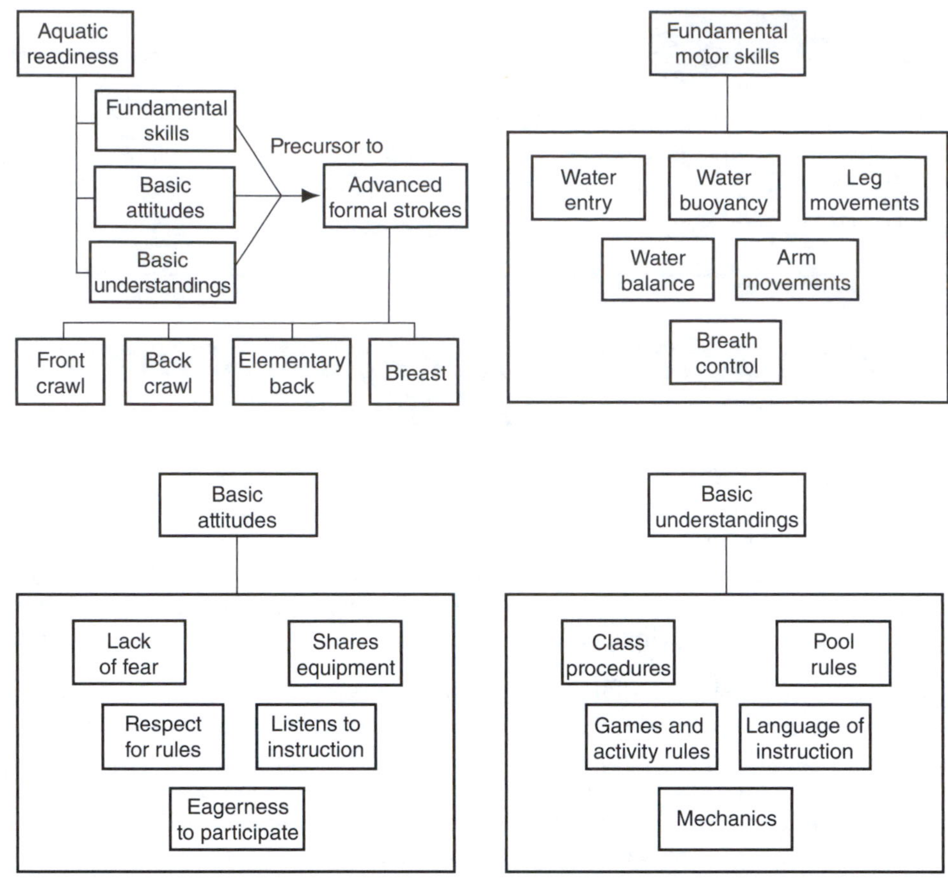

Figure 11.4 Water readiness not only includes fundamental aquatic skills but also attitudes toward participation in aquatic activities.

Reprinted, by permission, from S.J. Langendorfer and L.D. Bruya, 1995, *Aquatic readiness: Developing water competence in young children* (Champaign, IL: Human Kinetics), 5.

• **Transferring from the pool deck into the pool can be challenging for some individuals with physical or mobility differences.** Thus instructors must identify what type of device (e.g., chair, crutches, and walker) the participant uses to move as well as how independently or what level of assistance the participant may need to access the water. For some, transfers are a critical component of aquatic instruction and must be considered when working with individuals with disabilities.

There are different types of transfers and transfer techniques. Knowing the appropriate body mechanics and steps to follow when undertaking a transfer is key to increasing safety and minimizing the risk of injury for everyone involved. Practitioners unfamiliar with how to safely and effectively assist participants with transfers should collaborate with physical therapists or other health care providers well versed in these techniques for guidance and practice. Conversely, for participants with high functional ability, strength, and coordination, aquatics instructors should become knowledgeable of the different transferring techniques and spend time teaching these techniques to those individuals who will be able to independently transfer (Columna, 2011; Lepore, Gayle, & Stevens, 2007). Beyond person-assisted transfers, an array of equipment is available that can facilitate access to the water (figure 11.5). Pool lifts, ramps, transfer walls, stairs, mats, and zero depth (movable) floors can also help a participant transition from the pool deck to the water. However, as independent as a person may be, it still remains important to provide instruction on how to use these devices safely.

Figure 11.5 Many community pools now have pool lifts that allow greater access for all participants.

THINK BACK

Now that you have learned about aquatic readiness, skill development, and different transfers from the pool deck to the water, try to answer these questions:

1. What skills do you think Mr. Robert decided to teach Michael and Jake at the start of the program? Why do you think he might have decided to teach the boys these skills first?
2. How else might Mike and Jake use the water competence they attain beyond working with Mr. Robert?

MODIFICATIONS FOR AQUATIC ACTIVITIES

After identifying the critical elements integral to performing a variety of aquatic skills, instructors may need to make targeted modifications that increase capability and guarantee success for aquatic participants. In the following section we provide examples of how the FAMME model applies to some common aquatic activities and strokes. In all cases, the practitioner must discuss all modifications with participants and, when appropriate, include them in the process of planning and selecting the modifications.

Floating

Floating is a fundamental aquatic skill. Learning how to float is extremely important for water safety. Floating is also a basic skill underlying the learning of more advanced swimming skills such as the backstroke. Floating includes the front float and back float, and also involves learning how to recover from each floating position (i.e., returning to a standing position). Some participants might benefit from learning how to combine the arm and leg motions by holding onto the wall, using other flotation devices (e.g., floating belt or mat), or receiving physical support (e.g., holding underneath arms, back, and hips) from the instructor. Participants with poor head control can focus on the back float or use a snorkel (with supervision) for the front float. Table 11.1 lists other modifications for individuals with capability differences.

Table 11.1 Modifications for Floating

Capability difference	Modification
Body strength	Different depth of water
Balance and postural control	Flotation devices Physical support
Concept understanding	Break down skill Physical guidance
Flexibility	Physical assistance for positioning Flotation devices

Submersions and Breath Control

Strokes performed in a prone position typically require submerging the mouth, nose, and eyes and controlling the breath. Moreover, some skills and aquatic activities (e.g., scuba diving) require submerging the entire body. These skills might be challenging or scary for some individuals. However, this is an important skill to teach not only for safety but as a prerequisite skill for advanced strokes such as the butterfly. When teaching an individual to put his or her face in the water, the teaching progression should be specific and thoughtfully paced according to the comfort level and readiness of the participant. A flotation device (e.g., foam noodle) can be used to support the participant's body as he or she bends forward to practice breathing (Lepore, Gayle, & Stevens, 2007). Instructors can also engage participants in games to help them acquire these readiness skills. Table 11.2 lists modifications for submersion and breath control.

Front Crawl

The front crawl (i.e., freestyle) is the most efficient of the swimming strokes (Thomas, 2005). This stroke requires swimmers to be in a horizontal position and combine alternating arms and legs actions (i.e., flutter kicking) to propel the body from one place to another (American Red Cross, 2004). Performing the front crawl also involves submerging the face, controlling the breath, and breathing on the side. There are many modifications to employ to help teach the front crawl (table 11.3). Because making multiple changes at once can be confusing and difficult for some participants (American Red Cross, 2004), it is best to start by modifying one component of the skill and progressively changing other components one at a time. Beyond using flotation devices to assist some participants with buoyancy, participants can experiment with different arm strokes and kicking patterns depending on the functional differences they have in body structure or movement capabilities.

Table 11.2 Modifications for Submersion and Breath Control

Capability difference	Modification
Body strength	Support body and head when blowing bubbles. Use face mask and snorkel. Provide assistance by manually closing the lips, lifting head when breathing on front; or pushing down on the nonbreathing shoulder when breathing on the side.
Sensory perception	Provide tactile cues or auditory cues.
Balance and postural control	Provide support to the individual by holding his or her body, or have individual hold onto pool side or ladder.
Concept understanding	Teach through games (e.g., motor boat, Ping-Pong). Use pictures.
Attention	Use sinkable toys.

Table 11.3 Modifications for the Front Crawl Stroke

Capability difference	Modification
Body strength and endurance	Decrease the distance. Provide rest periods. Use fins or hand paddles.
Sensory perception	Bright equipment Lane lines Auditory signals for orientation Count arm strokes
Balance and postural control	Provide support from the side. Flotation devices
Concept understanding	Use pictures and cues. Use physical and verbal prompts. Demonstrate, simplify the information, and repeat as needed.
Attention	Walk/swim in front/side of the individual. Timers and cue cards Previewing and visual schedules Provide one aspect of the skill, instruction, or feedback at a time.
Self-responsibility	Create social stories related to swimming and personal space.
Flexibility	Warm-up Underwater arm recovery Stabilize other body parts. Exaggerate body roll. Roll on back to breathe.
Speed and agility	Decrease distance or avoid comparison with others through proximity.

Back Crawl

The back crawl (i.e., backstroke) is the fastest combination of alternating arm and leg movements performed in a supine position. One of the advantages is that the face is out of the water, allowing swimmers to breathe at will (Thomas, 2005). Individuals with disabilities can more easily execute this stroke because of the body's position. Underwater arm recovery, such as the one performed in the basic or elementary backstroke, can be used by individuals with limited range of motion in the arms.

The backstroke also allows for using a range of assistive equipment. Floating belts (e.g., water joggers), inflatable waterbeds or head floats, floatable toys, life vests, or foam noodles can be used to provide support, elevate the body, and stabilize the body in different positions to promote acquisition of the skill (Lepore, Gayle, & Stevens, 2007; Stopka, 2001). Table 11.4 lists other modifications that may assist participants with functional differences in learning the back crawl.

Table 11.4 Modifications for the Back Crawl

Capability difference	Modification
Body strength and endurance	Floating belts
Sensory perception	Lane lines Auditory signals for orientation Count arm strokes
Balance and postural control	Rest head of the individual in your shoulder. Provide support on back (one or two hands).
Concept understanding	Provide tactile feedback. Use associations—soldier, monkey, and airplane for the elementary backstroke arm-pull motion.
Attention	Encourage sight on a point in the sky (ceiling).
Flexibility	Modify arm and/or leg motion.

Think back to Mr. Roberts and the twins in his swimming class.

1. What strokes might be best for Mr. Roberts to teach Michael and Jake in his aquatics program? Why these strokes?
2. What modifications or equipment do you think might be necessary to increase the capability of the two boys in this program?

SUMMARY

A carefully designed aquatics program can improve the swimming skills of participants with disabilities. Enhancing water competence and aquatic skill can, in turn, facilitate access to a range of recreational aquatic opportunities and significantly contribute to the overall health and well-being of individuals with disabilities throughout their life. For these experiences to be positive, carefully considered and thoughtfully implemented modifications are necessary. Modifiable components of an aquatics program may include changes to instruction, equipment, strategies, specific swimming skills, and water safety skills. To identify the appropriate adaptations that facilitate successful participation in aquatic environments, instructors must consider the individual differences of participants, the complexity of the task, and the existing environmental factors.

What Do You Think?

1. In what ways do you think aquatic activities can support the goals of inclusive physical activity?
2. How do you think water competence can be used to achieve physical activity and health-related goals?
3. If indeed aquatics is the "great equalizer," then what must practitioners know and be able to do to make water environments and aquatic skills equally accessible to all?

What Would You Do?

Scenario 11.1

Maria is a young adult who once loved to be active. When she was not walking around the neighborhood, she was hiking in the mountains or jogging by the beach. However, she has recently become much less active because of joint stiffness and inflammation, especially in her knees. Walking and moving have become more difficult because of the joint swelling and pain. She knows that being active is important for improving joint function, muscles strength, and overall health, so she decided to consult her doctor about alternative activities. Her doctor suggested that she participate in aquatic activities. He informed her that the buoyancy of the water would reduce the pressure or stress on her joints, allowing her to move more easily and without pain. She visited her local aquatics facility to see what was available for her.

1. What activities do you think would be most appropriate for Maria in an aquatics program?
2. What modifications or equipment will Maria need to be successful in this program?

Scenario 11.2

Ramon is a nine-year-old child with Down syndrome. At school, he was receiving separate adapted physical education (APE) twice a week. His goals were related to balance, coordination, and muscular strength. The APE teacher was trying to accomplish these goals by using different traditional games and activities. However, he noticed that Ramon's attention span was short, and he was unable to keep him on task for more than 10 minutes. After talking with Ramon's father, the APE teacher learned that Ramon loves to swim. Luckily, Ramon's school has a swimming pool. The APE teacher has decided to work on Ramon's goals in the pool. He has talked to the aquatics instructor about ideas and activities for Ramon.

1. The aquatics instructor recommended that the APE teacher first conduct a formal assessment to determine Ramon's present level of performance in the pool. What steps do you think the APE teacher needs to follow to conduct this assessment?
2. What are some possible activities the teacher could use to help Ramon achieve his IEP goals?
3. Ramon is nine years old. What person-related factors might the teacher need to consider when working with a child of this age with Down syndrome in an aquatic environment?

CHAPTER 12

Outdoor Pursuits

© THEOBALD/age fotostock

LEARNING OUTCOMES

After completing this chapter, you should be able to

- describe the benefits and applications of outdoor pursuits;
- identify the core competencies of practitioners facilitating outdoor pursuits; and
- provide examples of variations for both land- and water-based outdoor activities.

INCLUDING ALL INDIVIDUALS

Ms. Emily Parks works for a community recreation program. She has been working with people of all ages and abilities in her programs, which have been primarily center-based classes in fitness, aquatics, and yoga. Many of these people have been referred from a local rehabilitation facility. Her boss has planned to expand the programs to include more outdoor pursuits, and the program participants have expressed a desire to participate in the new classes, such as hiking and canoeing.

Emily has little experience with outdoor curriculum and is a little uncertain about what she would need to know and be able to do to adequately teach some of these classes. However, she is interested and wonders how she can develop these classes and other outdoor activities. What equipment will she need? How will she go about starting such a program? What modifications might she need to make to include individuals of diverse abilities?

Outdoor pursuits are a growing trend nationwide as more people look for outdoor recreation and leisure activities. Many companies are aimed at offering outdoor enthusiasts varied touring and adventure trips. Outdoor activities are also being included more in school and recreation programs that teach skills to promote activities that last a lifetime. In this chapter, we review a variety of both land- and water-based outdoor pursuits and present a range of modification strategies likely to increase access and enjoyment for all who may want to participate.

OVERVIEW OF OUTDOOR PURSUITS

Outdoor pursuits are self-propelled activities performed in outdoor settings that involve personal goals and challenge and are approached from a low-impact environmental philosophy (Priest & Gass, 2005). They include outdoor activities done on land, such as hiking, climbing, and biking, as well as those pursued in the water, such as canoeing and kayaking. These pursuits can be done alone or in a group and allow for much flexibility in the level of challenge. For example, a person can chose to walk for 5 to 10 minutes, several hours, or days depending on skill level. One can kayak in the still waters of a lake or glide through rapids.

Regardless of level of challenge, outdoor activities are a wonderful way for people of all ages and abilities to enjoy physical activity and health promotion. From an activity as simple as a walk in the woods to the challenge of backpacking through high mountains for an extended period, outdoor activities have a multitude of benefits, such as these:

- Increased fitness through physical activity
- Increased coordination and agility
- Increased self-confidence
- Increased enjoyment and satisfaction in self and the environment
- Increased connection with nature and appreciation of the natural environment

Beyond these benefits, research comparing outdoor activities to activities done indoors has shown that outdoor activities allow for a greater decrease in tension, anxiety, and anger and more positive feelings of vitality, engagement, and satisfaction (Coon et al., 2011). In fact, some speculate that the lack of experience with nature and the outdoors has led to the increase in obesity, attention deficit/hyperactivity disorder, and depression (Louv, 2008).

COMPETENCIES OF OUTDOOR LEADERS

Over the past few decades there has been a significant increase in participation in outdoor pursuits; consequently, there has been an increase in the number of injuries and an increase in damage to delicate landscapes. This has led to the need for appropriate training and skill development for practitioners who lead outdoor activities for others. The Wilderness Education Association (WEA) is the national governing body for accreditation of training programs in this area of study (www.weainfo.org/outdoor-education). The WEA, along with the National Outdoor Leadership School (NOLS; www.nols.edu) also provides listings of accredited programs and provides training for future professionals. Professionals who become leaders of outdoor programs need to have a host of important skills, known as core competencies, because of the high-risk nature of many outdoor activities (Priest & Gass, 2005):

- Technical skills
- Safety skills
- Environmental skills
- Organizational skills
- Instructional skills
- Facilitation skills
- Professional ethics
- Flexible leadership style
- Experience-based judgment
- Problem-solving skills
- Decision-making skills
- Effective communication

DID YOU KNOW?

In the late 19th century before the development of antibiotics, sanitariums were established as a means of promoting health and well-being through experiencing high altitude, fresh air, and good nutrition via the outdoor experience.

In addition to having these skills, those who participate in outdoor activities should follow the guidelines of Leave No Trace. This principle is very clear: When you leave a natural space, it should be as if you were never there. While simple in theory, it is not as simple in practice. It means individuals should be certain to tread lightly, stay on marked paths, take out whatever is brought in, and leave no evidence behind. This also includes respect and care for all wildlife and plants. Specific details and guidelines for effective Leave No Trace practices can be found at http://lnt.org/learn/7-principles.

GOALS OF OUTDOOR PURSUITS

People of all abilities participate in outdoor activities for a variety of reasons. Thus, positive applications for participation in outdoor pursuits include the following (Priest & Gass, 2005):

- **Recreational**. Participation for fun and enjoyment in the outdoors for its revitalizing nature and pleasure.
- **Therapeutic**. Participation to improve some aspect of being, such as mental, physical, or emotional well-being. This approach can focus on coping strategies or dealing with personal issues. Examples of therapeutic application are the Surfers for Autism program, which helps individuals with autism spectrum disorder, and the Wounded Warriors Project, which assists military veterans in reducing stress and reconnecting with physical activity after injury.

DID YOU KNOW?

The National Audubon Society was founded in the late 1800s. The society has more than 500 chapters nationwide and a host of programs and resources. More information can be found at www.audubon.org.

- **Developmental**. Participation to challenge individuals to expand their abilities and test their limits. Challenge courses and many team-building programs focus on such goals. Participants learn new ways of interacting and improve behaviors and their ability to interact with others, whether at school or at work.
- **Educational**. Participation to learn about oneself, solve problems, and work as a team to meet new challenges. The focus of this application is helping people to think in new ways. In addition, many education programs focus on education about nature, the environment, and sustainable practices.

THINK BACK

1. What are some of the critical skills (competencies) that Emily would need in order to go about leading outdoor pursuits?
2. Where might Emily go to ensure she has the appropriate training?
3. What are some of the reasons her community participants might want to pursue an outdoor activity?

MODIFICATIONS FOR OUTDOOR ACTIVITIES

The increasing number of people seeking outdoor pursuits as a means of physical activity includes many with disabilities (Sugerman, 2001). While it would be difficult to describe every outdoor pursuit and all possible modifications of these activities in this chapter, the following examples highlight application of the FAMME model to some popular outdoor activities. We have divided these examples into land-based and water-based pursuits.

Land-Based Outdoor Pursuits

Outdoor pursuits are as diverse as the places and settings in which they take place. From hiking the woods in summer to skiing the slopes in winter, people enjoy participating in land-based outdoor activities every season of the year. The following paragraphs apply the FAMME model to hiking and backpacking, downhill skiing, bicycling, and in-line skating.

Hiking and Backpacking

Hiking is an outdoor activity that consists of walking or nonmotorized travel on trails or in scenic environments (figure 12.1). A day hike refers to a hike that can be completed in a single day, while multiday hikes with overnight camping are typically referred to as backpacking. The equipment required for hiking or backpacking depends on both the length of the hike (or number of days walking) and the terrain and natural environment covered. Table 12.1 offers some modifications for hiking and backpacking based on differences in functional ability.

Downhill Skiing

Downhill skiing, also known as alpine skiing, is an activity in which people ski down snow-covered mountains, typically making turns and various maneuvers. Downhill skiing includes recreational skiing, downhill racing, freestyle, and slalom ski racing. Most alpine skiing

Julien Leblay/fotolia.com

Figure 12.1 The use of animals to assist humans in bearing heavy loads has been a practice for thousands of years. In this case, a rickshaw is used to assist a hiker.

Table 12.1 Modifications for Hiking and Backpacking

Capability difference	Modification
Body strength and endurance	Support animals to carry weight Shorter trips Slope of terrain Rickshaw
Sensory perception	Guide animals or people Nature of surface (e.g., dirt, wood chips) Magnified or enlarged map
Balance and postural control	Assistive devices (trekking poles) Surface conditions
Understanding of concepts	Clearly and frequently marked trail Group activity versus individual
Attention	Clearly marked routes Short routes Frequent breaks
Self-responsibility	Shorter hikes Increased supervision

Note: Differences in flexibility and speed and agility are not as critical to successful hiking or backpacking.

occurs at ski resorts; however, some alpine skiers prefer backcountry skiing or skiing in less managed landscapes. Equipment such as the monoski (figure 12.2) and other technological advances have significantly increased access to the slopes for many people with disabilities. Table 12.2 presents modifications for a range of capability differences.

Rossmiller Photography

Figure 12.2 Everyone can enjoy the exhilaration of downhill skiing with minimal adaptations.

Table 12.2 Modifications for Downhill Skiing

Capability difference	Modification
Strength	Monoski Decreased slope Snow-plow technique versus stem turns Ski-bike
Coordination	Omit use of poles Limit number of turns
Visual perception	Guide people Auditory cues
Balance and postural control	Outrigger ski poles Monoski Bi-ski Four-track skiing (walker mounted with skis) Shorter skis Gentle slope
Speed and agility	Length and width of skis Nature of run (e.g., wide path, number of people on slope)
Endurance	Shorter or fewer downhill runs
Understanding of concepts	Verbal cues Physical guidance
Attention	Skiing partner Shorter downhill runs Fewer people on slope
Self-responsibility	Ski with partner Number of people in group or on slope
Flexibility	Particular skiing or turning technique

Bicycling

Two-wheeled vehicles requiring balance by the rider date back to as early as the 19th century. Since then, the bicycle has undergone many transformations and a host of designs. It was not until the late 1960s and early 1970s, however, that an increase in the value of exercise and the advantage of energy-efficient transportation led to increased popularity of bicycling in North America. With this increased interest came a corresponding increase in the technological advances of bicycles, including the tandem bicycle and the recumbent bicycle (figure 12.3). With these and other modern innovations, people of varying abilities can find many ways to enjoy the freedom of movement that comes with cycling. Table 12.3 lists some examples of modifications for bicycling.

L. Lieberman, courtesy of Camp Abilities.

Figure 12.3 Tandem or recumbent bicycles are a great way for those with limited strength to get out and enjoy cycling recreationally or competitively with friends or other athletes.

In-Line Skating

In-line skates are used all over the world for both sport and recreation. The skates typically have two to five wheels arranged in a single line under a boot and are designed for speed and maneuverability. In addition to in-line skating for fitness, recreation, or hockey, some people prefer to participate in aggressive in-line skating, which includes a variety of grinds, airs, slides, and other advanced tricks or maneuvers. Modifications for in-line skating are presented in table 12.4.

DID YOU KNOW?

In 1817, Baron von Drais invented a walking machine: two identically sized in-line wheels, the front one steerable, mounted in a frame that the rider straddled. The device was propelled by pushing the feet against the ground, thus rolling the person and the device forward in a sort of gliding walk.

Water-Based Outdoor Pursuits

Outdoor activities are not always on land. People also enjoy a variety of outdoor pursuits in and on the water. Following are

Table 12.3 Modifications for Bicycling

Capability difference	Modification
Strength	Tandem bicycle Recumbent bicycle Hand-cranked bicycle Gear ratios
Coordination	Tandem bicycle Straight course or route Limited obstacles and turns Flat and smooth terrain
Visual perception	Tandem bicycle Auditory cues Obstacle-free surface with bright markings
Balance	Three-wheeled cycle Tandem bicycle
Understanding of concepts	Verbal cues Tandem bicycle
Attention	Cycling partners Short routes Tandem bicycle Exciting and interesting rides
Flexibility	Recumbent bicycle Hand cycle
Self-responsibility	Ride with a partner Provide choices

modifications for those with capability differences participating in the water-based activities of canoeing and kayaking as well as sailing.

Kayaking and Canoeing

Traveling on water is an exciting way to participate in outdoor activities. Whether it be a peaceful, relaxing paddle on a flat lake or a thrilling whitewater kayak ride down the rapids, water travel offers an experience of the natural world that dry land does not offer (figure 12.4). Canoes are generally used on flat, slow-moving water because they are very stable and easy to keep moving in a straight line, while kayaks are designed for easy maneuverability in faster-moving water. Kayaks react quickly to the paddle and snap of the hips but are less stable and may turn over easily. Table 12.5 lists some modifications for kayaking and canoeing.

Sailing

Sailing has been around since early civilization, first as a means of transportation and in more recent times as a form of recreation. While outdoor pursuits is defined as a self-propelled activity, we include sailing because of its adaptability to all individuals and because it is a wonderful way to enjoy the outdoors. To a sailor, there is nothing more satisfying than catching a good breeze and sailing along to the gentle sounds of the water. Sailboats come in many shapes and sizes and are typically defined by the shape of the hull (monohull or catamaran) and the number and style of the masts and sails. Sailing can be done alone, with a partner, or with a group depending on the needs of the individuals and the size of

Table 12.4 Modifications for In-Line Skating

Capability difference	Modification
Strength	Incline or decline of surface Physical assistance Shorter or longer duration of skate time
Coordination	Forward rather than backward movement Slow speed Limited obstacles or turns Partner assist
Visual perception	Sighted guide Auditory cues Clear surface markings
Balance and postural control	Wide stance Use of support (e.g., trekking poles, hockey stick) Surface conditions
Speed and agility	Slowed movement Limited people in space
Endurance	Shorter time Frequent rests
Understanding of concepts	Physical guidance Verbal cues
Attention	Limited distractions Verbal cues or imagery Skill-development games
Self-responsibility	Peer support Limited distractions or people in space
Flexibility	Slow movement

iofoto/fotolia.com

Figure 12.4 Kayaks are an enjoyable way to experience many otherwise inaccessible natural settings.

Table 12.5 Modifications for Kayaking and Canoeing

Capability difference	Modification
Upper-body strength	Flat or slower-moving water Feathered paddles Lighter paddles Ergonomically designed paddles Paddle grips
Balance and postural control	Kayak with less rocker Kayak with more chine Kayak with more volume Increased deck height and width Inflatable kayak Postural-supported seats
Understanding of concepts	Verbal cues Physical guidance Partner paddling
Attention	Partner paddling Short sections of whitewater Tandem kayak
Endurance	Slower water Shorter trips Work with partner
Sensory perception	Sighted guide Verbal cues Partners
Self-responsibility	Shorter trips Positive reinforcement Choices

the sailboat. In addition, sailing can be as simple as going out for half an hour or as complex as sailing around the world. Individuals of all abilities sail for recreation and sport. In fact, sailing is one of the many activities enjoyed recreationally but also as a competitive sport in the Paralympics, Special Olympics, and World Cup. Modifications for sailing are presented in table 12.6.

1. Select an outdoor land activity for Emily to include in her new program. What are the functional components required for the activity? How might she make adaptations for individuals with disabilities?
2. Select a water activity. What kinds of modifications might Emily make based on the FAMME model to ensure that all individuals could participate?

Table 12.6 Modifications for Sailing

Capability difference	Modification
Upper-body strength	Sail in lighter winds Sail with a partner Modified rigging systems Sip-and-puff (or sip 'n' puff) rigging
Balance and postural control	Boats with greater stability Adapted bucket seats Adapted boat surface to prevent slipping Stability handles Pedal controls for hands or feet Transfer benches
Understanding of concepts	Sail with a partner Verbal cues
Attention	Shorter trips Racing against another boat Peer support
Range of motion	Sip-and-puff (sip 'n' puff) rigging Adapted rigging Swivel seats
Speed and agility	Simpler boats with less rigging Swivel seats Modified rigging
Endurance	Shorter trips Sailing with a partner
Sensory perception	Brighter ropes Sailing with a partner Sighted guide Visual cues Auditory compass Talking GPS
Self-responsibility	Sail with a partner Limit distractions Provide choices of roles and responsibilities

Note: Differences in eye–hand coordination are not as critical to successful sailing.

SUMMARY

The benefits of participating in outdoor pursuits are vast, especially for those who have previously been shut in. Various outdoor activities are available to meet the diverse interests and personal goals of all people regardless of ability. Whatever the reason or wherever the activity, practitioners should always be highly trained in the requirements and safety precautions as well as be aware of the environmental impact when facilitating outdoor activities, or they should know where to find appropriately trained facilitators. It is also important for outdoor leaders to continually assess participants' capability and modification strategies to ensure safe and successful outdoor experiences for all.

What Do You Think?

1. Given what you have read in this chapter, how might outdoor programming be relevant to your future professional role or practice?
2. Of all the core competencies identified for outdoor leaders, which ones do you already have? For which do you need further training and development?
3. Reflect on your personal experiences with outdoor pursuits. What modifications were used or could have been employed to accommodate other individuals in the group or those who could have participated if allowed access?

What Would You Do?

Scenario 12.1

Arturo, a new recreation leader for an outdoor program, will be taking a group on a weekend kayaking trip. One of the participants in his group is Joe, who had a head injury in a car accident three years ago. Before the accident, Joe spent many weekends rafting, camping, hiking, and enjoying the outdoors. He continues to enjoy the relaxation and challenge of outdoor pursuits. Joe currently has some difficulty with balance and is stronger on his left side. He walks independently but finds it helpful to use a walking stick when hiking over uneven terrain. He has limited range of motion on his right side and continues to stretch on a daily basis to help prevent contractures in his right arm and shoulder. Arturo has just collected all the release forms, health history, and medical information for the trip's participants. He is wondering if he will need to make any adaptations for Joe.

1. What are the functional requirements for kayaking?
2. What types of modifications, if any, might Arturo need to make for Joe?

Scenario 12.2

Sue is an instructor at her local university and teaches a skiing class. In one of her new sections this semester is a student named Ashley, an athlete who uses a wheelchair. Ashley competes in water skiing, downhill skiing, and wheelchair basketball. She is majoring in therapeutic recreation and plans on working with individuals with disabilities in the future. Sue has met with her class once and reviewed the syllabus. Sue is wondering what modifications Ashley will need for her ski class.

1. What are the functional skills needed for skiing?
2. What type of adaptations, if any, might be helpful for Ashley when skiing?

APPENDIX A

Person-Related Factors Influencing Capability

This appendix serves as supplementary information to the text regarding individual factors that might influence capability in movement experiences. Although classifications such as these can be helpful in providing general information, they do not provide deep insight into any one person's capability to perform. The task demands and nature of the context significantly affect performance outcomes and benefit. This information is provided to make practitioners aware of the possible influences on performance and, more important, to give them insight into the implications for physical activity participation, potential safety concerns, and activity recommendations and contraindications. Practitioners must take care not to generalize specific factors to all individuals or to make assumptions about capability should any given factor exist. Individuals will differ in terms of their functional capabilities regardless of any specific factor, thus assumptions about individuals based on categorical labels must be avoided.

Note: This appendix is organized according to the ICF classifications of body structure and function. However, this list is not an exhaustive list of all possible health conditions. The information provided within this appendix has been compiled from the websites referenced for each section.

MENTAL FUNCTIONS

Attention Deficit/Hyperactivity Disorder (ADHD)

Attention deficit/hyperactivity disorder (ADHD) is a condition in which individual differences include inattentiveness or distractibility, impulsivity, or hyperactive behavior, or a combination of the three. These difficulties usually begin before the person is seven years old but in some cases are not noticed until the child is older.

Selected Facts

- The behavioral differences of ADHD can be managed through helping the individual manage his or her behavior; creating a structured physical activity program that fits his or her needs; and providing medication, if necessary.
- One effective strategy for people with ADHD is exercise, preferably vigorous exercise. Exercise helps work off excess energy, focuses attention, and stimulates beneficial hormones and neurochemicals.

Tips and Techniques

- Practitioners must be clear, consistent, and positive. Set clear rules and expectations.
- Have a reinforcement program for good behavior.

- Employ effective strategies for managing behavior, such as charting, starting a reward program, ignoring behaviors, and using consistent consequences related to the behavior.
- Help individuals stay focused by making activities fun and rewarding.

Informative Websites

www.add.org

www.chadd.org

Autism Spectrum Disorder (ASD)

Autism spectrum disorder (ASD) is a developmental condition that is usually evident by age three and is a neurological condition that affects a child's ability to communicate, understand language, play, and relate to others. Other functional differences often associated with autism are engagement in repetitive activities and stereotyped movements, resistance to environmental change or disruption in daily routines, and unusual responses to sensory experiences, such as loud noises, lights, or certain textures.

Selected Facts

- Children with ASD vary widely in abilities, intelligence, and behaviors.
- Autism is one of the disability categories under IDEA.
- Children with autism display a variety of intellectual capabilities.
- ASD may also be present with other disabilities.

Tips and Techniques

- When teaching children with autism, try using physical guidance as the children learn movement skills; also try verbal and visual cues and prompts.
- Physical activity helps children with autism reduce self-stimulatory behavior and increase attention and play behavior.
- Use behavior-management techniques to promote on-task and safe behavior.
- Teaching methods should match learning styles and sensory needs.
- Provide a stable, structured environment for the child. Limit the amount of relevant stimuli or activity focus initially.
- Minimize unnecessary external stimuli or distractions.
- Sensory stimulation through activities such as music, dance, and aquatic activities might be successful for on-task and attentive behavior.
- Provide sensory breaks.

Informative Websites

www.autism.org

www.autismspeaks.org

www.autism-society.org

Down Syndrome

Down syndrome is the most common and readily identifiable chromosomal condition associated with mental retardation. It is caused by having 47 instead of the usual 46 chromosomes, which changes the orderly development of the body and brain. Down syndrome might result in slow physical development and cognitive differences.

Selected Facts

- There is a wide variation in intellectual abilities, behavior, and developmental progress in individuals with Down syndrome.
- There are over 50 clinical signs of Down syndrome, but it is rare to find all or even most of them in one person. Some common differences include poor muscle tone, hyperflexibility at the joints, and a variety of physical differences.
- Children with Down syndrome frequently have specific health-related problems, such as a lowered resistance to infection, making them more prone to respiratory problems.
- Differences in vision and hearing might exist.
- About 15 percent of people with Down syndrome have atlantoaxial instability, a misalignment of the first two cervical vertebrae. This condition makes these individuals more prone to injury if they participate in activities that overextend or flex the neck.
- Some individuals with Down syndrome might have congenital heart defects or cardiac problems.

Tips and Techniques

- Because of individual differences, it is impossible to predict future achievements of children with Down syndrome. Families and practitioners should place few limitations on potential capabilities.
- For some individuals with Down syndrome it can be effective to emphasize concrete concepts rather than abstract ideas.
- Teach physical activity tasks in a step-by-step manner with frequent reinforcement and consistent feedback.
- Find out what the individual enjoys most and begin with this activity first to promote increased involvement.
- Avoid activities that place undue pressure on the neck (e.g., gymnastics, diving, the butterfly stroke) unless otherwise informed by the participant's physician that these activities are appropriate.
- Be sure to obtain medical information regarding risks associated with cardiac or respiratory difficulties.

Informative Website

www.ndss.org

Emotional Disturbance

According to the Individuals with Disabilities Education Act, emotional disturbance is defined as "a condition exhibiting one or more of the following characteristics over a long period of time and to a marked degree that adversely affects a child's educational performance: (A) An inability to learn that cannot be explained by intellectual, sensory, or health factors. (B) An inability to build or maintain satisfactory interpersonal relationships with peers and teachers. (C) Inappropriate types of behavior or feelings under normal circumstances. (D) A general pervasive mood of unhappiness or depression. (E) A tendency to develop physical symptoms or fears associated with personal or school problems." [Code of Federal Regulations, Title 34, Section 300.7(c)(4)(i)].

Selected Facts

- Children who have emotional disturbances might exhibit hyperactivity and a short attention span, might show aggression or self-injurious behavior, might be withdrawn or have excessive fear or anxiety, might have poor coping skills, and might have learning difficulties.

- Children with the most serious emotional disturbances might exhibit distorted thinking, excessive anxiety, bizarre motor acts, and abnormal mood swings. Some are identified as children who have a severe psychosis or schizophrenia.
- Many children who do not have emotional disturbances might display some of these same behaviors at various times during their development, but these behaviors do not continue over long periods of time.

Tips and Techniques

- It is important to provide participants with positive behavioral support (PBS) so that problem behaviors are minimized and positive, appropriate behaviors are promoted.
- Physical activity settings should be highly structured with consistent routines and expectations that are frequently shared with participants.
- Repetition and small sequential, progressive steps should be incorporated into activity plans.
- Removal of distractions, reduction of wait time, and consideration of spacing and groupings can help maintain on-task behavior.

Informative Websites

www.nichcy.org

www.dbpeds.org

Epilepsy

Epilepsy is a neurological condition in which nerve cells of the brain occasionally release abnormal electrical impulses. Individuals with epilepsy have seizures that might be related to brain injury or family tendency, but the cause is usually unknown.

Selected Facts

- About 50 percent of people who have one seizure without a clear cause will likely have another one, usually within 6 months. If a person has two seizures, there is about an 80 percent chance he or she will have more.
- Recent research indicates that up to 70 percent of children and adults with newly diagnosed epilepsy can be successfully treated.
- Seizures can vary from mild to severe. Single brief seizures do not cause brain damage.

Tips and Techniques

- There must be a balance between safety and the desire to pursue a full life of activity.
- For persons with rare or fully controlled seizures, most activities can be safely pursued.
- For those with frequent seizures with loss of consciousness or a brief period of confusion afterward, certain activities might need to be restricted. Activities that include aquatics, high speed, or high places should be supervised and carefully monitored. Helmets should be worn when appropriate.
- Practitioners should be aware of safety and first-aid procedures for seizures.

Informative Website

www.epilepsyfoundation.org

Fetal Alcohol Syndrome (FAS)

FAS is a lifelong set of physical, mental, and neurobehavioral birth differences associated with maternal consumption of alcohol during pregnancy. Alcohol-related neurodevelopmental disorder (ARND) describes the functional or mental impairments linked to prenatal alcohol exposure, and alcohol-related birth defects (ARBD) describe malformations in the skeletal and major organ systems.

Selected Facts

- Individuals with FAS have evidence of central nervous system dysfunction. In addition to mental retardation, individuals with FAS, ARND, and ARBD might have other neurological deficits, including poor motor skills and poor eye–hand coordination.
- They might also have a complex pattern of behavioral and learning problems, including difficulties with memory, attention, judgment, and problem solving, as well as problems with mental health and social interactions.

Tips and Techniques

- Keys to working successfully with learners who have FAS are structure, consistency, variety, brevity, and persistence.
- It is important to provide external structure and to be consistent in response and routine. Give the learner lots of advance warning of activity changes or transitions.
- Because of attentional difficulties, it is important to give brief explanations and directions. Incorporate different ways to get and keep attention.
- Repetition of learning is critical. Break work down into small pieces so that the learner is not overwhelmed.
- Establish a few simple rules with consistent language.
- Allow the learner choices; encourage decision making.

Informative Website

www.nofas.org

Fragile X

Fragile X syndrome is the most common inherited cause of mental retardation. A person with fragile X syndrome has a mutation in the FMR1 (fragile X mental retardation 1) gene in the DNA that makes up the X chromosome.

Selected Facts

- Individuals with fragile X syndrome might have significant intellectual differences. The spectrum ranges from subtle learning "disabilities" to severe mental retardation and autism.
- Individuals might have a variety of physical and behavioral differences, including attention deficit disorders, speech disturbances, autistic behaviors, poor eye contact, and aversion to touch and noise.
- Connective tissue problems might lead to ear infections and skeletal problems.

Tips and Techniques

- Multidisciplinary approaches and therapy are helpful in addressing many of the physical, behavioral, and cognitive impacts of fragile X syndrome.
- Sensory integration activities and calming activities are useful when teaching some individuals with fragile X.

- Try to reduce sensory overload when considering the setting or context in which activities will be performed.
- See Intellectual Disability for additional tips and techniques.

Informative Website

www.fragilex.org

Intellectual Disability

Intellectual disability is a term used when a person has specific differences in intellectual functioning and adaptive functioning skills such as communication, daily living, and social skills manifested during the developmental period.

Selected Facts

- These differences might cause an individual to learn and develop more slowly.
- Individuals with an intellectual "disability" will learn, but it may take them longer. There might be some things they cannot learn.

Tips and Techniques

- Divide tasks into small, meaningful steps and present them to the learner sequentially. Limit distractions. Keep the activity area clean and well ordered; store equipment not currently in use out of sight.
- Encourage independence. Use reinforcement strategies and motivational techniques.
- Break tasks down into smaller steps.
- Demonstrations, verbal cues, and physical prompts are useful but should gradually fade to promote increased independence.
- Teach learners tasks across settings to promote generalization of skills.
- Physical activities and sports can improve fitness, increase confidence, and help build social skills.
- Programs should focus on age-appropriate activities.

Informative Website

www.aaidd.org

Learning Disability

Learning disability is a neurological condition that causes a difference in one or more psychological processes that presents an individual with difficulty in listening, thinking, speaking, reading, writing, spelling, or doing mathematical calculations.

Selected Facts

- People with learning "disabilities" generally have average or above average intelligence.
- There are different types of learning "disabilities." Each person is unique and might show a different combination and degree of difficulties.
- Learning "disabilities" might be accompanied by attentional difficulties.
- People with learning "disabilities" can be successful at school, work, and in the community given appropriate supports.

Tips and Techniques

- Teach using a multisensory approach (visual, auditory, and kinesthetic).
- Establish a routine and incorporate repetition.
- Break learning down into small sequential steps.
- Provide regular prompts and quality feedback.
- Allow sufficient time for processing and ample time for practice.
- Employ various techniques for memory and organization.

Informative Websites

www.ldonline.org
www.ldanatl.org

Traumatic Brain Injury (TBI)

Traumatic brain injury is an acquired insult or injury to the brain caused by an external force. TBI might result in a diminished physical and cognitive capacity or psychosocial difficulties. The term applies to open or closed head injuries resulting in changes in one or more areas, such as cognition; language; memory; attention; reasoning; abstract thinking; judgment; problem solving; sensory, perceptual, and motor abilities; psychosocial behavior; physical functions; information processing; and speech. The term does not apply to brain injuries that are congenital or degenerative or to brain injuries induced by birth trauma.

Selected Facts

- Traumatic brain injuries often result from motor vehicle, sports, and recreation accidents.
- Brain injuries can range from mild to severe, as can the changes that result from the injury. It is hard to predict how an individual will recover from the injury.
- In the case of children, as a child grows and develops, functional capabilities might change as he or she is expected to use the brain in new and different ways. The damage to the brain from the earlier injury can make it hard for the child to learn new skills that come with getting older. For an adult, brain injury can result in the loss of, or difficulty with, previously learned skills.

Tips and Techniques

- Give the learner more time to finish tasks.
- Break lessons down into small components and give directions one step at a time. For tasks with many steps, give the learner both visual and verbal cues.
- Show the learner how to perform new tasks. Give examples to go with new ideas and concepts.
- Have consistent routines. This helps the learner know what to expect. If the routine is going to change, let him or her know ahead of time.
- Assist the learner with organizational strategies, such as color-coding activities, using an assignment book, and keeping to a daily schedule.
- Realize that the learner might get tired quickly. Because of fatigue levels, avoid overloading; let the learner rest as needed.
- Reduce distractions.
- Offer choices; be flexible about expectations.

Informative Websites

www.neuroskills.com

www.biausa.org

www.headinjury.com

SENSORY FUNCTIONS

Blindness and Low Vision

Individuals who are legally blind have less than 20/200 vision in the better eye or a very limited field of vision (20 degrees at its widest point). Those who have low vision generally have a severe visual "impairment," not necessarily limited to distance vision. Low vision applies to all individuals with sight who are unable to read a newspaper at a normal viewing distance, even with the aid of eyeglasses or contact lenses. They use a combination of vision and other senses to learn, although they might require adaptations in lighting or the size of print, and sometimes Braille.

Selected Facts

- A young child with vision loss might have little reason to explore interesting objects in the environment and thus might miss opportunities to experience and learn about interaction with other people and other things. They might also miss opportunities to learn how to move in a variety of ways.
- Because the child cannot see parents or peers, he or she might be unable to imitate social behavior or understand nonverbal cues.

Tips and Techniques

- A sighted guide (peer tutor) can help an individual who is blind in any physical activity for positive learning.
- Make sure individuals know the size, shape, and boundaries of an activity area before they use it for sport or physical activity. Allow them to explore the area without others present.
- Arrange mats around the out-of-bounds area so participants know when they go out of bounds.
- Use beeper cones or music to mark boundaries. Use different surfaces to mark various playing areas.

Informative Websites

www.nfb.org

www.afb.org

Deafness and Hearing Loss

Deafness is defined as a hearing difference so severe that the individual cannot process linguistic information through hearing, with or without amplification. Deafness might be viewed as a condition that prevents an individual from receiving sound in all or most of its forms. In contrast, a person with a hearing loss can generally respond to auditory stimuli, including speech.

Selected Facts

- Loss in hearing can occur in loudness or intensity or in both areas; the condition might exist in one ear or both ears.

- Hearing loss is generally described as slight, mild, moderate, severe, or profound, depending on how well a person can hear the intensities or frequencies associated with speech.
- There are four types of hearing loss: conductive hearing loss caused by diseases or obstructions in the outer or middle ear; sensorineural hearing loss resulting from damage to the delicate sensory hair cells of the inner ear or the nerves that supply it; a mixed hearing loss or a combination of conductive and sensorineural loss; and a central hearing loss resulting from damage or impairment to the nerves or nuclei of the central nervous system.
- Hearing loss or deafness does not affect a person's intellectual capacity or ability to learn. However, children who are either hard of hearing or deaf generally require some form of support in order to receive an adequate education.

Tips and Techniques

- When planning a lesson, use visual cues, fewer rules, and less equipment. Creating peer tutor programs for learners helps keep them from isolating themselves from social gatherings. Teach your younger deaf learners neighborhood games such as jump rope and hop scotch. Knowing how to play these games helps them interact better with their peers.
- For those who are deaf or have severe hearing losses, early, consistent, and conscious use of visible communication modes (such as sign language, fingerspelling, and cued speech) or amplification and aural/oral training can help facilitate language development and communication.
- People with hearing loss use oral or manual means of communication or a combination of the two. Oral communication includes speech, lip reading, and the use of residual hearing. Manual communication involves signs and fingerspelling.
- Practitioners should attempt to learn some sign language in order to communicate directly with learners. If interpreters are used, be sure to speak to the learner and not to the interpreter.

Informative Websites

www.nad.org

www.deafchildren.org

Deaf-Blindness

Deaf-blindness is a combination of vision and hearing loss, not necessarily complete deafness and complete blindness.

Selected Facts

- Individuals who are deaf-blind sign tactually on the hand of the person with whom they are communicating.

Tips and Techniques

- Introduce an individual to roller-skating, swimming, biking, skiing, and gymnastics that allow for increased physical activity without the unpredictability of other players and equipment required in team activities.
- Modifications need to be made, such as changing the rules, equipment, or environment. For example, allow choices of activity and equipment. Link movement to language; teach the word for each skill learned.

Informative Website

www.aadb.org

FUNCTIONS OF THE CARDIOVASCULAR AND RESPIRATORY SYSTEMS

Asthma

Asthma is a lung condition characterized by wheezing, coughing, breathing difficulty, and lengthened expiration (prolonged exhaling).

Selected Facts

- Wheezing, coughing, tightness in the chest, and general fatigue are signs of an impending asthma attack.

Tips and Techniques

- When individuals with asthma exercise (particularly in cold weather), they can become short of breath and have an attack.
- Remind individuals with asthma to use their medication before exercising.

Informative Websites

www.asthma.org.uk

www.aaaai.org

Stroke

Stroke, often called cerebrovascular accident (CVA), is a sudden central nervous system impairment in which the flow of oxygen and nutrients to the brain is halted through a blood clot (ischemia) or bleeding (hemorrhage).

Selected Facts

- Risk factors associated with stroke include hypertension, coronary artery disease, hyperlipidemia, diabetes, obesity, and high amounts of alcohol, caffeine, and nicotine.
- Motor ability and control, sensation and perception, communication, and emotions might be influenced. Individuals might have partial or total paralysis on one side of the body.

Tips and Techniques

- Check with the participant's primary physician before starting an exercise program, and conduct exercise screening and assessments to ensure a safe and effective program.
- Know the implications of necessary medications (e.g., hypertension medications, water pills) on the body's ability to exercise or participate in physical activity.
- Monitor blood pressure periodically throughout an exercise program.
- Be aware of occurrences of orthostatic hypotension, which is dizziness, nausea, and lightheadedness from suddenly sitting or standing up.
- To avoid dangerous falls, make sure you have adequate support for balance while using exercise machines.

- If muscle groups are not functional because of spasticity, the opposing muscle groups might be strengthened to help normalize the spasticity. Any muscle groups incapable of being strengthened should be stretched.
- Spasticity can affect the respiratory muscles of the involved side. Cardiovascular exercise and deep rhythmical breathing can help strengthen respiratory muscles.

Informative Website

www.stroke.org

FUNCTIONS OF THE METABOLIC SYSTEMS

Diabetes

Diabetes is a disease in which the body does not produce or use insulin. Insulin is a hormone that converts sugar, starches, and other food into energy required for daily life. The condition results in too much glucose (sugar) in the blood.

Selected Facts

- When blood sugar is elevated or when basal insulin levels are low, exercise generally causes blood sugars to rise further.
- Symptoms of insulin shock are sudden fatigue, weakness, tremors, hunger, sweating, and double vision. If an individual with diabetes exhibits any of these during physical activity, have him or her stop exercising immediately and take a quick-acting sugar, such as sugar cubes or a regular soft drink.

Tips and Techniques

- Encourage exercise and participation in sports for individuals with diabetes.
- Be familiar with the signs, symptoms, and treatment of low blood sugar (insulin reaction).
- Make sure participants drink plenty of fluids. Dehydration can adversely affect blood glucose levels.

Informative Website

www.diabetes.org

NEUROMUSCULOSKELETAL AND MOVEMENT-RELATED FUNCTIONS

Amputee

Amputation refers to removal or loss of an entire limb or particular limb segment. Amputation can be congenital or acquired resulting from disease, tumor, complications of frostbite, injury, diabetes, arteriosclerosis (hardening of the arteries), or any other illness that impairs blood circulation.

Selected Facts

- Problems with thermoregulation could be present because of decreased skin surface.
- Prosthetic devices are typically used to increase functional use of the limb or body part.

Tips and Techniques

- Encourage participants to increase fluids during physical activity to prevent overheating.
- Allow time for participants with new prostheses to become familiar with them as necessary for performing an activity or task.

Informative Website

www.amputee-coalition.org

Amyotrophic Lateral Sclerosis (ALS)

Amyotrophic lateral sclerosis (ALS) is a progressive neurodegenerative disease that attacks nerve cells in the brain and spinal cord. The progressive degeneration of the motor neurons in ALS eventually leads to death. When the motor neurons die, the ability of the brain to initiate and control muscle movement is lost. With all voluntary muscle action affected, individuals in later stages of ALS become totally paralyzed.

Selected Facts

- Often referred to as Lou Gehrig's disease.
- At the onset of ALS symptoms can be so slight that they are overlooked.
- As motor neurons degenerate, functional differences might include muscle weakness in one of the hands, arms, or legs; weakness in the muscles involving speaking, swallowing, or breathing; cramping of muscles; difficulty in projecting the voice; shortness of breath; and difficulty in breathing and swallowing.
- Because ALS attacks motor neurons only, the sense of sight, touch, hearing, taste, and smell are not affected.
- For the vast majority of people with ALS, their mind and thoughts are not affected, and they remain sharp despite the progressive degenerating condition of the body.

Tips and Techniques

- Range of motion and stretching exercises can help prevent painful spasticity and shortening (contracture) of muscles.
- Gentle, low-impact aerobic exercise (e.g., walking, swimming, stationary bicycling) can strengthen unaffected muscles and improve cardiovascular health.

Informative Website

www.alsa.org

Arthritis

Arthritis is a rheumatic disease that causes pain in the joint or the muscle. The word "arthritis" is derived from the roots arth (joint) and itis (inflammation). The two most prevalent forms of arthritis are osteoarthritis, a degenerative joint disease that leads to deterioration of cartilage and formation of bone in the joint, and rheumatoid arthritis, a chronic and systemic inflammatory disease.

Selected Facts

- Many people report that regular exercise reduces the experience of pain and weakness from arthritis and provides a general feeling of well-being.
- Some arthritis medications might affect the cardiopulmonary systems and inhibit performance levels.

Tips and Techniques

- Heat or ice treatments (e.g., shower, ice, massage, whirlpool) before and after exercise can reduce pain and discomfort.
- It is best to do a variety of aerobic activities to avoid overstressing joints.
- Choose activities that expend less stress on joints, such as aquatherapy, biking, rowing, cross-country skiing, walking on soft surfaces, or low-impact aerobics. Choose activities depending on which joints are arthritic.
- Individuals with rheumatoid arthritis who experience morning stiffness should exercise later in the day.
- Focus strength training on increasing number of repetitions rather than amount of weight.
- A complete warm-up and cool-down stretching program should be done before and after each exercise program.

Informative Website

www.arthritis.org

Cerebral Palsy (CP)

Cerebral palsy is a nonprogressive but chronic disorder of movement and posture caused by a defect or lesion to the brain occurring before, during, or within two years after birth. The condition might be accompanied by associated differences in intellectual functioning, vision, hearing, communication, and seizures.

Selected Facts

- Movement differences might involve lower extremities (diplegia), one side of the body (hemiplegia), or all four extremities (tetraplegia). Motor differences might involve spasticity (increased muscle tone and tightness), athetosis (fluctuating muscle tone), or ataxia (low muscle tone and balance and coordination differences). Postural reactions and reflexive activity can influence movement efficiency and outcomes.

Tips and Techniques

- Flexibility is one of the important fitness goals for individuals with CP.
- Aquatic activity is often a preferred physical activity experience for movement, balance, and fitness development.
- Weight-bearing activity is important for bone density and reduced risk of osteoporosis.

Informative Websites

www.ucp.org

www.nichcy.org

Dwarfism

Dwarfism is defined as a medical or genetic condition that usually results in an adult height of 4 feet 10 inches (1.47 m) or shorter. In some cases a person with dwarfism might be slightly taller than this.

Selected Facts

- Although achondroplasia accounts for the majority of all cases of dwarfism, there are approximately 200 diagnosed types.

- Although the term "little person" is acceptable, most people would rather be called by their name than by a label. The term "midget" is not well received and considered offensive by most.
- There are three complications sometimes found in infants and toddlers with achondroplasia: compression of the brain stem, hydrocephalus, and obstructive apnea. These conditions do not always occur, but children should be evaluated.

Tips and Techniques

- Individuals are able to participate in physical activity and athletic events within the limits of their medical diagnoses. Swimming and bicycling are often recommended for people with skeletal dysplasias because these activities do not put pressure on the spine.
- Long-distance running or even extensive walking can be harmful because of the constant pounding or trauma to joints, although, as a rule, healthy individuals without any unusual orthopedic problems should be allowed to engage in typical activities and running games or sports.

Informative Websites

www.lpaonline.org

www.nlm.nih.gov/medlineplus/dwarfism.html

Multiple Sclerosis

Multiple sclerosis is a demyelinating disease of the central nervous system. Myelin, the fatty material surrounding the nerves, is destroyed, leading to symptoms such as muscle weakness, paresis, paralysis, spasticity, tremors, impaired balance, discoordination, heat sensitivity, and fatigue.

Selected Facts

- Some individuals with MS have cardiovascular dysautonomia in which irregular function of the autonomic nervous system (ANS) leads to a blunted heart rate and decreased blood pressure in response to exercise.
- Some people with MS have oversensitivity to heat, which might lead to fatigue, loss of balance, or visual changes.
- Balance and coordination difficulties can lead to dangerous falls.
- Be aware of side effects of medication and how they might affect exercise programming. Medication can affect energy level, muscle coordination, and muscle strength.

Tips and Techniques

- If cardiovascular dysautonomia exists, heart rate and blood pressure must be monitored throughout the exercise program; intensity might need to be decreased.
- Choose exercises and equipment that provide maximum support (e.g., swimming, recumbent cycling) and have participants work out in a safe environment (e.g., avoid slippery floors, poor lighting, and throw rugs).
- For those who are heat sensitive, create a cool environment with fans, air temperature between 72 and 76 degrees Fahrenheit (22-24 C), and pool temperature between 80 and 85 degrees Fahrenheit (26-29 C). If exercising outdoors in hot weather, exercise during early morning or evening hours. Wear clothing that "breathes," and use cooling aids as needed (e.g., cool vests, ice packs, cool baths).

Informative Websites

www.nationalmssociety.org
www.ncpad.org

Muscular Dystrophy

Muscular dystrophies are genetic disorders characterized by progressive muscle wasting and weakness that begin with microscopic changes in the muscle. As muscles degenerate over time, the person's muscle strength, power, and endurance decline. There are several types of muscular dystrophy, including Duchenne muscular dystrophy, the most common; Becker muscular dystrophy; facioscapulohumeral dystrophy (FSHD); and myotonic muscular dystrophy.

Selected Facts

- Muscular dystrophies are inherited, progressive disorders that gradually weaken the respiratory muscles and the muscles that move the limbs and trunk. The spinal muscular atrophies, and many other neuromuscular disorders can also lead to breathing problems and lung complications.
- Contractures and muscle atrophy are common.

Tips and Techniques

- Maintenance and improvement in muscular strength for performing activities of daily living, maintaining ambulation, and preventing contractures are important.
- Maintaining sufficient respiratory capacity is critical. Work with appropriate medical personnel to assess cardiovascular condition and potential complications.
- Strengthening postural muscles, which can slow the formation of scoliosis, should be included in the exercise program.
- Set reasonable goals involving activities that are achievable and enjoyable.
- Avoid overfatiguing muscles.

Informative Website

www.mdausa.org

Osteogenesis Imperfecta

Osteogenesis imperfecta (OI) is caused by a genetic defect that affects the body's production of collagen. Collagen is the major protein of the body's connective tissue and can be likened to the framework around which a building is constructed. In OI, a person has either less collagen than normal or a poorer quality of collagen than normal, leading to weak bones that fracture easily.

Selected Facts

- There are at least four recognized forms of OI, making for extreme variation in severity from one individual to another. A person might have just a few or as many as several hundred fractures in a lifetime.
- Individuals might have loose joints and low muscle tone.
- Some individuals might have underdeveloped lungs and respiratory problems.
- Spinal curvature is possible with the more severe types of OI.
- Hearing loss is also possible.

Tips and Techniques

- Treatment for OI is directed toward preventing or controlling symptoms, maximizing independent mobility, and developing optimal bone mass and muscle strength.
- Use of wheelchairs, braces, and other mobility aids is common, particularly among people with more severe types of OI.
- People with OI are encouraged to exercise as much as possible to promote muscle and bone strength, which can help prevent fractures. Swimming and water therapy are common exercise choices because water allows independent movement with little risk of fracture.
- Walking (with or without mobility aids) is excellent for those who are able.
- Individuals with OI will also benefit from maintaining a healthy weight, eating a nutritious diet, and avoiding activities such as smoking, excessive alcohol or caffeine consumption, and taking steroid medications—all of which might deplete bone and exacerbate bone fragility.

Informative Website

www.oif.org

Parkinson's Disease

Parkinson's disease is a chronic, progressive neurological disease. In Parkinson's, neurons in a specific region of the brain degenerate and result in the lack of a neurotransmitter responsible for the control of muscle movement. This can lead to tremors, muscle stiffness, and slower movements. Postural instability can also occur.

Selected Facts

- The functional differences of Parkinson's occur mainly between the ages of 50 to 65 years. Young-onset Parkinson's can occur in persons younger than 50.
- Signs and symptoms of Parkinson's change as the disease progresses.
- With Parkinson's, there might be behavioral and psychological changes including cognitive or memory difficulties, depression, anxiety, apathy, and fatigue.
- Medication plays a significant role in the treatment of Parkinson's.

Tips and Techniques

- Exercise and physical activity are strongly recommended to maintain functional ability and psychological well-being.
- Physical activity should be planned with consideration of medication schedules.
- Walking, swimming, and cycling are particularly good activities for maintaining health.
- Tai chi can promote postural control, balance, and smooth movement.
- Stretching exercises are particularly beneficial.
- Use light weights for maintaining as much strength and muscle tone as possible. Strengthening should focus on the extensor and postural control muscles.

Informative Website

www.parkinson.org

Post-Polio Syndrome

Poliomyelitis (polio), an acute viral disease, affects the lower motor neurons and causes muscle paresis, paralysis, and sometimes death. Post-polio syndrome, or PPS, is a name that has been adopted to indicate a constellation of new symptoms that occur between 20 to 40 years after the onset of the initial polio infection and after a period of "recovery" of at least 10 years. These symptoms often include new weakness, pain, breathing or swallowing difficulties, a variety of sleep disorders, muscle twitching, gastrointestinal problems, muscle fatigue, or "central" fatigue.

Selected Facts

- Symptoms can occur in previously affected muscles or in what were previously thought to be muscles unaffected at onset.
- Complications of PPS often include neuropathies, nerve entrapments, arthritis, scoliosis, osteoporosis, and, sometimes, additional atrophy.
- Onset of PPS is usually gradual, over a period of years, but sometimes abrupt, with major losses of function suffered over several months or a couple of years. Onset often occurs after a physical or emotional trauma, illness, or accident.

Tips and Techniques

- Physical activity is recommended for improvement in cardiovascular capacity and in performing activities of daily living.
- Energy management is important and achieved by striking a balance between rest and activity.
- Short-term exercise is indicated for affected muscles showing no signs of weakness and a full exercise program for muscles that have not been affected. Exercise is contraindicated for affected, severely weakened muscles.

Informative Websites

www.post-polio.org

www.ninds.nih.gov

Spina Bifida

Spina bifida is an incomplete closure of the spinal column during the first month of fetal development. In general, the three types of spina bifida (from mild to severe) are spina bifida occulta, an opening in one or more of the vertebrae (bones) of the spinal column without apparent damage to the spinal cord; meningocele, in which the meninges, or protective covering around the spinal cord, has pushed out through the opening in the vertebrae but the spinal cord remains intact; and myelomeningocele, in which a portion of the spinal cord itself protrudes through the back. In some cases, sacs are covered with skin; in others, tissue and nerves are exposed. Generally, people use the terms "spina bifida" and "myelomeningocele" interchangeably.

Selected Facts

- Myelomeningocele might include muscle weakness or paralysis below the area of the spine where the incomplete closure occurs, loss of sensation below the cleft, and loss of bowel and bladder control.
- A large percentage (70 to 90 percent) of children born with myelomeningocele have hydrocephalus or a buildup and accumulation of fluid in the brain. Hydrocephalus is controlled by a surgical procedure called "shunting," which relieves the fluid buildup in the brain. If a drain (shunt) is not implanted, the pressure buildup can cause brain damage, seizures, or blindness. Hydrocephalus might occur without spina bifida, but the two conditions often occur together.
- Children with spina bifida who also have a history of hydrocephalus might experience learning problems and difficulty paying attention, expressing or understanding language, and grasping concepts.

Tips and Techniques

- Participants might not have the ability to sweat and thus should take appropriate precautions to prevent overheating.
- Individuals with shunts should avoid activities that might result in physical contact to the head (e.g., soccer heading, boxing, headstands, forward rolls, tackles).
- Watch for symptoms such as headaches, dizziness, seizures, irritability, swelling, and redness along the shunt tract, which might indicate a blocked shunt.
- Flexibility in scheduling might need to occur to accommodate bowel and bladder management programs.
- Some individuals with spina bifida have latex allergies. If so, latex equipment (e.g., some types of rubber balls and balloons) should be avoided.
- Children with myelomeningocele need to learn mobility skills and often require the aid of crutches, braces, or wheelchairs. Even if the participant can ambulate on long leg braces, a wheelchair might make sport and game participation easier.

Informative Websites

www.spinabifidaassociation.org

www.easter-seals.org

www.marchofdimes.com

Spinal Cord Injury (SCI)

Spinal cord injury (SCI) is a complete or partial lesion to the spinal cord that results in functional loss of sensory, motor, and autonomic systems. The extent of functional differences depends on the level and completeness of the lesion. The physical ability of individuals with SCI is classified according to the amount of function retained. Common categories are paraplegia (SCI affecting level T2 and below, trunk and lower extremities involved) and tetraplegia (SCI affecting level T1 or above, all four extremities and trunk involved).

Selected Facts

- Individuals with lesions above the sacral level experience a loss of control with their bowels or bladder.
- Spasticity or high muscle tone and hyperactive stretch reflexes might occur in the muscles below the site of injury and be exacerbated by exposure to cold air, urinary tract infections, and physical exercise.
- Autonomic dysreflexia is possible, which is a sudden rise in blood pressure resulting from an exaggerated autonomic nervous system response to noxious stimuli such as bladder or bowel overdistension or a blocked catheter below the level of injury.
- Individuals with SCI often experience irregular body temperatures.
- Pressure sores (decubitis ulcers) or damage to the skin or underlying tissue caused by a lack of blood flow to the area might be problematic for individuals with SCI.

Tips and Techniques

- In extreme heat, individuals with spinal cord injuries at the sixth thoracic level and above have difficulty sweating. Some individuals with spinal cord injuries should avoid exercising in extremely cold or hot environments because of difficulty with thermal regulation.
- In response to autonomic dysreflexia, monitor signs of profuse sweating, sudden elevation in blood pressure, flushing, shivering, headache, and nausea; seek medical attention immediately if these symptoms occur.

- Monitor blood pressure throughout exercise, avoid quick movements, perform orthostatic training (if available), maintain proper hydration, and use compression stockings and an abdominal binder to avoid significant drops in blood pressure.

Informative Website

www.spinalcord.org

APPENDIX B

Eligibility Criteria for Infants and Toddlers

This appendix contains information on the criteria used to determine whether individuals from birth through two years of age qualify for early intervention services as required under part C of the Individuals with Disabilities Education Act (IDEA). The criteria to qualify for special services for infants and toddlers are much broader than for individuals aged 3 to 21. Based on state-determined guidelines, infants might fall into one of three categories of need: developmentally delayed, established risk for a developmental delay, or high risk for developmental delay. Each state must specify how they will meet the requirements under part C of IDEA in the federal law. Minor variations may exist. Be sure to be familiar with your state's guidelines. Following are the definitions of each of the terms based on current IDEA law and California Education Code.

(a) The term "eligible infant or toddler" for the purposes of this title means infants and toddlers from birth through two years of age, for whom a need for early intervention services, as specified in the federal Individuals with Disabilities Education Act (20 U.S.C. Sec. 1431 et seq.) and applicable regulations, is documented by means of assessment and evaluation as required in sections 95016 and 95018 and who meet one of the following criteria:

(1) Infants and toddlers with a developmental delay in one or more of the following five areas:

Cognitive development
Physical and motor development
Vision and hearing
Communication development
Social or emotional development
Adaptive development

Developmentally delayed infants and toddlers are those who are determined to have a significant difference between the expected level of development for their age and their current level of functioning. This determination shall be made by qualified personnel who are recognized by, or part of, a multidisciplinary team, including the parents.

(2) Infants and toddlers with established risk conditions, who are infants and toddlers with conditions of known etiology or conditions with established harmful developmental consequences. The conditions shall be diagnosed by qualified personnel recognized by, or part of, a multidisciplinary team, including the parents. The condition shall be certified as having a high probability of leading to developmental delay if the delay is not evident at the time of diagnosis.

(3) Infants and toddlers who are at high risk of having substantial developmental disability caused by a combination of biomedical risk factors, the presence of which is diagnosed by qualified clinicians recognized by, or part of, a multidisciplinary team, including the parents.

A multidisciplinary team determines a high risk for delay based on assessment and a combination of such factors as the following:

- Prematurity of less than 32 weeks gestation or low birth weight of less than 1,500 grams (53 oz)
- Assisted ventilation for more than 48 hours in the first 28 days of life
- Small gestation for age (below the third percentile)
- Asphyxia neonatorum associated with a five-minute Apgar score of 0 to 5
- Severe and persistent metabolic abnormality, including but not limited to hypoglycemia, acidemia, and hyperbilirubinemia in excess of the usual exchange transfusion level
- Neonatal seizures or nonfebrile seizures during the first three years of life
- Central nervous system lesion or abnormality
- Central nervous system infection
- Biomedical insult including but not limited to injury, accident, or illness that might seriously or permanently affect developmental outcome
- Multiple congenital anomalies or genetic disorders that might affect developmental outcome
- Prenatal exposure to known teratogens
- Prenatal substance exposure, positive infant neonatal toxicology screen, or symptomatic neonatal toxicity or withdrawal
- Clinically significant failure to thrive including but not limited to weight persistently below the third percentile or age on standard growth charts or less than 85 percent of the ideal weight for age or acute weight loss or failure to gain weight with the loss of two or more major percentiles on the growth chart
- Persistent hypotonia or hypertonia beyond that otherwise associated with a known diagnostic condition

High risk for a developmental disability also exists when a multidisciplinary team determines that the parent of the infant or toddler is a person with a developmental disability and the infant or toddler requires early intervention services based on evaluation and assessment.

APPENDIX C

Resources

This appendix suggests websites that might be useful to refer to when providing physical activity opportunities for individuals with differences in ability. The list is intended to provide a foundation for information and is in no way meant to be comprehensive or indicative of all the resources that currently exist or that could be accessed to support physical activity practitioners.

LEGAL INFORMATION

Americans with Disabilities Act
www.ada.gov

Job Accommodation Network
http://askjan.org

Individuals with Disabilities Education Act (IDEA)
http://idea.ed.gov/

Education Law
www.hg.org/edu.html

National Dissemination Center for Children with Disabilities
www.nichcy.org

DISABILITY SPORTS AND PHYSICAL ACTIVITY

American Association of Adapted Sports Programs
www.adaptedsports.org/

International Paralympics Committee
www.paralympic.org

International Platform on Sport and Development
www.sportanddev.org/en/learnmore/sport_and_disability2

Wheelchair Sports USA
www.wsusa.org

States Association of Blind Athletes
www.usaba.org

Disability Sports USA
www.dsusa.org

United States Quad Rugby Association
www.quadrugby.com

National Sport Center for the Disabled
www.nscd.org

International Blind Sport Federation
www.ibsa.es/eng

Special Olympics
www.specialolympics.org

International Tennis Foundation
www.itfwheelchairtennis.com

National Wheelchair Basketball Association
www.nwba.org

National Disability Sports Alliance
www.nationaldisabilitysportsalliance.webs.com/

World Organization of Volleyball for the Disabled
http://wovd.info

USA Deaf Sports Federation
www.usdeafsports.org

United States Racquetball Association
www.usra.org

Canadian Wheelchair Basketball Federation
www.wheelchairbasketball.ca/en/homePage.aspx

Wilderness Inquiry Outdoor Adventures
www.wildernessinquiry.org

United States Handcycling Federation
www.ushf.org

National Center on Physical Activity and Disability
www.ncpad.org

Special Populations Learning Outdoor Recreation and Education (S'PLORE)
www.splore.org

Cooperative Wilderness Handicapped Outdoor Group (C.W. HOG)
www.isu.edu/outdoor

Success Oriented Achievement Realized (SOAR)
www.soarnc.org

Adaptive Sports Center
www.adaptivesports.org/page.cfm?pageid=5134

ADAPTED PHYSICAL EDUCATION

Adapted Physical Education National Standards
www.apens.org

National Adapted Physical Activity Council (council within AAHPERD)
www.aahperd.org/aapar/people/councils/APAC.cfm

PE Central
www.pecentral.org

PALAESTRA: Forum for Sport, Physical Education, and Recreation for Those With Disabilities
www.palaestra.com

NCPERID: National Consortium for Physical Education and Recreation for Individuals with Disabilities
www.ncperid.org

APPENDIX D

Tests and Assessment Tools Currently Available

Test name (bold indicates common name)	Type or area tested	Age	Available
6MWT *Six-Minute Walk Test*	Functional exercise capacity	Adults/older adults	www.rheumatology.org/practice/clinical/clinicianresearchers/outcomes-instrumentation/6MWT.asp
Adult Fitness Test (2012)	Health-related fitness	Adults	www.adultfitness.org
AEPS *Assessment, Evaluation, & Programming System for Infants & Children from Birth to Three Years* (2002)	Early movement milestones, fundamental movement skills, functional movement skills	Birth-3 yrs.	Paul H. Brookes P.O. Box 10624 Baltimore, MD 21285-0624 www.brookespublishing.com
APEAS II *Adapted Physical Education Assessment Scale II* (2007)	Motor performance	5-18 yrs.	American Association for Physical Activity and Recreation 1900 Association Dr. Reston, VA 20191-1598 www.aapar-apeas.org
Assessment of Hand Skills in the Primary Child (DVD/web program) (2008)	Structured observation of hand and arm movements	5 yrs. and up	Clinician's View P.O. Box 458 Fairacres, NM 88033 USA www.clinicians-view.com
BDI-2 *Battelle Developmental Inventory, 2nd edition* (2005)	Motor abilities, early movement milestones, fundamental movement skills	Birth-7 yrs. 11 mo.	Riverside Publishing 3800 Golf Rd., Suite 200 Rolling Meadows, IL 60008 www.riversidepublishing.com
BEERY VMI *Beery-Buktenica Developmental Test of Visual-Motor Integration, 6th edition* (2010)	Visual perception integrated with fine motor skills	2-100 yrs.	Pearson Attn: Customer Service P.O. Box 599700 San Antonio, TX 78259 www.pearsonassessments.com
Berg Balance Scale (1989)	Balance and functional mobility	Adults	www.rehabmeasures.org/Lists/RehabMeasures

(continued)

Test name (bold indicates common name)	Type or area tested	Age	Available
BESTest *Balance Evaluation Systems Test* (2009)	Balance and gait	Adults	www.bestest.us
BOT-2 *Bruininks-Oseretsky Test of Motor Proficiency, 2nd edition* (2005)	Motor ability	4-21 yrs.	Pearson Attn: Customer Service P.O. Box 599700 San Antonio, TX 78259 www.pearsonassessments.com
Brigance IED II *Brigance Inventory of Early Development II* (2010)	Motor development	Birth-7 yrs.	Curriculum Associates Corporate Headquarters P.O. Box 2001 North Billerica, MA 01862-0901 www.curriculumassociates.com
Brockport *Physical Fitness Test Manual* (1999)	Physical fitness (for youths with "disabilities")	10-17 yrs.	Human Kinetics P.O. Box 5076 Champaign, IL 61825-5076 www.humankinetics.com
CARE-R *Curriculum, Assessment, Resources, Evaluation* (1998)	Motor development, early movement milestones, fundamental movement skills and motor ability	Birth-17 yrs. (varies for each area)	Adapted Physical Education Program, Southwest Support Services Center 1501 S. Peck Ave. Manhattan Beach, CA 90266
CCPSN *Carolina Curriculum for Preschoolers with Special Needs* (2004)	Gross and fine motor assessment and curriculum guide	2-5 yrs.	Paul H. Brookes P.O. Box 10624 Baltimore, MD 21285-0624 www.brookespublishing.com
DEVPRO Developmental Programming Gross Motor and Perceptual-Motor Skills (1999)	Developmental sequence and task analysis	Birth-11 yrs. (varies by area)	Carol Kofahl www.devprosoftware.com
Erhardt Developmental Prehension Assessment (1994)	Hand function and fine motor ability	All	Erhardt Developmental Products 2379 Snowshoe Ct. E. Maplewood, MN 55119 www.ErhardtProducts.com
FAQ *Functional Activities Questionnaire* (1984)	Independence in daily activities	Adults/older adults	Gerontological Society of America 1220 L Street NW, Suite 901 Washington, DC 20005 www.aviviahealth.com/media/pdf/elder-care/functional-activities-assessment-tool.pdf
Fitnessgram (2010)	Physical fitness	4th grade-high school	Human Kinetics P.O. Box 5076 Champaign, IL 61825-5076 www.humankinetics.com

Test name (bold indicates common name)	Type or area tested	Age	Available
GMFM *Gross Motor Function Measure* (GMFM-66 & GMFM-88) (2002)	Early movement milestones, fundamental movement skills	Persons with cerebral palsy under 20 yrs.	Mac Keith Press High Holborn House 52-54 High Holborn London WC1V 6RL www.wiley.com/WileyCDA/WileyTitle/productCd-1898683298.html
HELP *Hawaii Early Learning Profile* • *HELP 0-3* (for ages birth to 3) (1992-2007) • *HELP 3-6, 2nd edition* (for ages 3-6) (2010) • *HELP 3-6 Checklist, 2nd edition* (2010)	Structured observation and checklist with a gross and fine motor section	Birth-6 yrs.	VORT Corporation P.O. Box 60132-W Palo Alto, CA 94306 www.vort.com
KALMS(R) *Kounas Assessment of Limited Mobility Students* (revised 1999)	Functional motor skills of students with an orthopedic disability	3-21 yrs.	Sharon Kounas or KALMS (R) Test 6001 Wadsworth Ave. Highland, CA 92346 www.kalmstest.com
LAP-3 *Learning Accomplishments Profile (manual)* (2004)	Motor development	36-72 mo.	Kaplan Early Learning Company 1310 Lewisville Clemmons Rd. Lewisville, NC 27023 www.kaplanco.com
MOVE *Assessment Profile for Children* (1996)	Early movement milestones, fundamental movement skills	Infant-young adult	MOVE International 5555 California Ave., Suite 302 Bakersfield, CA 93309 www.move-international.org/products
Movement ABC *Movement Assessment Battery for Children Checklist, 2nd edition* (2007)	Motor abilities, fundamental movement skills, specialized movement skills	3-16.11 yrs.	Pearson Attn: Customer Service P.O. Box 599700 San Antonio, TX 78259 www.pearsonassessments.com
MVPT *Motor-Free Visual Perceptual Test, 3rd edition* (2003)	Sensory motor	4-8 yrs.	Western Psychological Services 625 Alaska Ave. Torrance, CA 90503-5124 http://portal.wpspublish.com
PDMS-2 *Peabody Developmental Motor Scales, 2nd edition* (2002)	Standardized	Birth-6.5 yrs.	Western Psychological Services 625 Alaska Ave. Torrance, CA 90503-5124 http://portal.wpspublish.com

(continued)

Test and Assessment Tools Currently Available (continued)

Test name (bold indicates common name)	Type or area tested	Age	Available
Physical Best (2011)	Physical fitness	5-17 yrs.	AAHPERD 1900 Association Dr. Reston, VA 20191-1598 www.aahperd.org/naspe/professionaldevelopment/physicalBest www.humankinetics.com/ppPhysBest/ppPhysBest
QNST II *Quick Neurological Screening Test II, 2nd edition* (1998)	Sensory motor	5 yrs. and up	Western Psychological Services 625 Alaska Ave. Torrance, CA 90503-5124 http://portal.wpspublish.com
SF-36v2 (2007)	Health-related quality of life	Adults	QualityMetric Health Outcomes Solutions http://sf-36.org
SFT *Senior Fitness Test Manual, 2nd edition* (2013)	Physical fitness	Older adults	Human Kinetics P.O. Box 5076 Champaign, IL 61825-5076 www.humankinetics.com
TGMD-2 *Test of Gross Motor Development II* (2000)	Motor development	3-10 yrs.	ProEd 8700 Shoal Creek Blvd. Austin, TX 78757 www.proedinc.com/customer/productView.aspx?ID=1776
Tinnetti Balance & Gait Test (1986)	Gait and balance	Adults	Lippincott Williams & Wilkins for copyright permission 351 West Camden St. Baltimore, MD 21201 www.lww.com
TPBA2 *Transdisciplinary Play Based Assessment, 2nd edition* (2008)	Early movement milestones, fundamental movement skills	Birth-6 yrs.	Paul H. Brookes P.O. Box 10624 Baltimore, MD 21285-0624 www.brookespublishing.com
TUG *Timed Up & Go* (1991)	Mobility	Adults	www.rheumatology.org/practice/clinical/clinicianresearchers/outcomes-instrumentation/TUG.asp
TVPS 3 *Test of Visual Perceptual Skills, 3rd edition* (2009)	Visual-perception using nonmotor response	4.1-18 yrs.	Western Psychological Services 625 Alaska Ave. Torrance, CA 90503-5124 http://portal.wpspublish.com

APPENDIX E

Sample Medical History and Referral Form

This appendix serves as a sample medical history and referral form. Practitioners can use this in community-based programs when working with individuals with disabilities. Before starting any physical activity program, individuals should consult with their physicians. A physician referral form is also important and should be completed by a physician before (or along with) the medical history form. All forms and records should be kept in the individual's confidential program file along with emergency contacts.

Health and Medical History

General Reference Information

Name: ______________________________ Age: _____ DOB: __________ Sex: ___

Address: ______________________ City/state: ________________ Zip: __________

Day phone: ______________________ Evening phone: ______________________

Emergency contact: ____________________________ Relationship: ______________

Career, Education, and Hobbies

Occupations: ____

____

____

Education: ____

____

____

Hobbies: ____

____

____

History of Physical Activity

Favorite physical exercises and activities to participate in: ______________________

____

____

Favorite sports and activities to be a spectator at: ______________________

____

____

Major exercise and fitness goals and objectives: ______________________

____

____

Information Regarding Physical Abilities

List and describe differing abilities: ______________________

____

____

Associated physical concerns: ______________________

____

____

Associated Health Information:

YES	NO		Briefly describe
☐	☐	Cardiac disorder	______
☐	☐	Angina	______
☐	☐	Chest pain	______
☐	☐	Irregular HR/murmur	______
☐	☐	Hypertension	______
☐	☐	Stroke	______
☐	☐	High cholesterol	______
☐	☐	Atherosclerosis	______
☐	☐	Arteriosclerosis	______
☐	☐	Embolism	______
☐	☐	Shortness of breath	______
☐	☐	Asthma	______
☐	☐	History of pneumonia and infections	______
☐	☐	Pulmonary disorders	______
☐	☐	Phlebitis	______
☐	☐	Diabetes	______
☐	☐	Sensitivity to heat or cold	______
☐	☐	Bleeding disorder	______
☐	☐	Recent illness	______
☐	☐	Thyroid disorder	______
☐	☐	History of smoking	______

Motor Condition

YES	NO		Briefly describe
☐	☐	Spasticity (tightness)	______
☐	☐	Reflexes	______
☐	☐	Tactile loss	______
☐	☐	Kinesthetic loss	______
☐	☐	Static balance	______
☐	☐	Dynamic balance	______
☐	☐	Equilibrium	______
☐	☐	Grip strength	______
☐	☐	Fine motor	______
☐	☐	Postural concerns	______
☐	☐	Numbness or tingling in extremities	______

Motor Condition *(continued)*

YES	NO		Briefly describe
☐	☐	Epilepsy	______
☐	☐	Fainting	______
☐	☐	Urinary tract infections	______
☐	☐	Kidney disorders	______
☐	☐	Arthritis	______
☐	☐	Gout	______
☐	☐	Hernia	______
☐	☐	Incontinence	______
☐	☐	Obesity	______
☐	☐	Corrective lenses	______
☐	☐	Hearing loss or hearing aids	______
☐	☐	Anemia	______
☐	☐	Cancer	______
☐	☐	Skin disorders	______
☐	☐	Chronic pain	______
☐	☐	Speech disorder	______
☐	☐	Ambulatory skills	______
☐	☐	Gait	______
☐	☐	Orthotics	______
☐	☐	Prosthetics	______
☐	☐	Assistive devices	______

Pulse rate: ______

Blood pressure: (Systolic) ______ (Diastolic) ______ (Opposite arm) ______

Family History

Are your parents living: Mother: ☐ Yes ☐ No Father: ☐ Yes ☐ No

If not, list their age and cause of death: ______

______

Have your parents, grandparents, or siblings suffered any of the following:

☐ Heart attack ☐ Hypertension

☐ Stroke ☐ Diabetes

☐ Obesity ☐ Cancer

☐ Arthritis ☐ Other ______

______

______

Medical Treatments

Physicians' name: ______________________ Phone number: __________

Address: ____

Physicians' name: ______________________ Phone number: __________

Address: ____

Physicians' name: ______________________ Phone number: __________

Address: ____

Physicians' name: ______________________ Phone number: __________

Address: ____

When did you last see a physician? ______________________________

____

Most recent hospitalization: ______________________________

____

History of surgeries: ______________________________

____

____

____

____

____

Medications, Dosage, Purpose, and Side Effects

____

____

____

____

____

____

____

____

____

Are you currently receiving physical or occupational therapy? ______________

Reason(s) for therapy: ______________________________

____

____

Name of therapist: ______________________ Phone number: __________

Location: ____

Exercise contraindications: ____

____

____

____

____

____

Personal general information: ____

____

____

____

____

____

Other relevant information: ____

____

____

____

____

____

Personal impression of level of health and wellness: ___________________________

____

____

____

____

____

What are your greatest concerns in participation in regular exercise? ______________

____

____

____

____

____

Potential individual risk factors associated with exercise participation: ______________

____

____

____

____

____

Recommendations for additional assessment: ______________________________

____

____

____

____

____

____

____

____

____

____

Medical Referral Form

________________________________ is interested in participating in the BE:WEL Program.

This program is an individually based exercise and wellness class that provides activities for individuals with disabilities.

The following types of activities are available to participants. Please indicate any activities that the individual *should not* participate in and list any special considerations for programming.

SHOULD
NOT

- ☐ Water jogging ________________________________
- ☐ Lap swimming ________________________________
- ☐ Water walking ________________________________
- ☐ Stretching ________________________________
- ☐ Range of motion ________________________________
- ☐ Diving ________________________________
- ☐ Weight training ________________________________
- ☐ Treadmill ________________________________
- ☐ Stationary cycling ________________________________
- ☐ Recumbent bicycle ________________________________

Please list any special considerations that we should be aware of: ________________________________

____

____

____

____

Please list any contraindications: ________________________________

____

____

____

____

Physician's signature: ________________________ Recommend participation: ☐ Yes ☐ No

Print name: ________________________ Phone number: ________________

Thank you for your time and consideration in reviewing this patient's program.

Sincerely,

Rebecca K. Lytle, PhD
Adapted Physical Education Program Coordinator
Department of Physical Education and Exercise Science
CSU, Chico 95929-0330

From S. Kasser and R. Lytle, 2013, *Inclusive physical activity: Promoting health for a lifetime, second edition* (Champaign, IL: Human Kinetics).

References

Almond, L. (1986). Reflecting on themes: A games classification. In R. Thorpe, D. Bunker, & L. Almond (Eds.), *Rethinking games teaching.* London: Exmonde Publications.

Altman, B.M. (2001). Disability definitions, models, classification schemes, and applications. In G. Albrecht, K. Seelman, & M. Bury (Eds.), *Handbook on disability studies* (pp. 97-122). Thousand Oaks, CA: Sage.

American Alliance for Health, Physical Education, Recreation and Dance. (1993). *Journal of Health, Physical Education, Recreation and Dance,* November-December.

American Association for Physical Activity and Recreation (AAPAR). (2010). Highly qualified adapted physical education teachers. Position paper. Available at www.aahperd.org/aapar/news/positionpapers/upload/Highly-Qualified-APE-Teacher_2010.pdf.

American College of Sports Medicine. (2011). Quantity and quality of exercise for developing and maintaining cardiorespiratory, musculoskeletal, and neuromotor fitness in apparently healthy adults: Guidance for prescribing exercise. *Medicine and Science in Sport and Exercise, 43*(7), 1334-1359.

American Red Cross. (2004). *Water safety: Instructional manual.* Yardley, PA: StayWell.

Anderson, W.L., Weiner, J.M., Finkelstein, E.A., & Armour, B.S. (2011). Estimates of national health care expenditures associated with disability. *Journal of Disability Policy Studies, 21,* 230-240.

Asch, A. (1984). The experience of disability: A challenge for psychology. *American Psychologist, 39,* 529-536.

Auxter, D., Pyfer, J., Zittel, L., Roth, K., & Huettig, C. (2009). *Principles and methods of adapted physical education and recreation* (11th ed.). Boston: McGraw-Hill.

Balan, C., & Davis, W. (1993). Ecological task analysis: An approach to teaching physical education. *Journal of Physical Education, Recreation and Dance, 64*(9), 54-61.

Balcazar, F.E., Keys, C.B., & Suarez-Balcazar, Y. (2008). Empowering Latinos with disabilities to address issues of independent living and disability rights: A capacity-building approach. *Journal of Prevention and Intervention in the Community, 21,* 53-70.

Bandura, A. (1977). Self-efficacy: Toward a unifying theory of behavioral change. *Psychology Review, 84*(2), 191-215.

Barth, B., Rimmer, J.H., Wang, E., & Schiller, W.J. (2008). A conceptual framework for improving the accessibility of fitness and recreation facilities for people with disabilities. *Journal of Physical Activity and Health, 5,* 158-168.

Baumgartner, T.A., & Jackson, A.S. (1995). *Measurement for evaluation in physical education and exercise science* (6th ed.). Boston: McGraw-Hill.

Behler, G.T. (1993). Disability simulations as a teaching tool: Some ethical issues and implications. *Journal of Postsecondary Education and Disability, 10*(2), 3-8.

Best-Martini, E., & Botenhagen-DiGenova, K. (2003). *Exercise for frail elders.* Champaign, IL: Human Kinetics.

Bishop, K.K., Woll, J., & Arango, P. (1993). *Family professional collaboration for children with special health needs and their families.* Family/Professional Collaboration Project: U.S. Department of Health and Human Services.

Block, M.E. (2007). *A teacher's guide to including students with disabilities in general physical education* (3rd ed.). Baltimore, MD: Paul H. Brookes.

Block, M.E., & Krebs, P.L. (1992). An alternative to least restrictive environments: A continuum of support to regular physical education. *Adapted Physical Activity Quarterly, 9,* 97-113.

Block, M.E., Lieberman, L., & Connor-Kuntz, F. (1998). Authentic assessment in adapted physical education. *Journal of Health, Physical Education, Recreation and Dance, 69*(3), 48-55.

Block, M.E., & Obrusnikova, A. (2007). Inclusion in physical education: A review of the literature from 1995-2005. *Adapted Physical Activity Quarterly, 24,* 103-124.

Block, M.E., Provis, S., & Nelson, E. (1994). Accommodating students with severe disabilities in regular physical education: Extending traditional skill stations. *Palaestra, 10*(1), 32-38.

Boslaugh, S.E., & Andresen, E.M. (2006). Correlates of physical activity for adults with disability. *Prevention of Chronic Disease* (online serial). Available at www.cdc.gov/pcd/issues/2006/jul/05_0207.htm.

Boyles, C.M., Bailey, P.H., & Mossey, S. (2008). Representations of disability in nursing and healthcare literature: An integrative review. *Journal of Advanced Nursing, 62*(4), 428-437.

Bradley, D.F. (1994). A framework for the acquisition of collaborative consultation skills. *Journal of Educational and Psychological Consultation, 5*(1), 51-68.

Brault, M. (2008). *Americans with disabilities: 2005, current population reports* (pp. 70-117). Washington, DC: U.S. Census Bureau.

Brehm, S.S., & Kassin, S.M. (1996). Social psychology (3rd ed.). Geneva, IL: Houghton Mifflin Company.

Brostrand, H.L. (2006). Tilting at windmills: Changing attitudes towards people with disabilities. *Journal of Rehabilitation, 72*(1), 4-9.

Brownell, M.T., Adams, A., Sindelar, P., & Waldron, N. (2006). Learning from collaboration: The role of teacher qualities. *Exceptional Children, 72*(2), 169-185.

Burgstahler, S., & Doe, T. (2004). Disability-related simulations: If, when, and how to use them. *Review of Disability Studies, 1*(2), 4-17.

Burton, A., & Miller, D. (1998). *Movement skill assessment.* Champaign, IL: Human Kinetics.

California Department of Education. (1998). Challenge standards for student success: Physical education. Sacramento, CA.

Cardinal, B.J., Kosma, M., & McCubbin, J.A. (2004). Factors influencing the exercise behavior of adults with physical disabilities. *Medicine & Science in Sports and Exercise, 36*(5), 868-875.

Centers for Disease Control and Prevention. (2007a). Physical activity among adults with disabilities: United States, 2005. *MMWR, 56,* 1021-1024.

Centers for Disease Control and Prevention. (2007b). Prevalence of regular physical activity among adults: Unites States, 2001 and 2005. MMWR, *56,* 1209-1212.

Choate, J., & Evans, S. (1992). Authentic assessment of special learners: Problem or promise? *Preventing School Failure, 37*(1), 6-9.

Coben, S.S., Thomas, C.C., Sattler, R.O., & Morsink, C.V. (1997). Meeting the challenge of consultation and collaboration: Developing interactive teams. *Journal of Learning Disabilities, 30,* 427-432.

Cohen-Mansfield, J., Marx, M.S., & Guralnik, J.M. (2003). Motivators and barriers to exercise in an older community-dwelling population. *Journal of Aging and Physical Activity, 11,* 242-253.

Columna, L. (2011). Assessing aquatics for children with disabilities. In E. Kowalski & L. Lieberman (Eds.), *Assessment for everyone: Modifying NASPE assessments to include all elementary school children* (pp. 65-76). Reston, VA: National Association for Sport & Physical Education.

Columna, L., Pyfer, J., & Senne, T.A. (2011). Physical recreation among immigrant Hispanic families with children with disabilities. *Therapeutic Recreation Journal, XLV,* 214-233.

Conaster, P., Block, M.E., & Gansneder, B. (2002). Aquatic instructors' beliefs toward inclusion: The theory of planned behavior. *Adapted Physical Activity Quarterly, 19,* 172-187.

Conaster, P., Block, M.E., & Lepore, M. (2000). Aquatic instructors' attitudes toward teaching students with disabilities. *Adapted Physical Activity Quarterly, 17,* 173-183.

Conoley, J.C., & Conoley, C.W. (1988). Useful theories in school-based consultation. *Remedial and Special Education, 9*(6), 14-20.

Cook, L. & Friend, M. (2010). The state of the art of collaboration on behalf of students with disabilities. *Journal of Educational and Psychological Consultation, 20,* 1-8.

Coon, J.T., Boddy, K., Stein, K., Whear, R., Barton, S., & Depledge, M.H. (2011). Does participating in physical activity in outdoor natural environments have a greater effect on physical and mental wellbeing than physical activity indoors? A systematic review. *Environmental Science and Technology, 45*(5), 1761-1772.

Covey, S.R. (1990). *The seven habits of highly effective people: Powerful lessons in personal change.* A Fireside Book. New York: Simon & Schuster.

Cowden, J., & Eason, B. (1991). Pediatric adapted physical education for infants, toddlers, and preschoolers: Meeting IDEA-H and IDEA-B challenges. *Adapted Physical Activity Quarterly, 8,* 263-279.

Cowden, J., Sayers, K., & Torrey, C. (1998). *Pediatric adapted motor development and exercise.* Springfield, IL: Charles C. Thomas.

Danforth, S., & Navarro, V. (1998). Speech acts: Sampling the social construction of mental retardation in everyday life. *Mental Retardation, 36*(1), 31-43.

Davis, L.J. (1997). Constructing normalcy. In *The disability studies reader,* L.J. Davis (Ed.). New York, NY: Routledge, 9-28.

Davis, R. (2011). *Teaching disability sport.* Champaign, IL: Human Kinetics.

Davis, W.E., & Broadhead, G.D. (2007). *Ecological task analysis and movement.* Champaign, IL: Human Kinetics.

DePauw, K.P., & Doll-Tepper, G. (2000). Toward progressive inclusion and acceptance: Myth or reality? The inclusion debate and bandwagon discourse. *Adapted Physical Activity Quarterly, 17*(2), 135-143.

DePauw, K.P., & Gavron, S.J. (2005). *Disability sports* (2nd ed.). Champaign, IL: Human Kinetics.

Dettmer, P., Dyck, N., & Thurston, L. (1999). *Consultation, collaboration and teamwork* (3rd ed.). Needham Heights, MA: Allen & Bacon.

Dishman, R.K. (1994). Motivating older adults to exercise. *Southern Medical Association Journal, 87*(5), 579-582.

Drum, C. (2003). Behavioral risk factor surveillance system project: Health status & disability. In Rehabilitation Research & Training Center: Health & Wellness Consortium (Ed.), *State of the science conference proceedings* (pp. 67-72). Portland, OR: Oregon Health & Science University.

Dunn, D.S., & Elliott, T.R. (2005). Revisiting a constructivist classic: Wright's physical disability: A psychological approach. *Rehabilitation Psychology, 50,* 183-189.

Durstine, J., Moore, G., Painter, P., & Roberts, S. (2009). *ACSM's exercise management for persons with chronic diseases and disabilities* (3rd ed.). Champaign, IL: Human Kinetics.

Dustin, D., & Ehly, S. (1984). Skills for effective consultation. *School Counselor, 32*(1), 23-29.

Edmonson, S.L., & Thompson, D.P. (2001). *The "role" of burnout among special educators: The relationship between burnout and role tension.* Paper presented at the Annual Meeting of the American Educational Research Association, Seattle, April 10-14, 2001.

Ellery, P.J., & Rauschenbach, J. (2000). Impact of disability awareness activities on nondisabled student attitudes toward integrated physical education with students who use wheelchairs. *Research Quarterly for Exercise and Sport, Supplement, Abstracts of Completed Research, 71*(1), A-106.

Emes, C., Longmuir, P., & Downs, P. (2002). An abilities-based approach to service delivery and professional preparation in adapted physical education. *Adapted Physical Activity Quarterly, 19,* 403-419.

Erickson, W., Lee, C., & von Schrader, S. (2010). *Disability statistics from the 2008 American Community Survey (ACS).* Ithaca, NY: Cornell University Rehabilitation Research and Training Center on Disability Demographics and Statistics (StatsRRTC). Available at www.disabilitystatistics.org.

Folsom-Meek, S.L., Nearing, R.J., & Kalakian, L.H. (2000). Effects of an adapted physical education course in changing attitudes. *Clinical Kinesiology, 54,* 52-58.

Foreman, P. (2005). Language and disability. *Journal of Intellectual and Developmental Disability, 1,* 57-59.

Friend, M. (1988). Putting consultation into context: Historical and contemporary perspectives. *Remedial and Special Education, 9*(6), 7-13.

Friend, M., & Cook, L. (2010). *Interactions: Collaboration skills for school professionals* (6th ed.). Columbus, OH: Merrill.

Friend, M., Cook, L., Hurley-Chamberlain, D., & Shamberger, C. (2010). Co-teaching: An illustration of the complexity of collaboration in special education. *Journal of Educational and Psychological Consultation, 20,* 9-29.

Galvin, R.D. (2005). Researching the disabled identity: Contextualizing the identity transformations which accompany the onset of impairment. *Sociology of Health and Illness, 27*(3), 393-413.

Gentile, A.M. (2000). Skill acquisition: Action, movement, and neuromotor processes. In J.M. Carr, R.B. Shepherd, J. Gordon, A.M. Gentile, & J. M. Hinds (Eds.), *Movement science: Foundations for physical therapy* (2nd ed.), pp. 111-187. Rockville, MD: Aspen.

Giangreco, M.F., & Doyle, M.B. (2004). Directing paraprofessional work. In C. Kennedy & E. Horn (Eds.), *Including students with severe disabilities,* (pp. 185-204). Boston: Allyn & Bacon.

Goyakla Apache, R.R., & Rizzo, T. (2005). Evaluating effectiveness of an infusion learning model on attitudes of physical education majors. *Perceptual and Motor Skills, 101,* 177-186.

Graham, G., Holt-Hale, S., & Parker, M. (2010). *Children moving: A reflective approach to teaching physical education* (8th ed.). Columbus, OH: McGraw-Hill.

Gutkin, T.B. (1996). Patterns of consultant and consultee verbalizations: Examining communication leadership during initial consultation interviews. *Journal of School Psychology, 34*(3), 199-219.

Gutkin, T.B., & Curtis, M.J. (1982). School based consultation: Theory and techniques. In T.B. Gutkin & C.R. Reynolds (Eds.), *The handbook of school psychology* (pp. 796-828). New York, NY: Wiley.

Hamel, R. (1992). Getting into the game: New opportunities for athletes with disabilities. *Physician and Sports Medicine, 20*(11), 121-122, 124, 126-129.

Harrison, T. (2006). Health promotion for persons with disabilities: What does the literature reveal? *Family and Community Health, 29*(1S), 12S-19S.

Haywood, K., & Getchell, N. (2009). *Life span motor development* (5th ed.). Champaign, IL: Human Kinetics.

Henley, M., Ramsey, R.S., & Algozzine, R.F. (2009). *Characteristics of and strategies for teaching students with mild disabilities* (6th ed.). Upper Saddle River, NJ: Merrill Publishing Co.

Hersman, B.L., & Hodge, S.R. (2010). High school physical educators' beliefs about teaching differently abled students in an urban public school district. *Education and Urban Society, 42,* 730-757.

Heward, W.L. (2006). *Exceptional children: An introduction to special education* (8th ed.). Upper Saddle River, NJ: Merrill Publishing Co.

Higgins, E.L., Raskind, M.H., Goldberg, R.J., & Herman, K.L. (2002). Stages of acceptance of a learning disability: The impact of labeling. *Learning Disability Quarterly, 25,* 3-16.

Hodge, S.R., Davis, R., Woodard, R., & Sherrill, C. (2002). Comparison of practicum types in changing preservice teachers' attitudes and perceived competence. *Adapted Physical Activity Quarterly, 19,* 155-171.

Hopple, C., & Graham, G. (1995). What children think, feel, and know about physical fitness testing. *Journal of Teaching in Physical Education, 14*(4), 408-417.

Horton, G.E., & Brown, D. (1990). The importance of interpersonal skills in consultee-centered consultation: A review. *Journal of Counseling and Development, 68*(4), 423-426.

Horvat, M., Block, M., & Kelly, L. (2007). *Developmental and adapted physical activity assessment.* Champaign, IL: Human Kinetics.

Huebschmann, A.M., Crane, L.A., Belansky, E.S., Scarbro, S.S., Marshall, J.A., & Regensteiner, J.G. (2011). Fear of injury with physical activity is greater in adults with diabetes than in adults without diabetes. *Diabetes Care, 34,* 1717-1722.

Huizinga, J. (1955). *Homo ludens: The play element in culture.* Boston: Beacon.

Hutzler, Y., Fliess, O., Avraham, A., Reiter, S., & Talmor, R. (2007). Effects of short-term awareness interventions on children's attitudes toward peers with a disability. *International Journal of Rehabilitation Research, 30,* 159-161.

Hutzler, Y., & Levi, I. (2008). Including children with a disability in physical education: General and specific attitudes of high-school students. *European Journal of Adapted Physical Activity, 1,* 21-30.

Idol, L. (1988). A rationale and guidelines for establishing special education consultation programs. *Remedial and Special Education, 9*(6), 48-58.

Idol, L., Nevin, A., & Paolucci-Whitcomb, P. (1994). *Collaborative consultation* (2nd ed.). Austin, TX: Pro-ed.

Idol, L., Paolucci-Whitcomb, P., Nevin, A. (1995). The collaborative consultation model. *Journal of Educational and Psychological Consultation, 6*(4), 329-346.

Johnson, L., Kasser, S., & Nichols, B. (2002). Including all children in standards-based physical education. *Journal of Physical Education, Recreation and Dance, 73*(4), 42-46.

Jones, G.C., & Sinclair, L.B. (2008). Multiple health disparities among minority adults with mobility limitations: An application of the ICG framework and codes. *Disability and Rehabilitation*, *30*(12-13), 901-915.

Joyner, A.B., & McManis, B.G. (1997). Quality control in alternative assessment. *Journal of Physical Education, Recreation and Dance , 68*(7), 38-40.

Kalyvas, V., & Reid, G. (2003). Sport adaptation, participation, and enjoyment of students with and without physical disabilities. *Adapted Physical Activity Quarterly, 20,* 182-199.

Kampwirth, T.J. (2003). *Collaborative consultation in the schools.* Upper Saddle River, NJ: Merrill Prentice Hall.

Kaplan, D. (2011). *The definition of disability.* The Center for an Accessible Society. Available at www.accessiblesociety.org/topics/demographics-identity/dkaplanpaper.htm.

Karge, B.D., McClure, M., & Patton, P.L. (1995). The success of collaboration resource programs for students with disabilities in grades 6 through 8. *Remedial and Special Education, 16*(2), 79-89.

Kauffman, J.M. (1998). Commentary: Today's special education and its messages for tomorrow. *Journal of Special Education, 32*(3), 127-137.

Kaye, H.S. (2001). *Disability watch: The status of people with disabilities in the U.S. (vol. 2).* Disability Rights Advocates, Inc. Volcano, CA: Volcano Press.

Kaye, H.S., & Longmore, P. (1997). *Disability watch: The status of people with disabilities in the U.S.* Disability Rights Advocates, Inc. Volcano, CA: Volcano Press.

Kelly, L., & Gansneder, B. (1998). Preparation and job demographics of adapted physical educators in the United States. *Adapted Physical Activity Quarterly, 15,* 141-154.

Kelly, L., Wessel, J., Dummer, G., & Sampson, T. (2010). *Everyone can.* Champaign, IL: Human Kinetics.

Kim, K.M., & Fox, M.H. (2006). Moving to a holistic model of health among persons with mobility disabilities. *Qualitative Social Work, 5,* 470-488.

Kinne, S., Patrick, D.L., & Maher, E.J. (1999). Correlates of exercise maintenance among people with mobility impairments. *Disability and Rehabilitation, 21*(1), 15-22.

Knoff, H.M., McKenna, A.F., & Riser, K. (1991). Toward a consultant effectiveness scale: Investigating the characteristics of effective consultants. *School Psychology Review, 20*(1), 81-96.

Knudson, D., & Morrison, C. (1996). An integrated qualitative analysis of overarm throwing. *Journal of Physical Education, Recreation and Dance, 67*(6), 31-36.

Knudson, D. (2013). *Qualitative diagnosis of human movement: Improving performance in sport and exercise* (3rd ed.). Champaign, IL: Human Kinetics.

Kozub, F.M., & Lienert, C. (2003). Attitudes toward teaching children with disabilities: Review of the literature and research paradigm. *Adapted Physical Activity Quarterly*, *20,* 323-346.

Langendorfer, S.J., & Bruya, L.D. (1995). *Aquatic readiness: Developing water competence in young children.* Champaign, IL: Human Kinetics.

Lepore, M., Gayle, G.W., & Stevens, S. (2007). *Adapted aquatics programming: A professional guide.* Champaign, IL: Human Kinetics.

Lewis, A. (2009). Disability disparities: A beginning model. *Disability and Rehabilitation*, *31*(14), 1136-1143.

Lieberman, L.J., & Houston-Wilson, C. (2009). *Strategies for inclusion: A handbook for physical educators* (2nd ed.). Champaign, IL: Human Kinetics.

Lieberman, L.J., James, A.R., & Ludwa, N. (2004). Impact of inclusion in general physical education for all students. *Journal of Physical Education, Recreation & Dance, 75*(5), 37-42.

Linder, T. (2008). *Transdisciplinary play-based assessment (TPBA 2)* (2nd ed.). Baltimore, MD: Paul H. Brookes.

Liu, J., & Pearson, D. (1999). *Teachers' attitude toward inclusion and perceived professional needs for an inclusive classroom.* Washington, D.C.: Resources in Education. (ED438274).

Lollar, D.J. (2001). Public health trends in disability: Past, present and future. In G. Albrecht, K. Seelman, & M. Bury (Eds.), *Handbook of disability studies.* Thousand Oaks, CA: Sage Publications Inc.

Longmuir, P.E., & Bar-Or, O. (2000). Factors influencing the physical activity levels of youths with physical and sensory disabilities. *Adapted Physical Activity Quarterly, 17*(1), 40-53.

Louv, R. (2008). *Last child in the woods: Saving our children from nature-deficit disorder.* Chapel Hill, NC: Algonquin Books.

Lund, J. (1997). Authentic assessment: Its development and applications. *Journal of Physical Education, Recreation and Dance, 68*(4), 25-33.

Lytle, D. (1989). *The crucial elements in cognition: Embodiment and playful action.* Berkeley, CA: California Folklore Society and the Association for the Study of Play Conference.

Lytle, D.E. (1999). Defining play: Problems, paradoxes and provocation. In T. Fahey (Ed.), *Encyclopedia of sports medicine and science.* Available at www.sportsci.org/encyc/encyc.html.

Lytle, R., & Bordin, J. (2001). Enhancing the IEP team: Strategies for parents and professionals. *Teaching Exceptional Children, 33*(5), 40-44.

Lytle, R., & Collier, D. (2002). The consultation process: Adapted physical education specialists' perceptions. *Adapted Physical Activity Quarterly, 19,* 261-279.

Lytle, R., & Hutchinson, G.E. (2004). Adapted physical educators: The multiple roles of consultants. *Adapted Physical Activity Quarterly, 21,* 34-49.

Lytle, R., & Johnson, J. (2000). Adapted physical education survey. *California Association of Health, Physical Education, Recreation and Dance Journal/Times, 62*(4), 12-13.

Magill, R.A. (2010). *Motor learning and control: Concepts and applications* (9th ed.). New York: McGraw-Hill.

Mann, K., Gordon, J., & MacLeod, A. (2009). Reflection and reflective practice in health profession education: A systematic review. *Advances in Health Science Education, 14,* 595-621.

Martin, J.N., & Nakayama, T.K. (2000). *Intercultural communication in contexts* (2nd ed.). Mountain View, CA: Mayfield Publishing Company.

Massie, B. (2006). *Participation—have we got an attitude problem*? Paper presented in the NDA 5th Annual Conference: Civic, Cultural and Social Participation: Building an Inclusive Society (paper available at www.nda.ie). Dublin, Ireland, November 16.

McAuley, E., Motl, R.W., Morris, K.S., Hu, L., Doerksen, S.E., Elavsky, S., & Konopack, J.F. (2007). Enhancing physical activity adherence and well-being in multiple sclerosis: A randomized controlled trial. *Multiple Sclerosis Journal, 13,* 652-659.

Melograno, V. (1994). Portfolio assessment: Documenting authentic student learning. *Journal of Physical Education, Recreation and Dance, 65*(8), 50-55, 58-61.

Meredith, M., & Welk, G. (2010). FitnessGram & Activitygram. Champaign, IL: Human Kinetics.

Milsom, A. (2006). Creating positive school experiences for students with disabilities. *Professional School Counseling Journal, 10*(1), 66-72.

Mintah, J.K. (2003). Authentic assessment in physical education: Prevalence and use of perceived impact on student's self-concept, motivation, and skill achievement. *Measurement in Physical Education and Exercise Science*, 7(3), 161-174.

Morris, C. (2009). Measuring participation in childhood disability: How does the capability approach improve our understanding? *Developmental Medicine & Child Neurology, 51*(2), 92-94.

Morris, D., & Stiehl, J. (1999). *Changing kids' games.* Champaign, IL: Human Kinetics.

Mosston, M., & Ashworth, S. (2002). *Teaching physical education* (5th ed.). San Francisco, CA: Benjamin Cummings.

National Association for Sport and Physical Education (NASPE). (2004). *Moving into the future: National standards for physical education* (2nd ed.). Reston, VA: NASPE.

National Association for Sport and Physical Education (NASPE) (2009). *Active start: A statement of physical activity guidelines for children from birth to age five* (2nd ed.). Reston, VA: NASPE.

National Center for the Dissemination of Disability Research (NCDDR). (1999). The socially constructed nature of race, culture, and disability. *Research Exchange, 4*(1).

National Dissemination Center for Children with Disabilities, Public Law 105-17. (1998, June). The IDEA amendments of 1997. *NICHCY News Digest,* 26 (Revised Ed.). Available at http://nichcy.org/laws/idea.

O'Brien-Cousins, S. (2000). My heart couldn't take it: Older women's beliefs about exercise benefits and risks. *Journal of Gerontology, 55B*(5), 283-294.

Obrusnikova, I. (2008). Physical educators' beliefs about teaching children with disabilities. *Perceptual and Motor Skills*, *106,* 637-644.

Obrusnikova, I., Block, M.E., & Válková, H. (2003). Impact of inclusion in GPE on students without disabilities. *Adapted Physical Activity Quarterly, 20,* 230-245.

Oliver, M. (1996). *Understanding disability: From theory to practice.* Basingstoke, Hampshire, UK: Macmillan.

Pangrazi, R. (2007). *Dynamic physical education for elementary school children* (15th ed.). San Francisco, CA: Pearson Education.

Pfeiffer, D. (2001). The conceptualization of disability. *Research in Social Science and Disability*, *2,* 29-52.

Pfeiffer, D. (2003). Attitudes towards disability in the helping professions. *Disability Studies Quarterly*, *23*(2), 132-149.

Pike K., & Salend, S. (1995). Authentic assessment strategies: Alternatives to norm-referenced testing. *Teaching Exceptional Children, 28*(1), 15-20.

Pratt, P., & Allen, A. (1989). *Occupational therapy for children* (2nd ed.). St. Louis, MO: C.V. Mosby.

Priest, S., & Gass, M. (2005). *Effective leadership in adventure programming* (2nd ed.). Champaign, IL: Human Kinetics.

Public Law 99-457. (1986). An act to amend the education of the handicapped act to reauthorize the discretionary programs under that act, to authorize an early intervention program under that act for handicapped infants and toddlers and their families, and for other purposes. S. 2294. 99th Congress.

Public Law 105-17. (1998, June). The IDEA amendments of 1997. *NICHCY News Digest,* 26, (Revised Ed.). Available at www.nichcy.org/pubs/newsdig/nd26txt.htm.

Pugach, M.C., & Johnson, L.J. (1995). *Collaborative practitioners, collaborative schools.* Denver, CO: Love Publishing.

Ramey, C.T., & Ramey, S.L. (2004). Early learning and school readiness: Can early intervention make a difference? *Merrill Palmer Quarterly Journal of Developmental Delay, 50,* 471-491.

Resnick, B. (2001). Testing a model of exercise behavior in older adults. *Research in Nursing and Health, 24,* 82-94.

Riley, B.B., Rimmer, J.H., Wang, E., & Schiller, W.J. (2008). A conceptual framework for improving the accessibility of fitness and recreation facilities for people with disabilities. *Journal of Physical Activity and Health, 5,* 158-168.

Rimmer, J.H. (1999). Health promotion for people with disabilities: The emerging paradigm shift from disability prevention to prevention of secondary conditions. *Physical Therapy, 79*(5), 495-502.

Rimmer, J.H. (2006). Use of the ICF in identifying factors that impact participation in physical activity/rehabilitation among people with disabilities. *Disability & Rehabilitation, 28*(17), 1087-1095.

Rimmer, J.H., Riley, B., Wang, E., & Rauworth, A. (2005). Accessibility of health clubs for people with mobility disabilities and visual impairments. *American Journal of Public Health, 95,* 2022-2028.

Rimmer, J.H., Rubin, S., & Braddock, D. (2000). Barriers to exercise in African American women with physical disabilities. *Archives of Physical Medicine & Rehabilitation, 81*(2), 182-188.

Rimmer, J.H., Rubin, S.S, Braddock, D., & Hedman, G. (1999). Physical activity patterns of African-American women with physical disabilities. *Medicine and Science in Sports and Exercise, 31*(4), 613-618.

Rink, J.E. (1998). *Teaching physical education for learning* (3rd ed.). Boston: McGraw-Hill.

Rink, J.E. (2005). *Teaching physical education for learning* (5th ed.). Boston: McGraw-Hill.

Ryan, R.M., & Deci, E.L. (2000). Self-determination theory and the facilitation of intrinsic motivation, social development, and well-being. *American Psychologist, 55*(1), 68-78.

Sanders, S. (2002). *Active for life.* Champaign, IL: Human Kinetics.

Scelza, W.M., Kalpakjian, C.Z., Zemper, E.D., & Tate, D.G. (2005). Perceived barriers to exercise in people with spinal cord injury. *American Journal of Physical Medicine and Rehabilitation, 84,* 576-583.

Schutzer, K.A., & Graves, B.S. (2004). Barriers and motivation to exercise in older adults. *Preventative Medicine, 39,* 1056-1061.

Scullion, P.A. (2010). Models of disability: Their influence in nursing and potential role in challenging discrimination. *Journal of Advanced Nursing, 66*(3), 697-707.

Shakespeare, T. (2006). *Disability rights and wrongs.* London: Routledge.

Sherrill, C. (1998). *Adapted physical activity, recreation, and sport: Crossdisciplinary and lifespan* (5th ed.). Boston: WCB/McGraw Hill.

Smart, J.F., & Smart, D.W. (1997). The racial/ethnic demography of disability. *Journal of Rehabilitation, 63*(4), 9-15.

Smith, J. (1997a). MR as educational construct: Time for a new shared view. *Education & Training in MR & DD, 32*(3), 167-173.

Smith, T. (1997b). Authentic assessment: Using a portfolio card in physical education. *Journal of Physical Education, Recreation and Dance, 68*(7), 46-52.

Smith, R.W., Austin, D.R., Kennedy, D.W., Lee, Y., & Hutchinson, P. (2005). *Inclusive and special recreation: Opportunities for persons with disabilities* (5th ed.). New York: McGraw Hill.

Spencer, S.A. (2005). Lynne Cook and June Downing: The practicalities in special education service delivery. *Intervention in School and Clinic, 5,* 296-300.

Spencer-Cavaliere, N. & Watkinson, J. (2010). Inclusion understood from the perspectives of children with disability. *Adapted Physical Activity Quarterly, 27,* 275-293.

Spiker, D., Boyce, G.C., & Boyce, L.K. (2002). Parent-child interactions when young children have disabilities. *International review of research in mental retardation, 25,* 35-70.

Stainback, S., & Stainback, W. (Eds.). (1991). *Teaching in the inclusive classroom: Curriculum design, adaptation and delivery.* Baltimore: Brookes.

Stainback, S., Stainback, W., & Ayres, B. (1996). Schools as inclusive communities. In S. Stainback & W. Stainback (Eds.), *Controversial issues facing special education* (pp. 31-40). Needham Heights, MA: Allyn & Bacon.

Stainback, W., Stainback, S., & Bunch, G. (1989). A rationale for the merger of regular and special education. In W. Stainback, S. Stainback, & M. Forest (Eds.), *Education of all students in the mainstream of regular education* (pp. 15-28). Baltimore: Paul H. Brookes.

St. Clair, S.A. (1995). Differences in gross motor performance among multihandicapped deaf children using inclusion versus special day class models in adapted physical education (Master's Thesis, California State University, Fullerton). *Masters Abstracts International,* 33-06, 1662.

Stopka, C. (2001). Equipment to enhance an adapted aquatic program part 1: New twist to conventional equipment. *Palaestra, 17*(1), 36-43.

Stuart, M.E., Lieberman, L., & Hand, K.E. (2006). Beliefs about physical activity among children who are visually impaired and their parents. *Journal of Visual Impairment & Blindness*, *4*, 223-234.

Stuifbergen, A.K., & Roberts, G.J. (1997). Health promotion practices of women with multiple sclerosis. *Archives of Physical Medicine and Rehabilitation*, *78*(Suppl. 5), S3-S9.

Sugerman, D. (2001). Inclusive outdoor education: Facilitating groups that include people with disabilities. *Journal of Experiential Education, 24*(3), 166-172.

Thelen, E. (1985). Developmental origins of motor coordination: Leg movements in human infants. *Developmental Psychology, 18,* 1-22.

Thelen, E. (1995). Motor development: A new synthesis. *American Psychologist, 50,* 79-95.

Thomas, C.C., Correa, V.I., & Morsink, C.V. (2001). *Interactive teaming: Enhancing programs for students with special needs* (3rd ed.). Upper Saddle River, NJ: Merrill Prentice Hall.

Thomas, D. (2005). *Swimming: Steps to success* (3rd ed.). Champaign, IL: Human Kinetics.

Tripp, A., & Rizzo, T. (2006). Disability labels affect physical educators. *Adapted Physical Activity Quarterly, 23,* 310-326.

Ulrich, B., & Ulrich, D. (1995). Spontaneous leg movements of infants with Down syndrome and nondisabled infants. *Child Development, 66*(6), 1844-1855.

Ulrich, D. (2000). *Test of gross motor development.* Austin, TX: Pro-Ed.

U.S. Department of Health and Human Services. (1996). *Physical activity and health: A report of the surgeon general.* Washington, D.C.: U.S. Government Printing Office.

U.S. Department of Health and Human Services. (2000). *Healthy People 2010: With understanding and improving health and objectives for improving health* (2nd ed.). Washington, D.C.: U.S. Government Printing Office. Available at www.healthypeople.gov/publications.

van der Ploeg, H.P., van der Beek, A.J., van der Woude, L.H.V., & van Mechelen, W. (2004). Physical activity for people with a disability. *Sports Medicine, 34,* 639-649.

Verderber, J.M., Rizzo, T.L., & Sherrill, C. (2003). Assessing student intention to participate in inclusive physical education. *Adapted Physical Activity Quarterly, 20*(1), 26-45.

Villa, R.A., Thousand, J.S., Nevin, A.I., & Malgeri, C. (1996). Instilling collaboration for inclusion schooling as a way of doing business in public schools. *Remedial and Special Education, 17*(3), 169-181.

Vogler, E.W., Koranda, P., & Romance, T. (2000). Including a child with severe cerebral palsy in physical education: A case study. *Adapted Physical Activity Quarterly, 9,* 316-329.

Wagstaff, M., & Attarian, A. (2009). *Technical skills for adventure programming: A curriculum guide.* Champaign, IL: Human Kinetics.

Weil, E., Wachterman, M., McCarthy, E.P., Davis, R.B., O'Day, B., Iezzoni, L.I., & Wee, C.C. (2002). Obesity among adults with disabling conditions. *Journal of the American Medical Association*, *288,* 1265-1268.

Wessel, J., & Zittel, L. (1995). *Smart start.* Austin, TX: Pro-ed.

Wiggins, K.C., & Damore, S.J. (2006). Survivors or friends? A framework for assessing effective collaboration. *Teaching Exceptional Children*, 49-56.

Wilson, S., & Lieberman, L. (2000). Disability awareness in physical education. *Strategies, 13*(6), *12,* 29-33.

Winn, J., & Blanton, L. (2005). The call for collaboration in teacher education. *Focus on Exceptional Children, 2,* 1-10.

Winnick, J.P. (Ed.). (2011). *Adapted physical education and sport* (5th ed.). Champaign, IL: Human Kinetics.

Winnick, J.P., & Short, F.X. (1999). *The Brockport physical fitness test manual.* Champaign, IL: Human Kinetics.

Wood, J.W. (2002). *Adapting instruction to accommodate students in inclusive settings* (5th ed.). Upper Saddle River, NJ: Merrill Publishing Company.

World Health Organization (WHO). (2001). *The international classification of functioning, disability and health (ICF),* 18. Geneva, Switzerland: WHO.

Yelin, E., Cisternas, M., & Trupin, L. (2006). The economic impact of disability in the United States, 1997. *Journal of Disability Policy Studies*, *17*(3), 137-147.

Yilmaz, I., Yanardag, M., Birkan, B., & Bumin, G. (2004). Effects of swimming training on physical fitness and water orientation in autism. *Pediatrics International, 46*, 624-626.

Yocom, D.J., & Cossairt, A. (1996). Consultation courses offered in special education teacher training programs: A national survey. *Journal of Educational Psychological Consultation, 7*(3), 251-258.

Young, E. (1992). *Seven blind mice.* New York: Philomel Books.

Zelazo, P.R., Zelazo, N.A., & Kolb, S. (1972a). 'Walking' in the newborn. *Science, 176,* 314-315.

Zelazo, P.R., Zelazo, N.A., & Kolb, S. (1972b). Newborn walking. *Science, 177,* 1058-1059.

INDEX

Note: The italicized *f* and *t* following page numbers refer to figures and tables, respectively.

B

D

E

About the Authors

Susan L. Kasser, PhD, is an associate professor in the department of rehabilitation and movement science at the University of Vermont at Burlington, where she teaches courses pertaining to inclusive physical activity. She holds a doctorate in movement studies in disability from Oregon State University.

Kasser has over 20 years of teaching experience in community and school-based physical activity programs involving individuals with diverse abilities. She has presented on both national and international levels in the area of inclusive physical activity. Kasser has also developed many community-based exercise programs for adults with chronic conditions and disabilities, including the Individualized Exercise for Active Lifestyles (IDEAL) program, which has served more than 75 adults with multiple sclerosis since 1998.

In 2012 she received the Outstanding Faculty Award from the College of Nursing and Health Sciences at the University of Vermont. Kasser also received the 2001 Outstanding Educator Award from the Vermont Association for Health, Physical Education, Recreation and Dance and the 2000 Kroepsch-Maurice Excellence in Teaching Award from the University of Vermont.

Kasser resides in Jericho, Vermont, where she enjoys hiking, kayaking, and backpacking in her free time.

Rebecca K. Lytle, PhD, is a professor in the department of kinesiology at California State University at Chico, where she teaches courses in adapted physical education and motor development. Lytle has been teaching in higher education since 1992. She also taught as an adapted physical education teacher in the public schools from 1988-1996, and was a school consultant from 2000-2002.

Lytle has published numerous articles for refereed journals and coauthored three books and six book chapters on adapted physical activity. She has presented at the state, national, and international levels and has served as consultant or coordinator for several community-based physical activity and motor skill assessment programs for both children and adults.

She is a member of the International Council for Health, Physical Education, Recreation, Sport and Dance (ICHPER-SD); Council for Exceptional Children (CEC); International Federation of Adapted Physical Activity (IFAPA); National Consortium for Physical Education and Recreation for Individuals with Disabilities (NCPERID); Adapted Physical Activity Council (APAC); Northern California Adapted Physical Education Consortium (NCAPEC); American Alliance for Health, Physical Education, Recreation and Dance (AAHPERD); California Association for Health, Physical Education, Recreation and Dance (CAHPERD); and California Teachers Association (CTA). Lytle also serves as chair of the National Adapted Physical Activity Council of AAHPERD and chair of the California State Council on Adapted Physical Education.

Lytle and her husband, Donald, reside in Chico. In her free time she enjoys playing with children, walking and hiking, and playing baseball and softball.